Léonide Massine and the 20th Century Ballet

To the memory of my mother
and to all the artists of the Ballet Russe

Léonide Massine and the 20th Century Ballet

LESLIE NORTON

McFarland & Company, Inc., Publishers
Jefferson, North Carolina, and London

Photographs provided by Jerome Robbins Dance Division, The New York Public Library for the Performing Arts, Astor, Lenox, and Tilden Foundations.

LIBRARY OF CONGRESS CATALOGUING-IN-PUBLICATION DATA

Norton, Leslie, 1952–
    Léonide Massine and the 20th century ballet / Leslie Norton.
      p.   cm.
    Includes bibliographical references and index.

    ISBN 0-7864-1752-8 (softcover : 50# alkaline paper)

    1. Massine, Léonide, 1895–1979. 2. Choreographers—
Russia (Federation)—Biography. 3. Ballet—History—20th
century. I. Title.
GV1785.M283N67 2004
792.8'2'092—dc22
                                        2004002721

British Library cataloguing data are available

©2004 Leslie Norton. All rights reserved

No part of this book may be reproduced or transmitted in any form or by any means, electronic or mechanical, including photocopying or recording, or by any information storage and retrieval system, without permission in writing from the publisher.

Cover photograph: Studio portrait of Massine, 1938 (Maurice Seymour)

Manufactured in the United States of America

McFarland & Company, Inc., Publishers
   Box 611, Jefferson, North Carolina 28640
   www.mcfarlandpub.com

Contents

Preface and Acknowledgments　　1

　1　July 1895–May 1917　　5
　2　June 1917–June 1920　　47
　3　July 1920–April 1926　　79
　4　June 1927–January 1932　　107
　5　May 1932–July 1936　　135
　6　August 1936–May 1939　　191
　7　June 1939–February 1943　　231
　8　March 1943–October 1954　　273
　9　July 1955–July 1960　　305
　10　The Final Years　　327
　　Epilogue　　333

Notes　　339
Bibliography　　359
Index　　365

Preface and Acknowledgments

Léonide Massine, consummate choreographer and performer, created hundreds of ballets for Diaghilev's Ballets Russes, the Ballet Russe de Monte Carlo, the American Ballet Theatre, and numerous major companies around the world. Throughout the 1930s, he was unquestionably the most important figure in the ballet world. While not a virtuoso, he remained a truly unique dancer and a peerless creator of character roles. Moreover, his versatility and scope made his choreography perhaps the most representative of the century. For an artist whose range was vast, his treatment was nearly always profound. Whatever period he portrayed, his style flowed freely and unselfconsciously. His character ballets dealt not with stereotypes but individuals, using the body alone to attain an actor's range of expression. His symphonic ballets proved how great music could be employed choreographically without being demeaned. They also revolutionized choreography with the first resolutely abstract ballet, as well as the first true fusions of ballet and modern dance.

With the outbreak of World War II, Massine, like many European artists, was confined to the U.S. But since the 1930s, American high culture, particularly the dance community, had been flush with a nationalistic renaissance. War brought this movement to its apogee with the dominance of homegrown American ballet and modern dance, its trendsetters such figures as Lincoln Kirstein, Agnes de Mille, Eugene Loring, and Martha Graham. In such an atmosphere, Massine's wide-ranging style could hardly be in vogue. Indeed, beyond the Ballet Russe de Monte Carlo itself, there was little room for any Russian ballet. Before long, Massine slipped from icon to critical scapegoat, his Americana works being particularly ill-received. Following his departure from American Ballet Theatre in 1943, Massine nonetheless continued to create fine ballets for major international companies. But he never regained the towering status of his years with Diaghilev and the Ballet Russe de Monte Carlo.

Throughout the subsequent half-century of neglect, Massine's contemporary relevance has remained controversial. More recently, however, his symphonic ballets have enjoyed revivals by a number of major companies, earning raves from respected critics. It seems clear that a genuine renascence of Massine's great art has at long last begun.

Dancers reaching the American stage in the 1970s and 1980s were often shaped by teachers and mentors who themselves were former members of the Ballet Russe de Monte Carlo. Like many of my generation, learning our craft in regional ballet companies across the United States, I absorbed not only their training but their philosophy and aesthetic ideology. From my earliest experience with Ilse Reese and the Rocky Mountain Ballet, to my days as a company member with George Verdak's Indianapolis Ballet Theatre, I was nourished by veteran Ballet Russe dancers. Performing in a few Massine ballets kindled my passion to learn more of this era and its master choreographer. The more I learned, the deeper my fascination, and the greater my artistic enrichment.

While offering a succinct biography of Massine, this book includes detailed analysis of the major ballets, subsectioned under "Synopsis," "Scenery and Costumes," "Music," "Choreography," "Critical Survey," and "In Retrospect." The study thus integrates discussion of Massine's life with multifaceted perspectives on his work. Following his mentor Sergei Diaghilev, Massine adopted the Wagnerian *Gesamtkunstwerk* as a model of inclusive artistic unity and strove to bring music, painting and literature of the highest caliber to the service of his ballets. In this spirit, the book touches upon the art of those composers with whom Massine collaborated, or where he found inspiration, from Scarlatti to Hindemith. It speaks as well to the history of opera, from opera seria and opera buffa to the "reform operas" of Gluck, the codified new forms of Rossini and the radically new music dramas of Wagner.

Massine was also notably influenced by his era's visual art movements—Cubism, Futurism, Neo-Primitivism, Constructivism, Neo-Romanticism, and Surrealism—and he collaborated with such seminal figures as Picasso, Braque, Matisse, Miró, Chagall, and Dalí. He called as well upon the literary and theatrical works of Boccaccio, Goldoni, Poe, Baudelaire, Cocteau, Valéry, and Thomas Mann. I hope readers will be pleased to encounter details of these rich symbioses.

But this book is more than a reassessment of one of history's great choreographers, now on the cusp of revival. For both novice and experienced choreographers, studying Massine's ballets yields much to ponder on the "do's" and "don'ts" of effective dance composition. For anyone intrigued by the era's dynamism, this study forms a lens through which the prodigious energies of many arts are brought sharply into focus.

While Massine's vast oeuvre contains many single-performance *pièces d'occasion*, these are necessarily excluded in my study, as are those ballets of which little record remains. At an original length of well over 500 pages, the first "finished" draft of this book required many subsequent omissions. Yet I have managed to retain a number of anecdotes, not merely to amuse, but to provide glimpses of what it was like to be a ballet dancer and a balletgoer in this fascinating era.

Writing this work has been a labor of love, albeit long and arduous. While hundreds of Massine collections, private and public, exist in the U.S., Europe, and South America, much is scattered. Comprehensive research has required two journeys abroad, as well as the usual delays for travel funds and interlibrary loan requests. At present, the most extensive and complete Massine resources are concentrated in the Jerome Robbins Dance Division, Library of Performing Arts, New York Public Library at Lincoln Center, and at London's Theatre Museum, Covent Garden.

To the many archivists and librarians who assisted me, I owe an unpayable debt. Special thanks are reserved for the staffs of the Dance Collection, Lincoln Center; the Theatre Museum, Covent Garden; the British Library, Bloomsbury; the Newspaper Library, Colindale, England; the Library of the Victoria and Albert Museum, South Kensington; and the Central Reference Library, St. Martin's Street, London. My deep gratitude as well to Tatiana Massine Weinbaum, who secured permission for me to view her father's films, now housed in the Jerome Robbins Dance Division of the New York Public Library; the late George Verdak, who allowed use of his private dance history archives in Indianapolis; Prof. Bonnie Krueger and Nathaniel Ver Gow, who translated my French and Italian material. Without the assistance of Hamilton College's Information Technology Services, and support specialist Gretchen Schultes in particular, the technical difficulties in translating draft software would have been nearly insurmountable. Her expertise, kindness, and patience have been extraordinary. Lastly, I thank my colleague, Prof. George O'Connell, for his close critical reading and invaluable suggestions.

1

July 1895–May 1917

Leonid Fedorovich Miassine was born in Moscow on July 27, 1895. Both of his parents were employed at the Imperial Theatre in Moscow, Mme Miassine as a soprano in the Bolshoi Theatre Chorus, and M. Miassine as a French horn player in the Bolshoi Orchestra. Leonid had three brothers—Mikhail, Gregori, and Konstantin—and one sister, Raissa. His closest relationship was with Konstantin, the brother nearest to him in age.

The year Leonid turned seven, he and the family spent the first of what would become many idyllic respites at their wooden dacha in Zvenigorod-Moskovsky, about forty miles from Moscow. Leonid and Konstantin often hunted partridge and guinea-fowl, and there were times when he joined the village children in games. But even at this early age, Miassine began to prefer solitude: "Although I enjoyed the warmth of family life, I was happiest wandering by myself through the dense pine forest."[1] When he was eight, his father took him to the nearby monastery of St. Saavo, where he saw the body of the monastery's patron saint, preserved under glass: "The sight of his mortal remains produced in me a curious sensation. I could almost feel his presence pervading the building, and in my boyish way I understood his renunciation of the material world, and his search for a contemplative, spiritual life.... I think some pattern or pervasive theme in my future creative life began to take shape on that morning."[2]

Until he was eight years old, Leonid was educated at home, but

Madame Chernova, a friend of Mme Miassine's, was struck by Leonid's good looks and obvious love of dancing. At her suggestion, he took the entrance exams to the Moscow Imperial Theatre School in 1904 and was accepted into the ballet division for the regular trial period of one year.

Fin-de-siècle ballet in St. Petersburg had become rather hidebound, steeped in the nineteenth-century classicism of Marius Petipa. In Moscow, however, Alexander Gorsky was leading the Bolshoi Ballet toward a new approach that would soon be embraced by Michel Fokine. Turning to the innovative theatrical ideas of Konstantin Stanislavsky, Gorsky revised the old ballets from the viewpoint of the logic of their plots and their fidelity to principles of realism. He carried these revisions to the point of oddity at times. In *Giselle*, for instance, he had the Wilis wearing nightgowns, since he felt they were more realistic than the traditional tutus.[3] During his tenure at the Bolshoi, Gorsky taught his students that fine acting and expressive use of the torso, arms and head were more important than technical virtuosity. The impact of this emphasis on Miassine during his formative years cannot be overstated.

Once the trial period was completed, a student examination was required for final acceptance into the school. Miassine passed and proved such a diligent and hard-working student that he caught the eye of Gorsky, who needed a small, dark student to play the role of the dwarf Chernomor in a new production of Glinka's *Russlan and Ludmilla*. The role of Chernomor ignited in Miassine the passion to become an actor. He must have made a good impression, for in the years 1908–09 he was cast in three juvenile roles at the Bolshoi and Maly theatres.

In September of 1909 Miassine suffered a personal tragedy which left "an ineffaceable scar."[4] During a hunting expedition with a friend at Zvenigorod-Moskovsky, his brother Konstantin was accidentally shot and killed. There was no one on earth to whom Miassine was closer than Konstantin, and it took him a lifetime to finally reconcile himself to this tragedy.

When he returned to school after the mourning period, Miassine's acting opportunities at the Moscow Imperial Theatres expanded, and he landed such choice roles as the young Tsar Feodorivich in *1613*. He also continued to perform juvenile roles in ballet productions at the Bolshoi. As the Monkey in *Pharaoh's Daughter*, he had a feature role in which he had to swing down from the branch of an exotic tree, perform a short solo on all fours, and swing back to the tree on his grapevine.

Leonid graduated from the Moscow Theatre School in August 1912 and was promptly accepted into the Bolshoi Ballet. In his first year as a professional, he danced solo roles in three ballets choreographed by

Gorsky. Even so, Miassine was still not wholeheartedly committed to being a dancer as opposed to an actor. By special permission from the Bolshoi's regisseur, he also found time to participate in theatre performances at the Maly.

The winter season of 1913 was a pivotal one for Miassine. At the beginning of December he danced the Knight of the Silver Moon in *Don Quixote* and the tarantella in *Swan Lake*. Sergei Diaghilev was present at these performances. Diaghilev had been the co-editor of *Mir Iskusstva* ("World of Art"), a pivotal journal which disseminated emerging artistic trends in Europe and revitalized interest in the native heritage of Russian art. The 1905 Exhibition of Russian Portraits, organized by Diaghilev at the Tauride Palace, was the first important representative exhibition of Russian paintings through the ages. With his 1906 exhibition of Russian art in Paris, Diaghilev began what could be called an "export campaign of Russian art." In the next two years, Diaghilev brought to Paris Russian concert music and opera, and in 1909 the impresario set his sights on the Russian ballet. Through his efforts, Western Europe would witness the revolutionary choreography of Michel Fokine, whose work, like Gorsky's, stressed realism and expressionism over the more artificial style of Petipa.

With Fokine, artists Alexandre Benois and Leon Bakst, and a group of dancers borrowed temporarily from the Imperial Theatres—among them the legendary Vaslav Nijinsky—Diaghilev launched his first season of Russian ballet in Paris at the Théâtre du Châtelet on May 18, 1909. The Ballets Russes was striking in its novelty, and it took Paris by storm. Not only were its purely artistic merits beyond dispute, but its spectacular boldness electrified audiences. For the next twenty years, excepting the war years, the Ballets Russes held regular Paris seasons and soon expanded its bookings throughout Europe.

In the winter of 1913 Diaghilev went to Moscow to recruit a leading dancer for his forthcoming production of *The Legend of Joseph*. When the ballet was first planned in 1912, it was intended that Vaslav Nijinsky would choreograph and dance the title role. However, Nijinsky's astonishing marriage to Romola de Pulszky in September 1913 led Diaghilev to sever contact with Nijinsky, who was not only the company's leading dancer/choreographer but Diaghilev's lover as well.

Diaghilev was captivated by Miassine's charismatic stage presence in the Bolshoi performances: he felt that he had found his ideal Joseph. He immediately enlisted Mikhail Savitsky, a new member of the Ballets Russes, to arrange a meeting at Diaghilev's temporary abode, the Metropole Hotel. The day when Leonid first encountered Diaghilev at the

Metropole was the most important one of his life: he "timidly" worked his way through the ornate lobby, the gold-braided porters, and Diaghilev's imposing valet. A moment later, Diaghilev appeared: "At first glance he appeared tall and imposing, but when I stood up I realized that he was only of medium height, but that he had an unusually large head and broad shoulders. The next thing I noticed was the streak of silver-white hair, like a feather, over his forehead. Peering at me through his monocle, he looked to me like a creature from another world."[5]

When Diaghilev offered him an audition for the role of Joseph, Miassine returned at once to the Theatre School for the advice of his friends. Most counseled against such a move, reminding Miassine that he was being considered for Romeo in the upcoming Maly production of *Romeo and Juliet*, a role that could launch his career as a leading actor. Days of "restless indecision" followed, but Leonid retuned to the hotel determined to refuse Diaghilev's offer. When he walked in, though, "I was just about to tell him that I could not accept his offer when, almost without realizing it, I heard myself say, 'Yes, I shall be delighted to join your company.'"[6]

Before arriving in Moscow, Diaghilev had deboarded in St. Petersburg to see Fokine, who had bitterly left the Ballets Russes when he saw that Nijinsky was supplanting him as the company's main choreographer. Now that Nijinsky had been ousted, Diaghilev was successful in persuading Fokine to choreograph *The Legend of Joseph*. Diaghilev now returned to St. Petersburg with Miassine, where the latter was to audition for Fokine. Fokine's "audition" was singularly odd: Leonid was asked to reproduce the positions of a Guilio Romano mural in Fokine's bedroom and to demonstrate his elevation by jumping over a three-foot chair. Miassine vaulted the hurdle without a graze and was accepted for the title role.

Miassine then returned to Moscow, got a discharge from the Imperial Theatres as of January 1, 1914, and rejoined Diaghilev in St. Petersburg. From there they went to Cologne to join the company. During their train journey, Diaghilev told him of his new concept for ballet—a modern-day *Gesamtkunstwerk*, or perfect blending of dance, drama, music and painting. Leonid listened, spellbound: "I began to feel that all my past experience had been negligible, and that I was now embarking on an entirely new career." He was "exhilarated at the prospect of working with such a man as Diaghilev,"[7] and he became infatuated with his new mentor. It was soon apparent that the attraction was mutual.

Miassine admired the depth and intensity of Fokine's characterizations and his natural, flowing movements. However, he did not adapt easily to Fokine's style. He wrote, "During the first week of rehearsals I

Sergei Diaghilev, 1928. *(Sasha)*

struggled to readjust my body so as to achieve the effortless rhythm which Fokine demanded.... I remained convinced that I had undertaken a task which was beyond me." By his own admission, Miassine "had almost no technique."[8] Tamara Karsavina wrote, "I don't think anyone, least of all myself, could have guessed the future top-rank choreographer ... in that frail-looking, shy boy. In the dance of the brothers he was, compared with the others, rather weak and uncertain of his steps."[9] Leonid was far more comfortable with the acting component of his role, especially since he could empathize with Joseph's plight. In the scenes where he tried to ward off the lurid advances of Potiphar's Wife, he found that "each time I struggled with her, I seemed to project into my acting all my own anguish and heartbreak at having left Russia."[10]

In the spring of 1914, the company arrived in Monte Carlo. There, Miassine met Misia Edwards Sert, Diaghilev's staunchest friend and supporter, and her lover, José María Sert, who was designing the sets for *Joseph*. While in Monte Carlo, Miassine took daily private lessons with the celebrated teacher Enrico Cecchetti, classes which continued when the company moved to Paris in May of 1914.

Miassine's first rehearsals on the Paris Opéra stage did nothing to relieve his insecurities. The stage was so steeply raked that he had great difficulty keeping his balance. For the May 14 opening-night performance, Leonid "was in a pitiable state of nervous tension.... Struggling to retain my balance on the huge sloping stage during my solo dance, I felt my ordeal was far worse than anything that Joseph had been called upon to endure."[11] Still, despite insinuations in the press that his dancing posed no threat to Nijinsky, Miassine was praised for his sensitive dramatic portrayal.

After Paris, the company began a London season at the Drury Lane Theatre on June 8. Miassine made his British debut in *Joseph* on June 23. As in Paris, reviewers complimented him on his striking appearance and stage presence even as they acknowledged his technical weaknesses. Overall, *The Legend of Joseph* was unsuccessful. It had a massive Renaissance setting and a bombastic score by Richard Strauss, neither of which were well suited to the simplicity of the parable. Charles Ricketts, the distinguished painter and stage designer, left us with a droll description of *Joseph*'s conclusion:

> At a gesture from Potiphar a burning cauldron is brought on to the stage, Joseph is wrapped in chains, and irons are heated.
> Then the music becomes vulgar beyond belief, a light breaks upon Joseph, the chains fall off, and a golden archangel passes across the upper stage, descends, and leads Joseph off to the Savoy Hotel—

I believe—to a sort of parody of Wagnerian apotheosis music of the worst type.[12]

During the London engagement, Diaghilev took Miassine on visits to London's great art museums and engaged an English tutor for him. Of course, the most important aspect of his education was rigorous daily training with Cecchetti. Despite his exciting growth in knowledge and facility, the sudden upheaval of his life in Moscow, not to mention his, by then, sexual relationship with Diaghilev must have been stressful for Leonid. Since leaving Moscow he had maintained a close correspondence with his family; both his letters and his memoirs repeatedly express "homesickness" during this period.

By July 1914 Diaghilev and Miassine were back in Paris. Shortly thereafter Austria-Hungary declared war on Serbia. By the time they arrived in Milan on August 4, Germany had declared war on Russia and France and had invaded Belgium. World War I had begun in earnest; Diaghilev realized that events in Europe were too serious to permit reassembling the company in Berlin in October as he had planned. At present, there was little he could do but enjoy a vacation in Italy with Miassine.

They spent a month and a half in Florence, where Miassine's artistic education accelerated. Under Diaghilev's tutelage, he acquired a fairly detailed knowledge of the Byzantine, Gothic, Renaissance and Baroque styles. Miassine was most deeply impressed by those paintings of Cimabue, Duccio and Lorenzetti whose theme was worldly renunciation. He wrote, "As I walked through the churches and museums of Florence I felt again that sense of peace and exaltation which I had experienced as a child of eight.... Perhaps it had been an unconscious identification of myself with St Saavo which had stirred my youthful emotions. Now I felt that my response to these primitive paintings derived from the same longing for a contemplative, spiritual life."[13]

Diaghilev stressed the technical aspects of the paintings under study. The impresario believed that meticulous analysis of a painting could teach a budding choreographer how to pose and configure dancers harmoniously onstage. One day in the Uffizi, Diaghilev said to him: "Do you think you could compose a ballet?" Miassine hedged at first, but then said, "Yes. I think I can create a ballet. Not only one, but a hundred, I promise you."[14] It was the sight of Simone Martini's *Annunciation* which gave him the courage to say "Yes." Nothing could be more indicative of Leonid's idealism, of his vision of life's calling as a relentless spiritual mission.

The two men left Florence for Rome where they took up residence at the Grand Hotel in November. In the first months of 1915, Diaghilev began negotiating a financially critical tour of North America with Otto Kahn, chairman of the board of the Metropolitan Opera. At the end of April, Diaghilev and Miassine left for Switzerland, where the company was to be reassembled to rehearse for their American debut in January 1916. Diaghilev rented a villa called Bellerive, located on Lake Geneva near the outskirts of Lausanne.

Once they arrived, Diaghilev cabled two Russian avant-garde painters, Natalie Gontcharova and Mikhail Larionov, to join him in Switzerland. They arrived on July 16, and he set them up in a studio in the garden of Bellerive. By hiring them, Diaghilev gave early evidence of his desire to turn towards modernist art.

Soon, dancers began arriving in Lausanne. Some were original members of the Ballets Russes who had scattered once the war broke out; others had been recruited in Russia and Poland by regisseur Serge Grigoriev. Miassine was in a powerful position once the company reconvened. It was obvious that most of their activity would center around Leonid's apprenticeship, and his intimacy with Diaghilev was tacitly acknowledged.

For Miassine's first project, Diaghilev suggested a liturgical ballet based on the Passion of Jesus Christ and taking the form of a series of tableaux in the style of Byzantine mosaics and Italian primitives. Gontcharova began work on designs based on geometrical Byzantine icons, while Larionov assisted with the choreography. Diaghilev asked Igor Stravinsky to compose the score for this new ballet, to be called *Liturgie*, but Stravinsky had other commitments. It was then decided that the ballet would be performed without music except for interludes of orthodox chants from Kiev. But when Diaghilev was unable to obtain the chants from Russia, the entire project was dropped, much to Miassine's distress.

In the fall, Diaghilev arranged two Red Cross benefit performances, one in Geneva, the other in Paris. He needed a new work to introduce before leaving for America, and he suggested that Miassine try his hand at a less ambitious ballet that could spring directly from his own experience, something straightforwardly Russian. A suite drawn from Rimsky-Korsakov's opera *Snegourouchka* ("The Snow Maiden") was chosen for a ballet to be entitled *Le Soleil de nuit*. The ballet was based on popular Russian folk legends. For about two weeks each June, the sun never sets in Northern Russia but lingers on to give the people nights of curious, incandescent beauty. It was a venerable custom in Russian peasant communities to pay tribute to Yarila, the sun god, in song and dance at the yearly advent of the "White Nights."

Mikhail Larionov, whose knowledge of Russian folklore was vast, was again assigned to assist Miassine with his choreography. The ballet was introduced on December 20 in a single performance at the Grand Théâtre in Geneva and at a December 29 charity matinee at the Paris Opéra. It was enthusiastically received at both performances, giving Miassine a great boost in self-confidence.

On January 1, 1916, the company sailed from Bordeaux to New York. Diaghilev was terrified of the sea and rarely departed from his cabin, never leaving it without donning a life jacket. Most of the time, his morbid fear kept him on his knees in fervent prayer during the Atlantic crossing (except at mealtimes, when he deputed his valet to do the praying). By journey's end, his phobia had nearly pushed his nerves to the point of collapse, and he kissed the soil of America upon landing.

For the American debut at New York's Century Theatre, the awkward name of "Miassine" was changed to "Massine" and Leonid's first name was Gallicized. *Le Soleil de nuit*, with Léonide Massine in the leading role, was on the first program. During the tour, he also danced the leads in *L'Après-midi d'un faune, Petrouchka, Scheherazade*, and *The Firebird*.

The Metropolitan première met with mixed reviews because of the absence of Vaslav Nijinsky and the Ballets Russes's prima ballerina, Tamara Karsavina. Press and public were also shocked or even outraged at the risqué, adult content of such works as *Scheherazade* and *L'Après-midi d'un faune*. After all, *Scheherazade* depicts an interracial orgy in which white women take black slaves as their lovers. What's more, in *L'Après-midi*, the Faun prostrates himself on a filmy scarf left by a nymph and masturbates atop this item as the curtain falls. Some offended New Yorkers demanded censorship action, and Diaghilev was summoned to a hearing in the chambers of Judge McAdoo on January 24, 1916. According to the *New York Sun*, "The Russians listened with the grave patience and the puzzled amusement with which intelligent folk from Continental Europe have often watched the working of the censorship of municipal authorities over the American theater. ... [They] naturally wearied of noisy bickering and agreed to alter certain items."[15]

As the *Herald Tribune* noted, "A moral *Scheherazade* is about as possible of realization as a continent Don Juan."[16] It was somewhat easier to give *L'Après-midi d'un faune* a quick fix. The very evening of the summons, *L'Après-midi* was on the Century's bill again. The *New York Times* reported that "the faun [Massine] placed the drapery gently on the rock and sat gazing dreamily at its silken folds. Then the curtain fell."[17]

The New York season ended on January 29. Two days later the company opened in Boston, the first leg of a tour that would include sixteen

Leaving Chicago, 1916. First U.S. tour of the Ballets Russes. Left to right: Adolf Bolm, Serge Grigoriev, Léonide Massine, Hilda Bhuck, unknown woman, Sergei Diaghilev, Lydia Lopokova, Lubov Tchernicheva, Olga Khokhlova.

more American cities. But did Diaghilev keep his promise to "alter certain items" once touring took him out of the range of Justice McAdoo? Certainly not, if the *Chicago Examiner* is any indication. For the Chicago Auditorium performance, critic Ashton Stevens reported:

> "The Faun," you may recall, is the *tableau chorégraphique* that suffered moderation recently at the hands of censorious New York. It was there held that Mr. Massine rode too realistically on the bit of drapery left behind by the tempting nymph.... But Massine did not seem to omit anything.... The faun fell—not supinated, as had been suggested by way of revision for the timid—over the scarf.... He was in the third dimension only when, in the climax, his right hoof parted from his left.[18]

Word of the degenerate ballet folks' shenanigans spread rapidly to Kansas City, and the Deputy Chief of Police, Captain Ennis, was ordered to give a warning to this troupe when they arrived in his fair city on April 3, 1916. Although Ennis was a little foggy on the Russian impresario's name, he called upon Diaghilev before the first performance and gave his version of their encounter to the *Kansas City Star*:

> They'd have tried to put something over if I hadn't seen 'em before it started. I dropped in to see Dogleaf before the curtain went up. Dogleaf, or whatever his name is, couldn't understand plain English. ... I told [an interpreter], "This is a strictly moral town and we won't stand for any of that highbrow immorality. Put on your show, but keep it toned down to the decency of a high class city where they don't stand for any monkey shines." What's more, I told him we didn't want to make trouble, but if the show was too rank I'd come right up on the stage and call down the curtain. Well, they took my advice. There were several places where they cut out some stuff lots of people would like to have seen, but I guess they remembered my warning.[19]

The American tour gave Massine the opportunity to perform several legendary roles. Of all of them, he found Petrouchka the "most rewarding" because he felt a strong sense of identification with the character.[20] Perhaps he was already subconsciously casting Diaghilev in the role of the ubiquitous, controlling Charlatan as well.

To everyone's amazement, Massine began to pay attention to a female company member. Lubov Tchernicheva was married to regisseur Serge Grigoriev, but she still loved to flirt—in private, Diaghilev referred to her as "Hotpants."[21] At a Red Cross benefit in Washington, D.C., Lydia Sokolova, Massine, and Tchernicheva sneaked into a deserted room. According to Sokolova, Massine and Tchernicheva were laughing and flirting when, to their horror, they saw Diaghilev watching them in the doorway. The next morning, a message came round via Diaghilev's servant, Vassili, "that anybody who interfered with the peace of the company by disturbing Massine in his work would be expelled immediately. Léonide and the lady did not speak to each other for many a day after that. As for the rest of us, any girl who valued her position in the company was careful to steer clear of Massine."[22]

Despite his ill will towards Nijinsky, Diaghilev had hoped to re-engage him for the American tour as the company's main box-office draw. However, during the war Nijinsky was interned in Budapest as an enemy alien. To free him, Diaghilev and Otto Kahn called upon the influence of Queen Alexandra of England, the dowager empress Maria Feodorovna, Emperor Franz Joseph of Austria, King Alfonso XIII of Spain and the Pope. The dancer and his family were finally released and landed in New York on April 4, the day after the Ballets Russes had its opening at the Metropolitan Opera.

Otto Kahn had organized a second American tour to follow the April 29 closing at the Met. Well aware of the hostility between Nijinsky and Diaghilev and recognizing that the latter was far more expendable, Kahn proposed to rent the company from the impresario for the second tour. Diaghilev knew that the tour was unlikely to be well-managed without him, but he also knew that it would be profitable. So he accepted Kahn's proposal on the condition that the company would first honor its engagements in Spain. Nijinsky would wait for the Ballets Russes in America.

The Ballets Russes had accepted an invitation from King Alfonso XIII to perform at Madrid's Teatro Real, beginning on May 26. King Alfonso XIII was no master of statecraft—by 1931, the country's economy would be in ruins, and he would have to abdicate—but he was a *bon vivant* of considerable savvy and good taste. His wife, Queen Ena, was so beautiful that when the royal family was in its box in the theater, the Ballets Russes dancers took turns peeking at her through the drop curtain. The royal couple loved ballet and were it not for their patronage, the Ballets Russes might not have survived the war years.

After the season at the Teatro Real ended on June 9, the company continued with engagements in Seville, Granada and Córdoba and then proceeded to San Sebastián, the court's fashionable summer resort. King Alfonso had asked Diaghilev to arrange two gala performances there at the end of August. Diaghilev wished to offer a ballet on a Spanish theme as a tribute to the Spanish monarch, who had formally declared himself Diaghilev's protector.

Diaghilev suggested that Massine create a work to Fauré's *Pavane*, a piece which reminded Massine of a Velásquez painting in the Prado which fascinated him. In this painting—named *Las Meninas*—two tiny girls can be seen wearing sumptuous court dresses with the exaggeratedly stiff, wide panniers of the period. "The children, aping their elders in clothes and deportment, were sad little Ladies-in-Waiting—waiting for maturity whilst childhood passed them by."[22] Massine's ballet kept the title of the painting and created a period piece in which the girls, now teenagers, had paramours.

Diaghilev also wanted to première one Russian novelty for the gala. He suggested to Massine one of the fairy-tale settings of the composer Anatole Lyadov. They decided to adapt the setting of a witch who kills her cat and named the ballet *Kikimora*.

Both *Kikimora* and *Las Meninas* premièred in San Sebastián on August 25, *Las Meninas* was doubly pleasing to the king because it paid homage to the traditions of the Spanish monarchy. Soon after its première, Massine reported that "we had become firm favourites with the Spanish Court."[24]

Following performances at the end of August in Bilbao, the Ballets Russes went to Bordeaux, where the bulk of the company sailed for New York on September 8. A splinter nucleus of dancers would remain in Europe. Diaghilev and Massine rented a furnished apartment complete with piano at the Corso Umberto in Rome. They were soon joined by Gontcharova, Larionov, and the Cecchettis. The apartment at Corso Umberto became the collaborators' artistic headquarters during their six-and-one-half-month stay in Rome.

For the next ballet, Diaghilev decided that an Italian subject would be appropriate and suggested that Massine read Goldoni's comedy, *Le donne di buon' umore* (in French, *Les Femmes de bonne humeur*). Goldoni's style of commedia dell'arte—a blend of mime, dance, and acrobatics—appealed to Massine's own sense of theatre. The comedy was a typical Goldoni imbroglio, dauntingly complex, with subplot piled upon subplot. To be in harmony with the period, Diaghilev decided that the music should come from Goldoni's contemporary, Domenico Scarlatti. He hired a pianist who played, often repeatedly, all 560 of the Scarlatti sonatas. Diaghilev and Massine finally chose twenty which would best enhance the comic action.

To evoke the style and manner of the period, Massine delved into the seventeenth- and eighteenth-century choreographic treatises Diaghilev had acquired for him at an auction in Paris. These included first editions of works by Carlo Blasis, Raoul Feuillet, Louis Pecour, and Jean-Philippe Rameau. The Goldoni ballet was choreographed almost entirely on the small nucleus of company dancers who had remained in Europe, and Massine had the luxury of several months in which to rehearse it.

Kikimora had been so successful when it premièred in San Sebastián that Diaghilev asked Massine and Larionov to expand the work into a longer ballet. The result, *Contes russes*, consisted of three Russian folktales—"Kikimora," "The Swan Princess and the Dragon," and "Baba Yaga." *Contes russes* was a sumptuous ballet which would seal Larionov's reputation when first performed in Paris in May of 1917.

The main company had returned from its American tour in April, and Diaghilev arranged some performances at Rome's Teatro Costanzi. The first performance on April 12, 1917, saw the première of *Les Femmes de bonne humeur*, and it was a hit with both press and public.

The most famous Ballets Russes creation of this Rome period was a cubo-futurist ballet called *Parade*. With decor by Pablo Picasso, a score by Erik Satie, a libretto by the French poet and dramatist Jean Cocteau and choreography by Massine, it was a distinguished collaboration indeed. *Parade* was planned and created in the winter of 1917, during the main company's second American tour.

Meeting Picasso was a momentous occasion for the impressionable twenty-one-year-old Léonide. One afternoon at the Corso Umberto, Massine noticed that Picasso was taking a "sudden and rather unusual interest" in a conventional eighteenth-century portrait which hung over the sofa. "Pablo, why are you so fascinated by that picture?" Diaghilev asked him. "I am studying it carefully," Picasso replied, "in order to learn how not to paint."[25]

By the end of April 1917, *Parade* was nearing its definitive form. With *Contes russes*, it was scheduled to première at a series of war benefit performances at the Théâtre du Châtelet May 11–18. Paris awaited *Parade* with breathless anticipation, and the Châtelet was sold out fifteen days before its May 18 première. This ballet was actually presented right in the middle of the Battle of Verdun. Reminiscing on a 1916 letter from Erik Satie, Misia Sert wrote, "I re-read the date three times before I could make myself believe that it really was at that time, at the peak of battle, that we kept minds so free as to be able to carry on with artistic undertakings important enough to mark a place in history."[26]

LE SOLEIL DE NUIT (Midnight Sun)

Ballet in One Act
Music: Nikolai Rimsky-Korsakov, the "Arcadian Revels" from the opera
    Snegourouchka ("Snow Maiden")
Scenic and Costume Design: Mikhail Larionov
Première: Grand Théâtre, Geneva, December 20, 1915

ORIGINAL CAST

Yarila, the Sun God: Léonide Massine
Bobyl the Innocent: Nicholas Zverev
The Snow Maiden: Lydia Lopokova

Synopsis

The ballet begins with a spirited children's game, similar to "hide and seek." The dancers' boisterous play breaks off into a stately khorovod, interrupted now and then by the village simpleton, Bobyl the Innocent, who tries to distract each couple in turn. The dancers sit down in a circle as an offstage soprano explains the rites to Yarila, the sun god, while the Snow Maiden interprets her lyrics in dance. Suddenly Yarila appears, dances a brilliant variation, and accepts his worshippers' homage. Four of his subjects form the wheel of Phaeton's chariot, and Yarila mounts to the heavens. The ballet concludes with the "Dance of the Buffoons," led by Bobyl and performed by men bearing pig bladders on the end of long poles.

Scenery and Costumes

Mikhail Larionov came to prominence in the West through his work for Diaghilev's Ballets Russes. In 1898 he entered the Moscow School of Painting, Sculpture and Architecture. There he met Natalie Gontcharova, who was to remain his lifelong companion. In 1906 he was invited to participate in the Russian art exhibition at the Salon d'Automne in Paris. The following year Larionov helped organize the 1908 Golden Fleece exhibition of modern French painting in Moscow, which influenced many young Russian artists to embrace the brighter palette and coarser brushwork of Post-Impressionism and Fauvism.

In 1911, though, Larionov and Gontcharova broke entirely with the French tradition and formed a new group and journal with the provocative name, "The Donkey's Tail." The title was suggested by the reviews of eminent French art critics who had recently lavished praise on a certain Russian painting exhibited in Paris. To their chagrin, the critics learned that the painting they had lauded was the work of prankster students who had tied paint brushes dipped into various paint pots onto a donkey's tail and then cajoled the ass to swish them about freely onto the canvas![27] The Donkey's Tail organized several non–French exhibitions from 1911 to 1913.

In 1913, Larionov created the art movement known as Rayonism, a non-objective style which theorizes that the eye does not see actual objects, but only the rays emanating from them. The artist uses the collision of these rays in space to create new forms. Concurrently, Larionov was also an exponent of Neo-Primitivism, a modern reinterpretation of Russian folk art. In 1914 Larionov went to Paris to see the Ballets Russes première of *Le Coq d'or*, which Gontcharova had designed in the neo-primitive style. Her sets took Paris by storm, and soon both Larionov and Gontcharova were being fêted as the art world's *dernier cri*.[28]

In 1919 Larionov settled permanently in Paris where he acted as Gontcharova's agent. He was an important member of the Ecole de Paris, a term which referred to non–French artists who had settled in Paris, most of them in Montmartre or Montparnasse. Larionov's Neo-Primitivism stemmed from his belief that Russian art had been impoverished by European values and should be reinvigorated by its own cultural traditions. His rayonist theory that a picture could be "constructed" according to a specific method strongly influenced the evolution of Russian constructivism as well as abstract art itself.

Larionov's decor for *Le Soleil de nuit* had a strong visual impact. The backdrop in deep blue and green set off the red-gold and white costumes, and there was a vivid red valance of sun figures across the front of the stage. The costumes were traditionally Russian with very tall, mitre-shaped headdresses known as *kitchki*. Lydia Sokolova complained that the costumes "were appallingly uncomfortable.... We had horrible thick pads tied round our waists, then we wore tight heavy costumes on top of them. The [kitchki] ... once they had slipped slightly to one side, just refused to stand up straight again."[29] Apparently, the dancers never found a way to stabilize the kitchki. Of the work's 1938 revival, Sir Lionel Bradley wrote that Bobyl the Innocent's "lack of precision was useful tonight as it enabled him to wander about the stage picking up the shoes and hats which other dancers had dropped."[30] All in all, though, Larionov's designs made a striking impression as a neo-primitive interpretation of Russian folk culture. Larionov's subsequent design creations for Diaghilev were *Contes russes* (1916), *Chout* (1921) and *Le Renard* (1922).

Music

St. Petersburg in 1860 depended on foreign sources for both the composition and performance of its operatic and concert repertory. A fundamental reason for the shortage of Russian musicians was the inadequacy of musical education in Russia. Even with a foreign education, a Russian composer had small chance of success. Neither the Theater Directorate nor the concert societies nor the general public showed an inclination for native music.

In the 1860s the musical world of St. Petersburg underwent a transformation that gave it an emphatically Russian identity. The most important catalyst was the founding of the Russian Musical Society in 1859. According to its charter, the Society would provide "the opportunity for native composers to hear their own compositions in performance."[31] The weekly RMS concerts of Russian music brought even the aristocrats around, and several contributed to the original charter of the St. Petersburg Conservatory. It opened its doors in 1861, the same year in which Nikolai Rimsky-Korsakov joined the group of amateur composers—Balakirev, Borodin, Cui, and Mussorgsky—dubbed "The Mighty Five."

Rimsky-Korsakov and The Five vaunted their amateurism and launched their nationalist music against the professional establishment. In 1871 Nikolai accepted a teaching post at the St. Petersburg Conservatory. Already a recognized composer, he had to teach himself the traditional musical techniques before he could teach his students. An unfortunate academicism then permeated his music, disappearing only in the 1880s with the appearance of such works as *The Snow Maiden* (1882) and *Scheherazade* (1888).

The Snow Maiden was based on an 1874 fairy tale of pagan sun worship by A. N. Ostrovski. Upon reading it, Nikolai's "warmth towards ancient Russian custom and pagan pantheism ... now blazed forth in a bright flame."[32] In composing *The Snow Maiden*, Rimsky-Korsakov made considerable use of Russian folk tunes, many with delightful titles. There is "Eagle—the commander-in-chief; quail—the court clerk"; "The beaver was bathing"; and "That I am dreadful, indeed you've told the truth!"[33]

Rimsky-Korsakov's conservatory students included Stravinsky, Lyadov, and Prokofiev. Besides teaching and composing, he undertook the task of orchestrating the works of his deceased friends Mussorgsky and Borodin. Eleven of his fifteen operas were written between 1895 and 1907, ending with *The Golden Cockerel*.

Choreography

Le Soleil de nuit fused—as did the opera—the legend of the sun god Yarila with that of the Snow Maiden, daughter of King Frost, who melts in the heat of the sun when she falls in love with a mortal. At his parents' summer home, Massine would often join the village children at play: "Our favourite game was one in which we formed a large group with one on guard in front of us. To distract his attention as we tried to slip past him without being caught, we shouted to each other, laughed and sang an old rhyme."[34] It was this children's game that provided the inspiration for the opening sequence of *Le Soleil de nuit*.

In the next section, the dancers performed a gentle round dance

Studio portrait of Massine as Yarila in *Le Soleil de nuit*. *(MAURICE SEYMOUR)*

known as a khorovod, while being pestered by Bobyl the Innocent. Massine gave Nicholas Zverev "loose uncoordinated movements and a sad, helpless expression" for this tragi-comic role. For the "Dance of the Buffoons," Massine devised a succession of interwoven leaps, twists, and turns. He wrote that these dancers had "tremendous gusto," and that "when the Buffoons entered carrying pigs' bladders on sticks, they banged them on the ground with such force that some of them shot into the orchestra pit."[35]

As Yarila, Massine created a solo for himself that showed his electrifying stage presence to great advantage:

> Larionov had designed for me a sumptuous glittering costume with a fantastic headdress of burning red suns which glowed against the inky-blue of the midnight sky. Attached to my hands by elastic were two more gold suns, the size of dinner plates, decorated with jagged red borders. As I danced, I flashed them in rapidly alternating rhythms, to the left, to the right, over my head, down below my knees. In order to sustain the illusion of a revolving sun, I was forced to keep every muscle in my body in constant motion until the end of the dance. But I could feel power pulsating within me, and by the end I had reached a fever pitch of excitement.[36]

Massine's first ballet made a good impression on his colleagues. Grigoriev saw that "With *Soleil de nuit* Diaghilev was assured that he no longer had any need of either Fokine or Nijinsky."[37] Misia and José María Sert came down from Paris to see the new work. The assurance of Massine's choreography came as a surprise, since they had blamed him for the failure of *The Legend of Joseph*. Now, in a letter to Cocteau, Misia described "Something completely new, very beautiful, in which Massine proves that he really is someone. And how prejudiced we were against him, Sert and I!!!"[38]

Critical Survey

Le Soleil de nuit was warmly received at its Geneva première. The *Journal de Genève* reported that "*Le Soleil de nuit* was a delight. It was like a box of Russian toys brought to life and laughter."[39] During the 1916 U.S.A. tour, *Le Soleil de nuit* proved to be popular with both press and public: the *New York Sun* thought Larionov's decor a "tour de force of effective stage decoration"; the *Christian Science Monitor* said that it had "an irresistible appeal because of the feeling of folk life that pervades it"; and the *Musical Leader* praised the "youth and promise of its choreographer."[40]

In Retrospect

Le Soleil de nuit stayed in the active repertory until 1918 and was revived for the Ballet Russes's 1928 season and for the 1938 season of the Ballet Russe de Monte Carlo. It was most recently revived for the Oakland Ballet in 1979. *Le Soleil de nuit* revealed at an early stage Massine's flair for humor, character dance and fast-paced theatricality. Inarguably, it was an auspicious first venture.

LAS MENINAS

Ballet in One Scene
Music: Gabriel Fauré
Set: Carlo Socrate
Costumes: José María Sert
Première: Teatro Eugenia-Victoria, San Sebastián, August 25, 1916

ORIGINAL CAST
First Couple: Lydia Sokolova, Léonide Massine
Second Couple: Olga Kokhlova, Leon Woizikowsky

Synopsis

Two ladies-in-waiting meet secretly—or so they think—with two courtiers. The couples perform a pavane as a dwarf makes her presence known and then rushes off, conveying in mime her intention to spread the scandal of illicit love. She is apprehended and a series of pas de deux in all possible combinations ensues, each designed to evoke the ambience of the court of Philip IV and the underlying sadness and strained formality of Spain's Golden Age.

Scenery and Costumes

Socrate's set depicted a garden overlooked by a balcony, and Sert designed costumes inspired by the work of Velásquez. *Las Meninas*' women wore huge hoop skirts which had to be put on in the wings, for they couldn't fit in the dressing rooms. Sokolova wore purple and gold and Kokhlova, salmon pink and silver. Their wigs were twice the width of their shoulders. According to Sokolova, the costumes were "so heavy that when you turned round you had to do it very carefully all in one piece."[41] For Edwin Evans, the women resembled "huge, hovering butterflies."[42]

Music

Gabriel Fauré developed a style that had considerable influence on many early twentieth-century composers. He attended the Ecole Niedermeyer in Paris, where he studied with Saint-Saëns. After graduating in 1865, Fauré became a regular visitor at Saint-Saëns's salon, but his work was generally esteemed only by the members of avant-garde salon circles.

In the 1890s, though, Fauré began to realize some of his ambitions. In 1896 he succeeded Massenet as professor of composition at the Paris

Conservatoire, and in 1905 he was appointed Director. His directorship from 1905 to 1920 made Fauré suddenly famous; his works were now frequently performed at important concerts.

In spite of Fauré's continuous stylistic development, certain traits characterize nearly all his music. Without destroying a sense of tonality, he freed himself from conventional tonal restrictions. His harmonic richness is matched by his consummate mastery of the art of unfolding a melody.[43] Fauré's most daring works were composed after 1890. The restraint, balance, lyricism and subtle detail characteristic of all his music is now enriched with a new sense of force, boldness of harmony and complex polyphony. He remained the most advanced figure in French music until the advent of Debussy. Fauré's outstanding works include the Piano Quartet in C minor (1879), the Requiem, op. 48 (1886), and *Pelléas et Mélisande* (1898).

The slow and majestic *Pavane* in F-sharp minor, op. 50 (1887) was humbly described by Fauré as "elegant ... but otherwise not important."[44] Its orchestral scoring, particularly the inspired woodwind writing, is delicate and airy; the opening flute melody is one of Fauré's most memorable inventions. The *Pavane* to some extent replaced the score that Diaghilev had requested from Fauré in July 1909, a project which was postponed because of other commissions and, later, by the outbreak of war.[45] Fauré, then, never composed a ballet, although quite a number of his works have been staged for ballet, notably the "Emeralds" section of Balanchine's *Jewels*.

Choreography

Las Meninas was expressly designed to be a low-keyed work, but one with meticulous attention to gesture. For Massine, Fauré's *Pavane* contained "haunting echoes of Spain's Golden Age." He spoke of the various pairings of the five dancers as a personal interpretation of Fauré's melancholy music and of the formality and underlying sadness he had glimpsed in Velásquez. However, he made "no attempt to re-create the grandeur of Spain's Golden Age."[46] His approach is well described by critic Alfredo Salazar: "When we saw that tiny delicate work performed on stage we understood clearly what exquisite and refined art was contained in the production; what fine and subtle talent had been involved in its creation."[47]

Critical Survey

Although it was a favorite of the Spanish court, Grigoriev maintained that *Las Meninas* was too understated for the general Spanish public.⁴⁸ In the spring of 1917, the ballet was presented in Naples and Rome, where *Il Giorno* even called it "a bad joke."⁴⁹ When *Las Meninas* was performed for the May 1917 Théâtre du Châtelet season, the ballet seemed pale to French critics, especially in comparison to sensational new works such as *Parade*.

In Retrospect

Diaghilev was fond of this rather unremarkable little ballet, and he kept it in the repertoire to the end of his days. In 1924 he revived the ballet for the Monte Carlo and London seasons, and he did so again for the 1928 London season. *Las Meninas* remained a slight but charming trifle which, to the *Observer*'s relief, was "Blessedly free from any esoteric problems."⁵⁰

LES FEMMES DE BONNE HUMEUR

Ballet in One Act
Based on *Le donne di buon' umore* by Carlo Goldoni
Music: Domenico Scarlatti, orchestrated by Vincenzo Tommasini
Scenic and Costume Design: Leon Bakst
Première: Teatro Costanzi, Rome, April 12, 1917

ORIGINAL CAST

The Marquise Silvestra: Mme Giuseppina Cecchetti
Mariuccia, her maid: Mlle Lydia Lopokova
Leonardo, husband of Felicita: M. Léonide Massine
Constanza: Mlle Lubov Tchernicheva
The Marquis di Luca: M. Enrico Cecchetti
Felicita: Mlle Kokhlova   Dorotea: Mlle Chabelska
Battista, Pasquina's Lover: M. Stanislas Idzikowsky
Pasquina: Mlle Antonova
Niccolo, waiter at the Café: M. Leon Woizikowsky
Rinaldo, Constanza's Lover: M. Sigmund Novak

Synopsis⁵¹

The setting is a small town near Venice in the eighteenth century. On her balcony, we see the elderly and vain Marquise Silvestra "busily engaged in repairing by artifice the ravages made by time" in the hopes of catching a beau at the Carnival. Her maid Mariuccia assists her and mocks her behind her back. Their labors at an end, they go indoors.

Count Rinaldo, "a very exquisite of exquisites," now arrives at the café and is served wine by the waiter, Niccolo. A maid brings him a letter which is really from his fiancée, Constanza, who wishes to test his love.

The note purports to be from a lady infatuated with him; she will reveal her identity by wearing a pink rose in her hair. Constanza comes in with her friends Felicita, Dorotea and Pasquina, and then leaves. All three wear pink roses in their hair, but all disdain Rinaldo's advances. Rinaldo despairs until the Marquise Slivestra, masked and wearing a pink rose, enters. Rinaldo accosts her, and this time there is no mistaking the success of his attack; she joins him in a glass of wine. "Alas! Just as the Marquise lifts her mask to drink, Rinaldo perceives the magnitude of his error." He struggles to escape from the Marquise, but the old lady firmly takes his arm and drags him off to the Carnival.

Left alone, Mariuccia welcomes to supper Leonardo, the husband of Felicita, and Battista, who loves Pasquina. A merry supper party takes place, and they are joined by the Marquis di Luca. Supper is followed by dancing—two variations for Mariuccia and Battista and a pas de trois in which they are joined by Leonardo. The party ends with the reappearance of Felicita, Dorotea and Constanza. Leonardo and Battista make hasty getaways at the sight of their lovers.

Now the Marquise and Rinaldo return. Leonardo and Battista come back disguised as women, with their faces veiled. They flatter the old Marquis until he is beside himself with delight and flings aside their veils. "Cursing his gullibility he collapses into a chair while his tormentors caper around him." Meanwhile, the good-humored ladies have dressed up the waiter Niccolo as a Prince, and they present him to the Marquise. The Marquise turns to all present and pompously announces her marriage to the supposed Prince. Then Mariuccia whips off his mask and poor Niccolo is soundly beaten by the angry old woman.

The Marquis has by this time retired to bed, but he is roused by the uproar and comes out in his nightshirt, brandishing a stick. He takes a wild swipe and knocks off the Marquise's elaborate wig. The bald-pated Marquise "drops to the ground, overcome with chagrin and ridicule." The young people, having resolved all their petty differences, rock with delight at the success of their stratagems.

Scenery and Costumes

Leon Bakst, with Alexandre Benois and Diaghilev, was a founder of the *Mir Iskusstva* ("World of Art") group in 1898. Bakst was largely responsible for the technical excellence of the group's influential journal. When the Ballets Russes was formed in 1909, Bakst was named artistic director. He had already created successful designs for productions at the Hermitage, Alexandrinsky and Maryinsky theatres in St. Petersburg; his designs for the Ballets Russes were to bring him international fame.

Bakst's most sensational success was his décor for the 1910 ballet *Scheherazade*. The audience was dazzled by the fabulously rich apartment of the Shah's harem. The walls and ceiling were resplendent with mosaics and paintings; the floor was covered with scarlet rugs which shot out against the emerald-green silk curtains. *Scheherazade* had a powerful impact upon both art and fashion. Oriental-style furniture, rugs, carpets, cushions, and textiles with vivid Persian designs hit the shops of Paris and London.

Between 1909 and 1921 Bakst designed more Diaghilev productions than any other artist. His preference was for retrospectivism in the style of Old Masters such as Rembrandt and Velázquez, Orientalism, and motifs from ancient Greece and Egypt. He did not experiment with Cubism, abstraction or other innovations of the early twentieth century, yet he modernized stage design, nonetheless. Through his kinetic forms and bold color schemes, he integrated vertical space with the movement onstage. His costumes, though lavish, did not restrict the dancers' movements. Josefin Peladan, symbolist founder of the Salon de la Rose Croix, hailed Bakst as "the Delacroix of the Costume."[52]

George Amberg points out that during its first active phase, the Ballets Russes "formed so compact an ethnic and cultural organism that it was practically self-sufficient."[53] But as time passed, Diaghilev began to gravitate to the newest trends in Western art. The first period of the Ballets Russes was essentially linked to Fokine, Benois, and Bakst; in the second period, with Fokine gone, Serge Lifar believed that the two veteran designers had to bow to Diaghilev's will and "reluctantly take part in a kind of revolution."[54]

By 1916 Bakst felt pressured to keep pace with the modernists, even though their style was completely alien to his own. So when Diaghilev asked for a small Venetian piazza with a bell tower for *Les Femmes*, Bakst painted the scene "in such a way as if it were seen through the medium of semispherical glasses."[55] The buildings all leaned inwards towards the center of the stage, like the reflection of a convex mirror. The consequent distortion and blurring seem to have been an attempt to vie with the experiments of both Cubism and Futurism. Grigoriev thought that Bakst's design was "pointless.... I could not see why everything was crooked."[56] While the convex set was used for the premières in Italy and Paris, Diaghilev asked Bakst to redo the drop with buildings shown in correct perspective for the London Coliseum opening in September 1918. Cyril Beaumont describes the Coliseum set: "A café with rude trestle-table and chairs forms the right wing, and on the left is a house whose main feature is a curved balcony overhanging a doorway. A fountain with a stone figure, some dilapidated palisades, and a ponderous oaken seat complete the scene."[57]

The costume designs showed Bakst in his true element. He created richly embroidered gowns for the women and dark velvet jackets and knee breeches for the men, all trimmed luxuriously in ruched ribbon or gold embroidery. Each costume was an eighteenth-century confection.

Music

Domenico Scarlatti was the son of the famous Alessandro, founder of the Neapolitan school of eighteenth-century opera. In 1709 Domenico entered the service of Maria Casimira in Rome. His renown grew as he wrote one cantata, one oratorio and six operas for the private court of this exiled Polish queen.

In August 1719 Scarlatti resigned from his position in Rome and went to Portugal, where he became *maestre* of the chapel in Lisbon. His duties included the training at the keyboard of King John V's talented daughter, the Infanta Maria Barbara. When Maria Barbara married the Spanish Crown Prince Fernando and moved to Madrid in 1728, Scarlatti followed among her retainers; there he spent the last twenty-eight years of his life.

Scarlatti flourished under Maria Barbara's patronage. In Italy, his bent for original composition had been stifled by a style in which the composer merely provided a blueprint for the vocalists. In Spain, Scarlatti had liberty to improvise and compose at the keyboard, exploring all the possibilities that his fingers could discover. The resulting five hundred or more single-movement sonatas in binary form resulted in a wide-ranging and original corpus of music.

Scarlatti's most characteristic harmonic feature is the *acciaccatura*, which can be defined as a lower auxiliary note struck together with its resolution. The other source of exceptional harmonic invention in the Scarlatti sonata is the "vamp": it is a section of indeterminate length, normally at the beginning of the second half of a binary movement, which precedes a main musical event. The themes at the opening of the first half are not recapitulated in the tonic in the second half: each half of a Scarlatti sonata preserves its own identity.[58]

Scarlatti's modern reputation has been bolstered by the revival of the harpsichord. Recitalists may go on playing Scarlatti on the piano, but for most of his sonatas there is no adequate substitute for the brilliance and clarity of a period or reproduction harpsichord.[59] Vincenzio Tommasini's orchestration of *Les Femmes de bonne humeur* was heavily amplified and scored. It did, however, retain use of the solo harpsichord, something of a novelty in 1916.

Choreography

Taking Goldoni's dauntingly complex story almost unaltered, Massine compressed the play into one act. Yet he was able to retain all the flirtations, disguises and deceptions of the plot by balancing two scenes simultaneously on both sides of the stage. This technique is seen, for example, at the point when Niccolo frantically dons princely attire stage left while the lecherous Marquis chases the mysterious masked "ladies" around the stage right table.[60]

No less essential to the successful compression of this play was the speed of the movement. André Levinson sensed "perpetual mobile, a movement falling on each note, a gesture on each semiquaver ... to which we owe the breathless and spirited animation of *Les Femmes de bonne humeur.*"[61] The pace was not for everyone: W. A. Propert complained that the ballet had "too much movement in it, everyone is so frightfully alive."[62]

Les Femmes was a portent of Massine's striking ability to create a coherent ensemble from a large number of characters without for a moment destroying the identity of those characters. He paid meticulous attention to the idiosyncrasies of each role. For instance, the foppish Leonardo offsets the virile Battista; the bubbly Mariuccia counters the soulful Constanza.

Les Femmes de bonne humeur taught Massine "the value of concentrating on detail, and giving full significance to even the most minute gesture."[63] His approach resulted in witty surprises springing from the rhythmic execution of everyday, pedestrian movements. The little dinner party, performed at lightning speed, is a case in point. The smoothing of the tablecloth, the setting of silverware and dishes, the anticipatory rubbing of the hands before the feast, and the chair dance, in which knives and forks clang in merry synchrony with crisscrossing legs, are all masterstrokes of ingenuity in the use of classical technique.

Critical Survey

By all accounts, *Les Femmes de bonne humeur* was the hit of the Ballets Russes's 1917 season. After short debuts in Rome, Paris, and Spain, the ballet was presented at the London Coliseum from September 1918 to March 1919. The *Observer* called *Les Femmes* "an artistic event of the first importance," and said that "it is the perfect precision with which every gesture is linked to its accompanying musical phrase that is the secret of this remarkable feat of stage production."[64]

In Retrospect

One obvious problem with reviving this work is the fact that Massine's choreography was custom-made for the talents and personalities of the original cast. Revival casts have simply been unable to duplicate their idiosyncrasies or to attain the uncanny degree of precision and mutual rapport made possible by the original ballet's long rehearsal period. In his *Complete Book of Ballets*, Beaumont unhesitatingly calls *Les Femmes* "a masterpiece." But, he warns, "to savour this ballet to the full you must have seen Lopokova, Tchernicheva, M. and Mme Cecchetti, Massine, Idzikovsky and Woizikowsky in their original roles."[65]

Of the de Basil (1936) and de Cuevas (1949) revivals of this ballet, critics claimed that many of the subtleties had vanished. In 1936, P. W. Manchester found the ballet to be "terribly dowdy."[66] By the time of the de Cuevas revival, Dynely Hussey rued that the characters looked "like ghosts of their former selves." When the Royal Ballet revived *Les Femmes* in 1962, Peter Williams believed that the company did not understand the style, and that Lydia Sokolova's "magnificently stylish" performance as the Marquise Silvestra "showed up only too clearly how the company at that time could never possibly make a success of such a revival."[67]

In the de Cuevas revival, the role of the old Marquise was tastelessly interpreted by a man in drag. Yet Hussey noted, "She is not a burlesque character. She is a pathetic old woman, and it was just because she realized the pathos beneath her ridiculousness that Mme. Cecchetti [the original Marquise] was superb." Hussey felt that Derain's crisp new set missed the point as well: "Bakst's mouldering, mysterious set realizes more completely the poetry of the ballet, with its underlying sadness and nostalgia, which raise it above the level of a heartless romp. It is this undercurrent of sadness that makes *Good-Humoured Ladies* the outstanding masterpiece that it is."[68]

CONTES RUSSES

Based on Russian folk legends: (1) *Kikimora* (2) *The Swan Princess* (3) *Baba Yaga*
Music: Anatole Lyadov
Scenic and Costume Design: Mikhail Larionov
Première of *Kikimora*: Teatro Victoria Eugenie, San Sebastián, August 25, 1916
Première of *Contes russes*: Théâtre du Chatelet, Paris, May 11, 1917

ORIGINAL CAST
Dance Prelude: M. Léon Woizikowsky
Kikimora: Mlle Lydia Sokolova   The Cat: M. Stanislas Idzikovsky
The Swan Princess: Mlle Lubov Tchernicheva
Bova Korolevitch: M. Léonide Massine

Baba Yaga: M. Nicholas Kremnev   **The Little Girl:** Mlle Antonova
Wood Demons: MM. Okhimowsky, Maximov, Jazvinsky

Synopsis[69]

Scene One. Kikimora's Loathsome Chamber. The grotesque and terrible Kikimora sleeps fitfully in her cradle, gnashing her teeth and clawing spitefully in the air. She awakens and beckons to her fluffy white cat. The Cat gently rocks the cradle until it succeeds in putting her back to sleep. Kikimora reawakens and explodes from the cradle in venomous rage because the Cat has left her side. She whips him with a straw rope as the poor cat "bounds convulsively into the air from sheer anxiety." The witch then draws from her cradle "a gleaming axe, then she dashes up to the Cat, grasps it by the throat, and crashes the weapon on its skull—once, twice, thrice!" The Cat rolls over dead, and Kikimora disappears up the chimney "to cast her evil spells upon the world." A street vendor enters and whips the Cat, who, "naturally alarmed at the strange conduct of its fellow-actor, scrambles to its feet and scampers on all fours out of the room."

Scene Two. The Banks of the Magic Pool. A beautiful princess has fallen victim to the enchantment of a fearsome Dragon. Each sunset, in the guise of a swan, she may glide across the lake in search of her rescuer. But at dawn she must resume human form and return to the palace of the Dragon. This scene is a gentle, undulating solo for the princess. At the sun's first rays, "she sinks to the ground, her body quivering with the plaintive movements of a wounded bird."

Scene Three. The Courtyard of the Palace. The Swan Princess reclines in the courtyard while on the other side crouches the three-headed Dragon, "a writhing mass of scaley coils." The Princess wears a ceremonial robe; her sisters creep under its voluminous folds and carry her up a great flight of steps. Suddenly there arrives on a white charger the valiant knight, Bova Korolevitch, "who travels the vast plains with no other thought than the doing of brave deeds in the righting of wrongs." The Knight dismounts and threatens the Dragon with his sword—a fight to the death is imminent. First, however, the Knight and the noblewomen kneel and pray to an icon of the Virgin Mary while the Dragon waits by respectfully. Next the Knight advances boldly to the attack, and he severs the Dragon's three heads at a single stroke. The Princess holds out her arms to embrace him, but the Knight bids the ladies farewell.

The drop curtain descends, and there is a mock funeral procession for the Dragon led by the Cat. As the Dragon's remains pass from view, the mourners form a single line, and a maid and her sweetheart step out to perform a peasant dance.

Scene Four. A Grotesque Cottage in a Sinister Forest Glade. Three revolting Wood Demons "leering and shaking with diabolical laughter, roll over on their backs with a horrid squirming of their gross bodies." They lurch to their feet at the entrance of their mistress, the ogress Baba Yaga. The ogress feeds on the bodies of little children who, having lost their way and fallen into her clutches, are "killed, boiled, and eaten." Now comes a young maid who has strayed from her path and entered the dreadful glade. Spying so "succulent a morsel," the ogress attacks her. The poor girl begs for mercy while the delighted ogress beats her with her cane. In despair, the young girl makes the sign of the cross. "Confronted with a power that none dare dispute and thus balked of her meal," the ogress stamps away viciously. Merry peasants enter and soon fresh arrivals swell the throng—the Cat, the Knight, and the Princess, her train supported by the Wood Demons, "now as jolly as the three good bears." The curtain falls on a joyful dance.

Scenery and Costumes

Characteristically, Larionov geometricized natural forms and used bold primary colors. For example, Kikimora's cottage had bright yellow walls pierced by a red-framed window, a green enamel stove, and huge, sharply faceted sunflowers sprouting from the cradle.[70] Larionov's costumes were remarkable for their richness of fantasy. He designed an elaborate *maquillage* for Kikimora which made her face appear grotesquely disfigured. Her stained, patched blouse and wig of dark matted hair completed the horrific effect. The "scaley coils" and six "bulging eyeballs"[71] of the Dragon, the huge pointed bone growing out of Baba-Yaga's heel, and Baba Yaga's "hut"—a cottage on chicken legs, danced by two males whose limbs alone were visible—were further touches of grotesquerie.

Elsewhere, Larionov created contrast with scenes of opulent beauty, such as the stage-spanning silk and ermine robe of the Princess. Dame Edith Sitwell described its effect: "The court gathers beneath the folds of her ceremonial robe, spreading them out till they float like a noontide lake, covered with water flowers."[72] By all accounts, *Contes russes* was a visual spectacle of the first order.

Music

Anatole Lyadov entered the St. Petersburg Conservatory in 1870. He was admitted to Rimsky-Korsakov's composition classes but was expelled in 1876 for failure to attend. He was, however, readmitted early in 1878 to prepare his graduation composition, and he subsequently became a teacher at the Conservatory.

Many of Lyadov's works are essentially a series of variations on pre-existing folk songs or other composers' themes. He was little concerned with the expression of human emotion in music, but he possessed a gift for musical characterization in the limited sphere of fantasy. The three descriptive orchestral pieces of *Contes russes* "Baba Yaga," "Kikimora," and "The Enchanted Lake"—are among his most successful works. Here the lack of purposeful harmonic rhythm, a serious fault in much of his music, produces a sense of unreality and excitement that is very well suited to fairy tales.[73]

Lyadov could be dreadfully indolent. Rimsky-Korsakov wrote that he "did almost no work at all." According to Rimsky-Korsakov, Lyadov came from a family of rowdy musicians notorious for their slipshod attitude towards work, which may help to explain why he never succeeded in applying himself wholeheartedly to composition for an extended period.[74] Lyadov's procrastination made musical history when he failed to deliver to Diaghilev a score which was due by the winter of 1909. His truancy paved the way for Igor Stravinsky's first important commission, *The Firebird*.

Choreography

As with *Le Soleil de nuit*, Massine's work-in-progress was reviewed by Larionov. The ballet's finale taught him a valuable lesson in choreographic counterpoint: it was so "frenzied" that "each group overshadowed the next, and it was impossible to see any of the movements clearly." Larionov helped him to simplify and to find connecting threads among the diverse movements he had given the various groups.[75] Effective use of counterpoint—to the music or among groups of dancers—would become a major hallmark of Massine's style.

Massine was already exploring the architectural massing of bodies that would also become a key stylistic trait. His dramatic use of levels is well illustrated in the Princess's ascent of the staircase. Recalling this scene, Tamara Karsavina admired Massine's "imaginative building in height of the groups. How much a vertical line is needed to relieve the prevalence of the horizontal."[76]

The most exciting choreography was for Kikimora and the Cat, danced by Sokolova and Idzikovsky. In their highly charged duet Massine wanted to capture "the specifically Russian violence inherent in the legend."[77] At Kikimora's leap from the cradle, the mood becomes an ambiguous blend of both humor and horror. Excitement peaks as the animal tries desperately to defend itself and is crushed to death. While this duet must have been disturbing to some viewers, it was obviously good theatre.

Critical Survey

On Chrismas Eve, 1918, the London *Times* reported that *Contes russes* "came out as a Christmas entertainment, but one quite out of the ordinary." The critic was quite right to point out that a ballet with axe murders and cannibalism was a bit of a departure from the normal Christmas fare. Nonetheless, he gave the ballet a glowing review: "the dance of the whole team is so exhilarating that one cannot wonder at the enthusiasm which greeted it."[78]

Cyril Beaumont praised Sokolova's "extraordinary presentation of venomous hate" and Idzikovsky's "remarkable elevation." He added that the Cat's "miming was excellent, especially his sorrow at the death of the dragon. The whimsical manner in which he despondently shook his head, and dabbed his eyes with an orange handkerchief dangling from a trembling hand, used to make Diaghilev shake with laughter."[79]

In Retrospect

Contes russes was an important stepping-stone in Massine's development: it was his first experience with large groups, and he used them to experiment with counterpoint and vertical design. *Contes russes*'s main shortcoming was that there was little cohesion among the stories. The union of the entire cast at the end of Scene Four was nonsensically unmotivated, but at least it filled the stage for a colorful finale. Overall, *Contes russes* was well paced and theatrical with varied incidents and contrasting types of movement.

PARADE

Ballet in One Scene
Based on a libretto by Jean Cocteau
Music: Erik Satie
Scenic and Costume Design: Pablo Picasso
Première: Théâtre du Châtelet, Paris, May 18, 1917

ORIGINAL CAST

The Chinese Conjurer: M. Léonide Massine
The Acrobats: Mlle Lydia Lopokova, M. Nicholas Zverev
The Little American Girl: Mlle Marie Chabelska
The Manager on Horseback: MM. Noval, Oumansky
The French Manager: M. Leon Woizikowsky
The American Manager: M. Stakiewicz

Synopsis

In France, "parade" is the term given to the efforts of circus performers to lure an audience into their tent before the show begins. Two circus managers appear outside a carnival tent, exhibiting their performers in a sample routine to drum up business. First the French Manager reveals his particular attraction, a Chinese Conjurer who regales the public with various tricks. Despite his best efforts, the Conjurer does not attract the public. The manager from New York now enters and introduces a little American Girl who mimes various adventures reminiscent of silent motion pictures. Now there appears a circus horse who prances along at a haughty gait and two acrobats, who go through their paces. The public is completely indifferent.

Next comes the finale of this pathetic parade. The two managers and the American Girl appear jointly to ragtime accompaniment. The Chinese Conjurer enters with the acrobats in feats of skill and daring. The horse gallops around the stage at full tilt. Still, no reaction from the public. The company lines up indignantly, the managers gesticulating that the turns presented are only samples of what can be seen inside. But no contact is established with the audience; the managers wilt, their artists pine, and the horse collapses from exhaustion.

Concept

Parade is remembered by most as a cubist ballet, but this is not entirely true. While the scenery was cubist, it was actually the futurist movement which inspired the birth and subsequent development of this ballet. Futurism was launched in 1908 by the Italian poet Filippo Marinetti. The publication of his Futurist Manifesto the following year gave it immediate international publicity, and Futurism spread throughout Europe. Exhilarated by the noise and speed and mechanical energy of the modern city, Marinetti wanted to obliterate the past—"Burn the museums! Drain the canals of Venice!"—and replace it with a new art based on dynamic sensations. "We declare," he wrote in the Manifesto, "that the splendour of the world has been increased by a new beauty: the beauty of speed. ... A screaming automobile that seems to run like a machine gun is more beautiful than the Victory of Samothrace."[80]

Unlike other modern art movements, Futurism was not confined to the static visual arts. Futurist artists conceived of their works as but small sections of continuing wholes. Action, rather than the form itself, was their true subject. Umberto Boccioni sought "not pure form, but *pure plastic rhythm*, not the construction of the body, but the construction of the *action* of the body."[81] Given the kinetic essence of their work, it is not surprising that many futurists had an interest in performance as well. Between 1913 and 1917, performance became a subject of intense theoretical enquiry in numerous futurist manifestos which articulate the concepts embodied in *Parade*.

In his 1917 manifesto, "The Futurist Dance," Marinetti railed against naturalism, narrative, and emotionality. He advocated dance that was fast-paced ("the body multiplied by the motor"); compressed ("Synthesis of war: an Alpine soldier singing under the unbroken vault formed by shrapnel"); simultaneous ("Fusion of human song with mechanical and destructive noise"); and dehumanized ("The dancer, lying on her stomach, will simulate by jolts and undulations of the body, the movements of an airplane which is taking off").[82]

A central tenet of futurist performance theory was that legitimate theatre was corrupt and that the serious must be supplanted by the comic, the sublime by the mundane. Futurists therefore embraced the circus, cinema, and music hall. With its jumble of animal, dance, magic and tumbling acts, low-brow entertainment had the speed, compression, simultaneity and non-linear structure that futurists adored.

The mastermind behind *Parade* was the ardent futurist, French poet and dramatist Jean Cocteau. Cocteau had wanted to do a circus ballet since 1914, when he had unsuccessfully tried to persuade Diaghilev to produce *David*, a ballet with clowns which took place outside a fairground booth. In April 1916 Cocteau and Erik Satie spoke of collaborating on a work to be called "Parade." That *Parade* was actually a reworking of *David* is strongly suggested by Cocteau's 1914 letter to Misia Sert in which he described *David* as "a short piece, not a play, just a parade."[83]

During the winter of 1916–17, Cocteau visited Diaghilev in Rome with a second attempt to interest him in a circus ballet. Picasso was also in Rome to discuss plans for the ballet *Le Tricorne*. He "was delighted by the whole concept and suggested that the costumes should be executed in cubist style."[84] Cocteau then persuaded Diaghilev to ask Erik Satie for the score, and so began this momentous collaboration.

During planning sessions, it was mainly Cocteau who kept throwing ideas into the ring, not always successfully. For instance, he suggested that the managers be given lines which they would deliver through megaphones and that an amplifier be used to spout gibberish between numbers. But Diaghilev felt that "the spoken word was entirely out of place in a ballet."[85] In the meantime, the French poet Guillaume Apollinaire was writing *Parade*'s program notes, in which he claimed that *Parade*'s artistic fusion produced a kind of "super-realisme."[86] With the 1918 production of Apollinaire's play *Les Mamselles de Tiresias*, the two words became one—"surrealism"—a movement with its own special significance.

Scenery and Costumes

Pablo Picasso was the most successful and influential artist of the twentieth century. Painting was his principal medium, but his sculptures, prints, theatre designs and ceramics all had an impact on modern art. In his earliest important works, Picasso adopted a predominantly blue palette, and his imagery focused on outcasts, beggars and prostitutes. This "Blue Period" was stimulated by his exposure to life and thought in Paris, where he made his home after 1904. By that year, both the color schemes and subject matter of Picasso's paintings had brightened. His pictures began to be dominated by pink and flesh tints and by delicate drawing: this phase is known as his "Rose Period." A fascination with images of *saltimbanques*, harlequins and clowns is evident; however, the underlying mood of spiritual loneliness of the Blue Period paintings is retained.

From 1907 to 1908, stimulated by the simplified forms of Cézanne, Picasso initiated the breakdown of illusionistic space that he was to pursue with greater intellectual rigor through Cubism. The restraint of Cubism, though, was preceded by works exhibiting a raw intensity and violence influenced by Picasso's study of pre–Christian Iberian bronzes and African and Pacific art. He began to make expressive use of distortion: *Les Demoiselles d'Avignon* (1907; New York, MOMA) was a shocking artistic departure. Picasso gave the painting a vertical format, amalgamated the simplified iconic forms of his primitive sources with Cézanne's geometrization of forms, and adopted new spacial relationships that were radical departures from the Renaissance traditions of perspective. Though not fully cubist yet, *Les Demoiselles d'Avignon* is the precursor of Cubism.[87]

In October 1907 Apollinaire introduced Georges Braque to Picasso. Braque, one of the few artists to see and understand *Les Demoiselles d'Avignon* at the time, immediately transformed his style to an early cubist idiom. In turn, Picasso responded to Braque's Cézanne-influenced landscapes by imposing an even more consistent control on the illusion of space. The invention of Cubism was such a joint effort that Braque later described their relationship as that of two mountaineers roped together.

In March 1909 the French critic Louis Vauxcelles referred disparagingly to Braque's style as one that "reduces everything to little cubes," thus giving the new style its name. Cubism developed from its embryonic phase to the more systematic style of 1910–12, known as Analytical Cubism. Requiring intense analysis of all elements in a painting, Analytical Cubism explored the representation of three-dimensional objects on a two-dimensional surface by means of facets, or cubes, arranged in overlapping, transparent planes with clearly defined edges that established mass, space, and the implication of movement. Despite this radical method of painting, fragments of the faces, guitars, or wine glasses that were the subject of these works can still be detected through the shifting facets or contours.

When Picasso and Braque invented collages and papiers collés in 1912, they entered a phase known as Synthetic Cubism. Synthetic Cubism describes visual reality without illusionistic painting by synthesizing the object, even to the point of including real components of it, in a collage, thus creating a new, separate reality for the object. The first collage to incorporate preexisting functional objects as part of the surface was Picasso's *Still-life with Chair-caning* (May 1912; Paris, Mus. Picasso). It is an oval picture surrounded by a frame made of rope. Onto the painted background Picasso applied a piece of oilcloth printed with an illusionistic chair-caning pattern. In the same year, Picasso applied similar principles to sculpture.

In the years following World War I, theoretical cubism became too formalized and dogmatic for Picasso, and he began to frequent a new social circle, that of the Ballets Russes. Roland Penrose notes the profound change that the ballet exerted on Picasso's work:

> It brought him into close relationship with the human form. Since 1906 his constant interest in the natural beauty of the figure had been overlaid by the stylistic problems of Cubism, in which the still-life composed of a quota of domestic objects had furnished the greater part of the subject matter. But humanity is the inexhaustible source of Picasso's inspiration, and the ballet accelerated his return to a less exclusive repertoire.[88]

Of Cubism's many evolutions, none is more pertinent to Picasso's décor for *Parade* than the invention of collage, for the managers were collages in motion. According to Massine, Picasso visualized the managers as animated billboards "suggesting the vulgarity of certain types of show business promoters."[89] Both were portraits of their particular cities decked out in forms appropriate to the native scenery. The back of the French Manager was outlined with shapes suggesting the chestnut trees of Parisian boulevards. He sported a regulation top hat and starched shirt-front and carried at the end of a grotesquely long arm a white pipe, while his other, real, arm pounded the stage with a heavy stick. The American Manager wore a towering stovepipe hat and bore the weight of the skyscrapers of Manhattan on his shoulders. He wore a red-pleated shirt and

Robert Talmage as the French Manager in the 1973 Joffrey Ballet of Chicago revival of *Parade*. (COPYRIGHT: HERBERT MIGDOLL, 2002)

the cowboy chaps of Buffalo Bill and held in his right hand a gaudy sign which read "Parade." The managers were over ten feet in height. Only the legs of the performers showed beneath the towering structures built up of cubist agglomerations. Alfred Barr notes that they "were intended by Picasso to dwarf and flatten out the dancers, turning them into unreal puppets."[90]

The dazzling Chinese Conjurer wore a costume of brilliant yellow, orange, white and black with bold patterns symbolizing a rising sun; his headdress in the same colors looked like a crown of flames. The acrobats wore tight-fitting costumes decorated in blue and white with bold volutes and stars. The haughty horse sported a head held high on a long wrinkled neck. The American Girl wore a navy blue sailor jacket, pleated white skirt, and an enormous hairbow.

Picasso's backdrop setting was a monochrome cubist streetscape of characterless buildings, trees and an improvised booth. The buildings were shuffled together in distorted perspective, and light was used arbitrarily, so that the windows of the building at the top center appeared lit up for nighttime, while those on either side were black rectangles, like shadows on a sunlit wall. The proscenium of the fairground booth was tilted in the center, with thick sagging columns and a lyre on the center of the pediment.

Picasso's drop curtain, depicting a group of circus people picnicking on a deserted stage, is in Picasso's realistic, Blue Period style. Picasso cannot have been ignorant of the fact that the whole point of having a drop curtain is to prepare the audience for what they are about to see by setting the artistic style. He surely had a reason for depicting the circus folk realistically. The mystery was finally solved by the brilliant detective work of Dr. Marianne Martin and Nesta Macdonald.[91]

Cocteau once said of Picasso, "he's a rag-and-bone man of genius,"[92] and Macdonald discovered where this "scavenger" found the source for his drop. Diaghilev, Massine, Picasso, Cocteau and Stravinsky made a trip to Naples in the winter of 1917. In any city, Diaghilev would drag his entire coterie to visit its local theatre. Naples' San Carlo Theatre has a permanent painted drop curtain depicting Mount Parnassus and surrounded by red velvet curtains with gold fringe. Picasso's drop curtain for *Parade* shows a stage framed in crimson, gold-fringed draperies. The background depicts the foothills leading to Mount Vesuvius. A drop curtain painted with curtains and a theatre "lifted" from another theatre was, however, only a small part of the scavenger's joke.

Noticing a distinct resemblance between the clown and Cocteau, Dr. Martin discovered the identities of all seven of the figures in short order:

the bareback rider is Lydia Lopokova; the Botticelli-like beauty, Picasso's wife-to-be, Olga Khokhlova; the Harlequin, Léonide Massine; the Blackamoor, Stravinsky; and the toreador, Picasso himself. Cocteau, who had been mad about clowns all his life, could hardly be cast as anything else. Funniest of all was the transformation of Diaghilev into a Neapolitan sailor: Diaghilev's utter terror of the sea was legendary.

Music

Erik Satie is best remembered as the composer of music which is deliberately modest and simple—he was the archenemy of pomposity. Satie's most discriminating admirers have always tended to praise his clarity, restraint, and purity of style. By stripping music to its bare bones, Satie forces the listener to concentrate and focus until the slightest shift becomes significant.

In 1879 he entered the Paris Conservatoire, but in 1882 he was dismissed for incompetence. Thereafter, Satie knew that his technique was severely limited, but pride and determination led him to try to bypass his deficiencies with intricate compositional systems of his own devising. His harmonic innovations are seen clearly in his earlier pieces—three *Sarabandes* (1887), *Gymnopédies* (1888) and *Gnossiennes* (1888), pieces in which unusual progressions are presented with purified melodies of quasi-archaic simplicity. Even today the *Gymnopédies* create the impression of being either very archaic or very modern.[93] Like the *Gymnopédies*, the *Gnossiennes* have melodic lines which never resolve: "The listener is kept at arm's-length. Elusive and withdrawn, these enigmas never yield up their mystery."[94]

From 1905 to 1908 Satie became a student at the Schola Cantorum and expanded his limited technique with studies in counterpoint, fugue and orchestration. The tide finally turned for Satie at the beginning of 1911 when Ravel and Debussy conducted performances of his *Sarabandes* and *Gymnopédies*. But Satie's meteoric rise to fame after World War I was due mostly to Jean Cocteau. He used his entrée to elite and wealthy circles to win Satie commissions and performances; he wrote and lectured about Satie, particularly in his journal, *Le coq et l'arlequin*.

Parade opened with a short chorale, dry and sparse. This was followed by the fugal exposition, "*Prélude du rideau rouge*." Next the Chinese Conjurer appeared to music that reached its climax with a pounding three-note phrase incessantly repeated on trumpet and trombone. Here occurred some of the extramusical sounds the composer selected—the noises of siren and lottery wheel. By contrast, the dance for the horse introduced a gentle melody on the horns. The American Girl's entrance was accompanied by a swirling tune played by woodwinds and strings; sounds of a typewriter and pistol shots accompanied her adventures. The dance for the acrobats began with a flourish on the bouteillophone and xylophone, which gave way to a clumping waltz expressing the vulgarity and nostalgia of the fairground. This dissolved into the managers' themes, complete with a thunderous siren. The ballet ended with a pianissimo variation on the earlier fugal prelude.[95] Unity is achieved by the fugue that opens and closes the work and by the managers' themes that recur throughout. For James Harding, "Even after more than half a century the music still sounds uncompromising in its modernity.... He mixed ragtime and music-hall in a blend which expressed both the ugliness of a mechanical, commercialized age and the spirituality that is crushed beneath it."[96]

Choreography

Magicians who assumed Chinese robes sufficiently voluminous to conceal rabbits and other assorted paraphernalia were popular acts in the music halls of this period. Massine envisioned his role as a "parody of the usual pseudo–Oriental entertainer with endless tricks up his sleeve."[97] As the solo begins, the Conjurer cleaves the air with eccentric *jetés*, knees and elbows at acute angles. Then, going to the center, he bows to the audience and begins his act. Cocteau's instructions for the miming were as follows: "He takes an egg out of his pigtail, eats it, finds it again on the end of his shoe, spits out fire, burns himself, stamps on the sparks."[98]

Nowhere is Cocteau's influence more evident than in the second solo for the American Girl. Movies fascinated Cocteau, and the American girl was a character transported directly from the silver screen. Moving at the staccato, rapid pace of a silent film, she had adventures typical of films like *The Perils of Pauline*. She jumped on a moving train, swam a river, had a running fight at pistol-point, imitated the shuffling walk of Charlie Chaplin, danced a ragtime, took a photo, and reached a "poignant conclusion when, thinking herself a child at the seaside, she ended up playing in the sand."[98] The action is so tightly compressed that it is the shrewd observer indeed who can catch each allusion as it passes.

The horse is danced by two cloth-draped men, one standing upright and sporting a papier mâché horse's head and the other bent over at a right angle and clasping the waist of the front dancer. The two men caper about the stage with classical *emboités*, galloping patterns, and steps from a soft-shoe routine. At one point, the front dancer rears up in a waist-supported *temps de flèche*, his legs scissoring high in the air. Not to be outdone, the horse's "better half" then hops out to the side from behind and vigorously shakes its "tail."[100] This clever duet had an emphatic vaudevillian flavor.

Gary Chryst as the Chinese Conjurer in the 1973 Joffrey Ballet of Chicago revival of *Parade*.

In its review of the 1973 Joffrey Ballet revival, the *Dancing Times* complained about the horse's "routine tricks."[101] However, this remark ignores the futurist spirit which animates *Parade*. As Massine wrote, "Rather than attempt a realistic presentation, I felt it would be more in the spirit of the production to use the old music-hall device of two men wearing a horse's head with a cloth draped over them."[102]

1. *July 1895–May 1917* 45

Between each of the acts, the managers stamped out a conversation. Even within these huge constructions, Massine managed to give the managers distinct ways of moving. The American Manager's steps have the flavor of tap dancing, while the French Manager's are prissy and amusingly synchronized with twirls of his cane.

The ragtime dance, in which each act makes a last desperate attempt to lure the audience inside, has the nature of a Petipa finale gone haywire. The dancers reappear and gradually fill the stage with wild and furious dancing. Though *Parade*'s overall tone is hardly solemn, there is a strong suggestion of sadness and futility in the exhausted collapse of the managers and circus folk at the end.

Critical Survey

When *Parade* had its world première, the appearance of the lovely drop curtain made some members of the audience sigh with relief that the inventor of Cubism had actually presented them with something they could understand. But this impression dissolved when the drop curtain rose. Much has been written about this scandalous première. Cocteau claimed, "I have heard the cries of a bayonet charge in Flanders, but it was nothing compared to what happened that night at the Châtelet."[103] As the ballet came to an end, the mounting anger of the audience boiled up into an uproar. Cocteau reported that cries of "Sales Boches" ("Dirty Germans"), the worst possible insult in the wartime atmosphere of Paris, were shouted at the company and that some viewers demanded that *Parade*'s perpetrators be sent to the front. He spoke of fistfights in the auditorium, of an irate female who accosted him and tried to put his eyes out with a hatpin, and of the man who said to his wife, "If I'd known this was going to be so silly, I'd have brought the children."[104]

Though Cocteau overdramatized the incident, there is no doubt that *Parade*'s seeming flippancy could appear unpatriotic at a time when so many soldiers were dying. In the newspaper *Les Carnets de la Semaine*, Jean Poueigh deplored this "ballet that outrages French taste" no more violently than most of his colleagues, but Satie singled out Poueigh for a bitter quarrel. What infuriated Satie was the fact that Poueigh had attacked him in print after congratulating him to his face after the performance.[105] Satie immediately sent him a series of dreadfully insulting postcards, the worst of which is reprinted below:

Fontainebleau, 5 June 1917
Satie to Monsieur Fuckface Poueigh
Famous Gourd and Composer for Nitwits

[...] Lousy ass-hole, this is from where I shit on you with all my force [...]¹⁰⁶

Poueigh hastened to take Satie to court on the grounds that these open postcards had no doubt been read by his own concierge. On July 12 Satie was sentenced to a week in prison and fined a thousand francs in damages to Poueigh. On appeal, Satie's punishment was suspended "on condition of good conduct."¹⁰⁷

Aside from Poueigh and other critics of his ilk, Massine observed that there were at least a few critics who "caught the serious undertones and recognized the efforts we had made to synthesize the new art forms."¹⁰⁸ Diaghilev hesitated to show this ballet to conservative London until November, 1919. Reviews were mixed: the *Sunday Times* was quite laudatory, calling *Parade* "craziness with a touch of genius,"¹⁰⁹ but many other critics were preoccupied with simply describing the work, as if *Parade* defied any attempt at lucid criticism.

In Retrospect

Parade has had three major revivals in the past forty years: by the Ballet du XXI Siècle in 1964; by the Joffrey Ballet in 1973; and by the London Festival Ballet in 1974. For the Joffrey revival, most critics used such terms as "slight," "utterly jejune,"¹¹⁰ and "decidedly unimportant"¹¹¹ to describe the choreography. Jack Anderson, though, said that the "principal reason for *Parade*'s vitality is Massine's choreography."¹¹²

In *Parade*, Massine wrote, "we were mainly concerned with creating something new and representative of our own age."¹¹³ James Monahan called *Parade* "a darling relic of passions long since spent,"¹¹⁴ and he is probably right. Even so, one hopes that *Parade*, the most famous collaboration in ballet history, will keep stepping off the pages of the history books in revivals to come.

2

June 1917–June 1920

At the end of May 1917 the Ballets Russes was back in Madrid. Nijinsky joined the company for their June 2 opening at the Teatro Real and, as usual, the Spanish monarchs attended every performance. After the engagement at the Teatro Real, the company spent June 23 to 30 in Barcelona at the Gran Teatre del Liceu. On July 4 the company, with Nijinsky, set sail for a tour of South America. Massine and Diaghilev stayed behind to plan new ballets.

Manuel de Falla had composed the opera-ballet *El amor brujo* for the itinerant theatre company of the noted poet and dramatist Gregorio Martínez Sierra in 1915. It wove together the musical forms, stories and legends of the Andalusian gypsies.[1] Falla's second work for the Sierra troupe was the pantomime *El corregidor y la molinera*. Massine and Diaghilev, who saw both of these works, were most impressed with the centrality of dance in their evolution and shaping and were delighted when Falla offered to revise *El corregidor* into a ballet to be called *Le Tricorne*.

During their first Spanish tour in 1916, Massine and Diaghilev had already begun to research *Le Tricorne* by going nightly to the cafés to drink manzanilla and watch the gypsy dancers. One night in Granada, they saw a brilliant virtuoso, Felix Fernandez García, a gypsy of that city who was a printer by day and a dancer by night. When the Ballets Russes returned to Madrid in 1917, Diaghilev and Massine became reacquainted with García, who was now dancing in a Madrid café. Diaghilev asked Felix to join the company, although Sokolova believed that "Diaghilev must have been in some doubt whether this fiery, ignorant boy would be able to work and fit in with his highly disciplined company."[2] Once hired, Felix immediately began to give Massine lessons in flamenco and a great variety of regional Spanish dances.

In July 1917 Diaghilev organized an excursion to enable Falla to finish his research on Spanish folk and popular tunes and to allow Massine to study Spanish regional dances at their source. Felix accompanied them, and he was a great asset. He not only arranged impromptu dance performances but also had much to teach Falla about regional music.[3]

Diaghilev suggested that Massine begin preparing another new ballet to a set of unpublished piano pieces by Rossini which the composer Ottorino Respighi had brought to their attention in Rome. His suggestion stemmed from Serge Grigoriev's idea to revive the Joseph Hassreiter ballet *Die Puppenfee*, which was first produced in Vienna in 1888 and was subsequently restaged for the Imperial Ballet in 1902. Massine and Diaghilev decided to base the libretto for the new Rossini ballet (to be called *La Boutique fantasque*) on *Die Puppenfee*.

After the South American tour, the Ballets Russes performed in Barcelona, followed by a season in November at the Teatro Real. But neither engagement was successful, for Spain was being swept by an influenza plague: in Madrid, half the populace had fled to the countryside. After the Teatro Real performances, prospects for the Ballets Russes were more uncertain than ever before. Aside from a December engagement in Lisbon, Diaghilev had no other bookings. With the rest of Europe at war and cut off from his Russian bank accounts because of the 1917 revolution, he saw that his company was now in serious danger of folding.

To make matters worse, the Portuguese Revolution, aimed at overthrowing the government of Bernardino Machado, broke out immediately upon the company's arrival in Lisbon. When the political turmoil came to an end, the Ballets Russes opened its season at the Coliseu dos Recreios. With this engagement, the last performance venue was exhausted. Diaghilev and Massine returned to Madrid in desperation. Fortunately, Manuel de Falla was able to put Diaghilev in touch with the impresarios Arturo Serrano and Méndez Vigo. They rescued Diaghilev by offering to organize a forty-seven-city tour throughout Spain. The Ballets Russes dancers, eighty-six members strong, began the tour at the end of March 1918 and traveled about four thousand kilometers before finishing in Granada.

At this point, Diaghilev's crisis intensified: three years into the war, he was nearly penniless and responsible for a huge company. Since March, Diaghilev had been in touch with Sir Oswald Stoll to arrange an engagement at the London Coliseum. Stoll was quite interested, but the problem was trying to transport the company to England via war-torn France. After trying in vain with connection after connection to arrange for transport through France, Diaghilev made a personal appeal to his "protector," King Alfonso. Through his intercession, the Spanish ambassador in London and the English ambassador in Madrid arranged for the French consulate to issue transit visas for the entire company.

On July 29, 1918, Massine and Diaghilev entered France. Once they reached Paris, Diaghilev and Massine were shocked at the city's devastation: its shops were boarded up and its people were "pale and drawn, drained of energy and fearful of the shells from 'Big Bertha' which burst over the town every few minutes."[4]

On August 9 Massine and Diaghilev left Paris for England. They got to work immediately, for their Coliseum debut was only four weeks away. Diaghilev held auditions to replace those dancers who had deserted the Ballets Russes in Spain during the company's darkest days. The names of the chosen English dancers were Russianized at once: Vera Clark, for instance, became Vera Savina.

The Coliseum was a lowly music-hall theatre, and the Ballets Russes was slated to do a forty-five-minute "turn" each afternoon and evening. Diaghilev detested seeing his ballets sandwiched in between dog acts, lewd comics and acrobats. Moreover, the size of the orchestra precluded the presentation of some of his most interesting ballets. The company opened on September 5 with the first London performance of *Les Femmes de bonne humeur*, and it was a sensational success.

London's artistic and literary intelligentsia, who had turned up their noses at Diaghilev's prewar seasons, now embraced the company. This new interest was partly motivated by an awareness of the artistic furor aroused by *Parade* the year before in Paris. Bloomsbury's Roger Fry was the person most instrumental in bringing the foreign art movements of Cubism and Futurism to the attention of the British public. Now that the Ballets Russes seemed committed to offering bold departures from conventional art, Massine and Diaghilev became the toast of Bloomsbury. (It was at a gathering of the Bloomsbury group that the great British economist John Maynard Keynes met his future wife, ballerina Lydia Lopokova.)

Aside from *Les Femmes*, Massine scored two other successes with *Le Soleil de nuit* and *Contes russes*, retitled *Children's Tales*. The unprecedented seven-month engagement at the Coliseum closed on March 29 with more than seventeen curtain calls and established Massine as an extraordinary choreographer and performer.

Sergei Diaghilev and Léonide Massine in London, 1919.

2. *June 1917–June 1920* 51

Throughout the Coliseum season, rehearsals for *Le Tricorne* and *La Boutique* continued. At the time that Felix García was hired, Diaghilev and Massine probably wanted him for the leading role of the Miller in *Le Tricorne*, and Sokolova is certain that he joined the company "in the confident expectation that Diaghilev intended to make him a world-famous star." But by September 1918 "it had been decided that Felix Fernandez was incapable of learning a sustained role such as that of the Miller. ... Massine's proficiency at Spanish dancing was now so great that he decided to take the part himself."[5]

All accounts indicate that Felix's mental condition was indeed deteriorating. Even Massine, himself an inveterate workhorse, wrote that "he would often rehearse far into the night, appearing next morning in a state of nervous exhaustion."[6] Felix even began to discipline himself by chewing his food to the rhythm of a ticking metronome, stopping now and then to readjust it to a different speed.[7]

Leon Bakst was another problematic person at this time. As the designer for the Imperial Ballet's 1902 *Die Puppenfee*, Bakst was the obvious choice for *La Boutique fantasque* and, indeed, Diaghilev commissioned him for the project in 1917. But according to Massine, when the preliminary sketches arrived, Diaghilev thought they lacked charm and gaiety. When Diaghilev heard that André Derain was interested in designing for the Ballets Russes, he gave the commission over to Derain instead. When he learned of this, Bakst became livid and threatened to sue. Massine wrote, "It was certainly a ruthless thing to do but it did not surprise me, for I had long ago realized that Diaghilev was ruthless in anything that affected the work of the company. ... He often told me that in the theatre there are no friends."[8] Prince Peter Lieven says that Bakst finally developed a hatred of Diaghilev because he "had betrayed the artistic principles which they had previously had in common."[9]

The Ballets Russes opened a second London season on April 10 at the Alhambra Theatre, also managed by Sir Oswald Stoll. Now in a more fitting facility, the company could present its customary three-ballet program. In late April and May Massine finished up rehearsals for *La Boutique* and *Le Tricorne*.

La Boutique fantasque's première on June 5, 1919, was one of the greatest triumphs in the history of the Ballets Russes. But Massine's winning streak was not to stop there. By mid–April Karsavina had rejoined the Ballets Russes to dance the role of the Miller's Wife in *Le Tricorne*. Although she had not seen Massine since *The Legend of Joseph*, she soon realized that he was a different person: "I found him now no more a timid youth ... he now possessed accomplished skill as a dancer, and his precocious ripeness and uncommon mastery of the stage singled him out, in my mind, as an exceptional ballet master."[10]

One crisis remained to be weathered before Massine's second great triumph at the Alhambra. Felix García was, after all, Massine's maestro in the Spanish dances of every region. Having lost the leading role, he was under the impression that he would at least be billed as *Tricorne*'s co-choreographer. But on the very morning of *Le Tricorne*'s première, he was stupefied to see that his name appeared nowhere on the playbills.[11] He left the Alhambra, rushed off to Trafalgar Square, and smashed through one of the windows of St. Martin-in-the-Fields Church. There, on the altar, he began to dance a demented farruca. Later that night he was discovered and arrested. He was subsequently certified insane and taken to a mental asylum in Epsom, where he remained until his death in 1941. Sokolova maintains that "Felix's reason was the price fate demanded for the creation of a masterpiece."[12]

At *Le Tricorne*'s première, the audience roared its approval, and so did London's cognoscenti the next morning. Writing in the *New Republic*, Clive Bell concluded that Massine possessed "a creative genius and therefore an authority, which has carried the ballet to a degree of seriousness and artistic importance of which Nijinsky can scarcely have dreamt."[13] T. S. Eliot also sang his praises: "[Massine] seems to me the greatest actor whom we have in London."[14] Léonide was no longer a mere satellite of Diaghilev: he left London a star in his own right.

After the Alhambra season ended on July 30, Diaghilev and Massine left for a vacation in Italy. In Naples, Massine renewed his ties with Mikhail Semenov, a former music critic from St. Petersburg. In the summer of 1917, Massine had accepted Semenov's invitation to spend several days with him and his wife at their retreat in Positano. During this visit he first glimpsed the Isole dei Galli. Massine yearned for a private retreat apart from his nomadic existence, and these islands were an irresistible lure. On his second vacation there in 1919, Massine renewed negotiations with the Parlato family, owners of the three islands. The islands are about three nautical miles from Positano. During the time of the Emperor Tiberius they were known as the "Islands of the Sirens," the mythological domicile of enchantresses who lured sailors to their deaths on the craggy rocks of the island with their hypnotic songs.

When Massine returned to Naples in August of 1919, he and Diaghilev made plans for a new ballet based on the commedia dell'arte character of Pulcinella. *Parade* had also been conceived in Italy. But while they were exploring the modernist present, Diaghilev and Massine had never neglected Italy's past. They had already gone back to Goldoni with

Les Femmes de bonne humeur, however, they fused its eighteenth-century content with modern styles and techniques. Likewise, *Pulcinella* would be a synthesis of treatments that were separated by at least two centuries.

Massine's interest in the commedia dell'arte began with his first trip to Italy in 1914, when he watched marionette plays that used stock commedia characters. His interest deepened with his second Italian visit in 1917 when he did extensive research at the Royal Palace Library in Naples and discovered a commedia dell'arte manuscript from 1700 entitled *Les Quatre Polichinelles semblables*. Fearing that "mere mastery" of the manuals of Blasis, Feuillet and Rameau (which he relied upon so heavily in *Les Femmes*) would make his choreography too dry and analytical, Massine hoped that commedia dell'arte, "with its emphasis on mime and its use of extempore acting, based only on a scenario, might hold the key to my artistic dilemma."[15]

By the end of August 1919, plans for *Pulcinella* were well under way, and Diaghilev obtained from the British Museum, the Bibliothèque Nationale and the Casa Musicale a bundle of compositions attributed to Pergolesi. Surprisingly, Stravinsky agreed to the humble task of orchestrating them. Picasso was commissioned to create the décor and by September 1919, all of the collaborators were at work in Paris.

Diaghilev also turned his attention to Stravinsky's *Le Chant du rossignol* for the upcoming season. As early as 1909, Stravinsky had completed Act One of his opera *Le Rossignol*. He wrote the last two acts right on the heels of his revolutionary *Le Sacre du printemps*. The result was a real difference in idiom between the music of the first act and that of the second and third. In 1916 Stravinsky used the last two acts only as the basis for a symphonic poem. This more homogenous composition, *Le Chant du rossignol*, was chosen by Diaghilev for a ballet adaptation of the 1914 opera.

With their plans for the next season firmed up, Diaghilev and Massine returned to London for a September 20–December 14 season at the Empire Theatre. The company moved on swiftly to the Paris Opéra, where the season was to be divided into two engagements. The first would begin on December 24 and would feature the world première of *Le Chant du rossignol*. The second would begin on May 8 and would include the world premières of *Pulcinella* and the opera *Le astuzie femminili*.

The Ballets Russes filled the interim before the second Paris Opéra engagement with performances in Rome, Milan and Monte Carlo, and they also began rehearsals for the opera revival of *Le astuzie femminili* (which can be loosely translated as "The Wiles of Women"). This opera was another yield from Diaghilev's research into Italy's pre-romantic past. His favorite hobby was searching for forgotten musical scores: his avid

Rome, 1919. From left to right, Léonide Massine, Natalia Gontcharova, Michel Larionov (standing), Igor Stravinsky, Leon Bakst.

pursuit of eighteenth-century Italian music had already netted him the scores for *Les Femmes* and *Pulcinella*. Now, according to Grigoriev, he burrowed in an Italian library, stumbled upon the score of this little-known opera by Domenico Cimarosa and was quite taken with it. *Le astuzie femminili* (1794) is a typical opera buffa—it abounded in elements of slapstick and disguise and had considerable success in Italy and abroad in the first two decades after its première.

Massine was to choreograph both the dance sequences and the movements of the singers. With so much responsibility, it was only natural for him to have strong opinions on how the opera should be treated. *Le astuzie femminili* was the source of the first heated disagreement between Diaghilev and Massine. Since the third act of the opera was actually entitled "Il Ballo Russo," Massine wanted to be true to the original staging and conclude the production with a divertissement. Diaghilev, however, wanted the dances to be interspersed throughout the opera. According to Grigoriev, "their arguments were interminable but Massine held out."[16] Although he was humiliated by Massine's unprecedented willfulness, Diaghilev gave in, and the divertissement was staged. But the clash marked the beginning of the end of their personal and professional relationship.

Four years later, the third-act divertissement was staged as a separate ballet, *Ballet de l'astuce feminine*, at the Théâtre de Monte Carlo. In 1925 the ballet was given with additional choreography by Bronislava Nijinska and a new title, *Cimarosiana*.

Following their Monte Carlo performances, the Ballets Russes proceeded to France for the second half of their Paris Opéra engagement. From June 10 to July 30 the company performed at Covent Garden, giving the first London performances of *Le astuzie femminili*, *Pulcinella*, and *Le Chant du rossignol*. *Le astuzie femminili* was politely received in Paris but failed to make the sensational impression that Diaghilev had hoped for. In London, the opera was far more successful.

LA BOUTIQUE FANTASQUE

Ballet in One Act
Suggested by the ballet *Die Puppenfee* by Joseph Hassreiter
Music: Gioacchino Rossini, orchestrated by Ottorino Respighi
Scenic and Costume Design: André Derain
Première: Alhambra Theatre, London, June 5, 1919

ORIGINAL CAST
The People
The Shopkeeper: M. Enrico Cecchetti
His Assistant: M. Alexandre Garivlov
A Thief: M. Okhimovsky
An English Old Maid: Mlle Klemeotowicz
Her Friend: Mme Miku Milina
An American: M. Jazvinsky   His Wife: Mme Alanova
Russian Merchant: M. Serge Grigoriev
His Wife: Mme Giuseppina Cecchetti

The Dolls

Tarantella: Lydia Sokolova, Leon Woizikowsky
Queen of Clubs: Lubov Tchernicheva
Queen of Hearts: Vera Nemchinova
King of Spades: M. Stakiewicz   **King of Diamonds**: M. Novak
The Snob: M. Stanislas Idzikovsky   **The Melon Hawker**: M. Kostetsky
Cossack Leader: M. Nicholas Zverev
Dancing Poodles: Vera Clark, Nicholas Kremnev
Can-Can Dolls: Lydia Lopokova, Léonide Massine

Synopsis[17]

The curtain rises to reveal a toyshop of the mid-nineteenth century. The owner and his apprentice open the store for the day, and the first to enter is a young shoplifter, who is quickly detected and given a sound thrashing. Next enter two English ladies who haughtily raise their lorgnettes and demand to see the dolls. They are interrupted by an American sporting a loud checked suit, his overbearing wife, and their two brats.

The Shopkeeper brings on the Tarantella Dolls. To the rattle and jingle of tambourines, the dolls break into a breathless dance. The porters remove these dolls and reappear with four new dolls representing the Queen of Clubs, the Queen of Hearts, the King of Spades, and the King of Diamonds. With mechanical precision, the four figures dance a lively mazurka.

When this dance is finished, in walks a tall, bearded Russian Merchant, his stout wife, and their four daughters. They are ill-received by the English ladies who exit disdainfully. Next are presented two dolls of opposing station—a Snob and a Gardener who wheels before him a barrow stacked with melons. The Gardener gives a slice of melon to the Snob, "who eats it in a manner suggesting the playing of a mouth-organ." When he is finished, the Snob resumes his strutting but is knocked over by the hawker's barrow. These dolls are replaced by six Cossack Dolls who march with exaggerated prancing and perform snappy rifle maneuvers. Next the Shopkeeper leads forward by the ears a pair of Dancing Poodles. The first is a "quiet, self-satisfied" male dog, and a sharp contrast to the flirtatious female. She attracts his attention by lifting up her hind leg just in front of him. Excited by this display, the male poodle jumps, scratches, and barks until both come to a halt.

The Shopkeeper announces that he will now exhibit his finest work, a pair of Can-Can Dolls. Once wound up, "the gentleman, alternately posed on each foot, throws himself backwards with such verve that his body almost assumes the horizontal. The lady alternately flings into the air each leg, which writhes, twists, turns, revolves amid a foaming sea of lace and ribbon." All of the visitors are delighted and eager to buy the Can-Can Dolls. After conferring, it is agreed that the dolls are to be divided—the Americans acquiring the male and the Russians the female. Both parties pay in advance and arrange to call the next morning for the dolls, which are to be boxed separately. The shopkeeper and his assistant lock up for the evening.

As the shadows take over, the dolls emerge from their resting places. The Can-Can Dolls are spirited from their separate crates and reunited under the sympathetic eyes of their toy companions. A poetic pas de deux ensues in which the pair, removed from the raciness of their customary dance, become the symbol of young love. The girl is borne away by her Cossack companions, and the dolls all disappear.

When the Shopkeeper opens the store the next morning, everything looks as he had left it, but when the customers arrive to secure the Can-Can Dolls, they are not to be found! The furious customers attack the unfortunate Shopkeeper and then invade the rear of the store, bent on the destruction of the dolls in revenge for the Shopkeeper's deception. At their advance, the dolls suddenly come to life with "terrifying militancy." They beat and kick the clients, overwhelm them, and drive them from the shop. As the band of invaders peers into the shop from the street, they can see the dolls dancing wildly in triumph. The Can-Can Dolls congratulate the delighted Shopkeeper; then, "as their legs fly into the air in three high kicks, the curtain falls."

Scenery and Costumes

"Fauves," or "Wild Beasts," was a derogatory label applied to André Derain, Henri Matisse and others of this group when they exhibited together in Paris in 1905. Their imagery defied all traditional canons of competent painting as they released painting from realism, freeing it to express the pleasures of pure, bright colors. By 1918, however, Derain had returned to the traditional virtues of figurative painting. Derain also began to take a lively interest in theatre at this time; his shift towards a relative degree of realism is evident in the stage designs he produced for Diaghilev.

Derain's setting was a toyshop set in an improbable arcade overlooking the Bay of Naples with a paddle steamer in the foreground. The backdrop did not remotely suggest a toyshop; moreover, furniture was painted straight onto the side flats of the boutique, jarring with the perspective of the real furniture onstage. But the sophisticated naïveté of Derain's flattened perspective and his use of broad masses of clear, bril-

Scene from *La Boutique fantasque* with Alexandra Danilova in foreground, 1935.

liant color proved ideal for the setting, which was a fantastic toyshop, after all—a deliberate and charming subversion of probability.

Music

No composer in the first half of the nineteenth century enjoyed the measure of popular acclaim or artistic influence that belonged to Gioacchino Rossini. Rossini threw off eighteenth-century formulae and codified new musical forms and orchestration and a new role for music in defining and shaping the opera. Not until the advent of Giuseppe Verdi was Rossini replaced as the center of Italian operatic life.

By 1815, Rossini had already composed thirteen operas, the best known of which was *Tancredi* (1813). The following year he premièred his most famous opera, *Il Barbiere di Siviglia*, in Rome. Other significant operas followed in the next few years: *Otello* (1816), *La Cenerentola* (1817), *La Gazza ladra* (1817), *La Donna del lago* (1819), *Semiramide* (1823), *Le Comte Ory* (1828), and *Guillaume Tell* (1829), a landmark in the history of romantic opera.

Guillaume Tell, the composer's thirty-ninth opera, was also his last, although he lived for almost forty more years. He moved to Paris permanently in 1855, where he lived in honored retirement. Essentially content to write for himself and his circle, he composed numerous short works grouped under the title *Péchés de vieillesse* ("Sins of Old Age"). Cultivated Paris flocked to hear these piano pieces and songs at Rossini's *Samedi soirs*, and they cast their spell on a younger generation of French composers. These pieces, sparkling with wit and irony, had such whimsical titles as "Asthmatic Study," "Here I am, Good-Morning Madame," and "Ugh! Peas!"[18]

Most of the music for *La Boutique* was assembled from the *Péchés de vieillesse*, and Respighi developed these rather slight pieces into music suitable for a full-bodied ballet. Constant Lambert was impressed with his orchestration of *La Boutique* : "Respighi has every trick of the orchestra at his finger's end."[19]

Choreography

When the Portuguese Revolution broke out upon their arrival in Lisbon, Massine, Diaghilev, and Grigoriev took shelter under the main staircase of their hotel for three days and nights. With shells raining down and bombs exploding twenty feet from his nose on the street outside, the unflappable Massine claims to have worked out much of the choreography for *La Boutique* under this staircase: "Throughout the revolution I remained in a highly creative mood and as a result, once the fighting had stopped, I was able to compose the major part of *La Boutique fantasque* in a few days."[20]

Each of the doll dances is a gem of characterization. Even in the nondancing roles, Massine created vivid and eccentric characters—from the loose-limbed, nose-picking Shopkeeper's Assistant to the pompous Russian merchant and his fussy wife. Massine also found ways to smooth out the often jarring transition from ballet dancing to the more pedestrian gestures of the shop people. For instance, rather than merely walking into the shop, the English spinsters make their entrance swaying to the rhythm of their crinolines.

Wearing a rakish black velvet suit with a checked waistcoat, "Massine was a Victorian wax doll" as the Can-Can Doll. His partner, Lopokova, was "the epitome of mischievous humor and charm," and Massine "delighted in her naughtiness. As she kicked above his head in a froth of lacy petticoats, he threw up his hands and ogled the audience to make sure everyone was appreciating just how naughty she was."[21]

Alexandra Danilova and Léonide Massine as the Can-Can Dolls in *La Boutique fantasque*, 1935.

Critical Survey

Sydney Carroll's remarks were typical. He could do nothing but rhapsodize: "*La Boutique fantasque* lets loose around me a flood of sensation too revolutionary to be tolerable. It makes me feel a child again."[22] Although Valerian Svetloff grumbled that "Massine continues obstinately to work in the realm of farce and grotesque,"[23] his was the minority opinion, and London flocked to see this ballet.

In Retrospect

La Boutique fantasque, a perennial favorite, remained in the repertoire from the days of Diaghilev until the demise of the Ballet Russe de Monte Carlo in 1962. This ballet's tenacious popularity can be partly attributed to brilliant performances by second-generation dancers. For example, Alexandra Danilova's Can-Can Doll was considered to be one of her greatest roles in the 1930s and 1940s.

Each of the characters is so vividly delineated in movement that convincing characterization is largely a matter of meticulously preserving dance and gestural details. Fifty years after *La Boutique*'s première, Peter Williams wrote, "in spite of the seemingly corny idea of dolls coming alive in a toyshop, what beautiful invention there is in this ballet—rich little cameos just waiting for the right interpreter."[24] Fortunately, Massine was able to take personal care of his ballet for an uninterrupted period from 1932 to 1941, and *La Boutique* was performed so frequently that details stayed fresh in his mind. *La Boutique* has suffered less attrition to the original choreography than any other Massine ballet. This must be a key factor in the success of recent revivals. Of course, any dancer in a Massine character ballet needs to show a high degree of showmanship. Mary Clarke attributed the success of the 1968 Royal Ballet revival to the willingness of everyone to throw British reserve to the wind and to "dance the ballet for all it is worth."[25]

LE TRICORNE (The Three-Cornered Hat)

Ballet in One Act
Libretto: Martínez Sierra, based on Pedro Antonio de Alarcon's novel,
 El Sombrero de tres picos
Music: Manuel de Falla
Scenic and Costume Design: Pablo Picasso
Première: Alhambra Theatre, London, July 22, 1919

ORIGINAL CAST

The Miller: M. Léonide Massine
The Miller's Wife: Mlle Tamara Karsavina
The Corregidor: M. Leon Woizikowsky
The Corregidor's Wife: Mlle Alanova
The Dandy: M. Stanislas Idzikovsky
Neighbors, Police, Peasants, Footmen, etc.

Synopsis

The drop curtain rises to reveal a sunny Spanish village. The Miller is standing before a birdcage, teaching his blackbird to whistle the hours of the day. As he gestures that it is two o'clock, his pet (through the medium of the orchestra) perversely answers "three." The Miller angrily tries to correct the bird, but only confuses it more. Now his beautiful wife appears. She whistles "two o'clock" and the blackbird gives the right answer.

Both the Miller and his wife are very much in love. They embrace, and then the Miller goes about his work. Suddenly a boyish Dandy is seen on the bridge over a nearby stream. He prances along and blows a kiss to the Miller's Wife. The Miller looks up from his work and runs in pursuit toward the bridge.

Almost immediately, the sound of marching men is heard and a litter borne by footmen appears. It conveys the Corregidor, governor of the province. The Corregidor, by nature a lecher, glances keenly at the Miller's Wife. He sends his escort on ahead and lets his elaborately woven handkerchief fall to the ground. The Miller's Wife returns it to him, and the Corregidor exits with a leering backwards glance.

Villagers enter and go about their work. The Miller notices a pretty village girl who has for him the same charm that the Dandy had on his wife; now it is her turn to be jealous. The village girl and the workers go their way, and husband and wife are reconciled after a chat about mutual fidelity. They dance an exultant fandango.

In the evening, a group of neighbors comes to the mill for a midsummer celebration, and they dance in homage to the Miller and his wife. Then the Miller draws himself to his full height. Snapping his fingers and advancing with determined steps, he begins an impassioned farruca, the climactic moment of the ballet. After his electrifying solo, the neighbors suddenly hear the tramp of marching men. Soon the bodyguards of the governor draw up before the house, place the Miller under arrest, and lead him away. The neighbors flee, and the Miller's Wife is left alone. She dances a plaintive solo, like a caged bird longing for freedom.

Studio portrait of Tamara Toumonova and Léonide Massine as the Miller and the Miller's Wife in Le Tricorne, 1939. *(MAURICE SEYMOUR)*

Suddenly she sees the Corregidor standing close by. Now that the Miller has been disposed of, the Corregidor's advances are bolder. He tries to embrace the Miller's Wife, grapples with her, is flung to the ground. He then chases her to the bridge, but the Miller's Wife pushes him into the stream. The Miller's Wife laughs to see the Corregidor in such an absurd and undignified state. She dances with the joy of a bird set free and hoists the Corregidor to the shore, but no sooner is he out of the stream than the chase resumes. This time the Miller's Wife threatens him with a musket and retreats into the house. The Corregidor takes off his soaking garments and lays them out to dry. Then, shivering with cold, he invades the Miller's home and falls exhausted onto his rival's bed. At dawn the Miller, escaped from the police, creeps toward his house. To his dismay, he sees the Corregidor's clothing, then the old man himself, stealing out of the house in a borrowed nightshirt. In revenge, the Miller takes the governor's clothes and his three-cornered hat and sets out to pay court to the Corregidor's wife.

The governor's troubles have only just begun. He is set upon by his own bodyguards—who mistake him in his borrowed nightgown for the escaped Miller. Drawn by the uproar, the village people come running to the scene, including the Miller and his wife. The ensemble dances a brilliant jota. Then, inflamed by the brutality of the Corregidor, the people revolt. The wretched Corregidor and his bodyguards make a hasty escape. A joyous anarchy reigns in the village. The Dandy appears on the bridge with a straw effigy of the Corregidor. As he tosses the dummy skyward, the crowd catches it and flings it up again. As the dummy whirls in the air, symbolizing the shattered rule of the three-cornered hat, the ballet ends in a riot of color, sight, and sound.

Scenery and Costumes

Viewers who associated Picasso with highly complicated essays in Cubism were startled to see *Le Tricorn*'s spare, sun-baked landscape. The backcloth gave a glimpse of a stone bridge through a gigantic pink and ochre archway against a pale blue sky filled with stars. It showed little trace of Cubism except in the organization of the angular walls of the houses.

Picasso's set was a landmark in stage design, introducing a new simplicity and subtlety. Diaghilev's scene painter, Vladimir Polunin, remarked that "Having dealt for so long with Bakst's complicated and ostentatious scenery, the austere simplicity of Picasso's drawing, with its total absence of unnecessary detail, the composition and unity, was astounding."[26] Picasso changed trends not only by simplifying and schematizing the set but also by softening his colors with the admixture of "zinc white" and "ivory black." His clear pastels brought a fresh new look to dance décor.

The pastel backdrop was an ideal contrast to Picasso's bright and authentic eighteenth-century costumes. They drew on the curves and zigzags characteristically used by Spanish peasants in their clothing, wagons, mule harnesses, etc.—patterns that probably descend from the calligraphic arabesques of the Moors.[27] The acid contrasts of greens, pinks, scarlet and black were equally evocative of Spain.

The foreground of Picasso's drop curtain shows a group of Spaniards looking over a balcony. In the arena is seen the end of a bullfight. Here again, the technique of Cubism was not in evidence, and the audience could take uncomplicated pleasure in the scene. Diaghilev later sold the center of this drop curtain, and it eventually found its way into the lobby of the Seagram Building in New York. Both the drop curtain and the backcloth for *Le Tricorne* are considered to be among the finest examples of scenic decoration within the last hundred years.

Le Tricorne came from the period of the painter's closest association with the world of dance, and his involvement was intense. At the time, Picasso was in love with the Diaghilev ballerina Olga Khokhlova. He came every day to Polunin's shop to supervise the transformation of his designs from sketch to stage and himself painted the stars which fall through the sky above the Andalusian landscape and shine by day as well as by night.

Music

Manuel de Falla is undoubtedly Spain's most important twentieth-century composer. In 1902 Falla began study with Felipe Pedrell, the founder of Spanish musical nationalism. Pedrell revealed to him a kind of nationalism that had its origins in folk music but was also blended with the classical techniques of Europe. It was in the opera *La vida breve*, composed in 1904–05, that Falla's distinctive style emerged for the first time. While it has an Andalusian flavor, little direct folkloric material is used, and its style—one in which the harmonization derives from the melodic substance—marks the work as uniquely Falla.[28]

In 1907 Falla left for Paris, where *La vida breve* was produced with great success at the Opéra-Comique in 1913. Concurrently, Falla was working on *Noches en los jardines de España* (1916). This important work shows the fusion of Andalusian material with French impressionism and the symphonic color of the Russian nationalists.[29]

The advent of World War I forced Falla to return to Madrid in 1915. Here, he collaborated with the noted poet and dramatist Martínez Sierra on *El amor brujo* ("Love the Sorcerer"), a *gitaneria* with dances, songs and spoken passages. The musical stimulus came from Falla's study of the rhythm, cadence, mode and sonority of the *cante jando*, the primitive flamenco song of Andalusia.[30]

The other large-scale work of this period is *Le Tricorne*. In adapting *El Corregidor y la molinera* into a ballet, Falla enlarged the orchestra, added the Miller's dance and expanded the ending into a fuller, more powerful finale. *Le Tricorne* is a work of humor, theatricality and magnificent orchestration. The first part, more limited because of its greater fidelity to the original pantomime, uses popular elements more directly; the second part is more abstracted and neoclassical.[31]

Choreography

There is a great deal of mime in *Le Tricorne*, done at "rat-a-tat-tat" tempo. One of the few sustained mime passages comes after the Miller's arrest when his wife, who has earlier taught a caged bird to sing, moves downstage on diagonal, arms stretched wide and fingers fluttering, like a bird vainly beating its wings against the bars of a cage. When the Corregidor tumbles into the river, she moves in the same diagonal, but this time in little spurts of energy, like a bird set loose and joyfully testing its wings. These two passages, as a unit, are considered a masterpiece of choreography.

Under the tutelage of Felix García, Massine quickly mastered flamenco technique. He created a super-national style by imposing ballet movements, plus many "twisted and broken" gestures of his own, on the forms and rhythms of regional Spanish dances. A good example is the pas de deux of the Miller and his wife. While it "was mainly inspired by the fandango with some flamenco passages, I added to it a variety of classical movements."[32]

In preparing this ballet, Massine also studied the paintings of El Greco, Goya and Velázquez to widen his understanding of the dignity and passion of the Spanish temperament. Through his study of bullfighters in the summer of 1917, he began to grasp the underlying ferocity present in such dances as the farruca: "I realized that it was essentially the same elements in the Spanish temperament which had produced both their dances and their national sport."[33] *Le Tricorne* had begun as an attempt to synthesize Spanish folk dances with classical techniques, but in the process of evolution it also emerged as a choreographic interpretation of the Spanish way of life.

Critical Survey

Le Tricorne was an immediate success at its 1919 première. The *Sunday Times* declared that "Serge de Diaghilev wears to the last moment his mantle of triumph.... The music is marvelous. Tamara Karsavina, Massine and Woizikowsky distinguished themselves and made us inarticulate with words and approval."[34]

In Retrospect

A few years before his death, John Gruen asked Massine which of his ballets he thought was the greatest. He replied, "Always *Le Tricorne* will stand out. I think it will be a classic."[35] Clive Barnes also flatly stated, "This is Massine's best ballet."[36]

Among this work's numerous revivals (most recently at the Paris Opéra in 1992), the best-known American revival was that of the Joffrey Ballet, staged by Tatiana Massine and Yurek Lazowski in 1969. Reviews were quite mixed, and Clive Barnes was in the minority when he stated that "the ballet has come up extraordinarily fresh."[37] Other critics pointed to problems in this revival which may help to explain the lack of Massine works in the repertories of many major ballet companies today.

For the successful revival of a ballet such as *La Boutique* or *Le Tricorne*, the dancers must deliver superlatively on two counts: first, they must perform even the most minute gesture with great precision and speed; and second, they must make a wholehearted commitment to robust and flamboyant characterizations. In their 1968 revival of *La Boutique*, the dancers of the Royal Ballet passed both tests handsomely. Reviews of Joffrey's *Le Tricorne* revival point to failures on both counts.

Because the mime must be performed with such speed and clarity, many of the scenes have either instant effectiveness or none at all, depending upon the performers. Jack Anderson observed that the Joffrey dancers failed to punctuate the action at critical moments, and as a result, "the entire point was lost: Take the scene in which the Miller is distracted by a girl with a jug, flirts with her, is discovered by his wife; they quarrel and are reconciled—and it all goes by like lightning. This vignette must be sharply etched; otherwise, it is nothing."

The choreography was not only blurry but even ignored in one instance. For the Miller's role, Robert Joffrey hired Luis Fuente, a professional flamenco dancer. For one of the performances, Fuente decided to show the audience a "real" farruca, and he completely trashed Massine's choreography. (According to Anderson, Joffrey fired him after the performance.) Anderson recognized that "This incident points up the essence of *Le Tricorne* which he [Fuente] evidently did not wish to accept. It requires the inner awareness and rhythms of Spanish dance ... but it is Spanish dance once removed, not genuine Spanish."[38]

Arlene Croce stated that the Joffrey dancers "looked like the kids in an expensive high school musical." They were unable to convey the "buoyant mood, the unshadowed psychology" of this comic fable: "It's such a square proposition and they're all too tense—with fear, I think, of being laughed at." She compared the Joffrey dancers to those in a 1939 film of *Le Tricorne* in the Massine Film Collection. The older dancers "move with sweep and sensual precision. The pantomime is conspicuously large and clear, carrying a full-throated force like singing.... Young dancers do not know how to make dancing look like mime or mime like dancing."

Massine revivals often suffer acutely from the loss of what was once known as "the Massine dancer." Here's a good example of what that dancer was like:

> I felt instinctively that something more than perfect technique was needed here [for the farruca], but it was not until I had worked myself up into a frenzy that I was able to transcend my usual limitations. The mental image of an enraged bull going into the attack unleashed some inner force which generated powers within me. I felt an almost electrical interaction between myself and the spectators. Their mounting excitement had the effect of heightening my physical strength until I was dancing with a sustained force that seemed far beyond my reach at other times. For a moment it seemed as if some other person within me was performing the dance [Massine, *My Life in Ballet*, 141 and 142].

In her conclusion, Croce observed: "perhaps revivals only succeed in telling us more about our own time than we thought we knew. That in itself is a value."[39]

Le Chant du Rossignol

Ballet in Two Scenes
Based on "The Nightingale" by Hans Christian Andersen
Music: Igor Stravinsky
Scenic and Costume Design: Henri Matisse
Scene Painting: Vladimir Polunin
Première: Théâtre Nationale de l'Opéra, Paris, February 2, 1920

ORIGINAL CAST
The Nightingale: Tamara Karsavina
The Mechanical Nightingale: Stanislas Idzikovsky
Death: Lydia Sokolova   The Emperor: Serge Grigoriev

Synopsis

(Act I of the original opera was omitted from the ballet, but it is necessary to recount it here.) In a wood in China, near the palace of the Emperor, dwells the Nightingale. Officials of the Chinese Imperial court appear in the wood. They are looking for this bird and have been sent by the Emperor, who has been told of its wonderful song. A little scullery maid, the only one in the palace to know the whereabouts of the bird, is their leader. When she locates the Nightingale, the officials are disappointed to see that it is small, gray, and unimpressive. When the Nightingale sings, though, she wins their hearts with her breathtaking notes. The Chamberlain invites the Nightingale to perform that evening at the Emperor's court.

Scene One. The Imperial Palace. A gauze curtain rises slowly, revealing the Imperial Palace. The Nightingale is borne to the throne room on a lofty perch, and the Emperor himself follows, carried in on a gilded throne. When the Nightingale sings, His Celestial Majesty's jaded senses are so touched that he begins to cry. He offers the Nightingale any reward she desires, but the bird replies that the tears glistening in the eyes of the Emperor are reward enough. At this point, three envoys arrive from the Emperor of Japan, bearing a large golden box on which is mounted the Mechanical Nightingale, gift of His Imperial Majesty to the Emperor of China.

The Mechanical Nightingale is wrought in gold and studded with gems. The song of the toy bird charms the Emperor and his court, and they forget the presence of the real Nightingale. When the Emperor grows weary of the toy and turns to ask the real bird to sing again, he discovers that she has departed without royal consent. The angry monarch thereupon banishes the Nightingale from his kingdom. He orders the Japanese toy bird to be mounted in the place of honor next to his Imperial bed.

Scene Two. The Emperor's Bedchamber. The Mechanical Nightingale stands by the dying Emperor's bedside. At the side of the gigantic bed sits Death, who has adorned herself with the Imperial crown. Specters are hovering about. They represent the Emperor's past deeds, good and bad. The Emperor calls for his musicians to drown out the noise of the accusing voices, but they are already pandering to his successor, and they do not come. Just as his life is at its lowest ebb, the voice of the Nightingale is heard outside his window. She has returned from exile at her own peril, and she sings so ravishingly that even Death pleads with her to continue. The Nightingale agrees, but only on the condition that Death will restore the crown to the head of the Emperor. Death makes this bargain, and under the spell of her heavenly music, Death surrenders and returns to her abode.

The Emperor is restored to good health and tearfully offers the Nightingale any reward she wishes. The Nightingale replies once more that the Emperor's tears are her best reward. Gently, she goes on to promise him that every night, without fail, she will nest in the shadows and sing to him until morning. Then she disappears.

A solemn march is heard. The courtiers, thinking that the Emperor is dead, enter the chamber gravely, then start in astonishment. Bathed in sunlight stands the Emperor in crown and full regalia. As the astounded courtiers prostrate themselves, he greets them all and says, "Good morning!"

Scenery and Costumes

Matisse's supreme accomplishment, which may be seen in all his work, was to liberate color from its traditionally realistic function and to make it the foundation of a decorative art of the highest order. In his early career, Matisse made his reputation as the principal protagonist of Fauvism. The subjects of Matisse's fauvist paintings are used as pretexts for exploring a new language of color. The greatest masterpieces of Matisse's early work are a series of large canvases entitled *The Dance* (1910; Hermitage, St. Petersburg). They show a technique dominated by flat planes of luminous, sometimes antinaturalistic color and a radical simplification of the human form; they are also distinguished by Matisse's fluid treatment of the contours of the figures in order to better express the idea of movement.[40]

Under the influence of Cubism, Matisse's palette became more somber—browns, ochres, and grays—and his shapes took on a geometrical severity for a time. His greatest painting of this period was *The Moroccans* (1916; MOMA, New York). To an unprecedented degree, the theme of this painting is obscured by the simplification of colored areas into basic geometric shapes.

In 1918, Matisse became a resident of Nice and developed a more naturalistic style. He observed the rules of classical perspective and concentrated on the female form, secluded interiors, landscapes, and still-lifes of flowers. During the 1920s, he adopted swirling, rhythmic decorative motifs which often seemed to be more important than the human subject of the painting. Characteristic of this period were his series of Odalisques, female nudes against Persian and North African fabrics. Matisse's new style reassured more conservative art collectors and dealers: not surprisingly, this period resulted in an increasing number of major exhibitions from 1919 to 1924.

Diaghilev offered Matisse a choice between new settings and costumes for *Scheherazade* or for *Le Chant du rossignol*. The picturesque Orientalism of *Scheherazade* seemed admirably suited to Matisse. However, after hearing music from both scores on the piano, Matisse decided in favor of *Le Chant*.[41]

Matisse had never designed stage scenery before, and he set to work, scissors in hand, cutting and piecing together a model. One of the problems, as noted by Vladimir Polunin, was that a three-dimensional model casts shadows and yields color tones at odds with those on a two-dimensional backdrop, where the colors are all on one plane. Polunin stated, "His complete ignorance of the stage was surprising, so that the very alphabet of it had to be explained to him," and Polunin apparently had to shepherd Matisse through many stages of the design process. Finally, though, he decided that despite numerous "changes of plan" and "alternating periods of depression and exultation," the final product passed muster: "His model was of a very simple, almost austere character, and its concentrated tones, well combined and balanced, produced at once a soft and brilliant impression."[42]

The backdrop was white with three overhanging friezes laced by black scalloped edges. Against this drop, the costumes stood out in the clear colors of Ming porcelain—green with pink, saffron yellow or white barred with orange and black. The Nightingale's costume was pure white, the Mechanical Nightingale was encased in a globular carapace and had a long beak, and Death wore scarlet tights and a necklace of skulls which was replicated on the crown of her head.[43]

One of Matisse's finest touches was the moment when the emperor was restored to life by the Nightingale's song. He rose to full height on his uptilted bed and loosened a black mantle with a magnificent vermilion lining, which billowed out to cover about sixty square feet of the stage. He then exited slowly, stepping upon the bowed backs of his courtiers.[44]

After the backdrop and costumes were completed, Diaghilev decided that *Le Chant du rossignol* must have a drop curtain. This was his sly way of obtaining huge canvasses from his most celebrated painters. Matisse's drop curtain represented two lions flanking a panel with three masks against a flowered background.

In Paris, Louis Laloy praised the "elegant simplicity" and "divine" color combinations of Matisse's designs.[45] London reactions were mixed. Valerian Svetloff called Matisse's scenery "bare and roughly planned."[46] When this project was completed, Matisse was so exhausted that he avoided the ballet medium altogether for the next two decades, evidently recalling his own anguished cry to Polunin, "Oh! how difficult it is to work for the Theatre!"[47]

Music

Igor Stravinsky is perhaps the greatest composer of the twentieth century. While still a law student, he began to study composition and instrumentation with Rimsky-Korsakov. Stravinsky's two earliest works, *Scherzo fantastique* and *Feu d'artifice*, made a deep impression on Diaghilev when they were first performed in St. Petersburg in 1909. Diaghilev believed that Stravinsky was the right composer for his artistic team, and he asked him to orchestrate *Le Festin* and two Chopin piano pieces in *Les Sylphides* for his 1909 Paris ballet season.

The first major event of Stravinsky's career was his commission from Diaghilev to compose the ballet *L'Oiseau de feu* ("The Firebird") for his company's 1910 Paris season. Here, for the first time, Stravinsky was faced with the challenge of composing an orchestral work nearly an hour in length. He was also stimulated to explore what turned out to be one of his most characteristic gifts, the ability to express physical gestures (and the psychological states that prompt them) in purely musical terms.

The score was thus praised for its picturesque orchestration. However, Vera Stravinsky and Robert Craft note that the Firebird's dance of supplication is pure Balakirev, and her "Berceuse" is heavily indebted to Ravel's *Rapsodie espagnole*.[48] Stravinsky also borrowed techniques from Rimsky-Korsakov, but even though one can object that *L'Oiseau de feu* is a thesaurus of current styles, this in no way weakens its impact in the theatre. Stravinsky was only twenty-eight when he composed *L'Oiseau de feu*, and its success was pivotal. Overnight he became known as the most gifted of the younger generation of Russian composers.

Concurrent with his work on *L'Oiseau de feu*, Stravinsky was working on a study for piano and orchestra called *Petrouchka*. Diaghilev persuaded him to turn the work into a ballet score, and *Petrouchka* was first performed in June of 1911. It proved just as successful with the public and critics as had *L'Oiseau de feu*. However, *Petrouchka* was a far more original work. The carnival scenes are more conventional, but Petrouchka's own music is radically different, marked by harsh polytonality, violent and percussive rhythms, and a dissonant harmonic idiom marked by the famous bitonal "Petrouchka chord" (combining C major and F-sharp major simultaneously).

After the Ballets Russes season that summer, Stravinsky retired to Ustilug where he wrote *Le Sacre du printemps*, the most famous work of his career.[49] While a great masterpiece of twentieth-century music, it was one which could have no sequel. Stravinsky's quest for a signature style was far from complete.[50]

In autumn of 1913 Stravinsky completed the last two acts of his opera *Le Rossignol*. Since it was introduced only a few weeks before the outbreak of war, the opera was quickly eclipsed.[51] Of the difference in idiom between the music of the first act and that of the second and third, Stravinsky stated that the first act owed much to "Tchaikovsky melodies too sweet and too cute even for that date."[52] Thus, the ballet adaptation of *Le Rossignol* would use the second and third acts only.

In his review for the première, Louis Laloy praised the music for achieving "the solidity of a symphony."[53] London critics, however, thought the score was ill-matched to the lyricism and romanticism of the story itself. The *Times* said, "there is something wrong between the dance and its music. It halts and wavers; the nightingale never seems to find her full voice."[54] Ernest Newman confessed that the music left him rather bored and continued, "This music ... has baffled even the genius of Massine to invent a satisfactory choreography for it."[55] Although Stravinsky's score was probably too avant-garde for this fairy tale, it still had moments of wonderful inventiveness. For Robert Lawrence, "Stravinsky's orchestral tone painting of the whirring mechanism of the artificial bird—identical in opera and ballet—is a stroke of instrumental genius."[56]

Choreography

Massine's choreography employed closely knitted groupings that suggested the odd masses of figures often found on Chinese porcelain, paintings, and screens. Massine and Matisse worked in close collaboration throughout the ballet, exploring ways in which individual costumes could be made to interact. Louis Laloy described the effect: "Matisse designed geometrically cut costumes for the Mourners and Mandarins that deliberately masked the curves of the body, thereby transforming the dancers into building blocks of Massine's accumulative architectonic structures ... they became part of an overall fluctuating pattern of stylized shape and color."[57]

It seemed to be Massine's own colleagues who were the most critical of his choreography. Diaghilev asserted that *Le Chant du rossignol*'s failure "was due to Massine's hermetic choreography, he had followed the principle of imposing a rhythm on the dance steps that was independent of the musical rhythm, having the dancers move against the beat. The result was that ... the ballet gave the impression of having been poorly rehearsed."[58] Karsavina, too, was disappointed with her supposedly lyrical role as the Nightingale. In her view, "this part was a pale, unloved creation of Massine. For the first time in my life I could not fall in love with my new role."[59]

Critical Survey

According to Serge Grigoriev, this ballet "turned out to be exactly what Paris liked."[60] Certainly Laloy's *Commoedia* review supports this impression. But London audiences were far less receptive. Valerian Svetloff termed it a ballet from which "all the poetry of Andersen's charming fairy tale has disappeared, and which has become changed in this rendering into cold dry mysticism."[61]

Several critics believed that one of Andersen's key symbols had been unwisely omitted: the lowly maidservant who brought the mandarins to find the Nightingale. She, the humblest, was the only member of the jaded Court who could discriminate between the costly and the priceless, and it was she alone who wept when the Nightingale was banished. This important point was lost in the ballet version. The *Times* said, "We miss most of all the little maidservant,"[62] and the *Observer* critic felt that Stravinsky had "spoiled his opera" by this omission.[63] Only the *Daily Herald* gave the ballet a favorable review, mostly for its costuming.[64]

In Retrospect

Le Chant du rossignol was revived in 1925, this time with choreography by George Balanchine. Massine's 1920 version had been forgotten by the dancers and was never much liked anyway. Though never a great success, *Le Chant du rossignol* was always in the Diaghilev repertory after 1925.[65]

PULCINELLA

Ballet in One Act
Based on the commedia dell'arte scenario *The Four Pulcinellas*
Music: Giovanni Battista Pergolesi, arranged by Igor Stravinsky
Scenic and Costume Design: Pablo Picasso
Première: Paris Opéra, May 15, 1920

ORIGINAL CAST

Pulcinella: M. Léonide Massine   **Pimpinella:** Mme Tamara Karsavina
Prudenza: Mme Lubov Tchernicheva   **Rosetta:** Mme Vera Nemchinova
Fourbo: M. Sigmund Novak   **Caviello:** M. Stanislas Idzikovsky
Florindo: M. Nicholas Zverev   **Il Dottore:** M. Enrico Cecchetti
Tartaglia: M. Stanislas Kostetsky

Synopsis

Dressed in a baggy white costume, Pulcinella is pursued by two charming ladies. Two gallants, who are suitors of the errant ladies, become jealous of Pulcinella's success. They attack Pulcinella and leave him for dead. Having only feigned death, Pulcinella escapes and returns in a magician's cloak, then attempts to revive the "dead" Pulcinella (now played by Pulcinella's friend, Fourbo). Meanwhile, the jealous suitors reappear, also dressed as Pulcinellas. When the real Pulcinella removes the magician's cloak, there are suddenly four Pulcinellas and two very confused ladies onstage. This comedy of sham and mistaken identity continues until the proper couples are eventually reunited in the finale.

Scenery and Costumes

Picasso's costumes were brightly colored except for the four Pulcinellas, who wore traditional flowing white shirts and shiny black trousers. Massine also wore a sugar-loaf hat and an authentic hook-nosed Pulcinella mask, with one side of the face laughing and the other crying.

As for the set, all that Diaghilev really wanted was a simple period drop evoking eighteenth-century Naples. Instead, Picasso's first proposal was based on an Italian Baroque theatre-within-a-theatre with a false proscenium opening onto a false stage and a further false opening revealing a harbor. Although the forced perspective and angular *trompe l'oeil* showed its cubist origins, Roland Penrose feels that the sum effect was one of "unabashed romanticism."[66] Diaghilev disliked Picasso's first proposal and, in the final version, all extravagances were suppressed. The final drop—tightly packed houses giving way to the night sky, with a large full moon and Mount Vesuvius above a boat in the harbor—was treated in a rigorously cubist style. The Neapolitan streetscape was strengthened by a somber palette of blue, gray, dark brown and white. Lighting, for the first time, was completely from above (no front or sidelights), and the entire stage was covered with a white dropcloth which, together with the lighting, created a suggestion of moonlight. The final result is one of the most beautiful stage settings ever designed.

Music

Giovanni Battista Pergolesi

Pergolesi lived during the heyday of the Italian opera seria, which acquired its definitive form during the 1720s. This genre was imbued with the classical ideals of clarity, dignity, purity of style and a hierarchical social order. Scholarly verse placed heroes of ancient times in highly conventionalized situations, usually involving a conflict of love and duty. Virtually all of the leading male roles were sung by castrati, male singers who had been castrated in boyhood so that their voices would remain in the soprano or contralto range. This practice produced adult voices of trumpet-like clarity and carrying power that, despite their high pitch, became associated with masculine heroes.

To temper the unrelieved solemnity of the opera seria, it became the custom to insert a comic intermezzo between its acts. This interlude had utterly nothing to do with the plot of the opera itself and was typically a scene for two or three singers in the roles of servants. As the eighteenth century went on, the structure of opera seria began to be challenged. Instead of the random coupling represented by the insertion of the intermezzo,

Alessandro Scarlatti and others began to compose entire comic operas with plots derived from love stories, escape dramas, and farce. This comic genre, known in Italy as the opera buffa, became popular throughout Europe and posed a threat to opera seria.

Although Pergolesi's life was short, his brief career had a powerful influence on the change of taste in opera. *Lo frate 'nnamoroto* (1732), his first opera buffa, was highly successful. When the opera was revived in 1748, the work was said to have been sung in the city streets for the previous fifteen years. Pergolesi's most portentous commission, the 1733 opera seria *Il prigionier superbo*, was most celebrated for its intermezzo, *La serva padrona* ("The Maid as Mistress").

Pergolesi's health began to fail in the summer of 1735, probably due to tuberculosis. Early in 1736 he moved into the Franciscan monastery in Pozzuoli. During his illness he composed his well-known *Stabat Mater*, a sacred work for voices and strings which became the most frequently printed single work of the eighteenth century. Pergolesi died on March 16, 1736, at age twenty-six; he was buried in the common pit next to the cathedral.[67] He enjoyed only limited success during his lifetime, but the almost universal fame he attained posthumously was due mostly to the traveling troupes of players who staged *La serva padrona* throughout Europe over the next two decades. Although lacking in profundity, Pergolesi's music is attractive for its sweetness and animation, and it was influential in the development of comic opera.

Igor Stravinsky

Diaghilev searched tenaciously for transcriptions of Pergolesi compositions and culled his favorite selections from libraries, auction houses and private collections. Stravinsky recalls that Diaghilev asked him one afternoon in Paris in 1919 if he would be interested in orchestrating some eighteenth-century music: "When he said that the composer was Pergolesi, I thought he must be deranged." At that time he knew only of Pergolesi's *Stabat Mater* and *La serva padrona*, neither of which interested him in the least. However, he did promise to take a look, and he claimed that he "fell in love."[68] Later, though, he reversed himself in chats with Robert Craft. Asked what he thought of Pergolesi, Stravinsky said, "Pergolesi? *Pulcinella* is the only work of 'his' that I like."[69]

Although Diaghilev had nothing more in mind than a straightforward orchestration, Stravinsky's imagination was deeply stirred by the project. Composing against the background of a harmonic and rhythmic system as predictable as that of Pergolesi made Stravinsky aware of how powerful an effect could be achieved by small and subtle dislocations.

There is scarcely a bar that does not reveal Stravinsky's genius in some felicity of phrasing, harmony or sonority.

Stravinsky's ultimate selection of pieces derived only partly from Diaghilev's discoveries, and it all came from Pergolesi's trio sonatas and operas. Perhaps the most extraordinary aspect of his orchestration was the decision to retain the vocal lines of the opera excerpts. While the vocal color fits the ambience of the stage action, the texts have no reference to the ballet's plot at all: this is a purely coloristic use of the human voice. Not the least of Stravinsky's achievements in *Pulcinella* was his transformation of markedly diverse musical selections into a coherent score with seamless transitions between movements.

When Stravinsky delivered his score, Diaghilev was amazed. Through the sensitive interpolation of his own ideas, Stravinsky had achieved an "utter transmutation"[70] of Pergolesi into Stravinsky. The critical importance of Stravinsky's encounter with eighteenth-century music cannot be overemphasized. *Pulcinella* pointed the way to Stravinsky's neoclassical period. It led to a consistent style in which he would adopt some mannerisms of eighteenth-century music and maintain an essential tonality, even while rejecting the conventional means of establishing it.

Choreography

Like *Les Femmes de bonne humeur*, *Pulcinella* integrated the qualities of commedia dell'arte gesture and attitude with classical ballet. In *Les Femmes* Massine had succeeded admirably in creating a variety of unique personalities. However, sharp characterization was much more difficult to achieve in *Pulcinella* because Massine opted to use the traditional commedia masks. For the title role, Massine decided to present Pulcinella as a "typical Neapolitan extrovert and a bit of a rogue." Since he was unable to rely on facial expression, he "used every possible flourish, twist and turn to suggest the unscrupulousness and ambiguity of Pulcinella's character."[71] Perhaps it was the very intricacy of this approach that led Stravinsky to describe *Pulcinella*'s choreography as "very good," but "sometimes mechanical."[72]

In order to save time, Stravinsky mailed Massine a piano reduction of each part of the score as he completed it. However, Massine assumed that *Pulcinella* was being scored for a large orchestra; when Stravinsky finally decided on a modest chamber orchestra, Massine's choreography was often out of scale for the music and had to be toned down on short notice.[73]

Critical Survey

While this ballet won acclaim from the critics, it was less popular with audiences. Stravinsky walked away with most of the kudos: "That

Stravinsky's adaptation and re-scoring of Pergolesi is not carried out in the spirit of self-effacement goes without saying," joked the *Observer*. "But somehow the lapses from Italian melodious purity into unadulterated Stravinsky do not jar."[74] Ernest Newman wrote, "Pergolesi and Stravinsky do not mix. Perhaps that is just the secret of the charm of this music ... it all seems pure *gaminerie* on Stravinsky's part, but as *gaminerie* it is first-rate."[75]

Pulcinella presented eye and ear with a complex synthesis of the past and present. Its Italian mate, *Les Femmes*, had novel choreography, but it was still firmly linked to the past by Bakst's realistic set and Tommasini's straightforward orchestration. As Edward Dent noted, "Observe the quintessence of Diaghilevism—*Pulcinella* is not a follower of *The Good-Humoured Ladies*, but it is merely engaged upon a more elaborate *Parade*."[76]

In Retrospect

Pulcinella survives mostly in the concert hall, although the ballet has been revived for historical purposes by La Scala in 1971 and by the New York City Ballet for the 1972 and 1981 Stravinsky Festivals. Even though it is rarely seen today, *Pulcinella* was a significant ballet for many reasons. It was the only Stravinsky/Picasso collaboration, it set new precedents in theatrical design and, most importantly, it was crucial to Stravinsky's subsequent musical development.

3

July 1920–April 1926

Following the spring premières of *Pulcinella* and *Le astuzie femminili*, Diaghilev's thoughts turned to *Le Sacre du printemps*. Its world première in 1913, with choreography by Nijinsky, had caused a famous theatre riot. Diaghilev may have been hoping for another *succès de scandale* when he decided to revive it in 1920 with entirely new choreography by Massine.

Diaghilev had arranged a season at the Théâtre des Champs-Elysées in December of 1920, but he couldn't afford any new productions. On the surface, a revival of *Sacre* might seem to be a practical alternative, since the backdrops and costumes were still in good condition. However, since the Stravinsky score demanded a large orchestra and an unusual number of rehearsals for dancers and musicians, the undertaking would actually be quite costly. During his summer vacation in Venice, Diaghilev saw Misia Sert every day. She was often accompanied by a young woman who would listen in silence as Diaghilev bemoaned his lack of funds. Misia's companion shortly made Diaghilev a gift of 300,000 francs on the condition that he was not to reveal her identity. The name of his benefactress was Coco Chanel.[1]

In the fall of 1920, the Ballets Russes toured the British provinces. Massine left the tour early and returned to London with Sokolova and Vera Savina. He needed more rehearsal time with Sokolova, the Chosen Virgin in *Sacre*, and he also offered to coach Vera Savina in her new role in the "Mazurka" from *Les Sylphides*.

Savina had joined the Ballets Russes in 1918. While rehearsing in

London, Léonide and Vera fell in love. Sokolova wrote that "Savina, being English and not speaking two words of Russian, was as innocent as a new-born lamb, and she was the only person in the company who had no idea of Massine's situation."[2]

When the British tour ended, the Ballets Russes went to Paris for the December première of *Le Sacre du printemps*, and Massine's pursuit of Savina intensified. After rehearsal one night, Sokolova discovered Savina alone onstage at the moment when Misia Sert walked through the stage door. Savina revealed to Mme Sert that she was on her way to a rendezvous with Massine at the Arc de Triomphe and asked for directions.[3]

Whether Misia dashed to Diaghilev and told him of the rendezvous or not, he was obviously getting suspicious. By New Year's Eve, when the company moved to Rome, Diaghilev had hired private detectives to follow Massine and Savina about. Tales of Diaghilev's jealous rage abound, the least savory of which has Diaghilev inviting Savina to his room, getting her drunk, stripping her naked, and then throwing her into Massine's room next door.[4]

One day in Rome, Grigoriev was summoned by Diaghilev and told, "I am definitely parting with Massine ... and I should like you, as régisseur, to inform him before today's rehearsal that I have no more need of his services."[5] When Grigoriev arrived at rehearsal he took Massine aside and gave him the news. Sokolova wrote that Massine "went deathly pale, turned and walked out of the room." Diaghilev disappeared for several days. His valet, Vassili, told Sokolova that "he nearly died."[6] Serge Lifar wrote that of all of Diaghilev's lovers, none but Massine had given him "so many moments of happiness or anguish."[7]

Massine was only twenty-five, and because his life had been wedded to the Ballets Russes since he left Russia, he felt "frightened and confused" at first. But he wrote that "once the initial shock had worn off I recovered my nerve and began to enjoy my freedom."[8] He had youth, fame, connections with the rich and powerful, and his lovely bride, Vera. They were married a few weeks after Léonide's dismissal.

By the end of the second week of February, Massine had his first offer of employment. The Italian impresario Walter Mocchi asked him to recruit a ballet company and appear in a syndicate of theatres which he managed in South America. Massine engaged some Polish dancers and some former Diaghilev dancers, and he sailed for South America on May 1, 1921, with a fifteen-member company. The repertory included excerpts from Fokine's and his own ballets. Léonide's grueling schedule required him to dance every night, rehearse a full repertory, choreograph new works and handle a myriad of administrative details involved in managing a company. The ballet troupe, billed as Compañia de Bailes Rusos, performed in Rio de Janeiro, São Paulo, Buenos Aires and Montevideo with great success. Léonide and Vera then sailed back for Europe early in 1922 and settled temporarily at the Hôtel Normandie in Paris.

It was London rather than Paris, though, that became Massine's home base for most of the 1920s. He negotiated with Hollywood producer Walter Wanger, who had leased the Royal Opera House at Covent Garden to book motion pictures and revues. This low-brow use of the opera house was a last-ditch effort to keep Covent Garden afloat in the wake of a severe postwar financial crisis.

During the 1921–22 Ballets Russes season at the Alhambra, Diaghilev had produced an opulent three-act *Sleeping Beauty* (retitled *The Sleeping Princess*) which lost so much money that by the closing, the impresario told the company that the most he could offer them was a two-pound-a-week retainer.[9] This was obviously inadequate, and several of Diaghilev's leading dancers were grateful for the chance to join Massine's Covent Garden enterprise.

The small troupe was billed as the Massine/Lopokova Company and also included Sokolova, Woizikowsky, Slavinsky, Savina and a few extras, one of whom was Ninette de Valois. They opened at Covent Garden on April 3, 1922, presenting a new set of divertissements from the Fokine, Massine and Petipa repertory every week in support of the weekly film. However, the movie series did not catch on; within one month Covent Garden had resolutely closed its doors to films. As he had in 1918, Sir Oswald Stoll came to the rescue by moving Massine and his dancers to the Coliseum.

At the beginning of 1923 Massine was asked to choreograph *You'd Be Surprised*, which opened at Covent Garden on January 22. This revue, coproduced by Walter Wanger and Sir Oswald Stoll, was further clarified under the hideous subtitle of "Jazzaganza." What it amounted to was a very indifferent production led by George Robey.

As with the earlier film series, much indignation was aroused at the impropriety of a coarse revue entering the hallowed portals of the Royal Opera House. Rumors of a demonstration in the gallery made opening-night jitters even worse than those already engendered by the wretched script. George Robey, however, disarmed potential troublemakers on the rise of the curtain: "With his finger on his lips he tiptoed straight down to the footlights. ... 'Hush, hush,' he announced, 'you mustn't laugh here.'"[10] For one month, the Royal Opera House disdainfully housed the revue. Afterwards, the whole production removed itself to the Alhambra

Theatre, where it was to play three times a day: "the arrangement definitely smacked of penance."[11]

By 1923 Massine saw the wisdom of going to Paris to renew his artistic and social contacts. He met with Satie, Milhaud, Picasso, Gontcharova, Larionov, Derain and, most fortuitously, Count Etienne de Beaumont. Etienne and Edith de Beaumont were great patrons of the arts, gathering under the roof of their magnificent mansion the leading artists of their day. An unlikely couple — he was a homosexual and she was a devotée and translator of Sappho — they were celebrated for their lavish masquerade balls, which were decorated and costumed by leading artists. Shortly after Massine's arrival in Paris, Beaumont asked him to collaborate with Picasso and Satie on a masquerade in the style of Louis XIV. At this point, Massine and Beaumont established a long-lasting friendship.

Soon after, Beaumont struck on the idea of organizing a series of public performances. By the autumn of 1923 he had rented the Théâtre de la Cigale, a small theatre in Montmartre, and was commissioning some of the most prestigious artists in Paris for the venture. These performances were to be called *Les Soirées de Paris*.

Diaghilev had been on friendly terms with Beaumont, but this new enterprise alarmed and infuriated him because it was commercial. Diaghilev was already facing competition from Rolf de Maré's Les Ballets Suédois, an avant-garde Swedish company that had caught the eyes of Paris. Now he saw yet another rival. Equally galling was the participation of dancers, composers and visual artists who were all associated with the Diaghilev ballet. The poster announcing *Les Soirées de Paris* prompted Diaghilev to say, "It's a Ballets Russes season where only my name is missing."[12] While preparing for his own 1924 season, Diaghilev intervened with several of these artists to dissuade them from taking part in the Beaumont enterprise. Their responses were uniformly soothing, but they went right ahead with their plans for *Les Soirées*.

Beaumont's mansion became Massine's headquarters. He moved into an annex, and two large rooms in the mansion served as rehearsal studios. The intensive rehearsal period began in February and, as opening night drew near, tensions escalated between Massine and his leading ballerina, Lydia Lopokova. Their rivalry probably had its roots back in the 1918 London season when they had shared honors as its most idolized dancers. Lopokova accused Massine of trying to upstage her in *Les Soirées*. In a letter to her husband John Maynard Keynes she wrote, "My friends find as ever that Massine does everything to shadow me and not make me his equal."[13]

For *Les Soirées*, Massine prepared three substantial works — *Salade*,

Mercure, and *Le Beau Danube*[14]—and four minor works. *Mercure* was inspired by a masked ball given by the Beaumonts in which Jean Cocteau appeared as the god Mercury: he donned gray tights and a winged helmet, carried Mercury's wand, and dashed about the ballroom with appropriate velocity. Satie and Picasso humored Cocteau by giving the Messenger their ballet's title role.

The conditions under which *Les Soirées* was rehearsed and mounted were characterized by wild disorder. Much of the chaos was due to the Beaumonts' absentmindedness. It was typical that, on one evening, the audience in the theatre should consist solely of Beaumont's mother and three of her lady friends. In a praiseworthy effort to help her son, she had bought every seat in the house—and then forgot to pass out the tickets.[15]

In the spring of 1924, the balletomanes of Paris all gravitated toward the Théâtre de la Cigale and the Théâtre des Champs-Elysées, where the battle of the impresarios was playing out. Although *Les Soirées* and the Ballet Suédois may have worried Diaghilev in 1924, his own new productions outclassed the new works of both companies. As Jean Hugo confirms, "it was Diaghilev who was always king of the season. Neither Rolf de Maré nor Étienne de Beaumont had succeeded in dethroning him."[16] Beaumont's Paris programs ran for only one season, and he soon renewed his connection with Diaghilev.

After *Les Soirées* closed on June 30, Massine returned to London, where his marriage ended. According to Massine, Vera Savina felt abandoned because of their long separations and his intense devotion to his work. Eleonora Marra, Massine's London student who had danced in *Les Soirées*, replaced Savina in Massine's affection for the next few years.

Léonide had made several attempts since 1922 to renew his professional relationship with Diaghilev, but nothing materialized. Since Massine's departure, Bronislava Nijinska had been the Ballets Russes's choreographer. When she left the company in 1924, Diaghilev was grooming George Balanchine with choreography for ballet scenes in several operas. However, Diaghilev wasn't yet ready to entrust Balanchine with an original ballet, and he suddenly needed an experienced choreographer. He sent word to Massine by way of Cecchetti.

A rendezvous was arranged at Cecchetti's London studio a week later. Diaghilev proposed that Massine choreograph two ballets—*Zéphyr et Flore* and *Les Matelots*—for the 1925 season. Grigoriev recounts that the Diaghilev-Massine meeting was "not very cordial" and that Diaghilev "distanced himself" from Massine's new works, "presumably because of hostility towards Massine."[17] Massine's version of the meeting is amusingly at odds with Grigoriev's: "When I saw Diaghilev again it was like a reunion with a member of my own family. I realized that my affection for him was as strong as ever, and I sensed that he felt the same. Our relationship was quickly re-established on its old footing."[18]

Negotiations concluded, Massine took Marra to Italy for a respite on the Isole dei Galli, which he had finally purchased in 1922. It was composed of three tiny islands—Isola Lunga, Brigante, and Rotunda. The task of cultivating these rocky islands was formidable, but Massine's caretaker eventually succeeded in growing cypresses, rosemary bushes and grape vines.

By 1925 Massine was back at work for the Ballets Russes, but it was no longer home to him. Diaghilev was cold and remote and to make matters worse, Vera Savina was back with the company again. Sokolova wrote that Massine ignored Savina and that he was "embarrassed and uncomfortable with the company."[19] Composer Vladimir Dukelsky also found his demeanor to be "inaccessible and reserved in the extreme."[20]

The Ballets Russes came forth with a rash of ultra-modern works in the 1920s, but beginning with the disastrous revival of *The Sleeping Princess* in 1921, Diaghilev also became fascinated with the grand siècle of Louis XIV. Works like *The Sleeping Princess* celebrated the aristocracy and were designed to appeal to upper-class patrons, whose financial contributions were critical.[21] At the time of *Zéphyr*'s planning, Lord Rothermere (Harold Sidney Harmsworth), an extremely wealthy newspaper magnate, was Diaghilev's main backer. Rothermere expressed the hope that there would be no "advanced" productions in the program for the 1925 season.[22]

This may well have influenced Diaghilev's decision to stage a ballet of the kind danced by serfs in companies maintained by Russian nobles during the eighteenth century. Diaghilev and the librettist, Boris Kochno, wanted to recreate the atmosphere of that period using the myth of *Zéphyr et Flore*. *Les Matelots* told a simple, farcical story of three sailors on shore leave. Grigoriev felt that it had an "exceedingly slight scenario in accordance with Diaghilev's dictum, with which I personally disagreed, that the public were bored with plots and only liked dances."[23]

Soon after Massine finished these two ballets, he returned to London in the spring of 1925. He had been hired by producer Charles H. Cochran to choreograph two revues, *On with the Dance* and its sequel, *Still Dancing*. During the run of *On with the Dance*, the Ballets Russes presented *Zéphyr* and *Les Matelots* in Monte Carlo and Paris. When the company moved to the London Coliseum in the summer of 1925, Massine rejoined them as guest artist, dancing the French sailor in *Les Matelots*. Diaghilev also spitefully paired Léonide and Vera Savina in the "Bluebird Pas de Deux" from *Sleeping Beauty*. In the fall of 1925, Massine plunged into rehearsals for *Still Dancing*. Cochran promptly negotiated his participation in his next show, *Cochran's Revue 1926*, scheduled to open on April 29.

LE SACRE DU PRINTEMPS

Ballet in Two Scenes
Music: Igor Stravinsky
Scenic and Costume Design: Nicholas Roerich
Première: Théâtre des Champs-Elysées, December 15, 1920

ORIGINAL CAST
La Vierge élue: Lydia Sokolova   **Vieux Sage:** M. Worontsaw
Les Femmes, Les Hommes, Les Adolescentes, Les Adolescents

Synopsis

Le Sacre du printemps is an evocation of the triumph and ironic cruelty of spring and the process of regeneration in the context of an ancient Slavic ritual sacrifice. The simple plot falls into separate yet mutually interdependent parts—the Adoration of the Earth and the Sacrifice. Primitive Slavs assemble for their yearly ceremonies, dancing their traditional rituals to propitiate the gods of the harvest. Finally, they select a virgin to be sacrificed to the gods of Spring.

Scenery and Costumes

Nicholas Roerich was a Russian painter and stage designer with wide-ranging cultural interests. As a stage designer, he worked between 1907 and 1915 for such directors as Nikolay Yevreinov and Konstantin Stanislavsky. His designs for the Ballets Russes productions of *Prince Igor* (1909) and *Le Sacre du printemps* (1913) have become classics.

During his time in Russia, Roerich's painting was strongly shaped by archeology and folklore. From 1924 to 1928 he led an American artistic-scientific expedition around Central Asia and then settled in the Himalayas. From the 1930s until his death in 1947, Roerich's paintings were strongly influenced by his interest in the Himalayas and in Eastern philosophy and religion. A large exhibition of his work forms part of Moscow's State Museum of Oriental Art; another important collection is in the Nicholas Roerich Museum, New York.

Roerich was best known for his distinctive and monumental landscapes. With their simplified outlines and flat areas of color, they emphasized atmosphere over detail. He had designed two backcloths for Nijinsky's *Sacre*. Massine's production used only the backdrop for Scene

Two, which represented the ancient Scythian steppe under a lowering black and yellow sky. The *Observer* declared that "the backcloth is the finest the Ballet has ever had, charging the atmosphere at once with an impression of bleak, wind-swept places, backgrounded by terrifying mountains."[24]

Music

Stravinsky's melodic themes in *Le Sacre du printemps* are simple and diatonic, often containing no more than four different notes. But their initial form is then subjected to radical and restless transformations of the note order, tempo, rhythm and meter. Occasionally a simple phrase is treated in canon, or two or more themes may overlap or be simultaneously deployed.

A tremendous internal tension is set up in the score between the simplicity of the thematic material and the discordant complexity of the harmonic texture. This essential dichotomy between melody and harmony is also seen at certain points in *Petrouchka*. The harmonic "germ" of *Sacre* is again a bitonal combination of two adjacent chords—this time E-flat major (with added minor 7th) and F-flat major. The bitonality appeared only momentarily in *Petrouchka*, but it is pervasive in *Sacre*, resulting in a work of much greater homogeneity.

The metrical aspect of the score is extraordinary. Either Stravinsky chooses a regular metrical pattern and upsets it with violently syncopated accents, or he allows his meter to follow the breakup of the melodies, calling for innumerable changes of time signature. The metrical framework of the score is often underlined by ostinatos, or short, constantly repeated phrases. In the "Sacrificial Dance" there is a complex ostinato, mainly for percussion, which fills a 5/4 bar. The time signature of the main subject oscillates between 5/4, 4/4, and 3/4, while the ostinato persists in its 5/4 shape and marches relentlessly across the bar lines.[25]

In his instrumentation, Stravinsky used highly sophisticated means to get a deliberately primitive effect. The orchestra is the largest that Stravinsky ever wrote for, and percussion is raised to the highest importance. Thus, the sheer volume of sound produced is almost overwhelming at points.

The opening night of *Le Sacre du printemps* (Théâtre des Champs-Elysées, May 29, 1913) gave rise to one of the great theatrical scandals of all time. Balletgoers who had been nurtured on tuneful Tchaikovsky melodies were outraged, and audience unrest was exacerbated by Vaslav Nijinsky's spasmodic choreography as well. Protests, counter-protests and fistfights multiplied. There were cries for "*Un docteur!*" and "*Une dentiste!*"

The police were called to expel the most violent demonstrators. The hubbub was so loud that the performers could not hear the music, and Nijinsky stood on a chair in the wings, shouting out numbers to the dancers.[26]

Sacre was an inspired score. However, it marks an extreme point along one line of technical development. E. Walter White points out that "it was a vocabulary that could essentially be used only once."[27]

Choreography

When Massine visited Stravinsky in Switzerland in August of 1920, Stravinsky told him that he thought that Nijinsky had followed the rhythms of the score too closely in trying to achieve a perfect metrical synchronization. Shortly thereafter, Stravinsky told the *Observer*, "The choreographic construction of Nijinsky was one of great plastic beauty but subjected to the tyranny of the bar."[28] Massine's choreography was based on phrases, an approach that allowed for a freer connection of choreography and music. Far from treating each bar of the music as an entity to interpret, Massine's movement phrases built long bridges over many bars of music, touching down occasionally to mirror the score and then alighting for the next bridge.

Massine focused on formal concerns, such as striking a balance between the mobile and the sculpturesque, the ensemble and the individual, and finding intellectual answers to challenging rhythmic problems. Human drama was secondary. As Shelley Berg noted, "for Massine *Le Sacre* was an interesting choreographic puzzle rather than a work of emotional significance."[29] Stravinsky and Massine discarded the original libretto. In part, the 1920 program notes read, "The work is divided in two parts and has no subject.... There is no story at all and no point in looking for one."[30] While this statement cannot be taken too literally, Massine did use a movement style that would bring him close to the abstraction he was seeking. Nijinsky's choreography was uncompromisingly anticlassical—twisted, spasmodic, and violent. Massine used a cleaner, more classical vocabulary.

Sokolova has left us with the most complete descriptions of the ballet's second scene. As the Chosen Virgin, she had to stand absolutely still for twelve minutes waiting for the "Danse Sacrale" to begin. To keep from blinking, she stared fixedly at the red exit light at the back of the theatre. The ensemble linked up and formed a human chain with Sokolova as its center, "gradually opening out like a concertina and closing in again." Afterwards, the men on either side of her broke hands and the "Danse Sacrale" began.

The lengthy solo was an exhausting ordeal for Sokolova: it was strenuous and, moreover, required continuous counting. She described herself as "a creature galvanized by an electric current." Towards the end of her dance, when she had no strength left to count, Leon Woizikowsky was allowed to call the counts out for her.[31] Of the solo's ending she wrote:

> At last I came to my final spinning jumps around the stage. These consisted of *grands jetés en tournant*, in themselves difficult steps to do, but between each, on landing, I had to bend sideways and place one hand on the stage while I raised the other in the air and beat my breast twice. Coming to a sudden halt in the middle, I pulled myself up on my toes, waiting for the curtain to begin to fall. I dropped to the ground and lay backwards, raising my body in a taut arch, like a victim meeting the knife.[32]

Although Massine's "Danse Sacrale" had a barbaric intensity, Nijinsky's certainly had no movement that critics and audiences could recognize as a *grand jeté en tournant*. Berg notes that Massine's *Sacre* seemed "less an evocation of the rites of a pagan Russian tribe than Nijinsky's ballet had been.... This new *Le Sacre* began to reveal the significance that the work would come to have as a universal drama."[33]

In 1929 Leopold Stokowski led the Philadelphia Orchestra in the American concert première of the score. The following year, he decided to present the full-scale ballet. Claire Reis, founder of the League of Composers, had assembled a distinguished board, including designer Norman Bel Geddes, Martha Graham, Doris Humphrey, Charles Weidman, Agnes de Mille, and Massine. Graham was to dance the Chosen Virgin, but she declined to choreograph because she had no experience in handling large groups. Massine accepted in her place.

The forty-member cast was assembled from The Group, Graham's all-female troupe, the Humphrey-Weidman Company, and the Roxy Theatre. Stories abound that Massine and Graham fought tooth-and-nail during rehearsals. Claire Reis reported that warfare broke out at the first rehearsal: "Massine wanted it done as it had been done in Paris and they crossed swords and neither one would give in."[34] John Martin declared there was "considerable bloodshed on both sides."[35] Eleanor King, a Graham dancer, recalls Graham sitting in a corner during rehearsal, with a shawl over her head. "When she did move, it was with condescension.... It was hard on Massine and for the dancers supporting her."[36]

It is quite possible, though, that these accounts are exaggerated. Most probably, the only serious bickering related to small changes which could alter the letter, but not the spirit, of Massine's choreography. When asked about the fighting, Graham replied: "I'm sorry to disappoint you on that.... There were certain things balletically that I changed a bit. But my style was beginning to develop at that time, and I would do the thing the way I would do it, you see, and usually Massine was very generous and he said, 'We'll keep that.'"[37] Massine wrote that he found Graham "a most subtle and responsive dancer to work with."[38]

Sacre was presented at Philadelphia's Metropolitan on April 11 and at New York's Met on April 22. It was considered one of the most important events in the music annals of New York, and the theatre was completely sold out for all performances.

Critical Survey

When Massine's *Sacre* premièred in Paris in December of 1920, reviews were quite mixed. Jean Bernier called it "an explosion of life,"[39] while André Levinson was hostile: "[Massine] denies, with—it would seem—the consent of the composer, the magnificently human motivating basis of the work to conform to a purely abstract conception, which has been consciously emptied of all significance."[40] Grigoriev was of the same opinion: "Massine's choreography was highly expert, but to my mind lacked pathos, in which it differed notably from Nijinsky's ... the result was something almost mechanical, without depth, which failed to be moving."[41]

In London, *Sacre* was heartily disliked because of its abstraction, and it was withdrawn after only two performances. The *Times* called it a "passionless ritual,"[42] while the *Morning Post*'s review was entitled "Ballet at Its Nadir."[43] Richard Capell, who had ridiculed Nijinsky's *Sacre* as "Cannibal Island Dancing" in 1913, made a complete turnabout: "they have spoiled a perfectly good ballet ... the Stone Age of 1913 appeared weird and impressive. The Stone Age, new version, is a bore."[44]

Massine's *Sacre* was performed on and off during the 1921–24 seasons of the Ballets Russes, and was revived again for the company in 1929. Interestingly, the 1929 revival had a great success in London. Perhaps the audience had grown more sophisticated, more accepting of abstraction in dance. The *Times* pronounced that Massine's *Sacre* was "the charter of the modern ballet."[45]

Response to *Sacre*'s 1930 American première was "explosive," according to Oliver Daniel.[46] John Martin had high praise for the choreography: "Through its complicated visual counterpoint and its terrific energy it is so young, so frank, so strong, that it seems a part of nature itself, a visualization of that rich depth which rolls through the music."[47]

In Retrospect

Massine staged *Sacre* for La Scala in 1948 and for the Royal Swedish Opera Ballet in 1956. Most recently, it was revived by the Nice Ballet in January 1995. Of this revival Clement Crisp wrote, "Massine was a brilliant man, and his view of the music astonishes by its control of a notoriously awkward score."[48]

The role of the Chosen Virgin marked a turning point in Graham's career. Berg believes that "Graham's fascination with the language of myth and the symbolic forms of ritual dates from her performance in *Le Sacre*."[49] In the Swedish revival, Bertil Hagman could "see resemblances to the work of Martha Graham, although in this case it is Graham who has manifestly been inspired by Massine."[50] *Sacre* was one of the first works to chip away at the artificial boundary between classical ballet and modern dance. One Graham dancer said, "I couldn't help thinking that there was a connection between the approach to dance as Martha Graham had and Léonide Massine had."[51]

You'd Be Surprised (Jazzaganza)

Musical Revue in Two Acts
Première: Royal Opera House, Covent Garden, January 22, 1923

DANCERS
Léonide Massine, Lydia Lopokova, Lydia Sokolova,
Taddeus Slavinsky, Ninette de Valois, and Leon Woizikowsky

For his first musical revue, Massine cooked up *Togo; Or, The Noble Savage* and *Chinese Dance*. *Chinese Dance*, Scene Sixteen, was an Oriental solo for Massine to a rigadoon by Louis Ganne. *Dancing Times* dubbed it "a very clever piece of choreographic portraiture."[52]

Togo, Scene Seven, was an Amerindian ballet set at the Wild Cat Inn in a small Arizona town. The characters were Togo (Massine), His Squaw (Sokolova), A Passing Negro (Taddeus Slavinsky), A Picaninny (Ninette de Valois), Mexican Gentleman (Leon Woizikowsky) and His Wife, Elaia (Lopokova). The not-to-be-missed plot of this ballet, quoted verbatim from the *Dancing Times*, is as follows:

> A Mexican gentleman and his wife, spending their honeymoon in Arizona, approach the "Wild Cat Inn," attended by their picaninny. Suddenly, Togo, an Indian chief, and his squaw are seen to capture a passing Negro. After securing their prisoner, Togo executes a ritual dance. The Mexican tourists are interested by this scene from savage

life until their Negress servant, recognizing her lover in Togo's victim, begs her mistress to intercede. Togo, overcome by Elaia's sweetness, ends by surrendering his weapons. Togo's wife, however, swiftly recalls him to his duty. The noble savage is returning to her, and to the execution of his Negro prisoner, when the Mexican gentleman asserts the claims of civilization with his revolvers. The reunited Negroes rejoice, and under the influence of their happiness, all ends in general married bliss.[53]

This bizarre, politically incorrect ballet had all the trappings of a Ballet Suédois production, with its novel African-Brazilian score by Darius Milhaud and modern décor by Duncan Grant. To some extent, Milhaud can be exonerated for participating in this project, because *Togo* used one of his preexisting scores, *Saudades do Brasil*. But it is bewildering that so distinguished an artist as Duncan Grant—an artist with no fewer than seven paintings in the permanent collection of the Tate Gallery—would have affixed his name to original designs for this dreadful ballet. The explanation must lie in the fact that Grant was a member of the Bloomsbury Group and a close friend of Sir John Maynard Keynes, the future husband of Lydia Lopokova, the "Elaia" in *Togo*.

By way of a critical survey, Sokolova's summary of *Togo* will suffice: "Massine's ballet was so poor I can hardly remember anything about it. I know I was dressed in all-over brown tights with a black wig and African make-up and did a war dance.... Massine had a chance to do something really good, but the programme he arranged was a disaster."[54]

LES SOIREES DE PARIS

A. Salade (Insalata)
Ballet in Two Acts
Libretto: Albert Flament, based on a collection of tales from the commedia dell'arte
Music: Seventeenth- and eighteenth-century Italian melodies, arranged and orchestrated by Darius Milhaud
Scenery and Costumes: Georges Braque
Première: Théâtre de la Cigale, Paris, May 17, 1924

ORIGINAL CAST
Polichinelle: Léonide Massine **Isabella**: Eleanora Marra
Rosetta: Mlle Allan **Tartaglia**: M. Witzansky
Coviello: M. Baikov **Cinzio**: M. Streletsky
The Doctor: M. Ignatov **Captain Cartuccia**: M. Sergiev

Synopsis

Act One. The beautiful Rosetta is secretly in love with Polichinelle but her father, Tartaglia, wants to marry her off to the rich Captain Cartuccia. Cinzio, the Doctor's son, comes in, accompanied by his beloved, Isabella. The Doctor does not approve of his son's love affair at all. Moreover, Tartaglia is also in love with Isabella, and he wants Cinzio out of the way. Polichinelle comes in, and Rosetta tells him that her father is trying to make her marry Cartuccia.

Polichinelle disguises himself as a doctor. He causes a great disturbance all around him, hoping that as a result, the real doctor will be arrested and sent to prison. Cinzio would then be free to marry Isabella. Next, Tartaglia asks Isabella if she will marry him. She responds that she will marry only if he administers a good beating to the doctor. Tartaglia finds the disguised Polichinelle and thrashes him soundly.

Act Two. Captain Cartuccia now arrives to ask for Rosetta's hand in marriage. He does not know that the mysterious damsel in the veil is actually Polichinelle in disguise. Suddenly, the supposed Rosetta flings a bag of flour over Cartuccia. He departs in a huff. In no time at all, a new plot is devised. Polichinelle and his servant disguise themselves as Persian slave merchants, while Isabella and Rosetta are dressed as slave girls. They offer these beautiful girls to the Doctor, who immediately buys one for Cinzio. He has in fact bought Isabella without knowing it. When the ruse is discovered, the Doctor and Tartaglia admit that Polichinelle is far too clever for them. So Tartaglia decides to let Polichinelle marry Rosetta while Isabella is allowed to marry Cinzio. The fathers give their blessing to the two young couples as we hear this shout: "Young people, never give way to your families!"

Scenery and Costumes

Georges Braque, with Pablo Picasso, was the co-founder of Cubism. In 1905 he became associated with Fauvism, but in the autumn of 1907, he began the transition to a more subdued style inspired by Cézanne. The transition was given additional impetus when Braque saw Picasso's *Les Demoiselles d'Avignon* in late 1907. Braque's response was his *Large Nude* (1908; priv. col., Mangin), in which Braque accepted the schematized structure, shallow space and subdued color of *Demoiselles*.

A trip to L'Estaque in the summer of 1908 led to his first works which were truly cubist in their flat treatment of landscape space.[55] While Braque's landscape exhibition of that year gave rise to Vauxcelles' description of Braque as a painter of "cubes," the term "cubism" as a critical label has a misleadingly geometric implication and was never proposed by either Braque or Picasso.[56] Braque's most important analytical cubist painting is *Portuguese Man* (1911–12; Basle, Kstmus). It was a landmark for its extreme fragmentation and unprecedented fusion of background and foreground. Moreover, the stenciled letters and numbers in the upper part of the canvas sit on the surface, challenging the boundaries of the conventional picture field.

By 1912, Braque and Picasso were using preexisting objects and materials in their paintings, partly to preserve a connection with reality in their works. Braque introduced papier collé: the artificial wood-grain paper (*faux bois*) that he stuck to paper on which he drew acted as an integral part of the structure of the drawing. By 1913 Braque began using colored paper; however, he still showed little interest in introducing other preexisting elements into his collages. Braque's austere and relentless formal interest in a narrow range of subject matter established his reputation as the most rigorous exponent of Cubism.

For *Salade*, Braque found a brilliant way to cope with the shallowness of the Cigale's stage. He devised a line of arches which spread across the full length of the stage, dividing it into two zones which were independently lit from one another and where simultaneous actions of the interpreters took place. For critic Raymond Cogniac, the zones created "the illusion of a space that would have been impossible to render by the use of perspective."[57] Braque's backcloth, with its sober grays and maroons, suggested to Massine "the raw, hard-working side of Neapolitan life with its street vendors and artisan families living in one room and ceaselessly struggling for survival."[58]

Les Six

The members of this music consortium were Georges Auric, Arthur Honegger, Louis Durey, Germaine Tailleferre, Darius Milhaud, and Francis Poulenc. It was at a song recital given in November 1917 that the entire six first appeared on the same program and were given their joint name. Originally a group of Conservatoire students, the group soon acquired an enthusiastic promoter and spokesman in Cocteau, whose *Le coq et l'arlequin* (1918) sounded forth on the principles for a new music. *Le coq et l'arlequin* rebelled against expressionism and French impressionism. Jabs were taken at Wagner, Debussy, Strauss, Ravel, Stravinsky and Schoenberg: Satie alone received praise.

The new music, said Cocteau, was to take its subject matter and its stimulus from everyday life; it was to learn from the music hall, the circus and the jazz band; its principal qualities were to be dryness, brevity and frankness. From 1924 to 1926, Satie and Les Six delivered scores for seven of Diaghilev's ballets. By the end of the decade, however, the group had lost any cohesion; only Poulenc kept faith with the group's original flippancy.

Music

In November of 1918 Darius Milhaud was drawn into Cocteau's circle and became one of Les Six. Membership helped to brand Milhaud as an outrageous composer for a time. During the 1920s, he offended traditionalists with his weird song cycles—*Machines agricoles* (set to descriptions of farm machinery in agricultural catalogues) and *Catalogue de fleurs* (to poems by Lucien Daudet inspired by a florist's catalogue). Music critics refused to take the song cycles in the perfectly serious spirit in which they had been conceived, and many performances of his work during the 1920s caused *Rite of Spring*–like theatre riots.[59]

From visits to the United States, Milhaud got his first experience of the authentic black jazz of Harlem. When he returned to Paris, he composed the ballet *La Création du Monde* (1923). This ballet score still commands respect when other hybrids of jazz and classical music have been forgotten, and it was the first of its kind, predating George Gershwin's *Rhapsody in Blue* by a year.[60] Milhaud acquired a patina of urban sophistication with Les Six, but his best work has the freshness and lyricism of his native folk materials. His additional tributes to the folk culture of North and South America in such works as *Kentuckiana* and *Saudades do Brasil* are sensitive mood evocations.

Milhaud normally composed in a readily accessible melodic style. He wrote twelve symphonies in addition to ballets, concertos, operas, oratorios, string quartets, and songs. He was one of the twentieth century's most prolific composers.

The libretto for *Salade* was sung in the orchestra pit as it was danced onstage. As the basis for the score, Massine gave Milhaud a variety of themes from antique Italian music for orchestration. Critic Arthur Honerée judged the score for *Salade* "one of the composer's best,"[61] but for the Paris Opéra revival twelve years later, W. H. Haddon Squire found that *Salade* "reminded one strongly of other scores by the same composer."[62] *Salade* was subsequently reworked and became *Le carnaval d'Aix* for piano and orchestra.

Choreography

Salade was the usual commedia dell'arte romp of farces, intrigues, and disguises. However, Madeline Milhaud said that Massine also gave the ballet a "tragic dimension, especially the scene in which Polichinelle is beaten and which Massine performed heartbreakingly."[63] To accentuate the haunting quality of Braque's set, Massine had the dancers carry candles, which they placed along the front of the stage before each scene. These threw a wavering light over the choreographic tableaux, which, Massine says, "came from my desire to emulate the sculptural effect of the works of Donatello and other Renaissance masters."[64]

Critical Survey

Salade was well received by critics. *The Little Review* stated, "The choreography is almost Massine's masterpiece."[65] Diaghilev told Massine that he thought the lighting and choreography of *Salade* "had marked a definite step forward."[66] However, Mme Sert put a damper on the response to *Salade* at its second performance: "The following day, at the first appearance of Massine [as Polichinelle], Beaumont cried 'Bravo' and noisily clapped his hands. There was scarcely an echo. Misia had entered. She incarnated the Russian ballet, which Massine had betrayed. She did not go unnoticed and when the curtain fell, many hesitated to applaud."[67]

In Retrospect

Massine never revived *Salade*, but the Paris Opéra did so in February of 1936 with new choreography by Serge Lifar. In 1938, *Salade* was given at the Royal Hungarian Opera House, Budapest, with new choreography by Gyula Harangozó. The ballet's last major revival was on June 11, 1955, for the Brandeis University Festival, with choreography by Myra Kinch and Léon Danielian in Massine's original role.

B. Mercure
Ballet in Three Tableaux
Music: Erik Satie
Libretto: Léonide Massine
Scenic and Costume Design: Pablo Picasso
Scene Painting: Vladimir and Elizabeth Polunin
Première: Théâtre de la Cigale, Paris, June 15, 1924 (First Ballets Russes performance: Théâtre Sarah Bernhardt, June 2, 1927)

Principal dancers: Vera Petrova, Léonide Massine, Lydia Lopokova

Synopsis

This ballet, presented in twelve scenes and three tableaux, has a mythological theme which is only faintly related to the ballet. After the overture, the curtain rises on *La Nuit, Danse de Tendresse, Signe du Zodiaque* and *Danse de Mercure*. The second tableau opens with the *Danse des Graces*, the *Bain des Graces, La Fuite de Mercure* and *La Colère de Cerbère*. The third tableau consists of the *Piège de Méduse*, followed by *La Nouvelle Danse, L'Apparition du Chaos* and Finale.

Scenery and Costumes

Picasso's drop curtain for *Mercure* showed two colossal, partially draped women striding across a beach. It had the character of fine calligraphy, a single sweeping stroke. From childhood, Picasso had enjoyed accomplishing the virtuosic feat of making a line twist itself into the illusion of a solid design without taking pen from paper.

Picasso's *tableaux vivants* ("movable scenery") included sculptures and constructs of enmeshed wire and canvas which were made mobile by hidden dancers or by strings. The *Mercure* designs are examples of what is called "free form" by architects and designers—a form generated neither by geometry nor by the direct imitation of natural forms, but rather by the freely curving movement of the hand which creates half-accidental shapes like those of clouds or amoebas. The properties of the drop curtain, repeated in the *tableaux vivants*, caused Gertrude Stein to comment that they were "Picasso's version of ultimate calligraphy adapted to the theatre."[68]

The Three Graces were danced by three figures *en travestie*, with raffia wigs, large papier-mâché breasts, and "plaited necks like telephone extension wires which stretched and contracted as their heads bobbed up and down."[69] The figures were many times as large as the dancers who carried them, as was true of the managers in *Parade*. In their strangest scene, the Three Graces swam in an inclined wooden bathtub. Otherwise, the male and female costumes were modeled after classical Greek tunics—with the incongruous addition of long white evening gloves for everyone except Mercure himself.[70]

Music

Satie, always meticulous in his composing habits, had yet to see the libretto for *Mercure* in the late winter of 1924. As he became increasingly anxious to get the precise details he needed, he went to see Beaumont and pleaded with him for clues as to the ballet's plot. "Ah, *mon cher ami*, that's very difficult," came the maddening answer, "because it's a surprise."[71] However, a libretto finally surfaced, and by April Satie had completed much of the score.

Satie described *Mercure* as "fairground music." Much of the score has a brash and rowdy quality. For instance, a crude-sounding tuba carries the melodic line in "*Signes du Zodiaque*"; "*Polka des Lettres*" is a cheesy popular tune for the trumpet. But James Harding writes that *Mercure* also "attains to passages of beauty and tenderness which are as fine as anything else in his work."[72] In 1940, Virgil Thomson put Satie's *Mercure* in the top echelon of twentieth-century ballet scores. Complaining that most modern ballet scores are "patchwork pieces that can't hold up," he praised the seamless transitions of Stravinsky's *Petrouchka* and Satie's *Mercure*.[73]

In 1925, Satie fell seriously ill from cirrhosis of the liver, not surprising in view of his forty years of heavy drinking in the bars of Montmartre. Because he became too weak to hoist himself up onto buses, his friends persuaded him to leave his home in Arcueil and take a hotel room in Paris. He died of his disease on July 1, 1925.

Satie's brother, Conrad, asked Milhaud and Roger Désormière to accompany him when the time came to open up Satie's long-deserted flat in Arcueil. For twenty-seven years no one had ever penetrated this inner temple. The intruders were overwhelmed to discover that the neat and impeccable Satie had lived in miserable penury. The windows were filthy and the curtains faded, rotten with age. The room contained strewn newspapers, a wretched bed, and a barren cupboard on which were piled a half-dozen unworn, and by now unfashionable, velvet suits. The pedals of Satie's ancient piano were held together with string. Wadded up behind the piano was discovered the score of *Jack-in-the-Box*, a composition which Satie thought he had lost years ago on a bus.[74]

In 1926 Beaumont turned over to the Ballets Russes the performance rights for Satie's *Jack-in-the-Box* as well as the music for *Mercure*. A year later, Diaghilev presented a memorial concert performance of *Parade* and the two works above.

Choreography

Massine's subsidiary role was quite apparent to the *Little Review* critic: "In *Mercure* the musician and the choreographer served purely as accompaniment to the painter. They felt this, and with remarkable art they acquiesced to this hegemony."[75] The libretto for *Mercure* was credited to Massine, but in a letter to Picasso dated February 21, 1924, Beaumont advanced the concept as his own.[76]

Critical Survey

At its première, all the kudos went to the "magnificent décor and costumes of Picasso."[77] As for the ballet as a whole, Richard Buckle wrote that most thought it "ridiculous."[78] Of the 1927 Ballets Russes revival of

Mercure, the *Times* wrote: "Mr. Diaghilev is to be congratulated on his wisdom in giving only one performance of it."[79]

In Retrospect

Although Diaghilev was not invited, he attended the opening performance of *Les Soirées de Paris*. His apprehensions were straightaway quieted when he realized the dilettantism of Beaumont's undertaking. *Mercure* alone was striking enough to worry him, and it has the distinction of being the only ballet that Diaghilev ever acquired from another producer.

C. Gigue, Les Roses, Premier Amour, Divertissement

Gigue, which Massine called "an elegant trifle," was a plotless suite of Baroque dances set to the music of Bach, Handel and Scarlatti and performed at the piano by Marcelle Meyer. It was danced by Massine, Stanislas Idzikovsky, and Vera Nemtchinova and was based on variations of steps from the dance manuals of Raoul Feuillet and Carlo Blasis. André Derain's backcloth depicted a corner of the garden of Versailles, and his costumes were in shades of shimmering gold and deep blue.[80]

Les Roses was a ballet in one scene danced to "Valse des Roses," composed by Oliver Métra and orchestrated by Henri Sauguet. It was danced by Idzikovsky, supported by Nemtchinova, Eleonora Marra, Vera Petrova, and Amalia Allan. Marie Laurencin's backdrop depicted a fragile lady on horseback. Because the scene was planned from a small watercolor, Polunin decided on the same technique as the best way "of rendering the feminine charm of Laurencin's work."[81]

Premier Amour was a solo sketch for Lydia Lopokova about a girl who dreams that she falls in love with a doll. Set to Erik Satie's *Trois morceaux en forme de poire* and *Petites pièces montées*, it was played at the piano by Erik Satie and Marcelle Meyer during performance. *Divertissement* was a plotless suite of dances featuring Lopokova and Idzikovsky and danced to Emmanuel Chabrier's *Bourée fantasque* and *Pièces pittoresques*. The most noteworthy aspect of *Divertissement* was its lighting design by Loie Fuller, a famous American pioneer of modern dance and stage lighting. Fuller flashed a constantly changing series of color projections onto the cyclorama as the ballet proceeded.

Zephyr et Flore

Ballet in Three Scenes
Libretto: Boris Kochno

Music: Vladimir Dukelsky
Scenic and Costume Design: Georges Braque
Première: Théâtre de Monte Carlo, April 28, 1925

ORIGINAL CAST

Flore: Alicia Nikitina   Zéphyr: Anton Dolin   Boreas: Serge Lifar

Synopsis

Scene One. Mount Olympus. The Muses pursue the dashing Boreas, who rejects their offers of love. He only has eyes for Flore, who appears in the company of the Wind God, Zéphyr. Boreas entices Zéphyr into playing a game of "Blind Man's Bluff." While Zéphyr is blindfolded, Boreas wounds him fatally with an arrow. Flore faints, and Boreas absconds with her to his lair.

Scene Two. The interior of Boreas' cave. This is the seduction scene, at the end of which the heroine, true to her type in such situations, swoons. However, Flore makes a speedy recovery and flees the clutches of the villainous Boreas.

Scene Three. Mount Olympus. The Muses perform an incongruous "Dance of Lament" to ragtime music around the body of Zéphyr. Following their funeral rite, he inexplicably recovers. Flore returns, with Boreas in hot pursuit. Boreas cowers in fear at the sight of the resurrected Zéphyr. The Muses tie Flore firmly to the wrist of Zéphyr so that he cannot again misplace her, and Boreas is chastised for his foul misdeeds.

Scenery and Costumes

In the winter of 1918–19 Braque began work on large-scale still-life compositions which continue to show some of the austerities of Cubism but are richer and brighter. In his Fireplace Series, begun in 1921, the still-life objects are seen against a mirror on an elaborate marble mantelpiece. The presence of marble in the Fireplace Series shows a new taste for luxuriant and decorative material. Braque increasingly displayed his gifts for impeccable good taste and refinement in color, texture, handling and other purely painterly qualities.

The flickering landscapes that Braque created for *Zéphyr et Flore* had nothing to do with Mount Olympus, but neither was there a sign of distortion to betray the designer as the co-creator of Cubism. Reviews for the backdrops were uniformly good: the *Observer* thought they had "a pure beauty of tone and color,"[82] and *Vogue* claimed that Braque "shows a delicacy of taste which is, I think, unrivalled."[83]

Critics were less impressed with Braque's costumes. The women wore

1920s flapper dresses of coarse woolen material in murky purples and browns, evolved from the backdrops' color schemes. Their accessories included "chic little pork pie hats and earrings."[84] Alexandra Danilova says that they were "dreadful costumes"[85]; Grigoriev "wondered how Diaghilev could have passed the designs."[86]

Music

Vladimir Dukelsky was an American composer of Russian birth. After studying at the Kiev Conservatory, he fled the Revolution with his family in 1919. *Zéphyr et Flore* was his first important commission, and he continued to compose music for the London stage for the next decade.

In 1938 Dukelsky moved to New York, where he became an American citizen. He adopted the pseudonym Vernon Duke for his popular songs and light music, continuing to use his Russian name for his serious, classical compositions. Because of his split personae, Anton Dolin claimed that "Unless one knew him, no one could believe that the two were the same person."[87]

Dukelsky's assignment in *Zéphyr* was to blend jazz music with a pastiche of eighteenth-century melodies and Bach fugues. Most critics seemed to think he met this daunting challenge successfully. Among many plaudits, the *Morning Post* called Dukelsky "a young man who, despite the discordant idiom of the times, knows how to shape a musical phrase and conceive a musical idea."[88]

Choreography

Massine's choreography had an eccentric, "jazzy" modernity which was at least in keeping with the costumes and score. Classical dancing was used only in the principal roles of Flore, Zéphyr and Boreas. Alicia Nikitina implies that the seduction pas de deux in the cave of Boreas was quite suggestive: "Lifar threw me down on the ground from his shoulders, then lay down on top of me, then seemed overcome by convulsions, and afterwards relaxed very suddenly and remained immobile for a time … the sight of this love dance made Diaghilev and his friends burst into peals of laughter—I only understood why much later."[89] Since Nikitina was the soon-to-be mistress of Lord Rothermere, the Ballet Russes's major financial backer at this time, it cannot have been *too* much later.

The dances of the Muses were an angular, stylized version of social dances like the Charleston. Danilova described the resulting style: "arm stiff from the elbow down. Very stiff and always zigzagging with the arms. There was [sic] no smooth movements."[90] Massine's colleagues have scant praise for *Zéphyr*'s choreography. Grigoriev said that the choreography was "deficient in both style and inspiration and devoid of any fresh ideas."[91] Dolin wrote that he had "an inaptitude to apply myself to the work that Massine was giving me to do."[92] Danilova found *Zéphyr* to be "dreadful," "floparoo," and "Massine's worst ballet."[93]

Critical Survey

After a cool reception at Monte Carlo, Diaghilev was fully conscious of the shortcomings of *Zéphyr et Flore*. As an emergency measure, he decided to add two more scenes, gambling that two more backcloths by Braque could save the ballet in Paris and London. Nonetheless, the ballet remained an obstinate failure. Horace Horsnell's response was typical: "The whole affair seemed to me a joke that was taken too seriously."[94]

In Retrospect

This work needed and lacked Diaghilev's magic touch to effect some semblance of artistic unity from the works of composer, designer, and choreographer. *Zéphyr*'s problem was not that it juxtaposed form and content; so did many of the postwar Diaghilev ballets, some of them ingeniously. In *Zéphyr*, however, this juxtaposition was a superficial one. The contributing artists abandoned the idea of evoking the spirit of a Russian court ballet, yet their final product was too schizophrenic to make an articulate contemporary statement. *Zéphyr* failed to convey meaning on any level.

ON WITH THE DANCE

Musical Revue in Two Acts
Première: London Pavilion, April 30, 1925

Principal Dancers: Alice Delysia, Eleanora Marra, Léonide Massine, Terry Kendall, Nicholas Zverev, with Amalia Allan, Laurie Devine, Josephine Head, and Pat Kendall

Massine choreographed three numbers for this revue: *Crescendo*, *The Rake* and *Hungarian Wedding*. The latter, a suite of Hungarian dances, was the finale for *On with the Dance*.

Crescendo, Scene Eighteen, was an attempt to portray the spirit of the Roaring Twenties. It was danced to a medley of popular jazz tunes with scenery and costumes by Gladys Calthrop. *Crescendo* was actually a collaboration between Massine and his co-star, Noël Coward, whom

Massine felt "had an instinctive, unsentimental grasp of the spirit of the 1920s."[95]

Massine was billed in the program as Bobo, the "Spirit of the Age." The Film Star was danced by Alice Delysia and the Manicure Girl by Eleanora Marra. Massine also devised a male jazz trio called "Three Nifty Nats" (Massine, Terry Kendall, Nicholas Zverev). A corps de ballet of flappers rounded out the cast.

As a parody, Massine began the work in blackout to the strains of the prelude from *Les Sylphides*, leading the audience to believe for a moment that they were about to see something classical. In an interview with the *Morning Post* Massine said, "Jazz represents us. It is an art form which represents the speed of modern life, worked out on a scientific basis ... more than we realise, Modern Choreography finds its highest expression in jazz."[96] Critics were not especially taken with *Crescendo*, but they seemed more put off by the decade itself than by Massine's interpretation of it. "The Sitter Out" remarked, "If we come away annoyed, let it not be with Massine for his clever satire, but rather with this restless spirit by which so many of us are dominated."[97]

The Rake, Scene Seven, was based on William Hogarth's drawings of "The Rake's Progress." It was danced to a score by Roger Quilter with scenery and costumes by William Nicholson. The principal roles were danced by Massine as the Rake and Eleanora Marra as the Corset Woman. To suggest the debauchery of eighteenth-century England, Massine "filled the stage with Hogarthian characters—obese women, grotesque musicians and deformed Bedlamites."[98] Artistically, this was one of Massine's better works for a Cochran revue: "It passes in one mad whirl which leaves one gasping at the finish. It is a brilliant work."[99]

All in all, *On with the Dance* got fairly good reviews. *Dancing Times* dubbed it "the most remarkable 'dance show' that has ever been placed before the London public."[100] *On with the Dance* was also the high point of Massine's contributions to the revue genre. Both *Crescendo* and *The Rake* were satires on high society which drew timeless parallels between eras as widely separated as the 1780s and the 1920s.

LES MATELOTS

Ballet in Five Scenes
Libretto: Boris Kochno
Music: Georges Auric
Scenic and Costume Design: Pedro Pruna
Première: Théâtre de la Gaité-Lyrique, Paris, June 17, 1925

ORIGINAL CAST
The French Sailor: Serge Lifar
The American Sailor: Taddeus Slavinsky
The Spanish Sailor: Leon Woizikowsky
The Fiancée: Vera Nemtchinova   Her Friend: Lydia Sokolova

Synopsis

Scene One: *Les Fiançailles et Le Départ*
Scene Two: *La Solitude*
Scene Three: *Retour et Variations des Matelots—L'Epreuve*
Scene Four: *La Tentation—Le Bar*
Scene Five: *Finale*

During their shore leave, three lively sailors amuse themselves by visiting the dockside bars and flirting with pretty girls. One of these lads, the French Sailor, forms a serious attachment and promises to marry his sweetheart on his return from naval duty. However, he then decides to test her fidelity with the help of his friends. Left alone, the girl gives herself up to a lyrical dance in which she expresses the sincerity of her love. Her friend tries to make her forget the affair and meet other sailors, but she firmly refuses. Meanwhile, the three sailors have gone back to their ships to disguise themselves. They return to the bar and try one after the other to seduce the young girl. She steadfastly resists all of their advances, thus convincing her fiancé of her fidelity. The mariners now discard their disguises and the girl throws herself happily into the arms of her beloved Frenchman.

Scenery and Costumes

Pedro Pruna was a twenty-year-old Barcelonean artist sponsored by Picasso and subsequently introduced to Cocteau and Diaghilev. Pruna was an easel painter whose "very light, school-of-Picasso paintings in pale colours they all admired at the time."[101] *Les Matelots* was Pruna's first work for the theatre.

For each scene, Pruna created colorful backcloths: the first drop depicts a sailboat; the second, a pensive sailor; the third, Cupid with his arrows; the fourth, a drinking booth; and the last, two colossal figures of a fisherman and his wife.

Music

Georges Auric began his studies at the Paris Conservatoire in 1913 and was a member of Les Six. His music for *Les Matelots* was a suite of hornpipes for woodwinds and brass based on themes from sea shanties. André Levinson admired the "joyous speed and insistence" of Auric's score. However, he added, "There is in these works [of Les Six] a similarity of essence and of form, a monotony of invention, a likeness in instrumental methods, which marks the end of a revolutionary period."[102]

Choreography

The most memorable choreography is the ingenious pas de trois for the sailors in Scene Three. Sitting down on three chairs, the sailors hop to stage center on the chairs' front legs and form a triangle. The performers tilt the chairs for precarious balances, perform intricate body percussion with their hands and feet, and, at one point, stick their heads through the opening of their chair backs and mime swimming the breast stroke. Afterwards, with their backs to the chairs, all three make a high leap onto the chair seats, rattle imaginary dice, toss them onto the floor and in a contest to see the results first, execute a daring nosedive onto their stomachs. This spectacular sequence with the dice is then repeated.[103] At the first performance of *Les Matelots*, Lifar's chair gradually came to pieces, and he finished by crashing through his chair seat onto the floor. Fortuitously, it happened that this accident coincided exactly with the last crashing chord of the music, and so it was thought to be intentional. Lifar received a tumultuous ovation.[104]

Les Matelots obviously relied heavily upon clowning, acrobatics, circus tricks and the music hall. Ballet vocabulary was used consistently only in the Fiancée's dance of loneliness in Scene Two and in the pas de deux for the Fiancée and the French Sailor in Scene Five. While the sailors' pas de trois is a gem of wit and originality, the classical sections are hackneyed at times. The opening of the pas de deux for the Fiancée and the French Sailor, for instance, is lifted straight from the opening of Petipa's "Black Swan" pas de deux for Odile and Prince Siegfried in *Swan Lake*.[105]

Critical Survey

Although *Les Matelots* was extremely popular with audiences, the only aspect of the ballet to win unanimous praise from the press was the superb dancing of its performers. As to the merits of choreography, music and décor, the ballet world has seldom witnessed such diversity of artistic opinion. The *Times* judged that "the scenery is the best we have seen since Derain's for *La Boutique fantasque*."[106] Svetloff, though, scoffed that Pruna's designs "created what was formerly known as feeling."[107] The *Observer* praised Auric's "deliciously tender music,"[108] while the *Times* bemoaned "the rather tiresome repetition of trivial phrases which we have come to expect of him [Auric]."[109] The *Queen* thought that Massine's choreography "approached perfection,"[110] while the *Times* thought it "funereal."[111]

In Retrospect

Les Matelots was a work which placed small value on unity of style, and in that spirit, Massine freely jumbled classical ballet, jazz, hornpipes, flamenco, circus stunts and eccentricities. *Les Matelots* was no less guilty of artistic schizophrenia than was *Zéphyr et Flore*. But unlike *Zéphyr*, *Les Matelots* was completely unpretentious and unabashedly nonsensical; it was well liked by audiences for just that reason.

This ballet was revived by the Diaghilev company in 1927 and for the 1933 season of Colonel de Basil's company. Although it has not been performed for decades, it still lives on in a sense: *Les Matelots* undoubtedly inspired Jerome Robbins' more worthy ballet, *Fancy Free* (1944), and so perpetuated the careers of "those three ubiquitous sailors on a spree."[112]

STILL DANCING

Musical Revue in Two Acts
Première: London Pavilion, November 19, 1925

Massine contributed four ballets to this revue: revivals of the successful *Rake* and *Hungarian Wedding* and two new works, *Pompeii à la Massine* and *Pyjama Jazz*. The latter, the finale of *Still Dancing*, was led by Alice Delysia and included solos for Massine and Eleanora Marra. For this number, the whole cast was clad in fashionable pajamas provided for the occasion by Selfridge and Company.

Pompeii à la Massine, Scene Fourteen, was danced to a potpourri of melodies, mostly by Louis Ganne. Scenery and costumes were designed by Doris Zinkeisen. According to the program notes, this fantasy represents an entertainment presided over by Ariadne (Eleanora Marra). It commences with a dance of flowers and a caterpillar, followed by Cupid's attempt to repair the heart of Ariadne, broken by the flight of Theseus. After an incident between the Alchemist and his clients, a Chinaman appears. The pavane, danced by Ariadne, leads up to the finale.

Rather improbably, Massine wrote that he based this work on "the frescoes at Pompeii."[113] It is just possible that he took a few liberties with classical antiquity, but *Pompeii à la Massine* did at least feature Léonide in a delightful solo as a Chinese Visitor who enters into this fanciful Roman goulash out of nowhere.

COCHRAN'S REVUE 1926

Musical Revue in Two Acts
Première: London Pavilion, April 29, 1926

Massine's *Gigue* from *Les Soirées de Paris* became Scene Ten in this revue, with Massine, Vera Nemtchinova and Nicholas Zverev in the principal roles. *La Carmagnole*, a new work, was danced to the music of Adolf Stanislas with costumes by Guy Arnoux. It was a plotless pas de deux in the romantic style for Eleanora Marra and Zverev.

The Tub, Scene Five, had music by Franz Joseph Haydn and scenery and costumes by William Nicholson. The cast included Nemtchinova as Peronella, Massine as Giannello and Zverev as Piero. The plot was based on one of the funniest stories from Boccaccio's *Decameron*—"The Tale of Giannello Strignario."

While her dull-witted husband Piero is away, Peronella receives Giannello, her lover, but to her distress, she sees her husband returning home early with a friend. Peronella quickly hides Giannello in the wine barrel; when the two men enter the house, Peronella learns to her horror that the friend has come to purchase a wine barrel! When they remove the lid and discover Giannello squatting inside the "tub," Peronella tries to convince Piero that Giannello, too, has come to appraise the wine barrel and simply needed to step inside for a closer look. Piero is satisfied with this explanation, and all ends happily.

4

June 1927–January 1932

For the next two years, Massine's life followed a pattern: he spent the summers on Galli and the rest of the year working for Diaghilev as guest choreographer. In 1927 he staged the revival of *Mercure*, a new version of Bronislava Nijinska's *Les Fâcheux*, and the world première of *Le Pas d'acier*. Apprehensive about the reactions of English critics to *Mercure*, Diaghilev gave the London press no advance notice of this ballet and billed it for only a single matinee performance on July 11, 1927.

Les Fâcheux, a modern adaptation of Molière's 1661 comédie-ballet, premièred on May 3, 1927, with a score by Georges Auric and décor by Georges Braque. Diaghilev had first produced this work in 1924, but according to Boris Kochno, the 1924 version failed because Nijinska "foundered in conventional, realistic pantomime."[1] Since original characterizations were Massine's forté, it was expected that he would fare much better; however, Massine's revival was no more successful than Nijinska's version.

In the spring of 1918 Diaghilev had introduced a red flag into the apotheosis of *L'Oiseau de feu* to commemorate the Russian Revolution. His interest in Soviet art deepened in March 1923, when he saw Moscow's Kamerny Theatre at the Théâtre des Champs-Elysées. The productions, directed by Alexander Tairov and designed by Georgi Yakulov, were Diaghilev's first glimpse of experimental Soviet theatre. He was keenly excited by the performances and realized that with its formal recognition by most of the countries of Western Europe, Soviet Russia had suddenly become topical. By June of 1925, he was at work on an all-Soviet ballet entitled *Le Pas d'acier*, with a score by Sergei Prokofiev and libretto and set designs by Georgi Yakulov. Diaghilev made efforts to bring Kaisan Golizovsky from Moscow to show Europe the innovative choreography so admired by George Balanchine. However, he refused to leave Russia, so the project actually went to Massine by default.[2]

Lifar recounts that Diaghilev's brother, P. G. Koribut-Kubitovitch, was avidly opposed to this project, arguing that Diaghilev would alienate not only the White Russian emigrants, but their aristocratic European supporters as well. When the "Soviet people" were received, administrator Walter Nuvel and Koribut-Kubitovitch "ostentatiously refused to carry out their secretarial duties, or have anything to do with them."[3] This, however, only made Diaghilev even more polite. For Diaghilev, an aristocrat by birth, education, and nature, these gestures of friendliness might seem out of character. Yet his credo deemed it unthinkable to pass over anything of outstanding artistic merit, no matter what its source. Grigoriev relates that Diaghilev had "long talks with Prokofiev for any news he could glean of artistic and cultural developments in Soviet Russia."[4]

During the June 1927 Paris performances of *Le Pas d'acier*, Massine met a fellow Russian named Eugenia Delarova at the ballet studio of Lubov Egorova, where he took his daily class. Having left the Soviet Union in 1926, Delarova was naturally most interested in *Le Pas d'acier*. Massine and Delarova began to meet often, at first to discuss Soviet politics and, later, more personal matters. She was dancing at the Folies-Bergère at the time, and Massine "missed her very much" when he had to return to London. By the summer of 1928, they would be married.

As the 1927 season ended, Massine began to feel that most of his possibilities for creative work in Europe had been exhausted. As he noted, "Now that Balanchine was doing so much of his [Diaghilev's] choreography, I felt there would not be enough work for the two of us."[5] Nor did he any longer have a say in the company's artistic direction—Boris Kochno was now Diaghilev's advisor and sounding board. Massine was merely being jobbed in to execute projects that had been conceived by others.

On February 7, 1928, Massine set sail for New York City. Upon landing, he discovered that finding work in the Big Apple was going to be much more difficult than he had anticipated. "New York," he wrote, "can be a cruel city, especially for young out-of-work foreigners. In Europe I had made something of a reputation, but in America I was just another dancer. ... It did not take long for me to discover that American interest in ballet was no greater than it had been when I made my first visit ten years earlier."[6] The only situation he could find there was a six-month provisional contract with S. L. Rothafel, manager of New York's Roxy Theatre, a large cinema house. Rothafel offered him a situation similar to what Massine had undertaken at Covent Garden: he would choreograph live shows in the interludes between films.

Massine returned to Europe and began work on his last Diaghilev ballet, *Ode*. As Danilova notes, "*Ode* was odd."[7] Composer Nicholas Nabokov actually started the whole thing: in 1927, he played Diaghilev his cantata, which was based on an ode composed in honor of the Empress Elizabeth Petrovna by her court poet, Mikhail Lomonossov. The ode was entitled "An Evening Meditation of the Majesty of God on Observing the Aurora Borealis," the Empress being equated with that northern phenomenon. Empress Elizabeth, daughter of Peter the Great, reigned from 1741 until her death in 1762. Diaghilev was greatly pleased by the poem's reference to Elizabeth because it was rumored that Diaghilev, on his mother's side, was a great-great-grandson of one of the Empress's illegitimate children. Wrote Nabokov, "He was flattered by this illicit relationship to the Imperial House of Russia because it made him a direct descendent of Peter the Great, and gave him a kind of 'morganatic' halo."[8] Diaghilev was instantly enthusiastic about presenting an eighteenth-century spectacle based on engravings of the court balls of the Empress Elizabeth, and Kochno concocted a scenario along these lines.

Pavel Tchelitchew was commissioned to create the décor. However, Tchelitchew did not like Lomonossov's poem, and he could care less that Diaghilev might be the great-great-grandbastard of Elizabeth. According to Nabokov, he thought the whole piece should be treated as a "surrealist vision" of the Aurora Borealis.[9] Tchelitchew promptly asked filmmaker Pierre Charbonnier to create special lighting effects for the Aurora Borealis and other natural phenomena.

Kochno claims that when Diaghilev learned that Tchelitchew had thrown the initial concept overboard, he "lost interest" and refused to have anything more to do with *Ode*.[10] At a subsequent production meeting, Tchelitchew presented Diaghilev with his expensive design concept, which included five film projectors on the first row of the balcony. Tchelitchew claims that Diaghilev got livid and told him, "You are insane and your ideas are terrible!" To Kochno, he reportedly said, "If you give birth to a monster, I'll disown you!"[11]

Discord escalated. When Nabokov arrived in Monte Carlo in April 1928, Diaghilev warned him that "Boris doesn't know what he wants to do with *Ode*, and Massine knows even less. As for Tchelitchew, I can't make heads or tails of his experiments.... If all of you finally decide to start working, don't pull the cart in three directions. It will get stuck and I'm not going to help you pull it out of *your* mud!"¹²

When he saw Massine's dance arrangements, Nabokov felt "an inherent anomaly" in their collaboration. Tchelitchew was not only uncommunicative but deliberately secretive. He weakened only once when, needing help in the timing of film sequences, he ordered Nabokov to hold the stopwatch. His film showed young men wearing fencing masks and tights simulating slow-motion diving. "I could not understand what this had to do with my ballet," wrote Nabokov, "but I was told by Kochno (Tchelitchew wouldn't speak to me) ... that this represented 'the element of water.'"¹³ Meanwhile, with time running out, Diaghilev was tearing around claiming that Massine's choreography was "utter rubbish."¹⁴ No one, it would seem, was on speaking terms with anyone else.

Three days before the opening, Nabokov was awakened by a phone call. It was Diaghilev. He barked, "Get dressed right away. ... This mess can't go on any longer." Diaghilev was going to pull the cart out, after all. He spent two entire days and nights in the theatre, directing the complicated lighting rehearsals and "shouting" at Tchelitchew and Nabokov whenever they slackened their pace. (Massine seems to have been absent.) Nabokov wrote, "I knew that it had been only thanks to this man's incredible drive and energy that *Ode* had been pieced together and that the curtain would be able to rise at all."¹⁵ The first performance was "quite well received."¹⁶

After Diaghilev's 1928 season, Massine and his new bride, Eugenia Delarova, spent their summer honeymoon on Galli. In the fall of 1928 they went to Paris, where Massine had been commissioned by Ida Rubinstein to choreograph two *mélodrames* for her newly formed company, Les Ballets Ida Rubinstein. Léonide and Eugenia had to leave for their new jobs at the Roxy before the ballets were finished; Massine agreed to return to Paris to supervise final rehearsals.

Before Massine arrived in New York, the press department of the Roxy Theatre issued a terse press release to the *New York Times* to the effect that Massine would "assist" director Léon Leonidoff and the Dance Captain, identified only as Miss Rogge. Dance critic John Martin was aghast, but hopeful:

> The idea of his [Massine's] assisting Miss Rogge and Mr. Léonidoff, clever and competent though they undeniably are, contains a certain element of grotesquery, when we stop to consider that he is one of the three maestro of the greatest ballet of modern times. ... Unless he is to do something manifestly different from the present type of production, however, there seems little need of Mr. Rothafel's

progressive gesture in engaging him. Why import a distinguished maitre de ballet to do what can be done better by any number of native routine devisers?[17]

While Massine may have arrived at the Roxy full of ideas for introducing America to twentieth-century ballet, Rothafel was obviously not interested. Massine's duties consisted mostly of cranking out one mundane dance routine after another. They were all vaudevillian, razzle-dazzle affairs with endless rows of sequined, high-kicking chorus girls moving on and off the vast raked stage:

> It was a staggering responsibility to have to create every week a ballet which would appeal to the enormous Roxy audience, particularly as my productions had to be co-ordinated with the weekly theme of the rest of the spectacle and in keeping with the season of the year. I composed Spring Ballets, Easter Ballets, Christmas Ballets ... I also danced four times a day, and five times on Saturday.... When I was not at the Roxy I was in my bed, asleep.[18]

David, Massine's first ballet for Ida, was the final première of her 1928 season at the Opéra. Since Massine was in New York, Bronislava Nijinska stepped in to finish the ballet, which only added to the confusion.[19] In April 1929 Massine and Delarova got a leave of absence from the Roxy. Feeling as if they "had suddenly been let out of prison,"[20] they sailed for Paris to supervise the final rehearsals for one of his Rubinstein productions, *Les Enchantements d'Alcine*. Massine began rehearsals on April 29, 1929, and *Les Enchantements d'Alcine* premièred on May 21.

Before Léonide and Eugenia returned to their Roxy drudgeries, they took a vacation on Virginia Beach. There, the local press gave them the awful news that Diaghilev had died on August 19. Massine wrote, "He had been the outstanding influence on my artistic career.... Having been so closely connected with him for so many years, I think I must have felt his loss more than anyone." With the often exasperating man of flesh and blood now gone, Massine began to idolize Diaghilev. More than anyone else of his generation, it was Massine who perpetuated Diaghilev's legacy of "bringing to the service of the ballet painting, music, and poetry at the highest level."[21] Massine's unflagging loyalty to this ethos would be the source of both his greatest triumphs and his most heartbreaking failures.

Back in New York, Cole Porter introduced Massine to Broadway producer Ray Goetz, who wanted to form an American Ballets Russes company. Goetz asked Massine to be the artistic director, and he attempted to purchase the Ballets Russes costumes and properties. These had been seized by the French government after Diaghilev's death; they were now stored in a warehouse on the outskirts of Paris. But the Great Depression brought Goetz's venture to an abrupt halt, and Massine's contract was cancelled. Nevertheless, Massine persisted doggedly in his efforts to secure the rights to the deceased impresario's properties and continually talked up the idea of re-forming Diaghilev's company. René Blum, director of the ballet at Monte Carlo, beat him to it, though. He had seen the 1931 Paris season of the Ballet de l'Opéra Russes, directed by Alexis Zereteli and Colonel Wassily de Basil. Blum met with de Basil early in 1931 to discuss a scheme of merging their mutual resources to form a Russian Ballet at Monte Carlo. By the end of 1931, de Basil had signed contracts to be co-director with Blum; Kochno, Balanchine and Grigoriev had signed on as *conseiller artistique*, ballet master, and *régisseur général*, respectively. Massine had no part in this development, which must have been discouraging.

Massine gladly quit his job at the Roxy when Ida Rubinstein engaged him from May 1 through July 15 to supervise rehearsals of *David* and *Alcine* and to stage a new production, *Amphion*. The Rubinstein engagement ended in July of 1931, and the Massines spent the rest of their summer on Galli. That autumn, Léonide signed with Milan's Teatro alla Scala to choreograph for the opera *Vecchia Milano* and to create an original ballet entitled *Belkis*. The latter was to be a lavish spectacle in six scenes with a huge budget and a cast of no less than four hundred dancers and extras.

In September of 1931, C. H. Cochran had asked Léonide to create the dances for *Helen!*, a new production based on Offenbach's operetta *La Belle Hélène*. It was to be directed by the renowned Max Reinhardt, a key figure in the development of realism in the theatre. *Helen!* had its first run in Manchester before moving to London's Adelphi Theatre on January 30, 1932.

Helen! was so successful that Cochran immediately paired Reinhardt and Massine in a revival of *The Miracle*, a play he had produced in 1911. Massine described *The Miracle* as "a wordless pageant in seven episodes based on the legend of a nun who breaks her vows for love of a knight, and returning to the convent after many years, finds that her place has been taken by the Madonna and no one has missed her."[22] Massine played the role of Spielmann, a trickster who persuades the nun to forsake her vow of chastity. *The Miracle* opened at the Lyceum on April 9, 1932, and had a considerable success.

LE PAS D'ACIER *(The Steel Step)*

Ballet in Two Scenes
Libretto: Georgi Yakulov
Music: Sergei Prokofiev
Scenic and Costume Design: Georgi Yakulov
Première: Théâtre Sarah Bernhardt, Paris, June 7, 1927

Principal Dancers: Alexandra Danilova, Felia Dubrovska, Lubov Tchernicheva, Alicia Nikitina, Léonide Massine, Serge Lifar
Peasants, Aristocrats, Peddlars, Commissars, Workers

Synopsis

Le Pas d'acier is a choreographic portrayal of Soviet life in the 1920s — an age of mechanization. The scenario has eleven episodes divided into two scenes. The first scene depicts rural destitution in the wake of the Revolution, and Scene Two depicts the lives of workers in the factories.

Scene One. Starving countesses dressed in tattered velvet curtains torn from their windows and wearing lampshades in place of hats appear on the stage and sell some colored rags to an itinerant food smuggler for a bag of flour. They make love to a beggar, each one trying to get the better of the others. Drunken sailors enter, one of whom wears a high boot on the left leg, while the trouser of the right hangs emptily to the ground. All the while, filthy, homeless children move from group to group like a pack of wild rodents. Into this scene of degraded humanity comes hope for the future in the entries of the new Russian proletariat. Peasants, commissars, newsboys, and workers dance successively and fill the stage. A sailor (Massine) is inspired by the noble vision of the working woman (Danilova).

Scene Two. The sailor dons a leather apron and joins his factory comrades in the march of progress. In the last three sections, the dancers form a kinetic, mechanized, interdependent mass to express the movement of cogs, levers, transmissions, wheels and pistons. In the finale, a climactic tribute to the Machine Age, the set pieces begin to move in synchrony with the dancers, and green, red and white lights flash down upon the grease-stained bodies of the workers.

Scenery and Costumes

Georgi Yakulov was a Georgian painter and stage designer who became a leader of constructivism, a progressive art movement which emerged in the confused and turbulent years after the Revolution. It had an essentially anti-aesthetic philosophy: the artist's mission was to express the national unity and technological progress of Soviet society and, also, to enhance its material well-being. In a spirit of utilitarian simplicity and respect for the logic of materials, constructivists eagerly accepted machine production and modern architectural engineering.

Yakulov's first major constructivist commission was a 1917 project to decorate the Kafe Pittoresk. The café interior is historically important as the first instance in Moscow where the methods of working with three-dimensional sculpture were applied to a practical, utilitarian situation in order to create a total environment.[23] A description was written in 1920 by K. Umanskii: "Splendid sculptural creations are suspended from the large domed ceiling. ... The observer's ability to recognise objects becomes numbed. However, he feels a presentiment of restless dynamism in these semi-machine, semi-decorative shapes, the construction of which emphasizes the enigma of modern machines."[24]

Yakulov made his debut as a stage designer in 1918 with Alexander Tairov's production of *Obmen* at the Kamerny Theatre, Moscow. He created two more successful constructivist designs for Tairov's productions of *Princess Brambilla* (1920) and *Giroflé-Girofla* (1922). In all three productions, he used dynamic sets with open, three-dimensional abstract structures which invited movement and actor improvisation.[25]

Of primary importance to Yakulov for a ballet depicting Soviet proletarian society was the representation of machines and tools. The dancers would portray the joy of communal industrial labor in choreography copying the movement of his machine-modeled scenery. Yakulov's set for *Le Pas d'acier* remained unchanged for the two scenes. It consisted of a very high rostrum, stage center, with steps leading up to it on either side. A number of machine parts, all in plain unpainted wood, were on the stage floor. The workers carried enormously oversized hammers and mallets which look cartoonish when seen in photographs today. Grigoriev wrote that the entire stage was "crammed with objects of various kinds so that it was almost impossible to move" and that "the general effect, though ugly, was yet forceful and exciting."[26]

Music

Sergei Prokofiev was among the greatest of twentieth-century Russian composers. A prodigy, he was admitted to the St. Petersburg Conservatory at the age of fourteen, and in 1911 he gave his first important public performance of his First Piano Concerto. The controversy engendered by this work was surpassed by his Second Piano Concerto, which premièred in Moscow in 1913. It sealed his reputation as what Harlow Robinson calls "the bad boy of Russian music." Here is the account of a contemporary music critic:

A youth with the face of a high school student appears on stage. This is Prokofiev. He sits down at the piano and starts either wiping off the keys or trying them out to see which ones produce a high or low sound.... The young artist concludes his concerto with a mercilessly dissonant combination of sounds from the bass.... Prokofiev bows impudently, and plays an encore. Exclamations resound all around: "The devil take all this Futurist music! We want to hear something pleasant! We can hear music like this from our cats at home!" Another group—the progressive critics—are in ecstasy: "It's a work of genius!"[27]

Prokofiev spent most of the war in St. Petersburg. His popular Classical Symphony (1917) was among the first of his works to gain international recognition. In May 1918, Prokofiev made the long journey to New York. Upon arrival, he found that his reputation as a virtuoso pianist and composer had preceded him. His solo recitals in New York and Chicago were greatly successful.

Prokofiev left the United States in April 1920 and went to Paris where his first Diaghilev ballet premièred on May 17, 1921. *Chout* was bright and witty and won favor with Paris audiences and critics. Prokofiev's career in western Europe looked promising; unfortunately, though, his 1924 Paris performances of the First Violin Concerto, the Fifth Piano Sonata, and the Second Piano Concerto were ill-received. Critics objected to certain anomalies in his music, such as its mixture of modernism with native Russian themes, of steely dissonance with tender lyricism.

Prokofiev's despondency was relieved in 1925 when Diaghilev offered him a commission for *Le Pas d'acier*. Perhaps the most successful pages of the score are those in which Prokofiev reproduces what he has seen and experienced in his own Russian past: "Only the characterizations of the commissars and the orator, with their rationality and automatic neutrality, do not perhaps ring true and indicate how difficult it was for the composer to reproduce those aspects of Soviet life which he had not yet witnessed."[28] Nevertheless, Prokofiev gives an important record of the period in *Le Pas d'acier*, of the dream of a fantastic transformation of backward Russia into a mighty State of Steel.

After Prokofiev's disappointing Paris concerts in 1924, he badly needed a hit, and he scored one. In London, the *Observer* noted that "Prokofiev's music is good stage music. It is noisy, but the scoring, though very thick is yet balanced."[29] The *Times* said that "Prokofiev certainly gets from the orchestra an extraordinarily vivid impression of the hum and roar of machines."[30]

Le Pas d'acier actually owes more to the influence of *Le Sacre du printemps* and to the machine music of Les Six than to anything specifically

Soviet. In their naïveté, Diaghilev and Prokofiev actually thought Soviet theatres might be interested in staging this ballet, and Prokofiev proposed it to the Bolshoi Theatre on a 1929 visit to the USSR. Not surprisingly, the bureaucrats of the Russian Association of Proletariat Musicians (RAPM) attacked *Le Pas d'acier* as a superficial, "distorted view of Soviet Reality." The bureaucrats on the RAPM expressed further outrage that the ballet had been created by a group of selfish émigré artists who, by abandoning their homeland, had lost any right to depict such a glorious and painful era in human history.[31]

This was not to be Prokofiev's last brush with the Soviet bureaucracy. He returned to Russia permanently in 1936. In 1948, he was attacked by the Union of Soviet Composers on the grounds of "formalism." Commissar Andrei Zhadanov stated, "Any listener will realize the vast difference between classical Russian music and the false, ugly, music of the formalist.... Not all that is accessible is a work of genius, but a real work of genius is one that is accessible ... disharmonious music undoubtedly has a bad effect on man's psycho-physiological activity."[32]

The term "formalist" was calculated to strike terror into the hearts of all Soviet artists during the last five years of Stalin's reign. The term applied to art that was excessively concerned with technique and insufficiently concerned with uplifting ideological content. Increasingly, "formalism" came to designate anti–Soviet subversion—untold numbers of prominent artists had already been sent to prison on the grounds of formalism.

A decree of the Party central committee was published on February 10 which declared the works of many prominent Soviet composers, Prokofiev among them, as marked with formalist perversions: "Disregarding the great social role of music, they are content to cater to the degenerate tastes of a handful of aestheticising individualists."[33] Those attacked at the January 1948 meetings suddenly found their well-established careers being tattered to shreds as concerts and commissions were abruptly cancelled. In his memoirs, Shostakovich wrote, "Everyone seemed to go mad and anyone who felt like it expressed an opinion on music."[34] After 1948, and doubtless exacerbated by this misfortune, Prokofiev's health failed rapidly. In March 1953 he died of a brain hemorrhage—ironically, on the very same day that Stalin died.

Today *Le Pas d'acier* is one of Prokofiev's least-known scores. Yet its initial success reaffirms just how essential Diaghilev's direction and support were for his career. Prokofiev's other ballets are *The Prodigal Son* (1929), *Peter and the Wolf* (1936), *Romeo and Juliet* (1940), *Cinderella* (1941), and *The Stone Flower* (1954).

Choreography

Massine created two scenes which contrasted the old order with "the force and virility of Communist youth." The link between the two scenes is provided by the sailor-turned-worker, danced by Massine. For this role, he "used strenuous character movements to suggest the conflict in the mind of a young man torn between his personal life and his nation."[35]

Massine gave poignant and compelling stage actions to the impoverished refugees in the first section. However, the remaining five sections of the first scene apparently lapsed into a suite of dance *entrées*—peasants, commissars, workers—which brought the dramatic impetus to a halt. Just where these people found vacant spaces for dancing is a matter of conjecture, since the stage was strewn with Yakulov's "factory equipment." The second-scene choreography required the dancers to move up and down ladders and around machine-like constructions. In the finale, Massine synchronized the hammering movements of the young factory workers to the movements of the wheels and pistons on the rostrums, and he strengthened the closing tableau with a "large ensemble group in front of the rostrums, so evolving a multi-level composition." He believed that he "was able to create a climax of overwhelming power."[36]

Critics agreed unanimously. The *Observer* praised the "remarkably good steps and figures."[37] Even Valerian Svetloff, rarely a Massine fan, said that "it requires the talent of a Massine, and his extraordinary capacity for work to succeed in mastering this rhythm of mechanism; dilettantes should leave it strictly alone."[38]

Critical Survey

Like all Ballets Russes Paris premières, the opening night of *Le Pas d'acier* was attended by the artistic crème de la crème. Rumors of a protest by White Russian émigrés were flying. In the end, there were no demonstrations, and Parisian critics and audiences liked *Le Pas d'acier*. Critic André George wrote, "the bodies resemble living cam-shafts, but something beautiful—like a human smile—is superimposed on their implacable metallurgical precision.... Perhaps this is no longer dance, but whatever you call it, it is a new and powerful form of art."[39]

The London première of *Le Pas d'acier* was potentially far more volatile than the one in Paris. England was very anti–Bolshevik, and the previous year's general strike in London was still fresh in the minds of its upper class. Lifar claimed that "we were all in a state of extreme tension for the London opening." According to Lifar, Diaghilev sat in the orchestra with a revolver which he would fire in the air at the first signs of trouble. At the end of the performance, the audience looked anxiously at the Duke of Connaught's box (the Duke was the first cousin of the assassinated Tsarina Alexandra). There were "anxious moments of absolute dead silence," said Lifar. Finally, the Duke rose, came to the edge of his box, and began to applaud, whereupon "the whole house immediately did likewise, to loud cries of 'Brava! Bravo!' The Duke of Connought had saved our honour, and thenceforth *Le Pas d'acier* enjoyed an incomparable success."[40]

Le Pas d'acier was hailed by London critics. The *Times* called it a "masterpiece," "impressive and even terrifying."[41] For the *Observer*, *Le Pas d'acier* was a grim metaphor: "they [the dancers] strain nerve and muscle to keep time with the purposeful cacophony. Great hammers clang and boilers let off steam: the soul of man is but a variant of the fuel force."[42]

In Retrospect

Despite its initial success, *Le Pas d'acier* had only one revival in 1928. It should be noted that Europeans lacked a true frame of reference for the ballet's Soviet allusions. For Alexandra Danilova, who survived the horrors of the Revolution with George Balanchine, *Le Pas d'acier*'s images brought back chilling memories: "Because at that time there was nothing ... if you get out and didn't have that hat, you take a lampshade and put it on your head if it's raining. So it was full of these strange figures that people didn't understand. Only the Balanchine group knew."[43]

In the audience, though, there actually were a few others who knew. For White Russians who had gone hungry in the new Russia, the painful imagery of the first section was, for Alexandre Benois, a "shameful mockery of the old regime."[44] Though Europeans may have found the wretches of the opening section fantastic and incomprehensible, they may have been the only part of the ballet that rang true for most Russian emigrants. For them, the last scene's vision of "Factory as Utopia" must have seemed a fantasy on par with the gigantic hammers and rainbow of flashing lights on Yakulov's rostrum.

ODE

Ballet in One Act
Based by Boris Kochno on a poem by Mikhail Lomonossov
Music: Nicholas Nabokov
Scenic and Costume Design: Pavel Tchelitchew
Lighting Design: Pierre Charbonnier
Première: Théâtre Sarah Bernhardt, Paris, June 6, 1928

ORIGINAL CAST
The Poet and the Light Fleck: Serge Lifar   **Nature:** Mlle de Belianina
Principals in Nature's Festival: Felia Dubrovska, Alicia Nikitina,
Léonide Massine, Nicholas Efimov, Alexandra Danilova,
Constantin Tcherkas, Leon Woizikowsky

Synopsis

With luminous diadem and robed in phosphorescent white, Nature looks down from her pedestal while clouds move slowly behind her. Awaiting her is the Disciple of Isis. Nature descends from her pedestal and initiates the Disciple into the mysteries of the universe. The blue gauze curtain separates, disclosing Earth, the moon, the constellations, nebulae and comets. The glories of nature present dances which culminate in the Aurora Borealis. Captivated by its beauty, the pupil darts forward, enters Nature's Festival, and destroys by his presence the vision of the Aurora Borealis. The charm is broken; Nature returns to her pedestal and is turned again into stone.

Scenery and Costumes

Pavel Tchelitchew is best known for his tormented metamorphic paintings and his imaginative stage designs. In the 1920s, he specialized in dreamlike landscapes and figures in somber tonalities. By the end of the decade, Tchelitchew's work was showing strong surrealist elements, with fantastic distortions of everyday objects.

In 1926, he had shared an exhibit with neon lighting pioneer Pierre Charbonnier, which led to Charbonnier's involvement with *Ode*. *Ode* was novel in its use of motion picture projections. It began with Nature standing on a pedestal while a film of slowly moving clouds was projected from behind. The blue gauze curtain separated, disclosing a large globe lit in blues and browns to resemble the Earth. Visible behind it was a circular platform on which dancers with tiny batteries and lights fitted onto the backs of their unitards depicted the constellations. As they danced, distant nebulae and comets were projected onto the backcloth. In the most stunning projection, a flower bud expanded by jumps into full blossom through the agency of a time-exposure cinematic camera.[45] For A. V. Coton, "*Ode*'s strongest remaining impression is of the unearthly beauty created in most of the scenes by a revolutionary use of light never before seen in any form of Theatre."[46]

For the section called "Man's Bondage," Tchelitchew created an irregular framework of white cords which enclosed the stage action. Masked dancers in white phosphorescent costumes manipulated the cords to create

Serge Lifar (center) as the Disciple of Isis in the Aurora Borealis scene from *Ode*, 1928. Set design by Pavel Tchelitchew.

a succession of moving Euclidean forms. For the Aurora Borealis, he strung up two lines of dolls on wires extending from stage center to the wings on either side. They were dressed in gray crinolines of the era of Empress Elizabeth, and identically dressed dancers appeared in front of the dolls for a dual perspective. Although *The Sketch* complained that "no one has yet explained the reason the rows of gibbeted dolls appear,"[47] the dolls may well have been Tchelitchew's malicious nod to Diaghilev—as if to say that the Empress had been deposed, but not entirely forgotten.

Music

Nicholas Nabokov was an American composer of Russian origin. His inspiration was basically lyrical, and his best music shows strong dramatic powers and eloquent orchestration. Nabokov's score for *Ode* was an oratorio and required a large choir. Reviews were mixed. Svetloff said that the music had "nobility of aims" and was "the best part of *Ode*."[48] But the *Morning Post* thought it "redolent of the circus"[49] and for the *Times*, it "made little impression."[50]

Choreography

With Tchelitchew zealously guarding his secrets and Nabokov declaring an "anomaly" between music and movement, Massine faced the task of trying to devise compatible movement for a designer and composer who were deliberately avoiding him. If Diaghilev accused him of knowing "even less" than Kochno about what he was supposed to be doing, it is small wonder.

This was very much the period of the designer's ballet, and Massine's scope for movement invention was largely confined to the "Nature's Festival" and "Man's Bondage" sections. For the latter, he created a succession of shifting geometrical patterns for the dancers within Tchelitchew's cord framework. To the *Morning Post*, this dance "looked as if it had strayed from the gymnasium of the Bath Club,"[51] and it was described as static and tedious by other critics.

Massine devised a novel pas de deux for "Nature's Festival" in which he and Alexandra Danilova held overhead a long pole from which lengths of gauze were suspended on either end, leaving a gap in the middle. The dancer behind the gauze had an ectoplasmic quality compared to the solid form visible in the gap. Danilova was utterly baffled as to what the stick and the curtains were supposed to represent. She said, "I always asked, 'But what is it? Who am I?' He said, 'Keep quiet and do your movement.'" All she knew for certain was that the pole was very awkward: "I had a lift sitting on the shoulder and in one hand this damn ... excuse me ... stick."[52]

Critical Survey

Not surprisingly, the designers stole the show. Cyril Beaumont described *Ode*'s decor as a work of "celestial beauty."[53] The *Morning Post* said that *Ode* was "revolutionary and ahead of its time, most especially in the work of Tchelitchew and Charbonnier."[54] Massine is rarely even mentioned, although Svetloff did call his choreography "something of a cross between circus-tricks and Swedish exercises."

Critics were quick to see that *Ode* was illogical and disjointed. A recurring complaint, here by Svetloff, was that *Ode* was "very clear from the programme notes, but misty in the stage version."[55] The *Times* asked, "Why the gibbeted dolls? It is this habit of leaving too many questions unanswered, in fact of failing to carry through a design, that marks too many of the company's new productions."[56]

In Retrospect

Grigoriev said, "*Ode* indeed was a failure; for once the collaboration of librettist, composer, choreographer and designer failed to produce a work of much value."[57] However, there was precious little collaboration here, and the words "for once" seem to indicate that Grigoriev saw *Ode* as an isolated accident. In fact *Ode* followed a course nearly identical to that of the earlier *Zéphyr et Flore*. First, Diaghilev turned to an eighteenth-century theme. Second, he distanced himself from the project when his original concept was tossed out. Third, his absence resulted in the loss of any semblance of coherence. Fourth, Diaghilev saw disaster looming and made a last-ditch effort to save the ballet. But his efforts were too little and too late.

DAVID *(Le Roi David)*

A Choreographic Pageant in Two Acts
Libretto: André Doderet
Music: Henri Sauguet
Scenic and Costume Design: Alexandre Benois
Première: Académie Nationale de Musique et de Danse, December 4, 1928

ORIGINAL CAST

David: Ida Rubenstein   **Goliath:** M. Lapitzky   **King Saul:** M. Dolinoff

Ida Rubinstein

Ida Rubinstein was born in Kharkov in 1885 to an extremely wealthy grain magnate father. When she announced her determination to become an actress, her family refused to let her study. Denied conventional entrée into the professional theatre, Ida simply used her own money to buy herself a public performance when she came of age.

Her 1908 production of *Salomé* was designed by Bakst and choreographed by Michel Fokine. In the "Dance of the Seven Veils," she stripped down almost to her birthday suit, causing a local scandal. Sergei Diaghilev saw her in *Salomé* and was impressed with her charisma and beauty. He offered her the title role in the Fokine ballet *Cléopatre* for the Ballets Russes' first (1909) season. Beyond her purely physical charms, the shrewd impresario also realized that she was so rich that she could be counted upon to work for nothing.

In 1910 Rubinstein danced the leading role of Zobedie in Fokine's *Scheherazade*. Even though she was no dancer, critics raved over her mesmerizing stage presence. However, Ida was unwilling to accept her own limitations, and her desire to dance rather than simply mime leading roles led her to leave Diaghilev and finance her own productions. She became the toast of Paris as she bought her way into its most distinguished houses.

In the summer of 1910 she threw herself into the project of mounting a production of *Le Martyre de Saint Sébastien*, a grandiose verse-drama in which Ida portrayed the title role. Thereafter, performing in titillating transvestite roles became her trademark. After World War I, Rubinstein staged numerous lavishly expensive *mélodrames* and ballets at the Paris Opéra. While her collaborators included a few modernist writers and composers, her designers—primarily Bakst and Benois—clung steadfastly to the styles associated with the prewar Ballets Russes.

At this time, Rubinstein was concentrating on dramatic works, which Diaghilev did not regard as competition, except when she lured away his designers and composers with fees much higher than he could afford himself. But by November 1928, Ida had decided to form her own ballet company, Les Ballets Ida Rubinstein. Undeterred by the fact that she was now in her forties, Rubinstein assembled a company and made herself the star of every ballet she produced.

The enterprise was to be on a large scale with a repertoire of nine new ballets. One of the original scores she commissioned for the 1928 season was Ravel's great classic, *Boléro*. Her other first-season composers were Honegger, Milhaud, Sauguet and Auric. Her choreographers included Fokine, Nijinska, Massine, and Kurt Jooss.

Synopsis

The story of *David* is quite simple. Doderet's libretto is a balletic version of the life of David, from the curing of King Saul with the therapeutic strains of David's harp to David's victory over Goliath with his equally efficacious sling.

Scenery and Costumes

A man of great knowledge and sophisticated taste, Alexandre Benois played a crucial role in the vitalization of Russian culture during the first quarter of the twentieth century. He became a founder and leading member of *Mir Iskusstva* and of the exhibition society that succeeded it in 1910. From 1909 to 1914 he was artistic director of the Moscow Art Theatre, and he was director of the picture gallery at the Hermitage, Petrograd, from 1918 to 1926, at which time he left Russia to settle in Paris.

Benois was decidedly retrospective. He was captivated by the court of Louis XIV at Versailles, and the greater part of his artistic oeuvre was given to depicting Louis' court, as well as that of Peter the Great in St. Petersburg. He achieved his greatest artistic successes in the ballet and the theatre. Benois' obsession with Versailles was first realized in his historically accurate designs for *Le Pavillon d'Armide* (1907) for the Imperial Ballet of St. Petersburg. His Ballets Russes designs for *Petrouchka* (1911) are perhaps his most celebrated.

Music

Henri Sauguet was born in Bordeaux and moved to Paris in 1923. With several colleagues from the provinces, he formed the *Ecole d'Arcueil*; their inaugural concert at the Sorbonne was presided over by Cocteau and Satie. These connections opened up the field in which Sauguet was to excel: the ballet. His orchestration for the 1924 Massine ballet *Les Roses* marked the beginning of his professional career.

In the ensuing years, this career proceeded smoothly; his second ballet score for Balanchine's *La Chatte* (1927) was one of Diaghilev's successes and prompted Rubinstein to commission him for *David*. The resulting score was considered one of the most original works of the Rubinstein repertory.[58]

Sauguet also composed several operas, concertos, and four numbered symphonies. He remained opposed to particular systems, and his music evolved little over the years. For him the essentials were melody, harmony, and rhythm, and he maintained an art of clarity, simplicity and spontaneous ease.

Choreography

Rubinstein's assumption of the title role in *David* gave her yet another chance to display herself as an androgynous hero. Although this gimmick excited her fans, Massine seems to have been rather bored with Ida and frustrated by her limitations. He wrote that "it was difficult to get her to move gracefully. As she was dancing the part of David, and the whole ballet was centered on her, I had very little opportunity for original choreography."[59]

However, some critics seemed to admire Massine's choreography for *David*, whatever he may have thought of it. The *Times* critic found it to be "energetic and effective."[60] Likewise, Arnold Haskell thought that "Massine's *David* had a simplicity and grandeur that gave one a taste of his new development."[61]

Critical Survey

Sir Francis Rose was impressed by "the wonderful music and unique collaboration of the creators," but he could not resist recounting the hilarious mishap that occurred when Ida "dragged an enormous papier-mâché head of Goliath across the stage. ... The hair came off, and there was nearly a disaster when the head rolled off her platter into the footlights and practically onto the drums in the orchestra."[62]

There were those critics who thought this piece showed "neither talent, nor invention nor intelligence."[63] There were the usual complaints about Ida's inept dancing: "This slim boyish figure becomes awkward and gauche the moment a simple pose en arabesque or any step of elevation is attempted, and in her pas de deux, one trembles lest a catastrophe should occur."[64] These reactions to *David* were quite typical—rarely was there a consensus of opinion on the quality of Rubinstein's works.

In Retrospect

Michael de Cossart writes, "when the curtain finally came down at the Opéra on December 4, 1928, Ida had the personal satisfaction of knowing that, in the briefest of seasons, she had succeeded not only in mounting more original works than any independent impresario in living memory but also in starring in each and every one of them herself."[65] Massine shared only modestly in her glory. He was simply a hireling, bound to obey the diva's every command, and he always took scant pride in creations where the main artistic decisions were not his.

LES ENCHANTEMENTS D'ALCINE

Choreographic Pageant in Two Acts
Based on a Scenario by Louis Laloy after Lodovico Ariosto's *Orlando Furioso*

Music: Georges Auric
Scenery and Costumes: Alexandre Benois
Premiere: Académie Nationale de Musique et de Danse, Paris, May 21, 1929

ORIGINAL CAST

The Rose Fairy: Ida Rubenstein   **Roger:** M. Lipatov
Angélique: Mlle Winthrop   **Tancrède:** M. Lapitzky

Synopsis

Two suitors, the poet Roger and the warrior Tancrède, compete for the hand of the fair Angélique. She favors the manly soldier and trips off from her palace with him. Just then the thorns of a rosebush catch her dress, and her beau proceeds to free her by hacking off the offending branch. The rejected poet stops him in time and gently frees the dress without harming the bush.

Left alone, Roger is waylaid by the Rose Fairy, Alcine (Ida Rubinstein), who presents him with a rose in gratitude for his kindness. Roger fails to realize that Alcine is in love with him, and he tactlessly gives the rose to Angélique. To punish him, the fairy transports him to a garden and changes him into a tree. Not content with that, she turns the rocks and flowers into monsters and amazons to harass him. But Angélique breaks the fairy's spell with the aid of the magic rose and offers her hand to Roger instead of Tancrède—who takes it all with as much good grace as does the evil fairy.

Scenery and Costumes

A simple enough story in itself, *Alcine* was rich in possibilities for an elaborate and luxurious production: it existed more than anything else as a series of exotic backgrounds for Rubinstein's striking presence. Benois was in his true element and, as usual, critics raved over his splendid sets and costumes.[66]

Music

Les Enchantements d'Alcine was Auric's fourth score for a ballet. It was very eclectic, and James Harding detected hints of Satie, Messager and Chopin, along with popular tunes of the 1920s: "The Flowers sway gracefully to a little melody like those sentimental songs that were to be heard at the tea dances in the Twenties, and Alcine's slow waltz is nothing more or less than a popular café concert tune."[67] Paul Bertrand was far more positive, summing up Auric's achievement as "perhaps the most complete and richest in effects in all his already abundant output."[68]

Choreography

Since Massine is not even mentioned in any of the reviews for *Alcine*, one must assume that choreography played a very marginal role. Bertrand wrote, "as always, one had to applaud the supreme harmony of her [Ida's] poses,"[69] indicating that much of Massine's work was limited to gesture and static design.

Critical Survey

Les Enchantements d'Alcine was quite in line with Rubinstein's previous productions and was greeted with the usual mixed reviews. All in all, though, Ida came in for much harsher personal criticism during her second Paris season. Perhaps it was in response to this and to the worldwide depression that Rubinstein was prompted to cancel her 1930 engagements.

In Retrospect

During the first years of Les Ballets Ida Rubinstein, Diaghilev's fear and jealousy knew no bounds. His frequent outbursts on the subject certainly didn't keep Ida from going right ahead with her plans, but Diaghilev's final days were adversely affected. Lifar, Grigoriev, and many others worried about the effect of the "desertion" of his most trusted painters and composers on Diaghilev's already failing health.

AMPHION

Ballet in One Act
Based on a Poem by Paul Valéry
Music: Arthur Honegger
Scenic and Costume Design: Alexandre Benois
Costume Execution: La Maison Mathieu-Solatgés
Costume Execution for Mme Rubinstein: La Maison Paquin
Première: Académie Nationale de Musique et de Danse, June 23, 1931

ORIGINAL CAST

Amphion: Mme Ida Rubinstein   La Voix d'Apollon: M. Panzera
Une Proie: M. Lapitzky   Le Monstre: M. Feodorov
Les Chauves-Souris: Mlles Berry, Winthrop
Le Roi d'Argent: M. Plucis
Le Songe Amoureux: M. Dolinoff, Mlles Larin, Chmatkova
Les Biches: Mlle Ouchkova, M. Lipatov
Deux Guerriers: MM. Jasinsky, Ciwinsky

Concept

Valéry was the last of the great symbolists. His experimentation with the musical and psychological nuances of the voice produced some of the most resonant poems in French verse. *La Jeune Parque* (1917) made his reputation and also inspired his concept of poetry as song in subsequent works.[70]

Valéry's essays on painting, architecture, music, and dance illustrate the symbolists' characteristic interest in the parallels to be drawn among the arts. In the 1890s, he became fascinated by the close correlation between structure and form in architecture and the French language. And, when one went further, both also had close affinities with structure and form in music. Valéry's ruminations led him back to the Greek myth of the invention of music and, through music, the birth of architecture.

As early as 1894 Valéry had sketched out a plan for a stage spectacle to be called "Amphion." He approached Debussy for a score, but he was unavailable. Valéry then put the project aside for another thirty-five years; it may well have been the Rubinstein performances that finally rekindled his interest. An introduction to Ida was easily arranged; the poet discussed his ideas with her and, as he noted, Rubinstein acted as the catalyst that made them crystallize into something tangible.[71]

Synopsis

Amphion, Jupiter's son by Antiope, leads a rough and savage existence in the forest. Tired from his hunting chase, he falls into a deep sleep. In his dream Apollo reveals that a special mission has been entrusted to him ... as soon as Amphion awakens, he sees a lyre before him on the ground. Plucking the strings gently, he produces a caressing sound that enchants all things, animate and inanimate. As he practices, he discovers scales. He has invented music. Rocks are charmed by his melodies; they arrange themselves in impeccable order and form the city of Thebes. A temple in honor of Apollo is formed, and the people acclaim the man whose art has just given birth to the science of architecture. They decide to take Amphion into the temple and set up a cult to him. Suddenly, a woman shrouded in mourning veils snatches the lyre away from him and throws it into a stream. She then drags him off to nothingness and thus, Amphion is the only one not to benefit from his discovery.

Scenery and Costumes

Alexandre Benois' sumptuous décor in the grand opera style was lauded by the *Revue de France* as a stage picture that "opens the door to all fantasies."[72] André George, on the other hand, deplored its "dark heaviness." [73] Henri Malherbe lamented that the naturalistic designs contradicted the symbolic intention of Paul Valéry, who was seeking to free himself from the realistic style.[74]

Music

Towards the end of World War I, Arthur Honegger became one of Les Six, but the arbitrary nature of this grouping was particularly evident in his case: "he had little sympathy with any aesthetic claimed for the movement, his dislike of Satie's work was reciprocated, and his musical affinities were as much German as French."[75]

From the 1931 première of *Amphion* through World War II, oratorios based on legend and history occupied much of his attention. The oratorios *Judith* (1926), *Antigone* (1927), *Jeanne d'Arc au bûcher* (1938) and *Nicolas de Flue* (1945) use a narrator to objectify the drama. In all of them, Honegger aimed at a more pronounced accentuation of the French language. His varied handling of the voice—speaking, whispering, screaming, murmuring, humming—was a novelty and has had wide influence. Honegger may be regarded as an austere composer in his attention to structure and complex polyphony, in his somber and tragic subjects, and in his distaste for pictorial orchestration, even in works for the stage.[76]

In composing the score for *Amphion*, Honegger was well aware that he was tackling a project which Valéry had previously entrusted to Debussy, and he considered this "a heavy responsibility."[77] He wondered if he would be able to depict musical evolution "from original chaos to forms of the highest sophistication."[78] But he set to work with a will, and he created an impressive score for the narrator (Amphion), baritone solo (Apollo), female soloists (the Muses), chorus, and orchestra.

Some critics were disturbed that Honegger had written a dramatic, theatrical score which covered the full range of dynamics and intensity while Valéry, on the other hand, had produced one of his most "Apollonian" works—elegant, graceful, serene. Boris de Schloezer noted that the music cramped the free flow of the text at times and that Honegger's occasional attempts to adjust his music to the text resulted in "a very uneven score."[79] Henry Prunières, though, praised Honegger's sensitivity to the text: "This time he has devoted his talent to the service of a great poet's thought."[80]

Choreography

As one would expect given the subject matter, the use of bodies as building blocks figured prominently in Massine's choreography for

Amphion. For André Levinson, the choreography's "monumental gymnastics" were "not exempted of grandeur."[81] Massine seems to have been even less enthusiastic over *Amphion* than he was for *David* and *Alcine* and does not even mention *Amphion* in his memoirs.

Critical Survey

Valéry's involvement with the Rubinstein company created high anticipation in the Paris press. Gustave Bret praised the "mystery and harmony" of Rubinstein's gestures.[82] Georges Guy also commended Rubinstein for bringing about a splendid collaboration between Valéry and Honegger.[83]

However, other critics thought that *Amphion* was a garbled mess: "The simultaneous use of a large chorus on the stage, with five soloists in the orchestra pit and a troupe of dancers executing movements that were closer to mime than dance, resulted in a disquieting mélange of sound and sight."[84] F. Bonavio wrote that the entire piece seemed "written by amateurs, to be performed by amateurs, for the exclusive enjoyment of amateurs."[85]

Once again, Rubinstein was lambasted for producing works that kept her own persona firmly at center stage. Levinson rued, "How sad that Mme Rubinstein, who stages so many important productions, persists in spoiling everything by becoming a star."[86] And what of Massine? As was true of *Alcine*, Massine's contribution to *Amphion* was practically ignored by the press.

In Retrospect

Rubinstein clung to her false self-image as a great actress and dancer and spent the fortune which enabled her to do so year after year. In Lynn Garafola's assessment, "[She] noticeably failed to commission a single work that was not a vehicle for herself ... the vast majority of her works were dinosaurs—pretentious, old-fashioned, unwieldy, tedious. Rubinstein never got over her infatuation with the *fin de siècle*, and she never ceased to be a spoiled rich girl."[87]

However, Garafola also acknowledges that Rubinstein's very wealth advanced the development of music and dance by enabling her to commission important original works from great masters. The overall failure of her 1931 season in Paris and London, coupled with harsh personal criticisms, seems to have wounded Rubinstein more severely this time and resulted in her absence from the stage for the next two years. Les Ballets Ida Rubinstein gave its final performances at the Paris Opéra in 1934.

BELKIS

Ballet in Six Scenes
Libretto: Claudio Guastalla, based on the Biblical story of King Solomon and Sheba
Music: Ottorino Respighi
Scenic and Costume Design: Nicola Benois
Costume Execution: S. A. Casa d'Arte Caramba
Première: La Scala, Milan, January 23, 1932

ORIGINAL CAST

Belkis, Regina di Saba: Lelia Bederkhan
The Araba Fenice: Attilia Radice
King Solomon: David Lichtenstein[88]
Un Principe Sabeo: Vincenzo Celli   **Taklé Aymanot:** Serverino Verri
Il profeta Ménylek: Ermanno Savaré
I consiglieri di Belkis: Ebna Hakim, Erminio Télo
Zagdur: Mario Beretta

Synopsis

Scene One. The interior of an Arab tent. The narrator begins telling the ancient tale of Belkis, the beautiful queen who languished for love of Solomon and of how the great king, hearing of her plight, dispatched forthwith his winged messenger, the Araba Fenice, who invited Queen Belkis to meet the king.

Scene Two. The court of King Solomon. The king and his seventy wives await the coming of the Araba Fenice. There follows the "Dance of the Birds," the "Dance of Offering," and the "Dance of the Winds." On the wings of the latter, the Araba Fenice returns to tell Solomon of the beauty and love of Belkis and then flies back to Sheba.

Scene Three. The terrace of the queen's garden in Kitor. The Araba Fenice delivers a letter from the king to Belkis. After due invocation to the gods ("El Passo del Gallo" and "Dance of the Seven Perfumes"), the queen prepares to start her journey.

Scene Four. A great caravan winding across the desert. A rich train passes before the throne of Solomon: camels in lavish trappings, litters of costly gifts, troupes of dancers and at last, on a milk-white elephant, the lovely Belkis. She descends and dances before Solomon ("Dance of the Mirror"). Her beauty so overwhelms him that he falls prostrate at her feet.

Scene Five. King Solomon's pavilion. Belkis enters swathed in veils. Then, garment by garment, the slaves disrobe her until she stands before her king in nude beauty ("Dance of the Garments"). Solomon conducts her to his throne and dances for her ("Mystic Dance"). Next the royal couple dance together and then ascend the stairs to the throne. There follows a glittering fête in their honor ("Dance of the Amphoras," "Dance of the Tambors," and "Orgy").

Scenery and Costumes

Nicola Benois was the son of Alexandre. For the décor, Benois produced a stunning array of opulent backcloths and sets, plus the designs for over six hundred costumes. According to *Dancing Times* the staging cost nine thousand lire and "indeed one sees it!" The critic continued: "Taking advantage of the kaleidoscope of colour offered by the Hebrew-African-Arabian theme, M. Benois, the scenic artist, has designed settings and costumes of a fantasy founded on ethnographic authenticity which is at once artistic and convincing." [89]

Music

Though not the most important Italian composer of his generation, Respighi was the most successful internationally. John Waterhouse wrote that Respighi was especially receptive to visual impressions and that it follows that his best works tend to be "sensory" in character: "his preoccupation with vivid orchestral colors and his eager appropriation of the purely decorative elements in the styles of predecessors and contemporaries were symptomatic."[90] In 1916 Respighi completed the justly celebrated *Fontane di Roma*, in which influences from Ravel and Strauss, among others, are completely assimilated. "Here, Respighi shows both a perfect knowledge of his formatic and structural limitations and a superb command of his gifts."[91]

In 1922 Mussolini and the Fascist Party came to power. Respighi did not pander to the Fascist Party, however. He was the one composer of his generation whom the regime backed without being courted and, unlike many other Italian composers of the period, Respighi never became a member of the National Fascist Party.[92]

In his works subsequent to *Fontane*, Respighi maintained his pictorialism but also began to use archaic elements more frequently. Respighi's score for *Belkis* is an excellent example of his archaizing principles. He drew on two sources: the melodic characteristics of ancient Hebrew songs and Arabic rhythms with a vast assortment of native percussion instruments. The *Dancing Times* praised Respighi's imaginative use of ancient source material: "Respighi has woven them [Hebrew and Arabic themes] into a work whose composition only is modern.... The frequent use of barbaric and primitive instruments, in which this composer excels, does much to heighten the fantastic atmosphere."[93]

The full eighty-minute ballet required an enormous orchestra, including such unconventional instruments as sitars and wind-machines, and a phalanx of offstage brass. In the *New York Times*, Raymond Hall extolled the ballet's finale, the "Orgiastic Dance," as "a deafening tumult of sound and a paroxysm of rhythm that finds a par only in the Dionysian climaxes of the *Sacre du Printemps*.... At the Scala premiere it brought the audience to its feet in a frenzy of excitement."[94]

Choreography

Apparently, the choreography was dull and repetitious. For *Dancing Times* it was

> far inferior to the grandiosity of the line achieved by the composer and sceneograph.... An endless repetition of "arabesque" and "jeté en tournant" marred nearly every number, especially as the nearly limitless possibilities of choreography in this eastern fantasy could have rendered it entirely deserving of the settings. Had M. Massine taken a hint from M. Benois and founded genial fantasy on ethnologic knowledge, his audience would not so soon have become surfeited.

To some extent, Massine was hampered by the inadequacy of the Persian princess-turned-dancer, Lelia Bederkhan, since the whole ballet revolved around the seductive and magnificent dancing of Queen Belkis. Even so, *Dancing Times* believed that Massine's choreography for Solomon (David Lichtenstein) "was not routined to do him justice."[95] Some dance numbers were successful, though, especially those featuring Attilia Radice, a rising star of La Scala, as the Araba Fenice.

Critical Survey

The general consensus was that *Belkis*, "one of the most important ballets in recent years,"[96] was seriously flawed by Massine's choreography. It failed to match either the splendor or the scrupulous research manifested in the score and setting.

In Retrospect

One is inclined to be skeptical of Massine's defense that *Belkis* "did not offer me much opportunity for inventive choreography."[97] In addition to superb creations by Benois and Respighi, La Scala handed him a huge budget and cast to work with. Massine's endless repetition of *pas* from the traditional ballet vocabulary was a shallow, perfunctory response to the more penetrating research of his collaborators.

Massine's exhaustive study of the ethnic dances of Spain had resulted in a masterpiece: *Le Tricorne* (1919). Had he put the same effort towards a study of the ethnic dances of Hebrew and Mediterranean cultures, he might have found a treasure chest of "opportunity for inventive choreography." It is possible that *Belkis* taught Massine a lesson. His work from 1932 onwards shows consistently thorough investigation into the historical, anthropological, religious and socio-political aspects of his source material.

5

May 1932–July 1936

Between his stints with *Helen!* and *The Miracle*, Massine went to Monte Carlo to choreograph a new work called *Jeux d'enfants* for the debut season of the Blum/de Basil Ballet Russe de Monte Carlo. Many former Diaghilev dancers had joined this company, but it would be a new generation of young dancers who would define its style and personality. Mostly Russian-born, they had been trained in Paris in the strictest Russian technique by former Imperial Ballet stars Olga Preobrajenska, Mathilde Kchessinskaya, and Lubov Egorova. When Balanchine went to these teachers' studios, he discovered three girls, aged twelve to fourteen, who possessed dazzling technique. They joined the Ballet Russe de Monte Carlo at the rank of principal and were promptly dubbed "The Baby Ballerinas." Despite their youth, all three had developed highly individual dance styles and personalities: Tamara Toumanova was the most glamorous and exotic; Irina Baronova, the most wholesome and womanly; Tatiana Riabouchinska, the most fragile and ethereal. Good copy for journalists, the Baby Ballerinas were a perfect sales pitch for launching the new company. They were guarded by jealous stage mothers whose fierce loyalty to their charges rivaled that of watchdogs. One of the mothers accosted prima ballerina Alexandra Danilova and said, "You know, it's time for you to retire." Danilova had just turned thirty.[1]

Massine's arrival in Monte Carlo had been eagerly awaited. His reputation as a stern taskmaster had preceded him, and the veterans of the company were relieved to see the changes wrought in Massine's demeanor by his sparkling and talkative wife. Soon Eugenia had charmed everyone, and she and Massine became a welcome part of the company's social life.

Although George Balanchine was the Ballet Russe de Monte Carlo's *maître de ballet* and Massine was merely a guest choreographer, it is quite likely that Léonide was waiting in the wings for Balanchine's position. He not only had a more important name as a choreographer but, unlike Balanchine, he was also a star performer. Moreover, Massine possessed the notation for a number of surefire Diaghilev revivals. When quarrels arose between Blum and de Basil on the one hand and Balanchine and Boris Kochno on the other at the end of the 1932 season, Massine was offered Balanchine's position as ballet master. Kochno and Balanchine formed the short-lived Les Ballets 1933.

After their Galli vacation, Léonide and Eugenia came to Paris in late autumn of 1932 to start preparations for the second Monte Carlo season. The year 1933 would see the debuts of five new Massine ballets. Unswayed by the dire warnings of Blum and de Basil that the music of a familiar symphony was off limits to the ballet, Massine forged ahead with *Les Présages*, a choreographic interpretation of Tchaikovsky's Fifth Symphony. *Les Présages* was a triumph at Monte Carlo. But it was the Paris and London premières during the summer that launched the symphonic ballet controversy that was to rage for years. Some musicians deemed the use of a symphony to accompany a ballet nothing less than a sacrilege, while others contended that ballet should not have to acknowledge musical boundaries.

The second new work of the Monte Carlo season was a revival of *Le Beau Danube*, originally staged in 1924 for *Les Soirées de Paris*. Massine also wanted to create a ballet that would be a gesture of gratitude to the principality of Monaco, which had given him such staunch support throughout all the years of his career. *Beach*, the third new ballet, evoked the chic, privileged atmosphere of the Riviera and the Jazz Age. In its topical content and style, *Beach* was practically a sequel to the Cocteau-Nijinska *Le Train Bleu* of 1924.

The final Monte Carlo première was *Scuola di ballo*. This was Massine's second ballet (after *Les Femmes de bonne humeur*) to be based on a Goldoni comedy. In the winter of 1932–33, he reread some of Goldoni's plays in search of a subject and decided that *Scuola di ballo* "might have been written for my purpose."[2]

Massine enjoyed the greatest success of his career in the 1933 season, both as choreographer and leading dancer for a brilliant company. The Ballet Russe de Monte Carlo's historic engagement at the Alhambra,

Studio portrait of Léonide Massine, 1938. *(Maurice Seymour)*

scheduled for three weeks beginning on July 4, was extended to nineteen. The company performed nightly to sold-out houses, and Massine became ballet's superstar (although that word had not yet been coined). *Choreartium* was the last première of the London engagement. The success of *Les Présages* in the spring of 1933 encouraged Massine to create a second symphonic ballet to Brahms' Fourth Symphony in the fall of the same year. He wrote, "Although I had been pleased with *Les Présages* on the whole, I felt I had relied too heavily on a clearly defined theme, and I wanted to try and achieve a more abstract choreographic interpretation."[3] He proceeded to create a resolutely abstract ballet sans theme, symbolism or allegory.

At its public première, *Choreartium* created a sensation. Agnes de Mille, then a struggling novice with the Ballet Rambert, described the frenzy at the Alhambra: "Seeing a Massine ballet had become one of the erotic pleasures of the London season. The expensive spectators in the stalls contented themselves with 'Bravos' and gush. The devotees upstairs gave themselves unrestrainedly to screaming, jumping up and down, beating the railing, hugging one another, slathering at the mouth."[4]

In musical circles, the controversy over symphonic ballets peaked. Some critics, indignant enough that Massine had choreographed to Tchaikovsky's Fifth, were utterly incensed when Massine dared to lay his hands upon Brahms. The heated debate spread quickly in news columns throughout Europe and established Massine as the most avant-garde choreographer of his day.

Constant Lambert, remarking that the first note of a symphony should imply the last, made the point, "I should have thought myself that the man who imagines that the recapitulation of a symphonic subject can be represented by the reappearance of a particular dancer, or that a separate leap on each note is an adequate translation of a theme which came into the composer's head as a unit, shows an appalling lack of musical sensibility and insight."[5] Edwin Evans gave guarded support to symphonic ballets:

> The essence of a symphony is that it should create the impression of being "all of a piece." Music has a thousand ways of producing that impression. Choreography, in spite of recent accretions to its resources, has fewer at its disposal with which to face this problem of creating unity in diversity.... As for the general question whether symphonies should be used for ballets, I can only retort "Why not?" ... The difference between keeping step to a march and dancing a symphony is one of degree, not of principle—but from one to the other is a long way.[6]

Despite these reservations, leading world conductors of the time (Sir Thomas Beecham, Leopold Stokowski, Eugene Goossens, Eugene Ormandy) conducted performances of *Choreartium* in England and the United States throughout the decade, and Massine had many powerful supporters among the music intelligentsia. Ernest Newman of the London *Times* became Massine's staunchest supporter in a long series of articles which followed the première of *Choreartium*:

> The fact that some parallelisms are much more difficult than others, and have consequently not been attempted hitherto, is no reason for denying a choreographic genius like Massine the right to attempt them.... The rational thing to do when watching *Choreartium* is not to concentrate stubbornly on what is exclusively musical in the music, and therefore alien to this or any other action, but to seize upon, and delight in, the many things in the music that can be paralleled in choreography.... In a truly extraordinary way Massine has given us a transvaluation into choreographic values of a hundred musical features of the symphony.[7]

As the Alhambra season drew to a close, the company's dazzling success enabled de Basil to set up an elite sponsoring committee that won his troupe an annual residency at the Royal Opera House at Covent Garden. The company scored a second major coup when the powerful American impresario Sol Hurok offered to bring the company to the United States for the first time in December of 1933.

Back in 1933, the marketing of ballet in the United States was viewed as a foolhardy, if not insane, endeavor. Any American public for ballet would have to be created from scratch. Sol Hurok quickly proved that he was neither foolish nor crazy, but a shrewd gambler. He wagered correctly that de Basil's Baby Ballerinas, who had already captivated Western Europe, would be especially appealing to Americans. The company opened in New York to half-empty houses. But the publicity engendered by Massine, Danilova and, above all, the Baby Ballerinas was fantastic. By the end of the tour, Hurok had turned loss into profit. Subsequent New York engagements would be characterized by a great clamor for tickets and long queues waiting for standing room.

In the seasons which followed, the troupe toured the United States, Canada, Mexico and Cuba for half the year. The rest of their schedule was packed with bookings in Europe. Massine became an international celebrity. He was, without question, the most famous dancer and choreographer in the world in the decade of the 1930s.

Throughout the American tours, Léonide and Eugenia traveled in a two-room trailer attached to the choreographer's Lincoln. A Lithuanian couple, Alexander and Elizabeth Drevinskas, served them as chauffeur and cook. This arrangement allowed them to escape Pullman trains and grab a few hours of privacy on the lengthy tours.

The 1934 American tour saw the première of *Union Pacific*, based on the first transcontinental railroad, completed in 1869. It was built in two sections by rival capitalists, one section from the East towards the West with Irish workmen, the other from the West towards the East with a Chinese crew. The final stages of construction accelerated into a competitive race ending at Promontory Point, Utah.

During the first American tour of 1933, Massine and Sol Hurok decided that a ballet on an American theme would have great publicity potential. They met with composer Nicholas Nabokov, who suggested an unusual collection of American recordings assembled at the turn of the century by Thomas Edison and owned by American expatriate Gerald Murphy. Nabokov also advised Hurok that the U.S. poet and playwright Archibald MacLeish had spoken to him about composing a score for his recent ballet libretto concerning the construction of the Union Pacific.[8]

MacLeish had already approached Massine with his ballet libretto, but Massine found the idea of a ballet based on railway construction to be "lifeless and unimaginative." For him, the insuperable problem was the presentation of the actual laying of the wooden sleepers and rails. For days he mulled over the problem without inspiration, but "Then, one day, I suddenly saw dancers, absolutely rigid, being carried on stage like planks.... I got very excited about the whole project, and now felt that I could make something highly original out of it."[9] Massine then agreed to work with MacLeish and Nabokov, and Gerald Murphy not only granted music rights, but even became one of the ballet's principal backers.[10]

Union Pacific was created under extenuating circumstances. Crisscrossing the vast United States, the company's touring schedule was much more hectic than it had been in Europe, and there was scant rehearsal time. Massine resorted to stage rehearsals after performances, in hotel lobbies, and even in train corridors. The strain was felt by everyone, not just the dancers. Nabokov had only twenty-three days to transcribe the recordings and orchestrate the music. As the April 6 première drew near, Nabokov relates that prospects for the new work looked bleak indeed:

> Massine was in a frenzy and so was I. The parts were peppered with mistakes; the orchestra played like pigs; Efrem Kurtz complained that the penciled score was illegible; the dancers did not remember their

steps; the group scenes did not work; the sets weren't dry and could not be hung; none of the sizes given to Johnson proved to be correct; props were falling down; the curtain was too short; the tent was too small.... We worked until midnight of the 5th, and still it all looked and sounded like inevitable disaster.[11]

At the eleventh hour, though, the ballet actually coalesced and was a hit in the United States.

When the American tour ended, the company returned to Europe for its spring and summer seasons in Monte Carlo, Paris and London. Whenever he was in Europe, Massine sent his wife to new shows to scout for young dance talent. After attending a performance of the play *Ballerina*, Eugenia urged Léonide to hire a beautiful featured dancer named Eva Hartwig. Hartwig joined Ballet Russe during the 1934 Covent Garden season with the stage name of Vera Zorina.

By the time of the fall 1934–35 North American tour, Zorina had fallen in love with a man she admitted was "old enough to be my father." Léonide reciprocated her ardor, and they launched into an affair. This development was obvious to all: Zorina wrote, "No secret could remain a secret in the tight insular world we lived in." Eugenia, perhaps in a last-ditch effort to save her marriage, accepted Zorina into the life she shared with her husband. Incredibly, Zorina became the third member of the Massine trailer caravan. Zorina wrote, "I could not bear his wife and I daresay she could not stand the sight of me. How could it have been different? We were both forced into a position which we detested. One does things for love that one cannot comprehend having done once love has died."[12]

Massine's only new work of 1935 was *Jardin public*. In the fall of 1934, Léonide had met with Vladimir Dukelsky to discuss a passage from André Gide's novel *Les Faux-monnayeurs* ("The Counterfeiters") as a potential subject for a ballet. Gide's 1926 novel deals with the relatives and teachers of a group of schoolboys subject to corrupting influences both in and out of the classroom. It treats this author's favorite theme—the self-aware and sincere individual as the touchstone of collective morality—in a progression of discontinuous scenes that approximate the texture of daily life itself. The passage selected by Massine describes the corner of a public park through which, from morning to night, pass a stream of contrasting characters.

Massine also created a new version of *Le Bal* in 1935.[13] This ballet was originally choreographed by Balanchine for Diaghilev's Ballets Russes in 1929. As with *Union Pacific*, rehearsals for both *Jardin public* and *Le Bal* had to be squeezed into an already grueling touring schedule. Final rehearsals for *Jardin public* took place in the basement grill of New York's Hotel Piccadilly on West Forty-fifth Street.

In the summer of 1935, the company reassembled at Covent Garden for a season which was mostly successful, except for *Jardin public* and *Le Bal*. Afterwards, Massine invited Zorina to join Delarova and himself on Galli. Zorina wondered "why a man would want to subject two women who loved him to such an unhappy arrangement—both of whom complied in the hope that they would be left alone with him one day."[14]

During the United States tour that fall, Léonide retained counsel to get a divorce, but his relationship with Zorina was beginning to cool off. De Basil had forbidden her to travel in the Massine trailer this season, and Zorina was in so much anguish over their separation that she slashed her wrists with a razor blade in Orlando, Florida. She did so because "It seemed that by inflicting physical pain, I might stop the mental pain I was no longer able to endure. It was a cry for help but Massine, when he was told, paid no attention. In fact, he seemed annoyed and angry. I was made to feel that I had done something disgraceful."[15] After the 1936 summer season at Covent Garden, Zorina left the company, became Balanchine's wife for a while, and had a successful career in musical comedies and films.

At the time of her departure, London was buzzing over the spectacular Covent Garden première of Massine's *Symphonie fantastique*. The success of *Les Présages* and *Choreartium* encouraged Massine to plan a third symphonic ballet, this time to Berlioz's famous five-movement symphony. Ballet Russe conductor Anatol Dorati says that he recommended this symphony because the composer himself had provided a programme.[16] Massine's goal was to fuse the two different approaches that he had used in *Les Présages* and *Choreartium*, integrating "abstract choreographic passages with a romantic and melodramatic plot."[17] The ballet was a dazzling success, even with elitist music critics.

JEUX D'ENFANTS (Children's Games)

Ballet in One Act
Libretto: Boris Kochno
Music: Georges Bizet
Set Design: Joan Miró, executed by Prince A. Schervachidze
Costume Design: Joan Miró, executed by Madame Karinska
Première: Théâtre de Monte Carlo, April 14, 1932

ORIGINAL CAST

The Spirits Who Govern the Toys: Lubov Rostova, Roland Guérard
The Top: Tamara Toumonova   **The Child:** Tatiana Riabouchinska
The Rocking Horses: MM. Petrov, Hoyer, Katcharov,
Lipatov, Dolotine, Shabelevsky
Two Rackets: MM. Borovonsky, Jasinsky
A Shuttlecock: Valentina Blinova   **The Traveler:** David Lichine
Three Sportsmen: MM. Ladré Woizikowsky, Guérard
Amazons: Mlles Obidenna, Marra, Kervilly, Strakhova
Soap Bubbles: Mlles Kirsova, Slavinska, Tresahar,
Morosova, Blanc, Sonne, Chabelska

Synopsis

A little girl wishes to share in the mysterious life which playthings are said to enjoy at nighttime. The curtain rises to reveal an enigmatic disc and cone, structures which house the Spirits Who Govern the Toys. The two spirits, the animators of toy-folk, emerge from the disc and cone to do their magic.

The first toy that they bring to life is a striped Top, who spins brilliantly on the spot and around the room. At this juncture, the Child comes into the magical room to watch her toys at play. Six wooden Rocking Horses do a stationary dance followed by the dance of the Rackets and Shuttlecock. The two rackets mime volley and release and exchange the shuttlecock in swung lifts backwards and forwards. Next four Amazons emerge from behind four large canvasses to perform military exercises and mock combat. Nine Soap Bubbles float about the stage; next appears the Traveler.

The spirits place two signs, one reading "Paris" and the other, "New York," on either side of the stage. The Traveler dances to the four corners of the world, and the Child loses her heart to him. They dance together, then the three Athletes enter and show off their skill as runners and tumblers. The Child dances with the Tumbler, but the jealous Top swirls in and tries to separate them. The Tumbler, pulled in two directions, tries to partner the Child with one hand, the Top with the other.

The ballets ends with a finale in which the toys fill the stage in the order of their dances in a kaleidoscope of movement and color. With the coming of dawn, the spirits return to reclaim the life they have temporarily bestowed on the playthings. The child wanders dreamily among the stiff, inanimate toys. The arm of a Spirit appears through the center of the white disc and gives the final command for the curtain to fall.

Scenery and Costumes

Joan Miró, the great Catalonian painter, experimented with Fauvism, Cubism and Dadaism before being drawn to Surrealism in 1924. This was the year of André Breton's first Surrealist Manifesto, signed at the bottom by Miró and other artists. The aim of this manifesto was to explore the psychic world revealed by Sigmund Freud and, in Breton's famous words, to transmute "those two seemingly contradictory states, dream and reality, into a sort of absolute reality, of surreality."

Under the influence of Surrealism, Miró forsook representational painting to engage in abstract personal fantasies, which by their spontaneity and seeming lack of predetermined arrangement, won him the approval of the group. Surrealist spokesmen championed "automatism," or the recording of signals sent out by the subconscious without the interference of conscious thought. However, the personal language that Miró developed for his externalization of inner visions, far from being autonomous, was actually the result of profound study and diligent labor. When Breton wrote that Miró "may be considered the most Surrealist among us"[18] in his book *Surrealism and Painting*, he was mistaken on one essential point. Miró was too obsessed by an almost pedantic striving to "delimit the extension of his shapes and lines to the fraction of an inch"[19] to be satisfied with any unverifiable language of symbols. Surrealism had been a catalyst to Miró's development, but his genius was not bound to any "ism."

Miró's play of fiery-colored elemental forms, reinforced by lines of equal simplicity, resulted in unified, vivacious, and majestic works. His fluid and curvilinear designs, like those of Picasso in *Mercure*, have been labeled "free form" or "biomorphic abstraction." The shapes in Miró's paintings seem to change before the viewer's eyes, expanding and contracting like amoebas.

Starting with *Jeux d'enfants* and continuing with the etchings that he began to engrave in 1933, Miró's inclination toward an art that was monumental in conception became increasingly stronger.[20] For *Jeux d'enfants*, Miró did not completely desert all relationship to the recognizable form of objects, but he conceived them as seen through the eyes of a child, an approach that fit the ballet perfectly. To set the mood, Miró designed a front curtain with splashes of basic colors, like a child's drawing, and a *gouache* ring construction, floating and rotating in the air.

The curtain rose to reveal a surrealistic playroom—a large black cone to the left and a luminous white disc to the right. P. W. Manchester said they had that "lovely look of child's toys. You know, when you were a child, you would lick a ball because it was a bright color. Well, that's the kind of feeling that he gave you. It was all bright, and it looked as if it were still a little bit wet from the fresh paint."[21] During the ballet, dancers brought in four plaques bearing paint smears, rods, string, and pieces of fabric which were subsequently mounted on easels at the edges of the wings. A. V. Coton found a parallel between "those innocently smeared patterns such as a child will make with any apparatus, and the conscientious simplicity of the Bretonites."[22]

Miró dressed many of the characters in unitards, quite a risqué decision for 1932. The hooded spirits were dressed in pure white, the Soap Bubbles in unitards of various pastel shades. The hooded Top wore a striped unitard of red, green, and yellow. The Top's revolving leg was striped and the whipping leg was solid red, giving the viewer a sense of vertigo as she executed her riveting series of *fouettés*.

Music

Georges Bizet showed so much musical talent as a child that he was admitted to the Paris Conservatoire in 1848, at the age of nine. In the autumn of 1855, Bizet, just seventeen, wrote the Symphony in C. It probably has no rival in the work of any other composer of that age and proclaims him already a master of orchestration.[23] In 1857 Bizet was the co-winner of the Conservatoire's coveted Prix de Rome for composition, which endowed him with a stipend to study abroad for three years.

One of the conditions for the Prix de Rome was to submit sacred music, including a mass, and Bizet had no feeling for sacred music. When he was prevented from following his own natural instincts, his work could become self-conscious and pedantic. Bizet completed only three lackluster compositions during these years.

His first important opera, *Les Pêcheurs de perles*, was performed without success at the Théâtre-Lyrique in 1863. While his second opera *La Jolie Fille de Perth* (1867) was successful, Bizet was in a state of spiritual crisis by 1868. It began with a spate of abortive works and in the summer, he suffered an acute attack of quinsy, a serious throat ailment. Possibly as a result, he experienced an extraordinary change in his attitude towards music—he was no longer afraid to take risks. This change is clearly seen in the masterpieces which followed—*Jeux d'enfants*, the incidental music to *L'Arlésienne*, and *Carmen*. With these, Bizet finally found his true voice.

Jeux d'enfants (1872), based on the theme of childhood, provided French piano music for four hands with its first authentic masterpiece.[24] There were originally ten pieces; two more were added later. The following year, Bizet orchestrated five of them as a *Petite suite d'orchestre*.

In 1872 Bizet wrote the incidental music for Alphonse Daudet's mélodrame, *L'Arlésienne* ("The Girl from Arles"). It was revived with great success at the Odéon in 1885. Although *L'Arlésienne* cannot be fully appreciated apart from the play it was intended to illustrate,[25] the suite still never stales as concert music.

At the first performance of *Carmen* on March 3, 1875, at the Opéra-Comique, the audience was shocked and puzzled. Most critics maintained that the story was too obscene and the characters too repulsive. The voice was sacrificed to the confused clamor of the orchestra. The music was unoriginal and undistinguished in melody, and so on. Bizet's depression over the reviews may well have contributed to the aggravation of his throat ailment. He died a few hours after the thirty-first performance of *Carmen*, and the production closed after only forty-eight performances. Eventually, the Vienna revival of October 1875 led to *Carmen*'s worldwide triumph.

Since the beginning of the nineteenth century, *opéra comique* had been light, sentimental, and trivial. Even discounting the music's brilliant structure and orchestration, *Carmen*'s impact towers over that of any previous *opéra comique* because Bizet extended the genre to embrace true passion, believable characters, and a tragic ending.

Choreography

Massine avoided treating the dolls as mechanical wind-ups, the method used in *La Boutique fantasque*. Because they existed only in the child's subjective fantasy, they were quite free to take on human movement and human expression. For the Top, Massine made superlative use of Toumanova's phenomenal gift for turning. Adrian Stokes wrote that she conveyed "a most vivid memory of the ricocheting, hard-used nursery top. The music makes a sudden utterance; the top is wound and poised; she is loose, she spins twenty-three *fouettés en tournant* with double ones mixed in."[26]

For A. V. Coton, the dance of the Soap Bubbles was "a superb balletic patterning of thistledown softness and airiness."[27] As the Child, Riabouchinska conveyed the character "by jumps, running steps, handclappings, childish grimaces and seemingly spontaneous laughs and leaps, the ecstasies of an Alice come at last to a crazy Wonderland."[28] For the pas de deux of the Child and the Traveler, Massine "created a romantic pas de deux which showed her falling in love with this handsome, dashing stranger, the personification of the dreamworld in which she finds herself."[29] One sees a parallel here with the Nutcracker Prince, the embodiment of Clara's adolescent fantasies.

The *Times* reported that "There are some weak episodes—for example, the dance of the Amazons and the entrance of the Rocking Horses."[30] The rocking horses may have been too unkinetic for a successful dance, and photos of the Amazons reveal four petite, well-groomed young ladies in floating chiffon tunics. If they were meant to be bloodthirsty Amazons, they were hardly dressed for the occasion.

Critical Survey

Jeux d'enfants triumphed in Monte Carlo and in Paris. When it premièred at the Alhambra in July 1933, Ernest Newman wrote, "One's first impression is that Bizet's charming music does not lend itself to action. ... Yet in a very little while it becomes clear that Mr. Massine has achieved the almost impossible by a boldness of translation that soon converts our first skepticism into willing belief. *Jeux d'enfants* is a delightful fantasy."[31]

In Retrospect

When *Jeux d'enfants* was revived for the 1937 season, it was not received so enthusiastically. The *Times* wrote that it "has fewer of those delightful touches of sentiment and humour which Massine contrived for in *La Boutique fantasque*."[32] Fernau Hall felt that Massine "set out to create a ballet which should be ultra-modern—with the inevitable result that it now dates considerably."[33] Nevertheless, *Jeux d'enfants* remained in the Ballet Russe repertory until 1941. It had important revivals for the Royal Ballet in 1947 and 1962, for the Teatro Colón (Buenos Aires) in 1955, for the Opéra-Comique in 1952 and 1957 and for the Oakland Ballet in 1978.

Jeux was quite important to Massine's career because its success set the seal on his replacement of Balanchine as the new *maître de ballet* in 1933. This ballet also marked the introduction of Surrealism onto the ballet stage; however, it remained a ballet in which the dance element predominated over both décor and libretto.

LES PRESAGES

Symphonic Ballet in Four Movements
Libretto: Léonide Massine
Music: Peter Illych Tchaikovsky, Symphony No. 5 in E minor
Set Design: André Masson, executed by Prince A. Schervachidze
Costume Design: André Masson, executed by Madame Karinska
Première: Théâtre de Monte Carlo, April 13, 1933

ORIGINAL CAST

First Movement
Action: Nina Verchinina
Temptation: Nathalie Branitska, Nina Tarakanova, Roland Guérard

Second Movement
Passion: Irina Baronova, David Lichine

Third Movement
Frivolity: Tatiana Riabouchinska
Variation: Mlles Berry, Branitska, Delarova, Kobseva, Larina, Nijinska, Obidenna, Chabelska

Fourth Movement
The Hero: David Lichine **Fate:** Leon Woizikowsky
Passion, Frivolity, Action The Ensemble

Synopsis

First Movement. To a somber melody, the curtain rises on an amazing stage picture of a sky full of signs and portents, shooting stars and a single eye. Onto this already charged stage comes Action, circling the space counterclockwise with strong, rhythmically abrupt sweeps and thrusts of her arms. Soon she is followed by other dancers in massed groups, pairs, or alone. A prominent group of one man and two women symbolize Temptation. They have softer, sensual movements, which Action herself is lulled into joining.

Second Movement. The stage darkens to all but a path of light, and down this comes a man in a white suit, worn over a top with a cryptic design, and a woman in red. This couple's duet intensifies into a tumult of young love as he lifts, carries, tends to and embraces her. The Temptation trio returns briefly. Then, as Tchaikovsky introduces a harsher theme, the ugly and grotesque figure of Fate appears. He disrupts the idyll, but he finally departs with his striking motif of walking backwards on his heels. The man lifts his beloved and exits, with the woman still walking in mid-air.

Third Movement. A scherzo entirely for the women ensues, led by Frivolity, a single figure in pale blue. This episode for soloist and ensemble is all speed, skimming lightness, swift turns, intricate *batterie.*

Fourth Movement. The backcloth has darkened and glowers with a red light behind. Fate leads on the men in disciplined squadrons. It is War. The man of the second movement, now called the Hero, bounds among them, although Passion, Action and Frivolity plead with him not to join the conflict. At the climax, the female principals from the earlier move-

Fourth movement of *Les Présages*, 1933. Set design by André Masson.

ments are borne feet first across the back, each held high by a pair of men, as if to be consigned to a funeral pyre. Lightning flashes; the crowd shake their fists vainly at heaven. But finally the Hero soars once more through their ranks and is raised in triumph as the women return, saved from their fate (or from Fate), to kneel before him as the final chords blare out. He, the victor, restores peace.

Scenery and Costumes

André Masson's work played an important role in the development of both Surrealism and Abstract Expressionism. In 1923, he was invited by André Breton to join the Surrealists. Under their influence, both Masson and Joan Miró experimented with automatic drawing. By sprinkling colored sands on canvas prepared by drawing "automatically" with glue, Masson was able to obtain an imagery of conflict and metamorphosis in his biomorphic abstractions.

Masson became identified with Abstract Expressionism when he broke away from the Surrealists in 1929. His work from 1930 to 1933 became more exclusively and intensely violent than it had been before. The Massacre Series began with drawings of frantic, bestial battles in which man murders man, but as the series progressed, women became the exclusive victims of violence. Man tries to circumvent the cycle where copulation leads to birth and birth to death in his primal desire to murder the female.[34] The drawings of this series are done with great speed, and each line is broken by abrupt, spasmodic changes of direction. These "arrow lines" echo the knives and penises that are invariably present in the drawings.[35] It was during this artistic phase that Masson designed the sets and costumes for *Les Présages*. There is a striking similarity between *Massacre in a Field* (1933; New York, Lerner-Heller Gallery) and Masson's backcloth for *Les Présages* in their lines, union of foreground and background and dynamism. Both works share the same color scheme: bright reds, greens, yellows, purples, blues.[36]

In his backcloth for *Les Présages*, Masson focused on pure abstract symbolism. Comets, stars, flames and waves surged stridently in a wild swirl of vibrant contrasting colors. Black and white pictures cannot convey the sinister effect of these sharp and acid shades.[37] From one high corner of the backcloth stared the huge symbol of an eye—what *Dancing Times* called "a Blake-like vision.... Amid the maelstrom of the astrological nightmare this eye was constantly alert; it had the fixity of the eternal."[38] To each side of the drop hung three tall wings which, repeating the colors, enhanced the verticality of the set.

The female dancers' costumes were modeled on classical Greek tunics and appliquéd with bright symbols of the occult: clubs, daggers, half-moons and spades. The costumes' mild range of coloring kept them from being swallowed up into the vivid background. However, they were trimmed for wild contrasts: costumes of lavender were whipped to life with red, gowns of petunia were made stern with dead black, Passion wore a tomato-red tunic with pink tights and Fate wore shades of gray trimmed in pink. With the exception of Fate, costuming for the males had a contemporary look. In the second movement, David Lichine wore a white suit over a yellow top with a mysterious design. The male corps wore green tights and mauve shirts in the first two movements and, in the finale, long-sleeved coveralls in shades of brown.[39]

Music

Peter Illych Tchaikovsky, probably the most popular nineteenth-century Russian composer, attended the School of Jurisprudence and was assigned on graduation to the Ministry of Justice. But music remained his avocation, and in 1862 he left his job and entered the just-founded St. Petersburg Conservatory.

Tchaikovsky joined the faculty of the Moscow Conservatory in September of 1866. During his eleven years there, he composed the ballet *Swan Lake* (1876), piano concertos, four operas, three symphonies and many smaller works. He also established close ties with the composers of the Russian nationalist group, the Mighty Five. What principally distinguished Tchaikovsky from the Five was his formal conservatory grounding in Western musical techniques, which entrenched him in concepts that were often inimical to Russian folk themes. Since each member of The Five had acquired his technique empirically, contact with such men had a broadening, even liberating effect on Tchaikovsky. Due to their influence, Tchaikovsky's lyric gift owes much to Russian folk song, either quoted or interpreted.[40]

Marriage in July 1877 to Antonina Miliukova triggered an emotional crisis, doubtlessly related to his homosexuality, that brought him near suicide. An annuity from Nadezhda von Meck, granted during his crisis, allowed him to quit teaching in 1878. His correspondence with von Meck, begun in 1876, was sustained voluminously over thirteen years, although they never met.

On November 26, 1878, the day following the première of the Fourth Symphony, he wrote to von Meck, "you understand better than anyone else the many things the symphony expresses."[41] After the Fourth, von Meck urged Tchaikovsky to create an explicit programme on the theme of fate for the Fifth.

Accordingly, Tchaikovsky set down the first drafts for his Symphony No. 5 on April 15, 1888. The earliest notebook sketches include general indications of emotional states rather than a detailed scenario: "Complete submission before Fate, or which is the same, before the inscrut[able] predestination of Providence." Beside the sketch of a musical theme, he wrote, "Consolation. A ray of light," and below the sketch stand the words "No, no Hope."[42] Ultimately, the Fifth reverted to a fairly traditional structure with little evidence of a consistent programme on the theme of fate. The only truly cogent factor is that the principle of a motto theme, established only in the first movement of the Fourth Symphony, is here extended to all four movements.

The most novel feature of the first movement is the waltz-conditioning in much of the three-stage exposition of themes. This paves the way for the explicit waltz which does duty as the third-movement scherzo. Between these two movements is the *Andante cantabile*, an extended flow of yearning melody that is quintessential Tchaikovsky. Critical consensus has it that the fourth movement is the weakest, especially in its recapitulation, which brazenly restates the motto theme in a blatant attempt to synthesize extra power. It results in a rather crude ending for the Fifth.

The Fifth Symphony was first performed in St. Petersburg on November 5, 1888. Some critics were outraged by the replacement of the usual scherzo with a waltz. With reference to the additional waltz episodes in the first and second movements, one reviewer even mockingly called it "the symphony of three waltzes." Tchaikovsky, as he so often did, agreed with these negative comments, telling Mme von Meck that "there is something repulsive in it, a kind of excessive diversity of color and insincere artificiality."[43] Of course, he was being too hard on both himself and on a work which, if not his best, still resounds in every bar with the same intense emotions of his Fourth Symphony.

In 1890 Tchaikovsky suffered another personal crisis when Mme von Meck arbitrarily terminated both his annuity and their long friendship. Despite this blow, which deeply affected Tchaikovsky's self-torturing ego, he composed in that year one of his finest scores, the three-act ballet *Sleeping Beauty*. Tchaikovsky's *Swan Lake*, *Sleeping Beauty*, and *Nutcracker* (1892) helped to reestablish the full-length ballet as an important art form.

Tchaikovsky's *Pathétique* Symphony had its première performance in St. Petersburg on October 28, 1893. A little more than a week later, on November 6, Tchaikovsky died in St. Petersburg after taking arsenic to avoid a scandal when he was threatened with exposure of his homosexuality.

Choreography

Massine invented a story of man's struggle with his destiny to accompany this symphony. In part, his interpretation involved allegorical visualizations of the music. Each main musical theme found its counterpart, as exemplified in the roles of Action and Fate.

But Massine used the ensemble to interpret the structural as well as the thematic content of the score, often to the point where each dancer in the ensemble became an independent entity with personalized steps and patterns. Massine wrote that he "decided to avoid all symmetrical compositions and to render the flow of the music by fluctuating lines."[44] In an interview, ballerina Tatiana Leskova recounted that it was very difficult to reconstruct because "Some dancers move to eight bars of the music, some to four—but at the same time, another would be dancing to a totally different rhythm."⁴⁵ Almost sixty years after the première of *Les Présages*, John Percival marveled that "their dances are more complex than almost any choreographer today would give the corps de ballet. ... Massine in 1933 was anticipating the unfocusing of the stage which we thought Cunningham had invented forty years later. Yet the picture always holds together, because every entry, crossing of the stage or exit arises naturally from the musical score."⁴⁶

To visualize the musical climaxes in the Fifth, Massine employed the corps in mass architectural constructions. He wrote, "I drew my inspiration from the ancient ruins of Selinius, Agrigento and Paestum. It was the mass and volume of these structures which offered a challenge."⁴⁷ As dictated by the music, dancers would form three-dimensional mass designs which broke up at the instant of realization in a constant flow of movement to parallel the flow of the music.

Massine tried to strike a balance between the score's structural and emotional evolutions with his allegorical designations of the principals. Yet he was sensitive to the music's emotional tone without being slavish to it. For example, Frivolity and her ensemble cavort merrily for the entire duration of the third movement: "When a more sinister theme is heard in the music towards the end, the effect is the more poignant because they ignore its warning."⁴⁸

Les Présages was remarkable in its day for its fusion of classical ballet and the principles of German expressionist modern dance, as formulated by Rudolf von Laban and Mary Wigman. Nina Verchinina, who danced the role of Action, went to Germany to study for a year with Wigman. Yet her prior rigorous ballet training gave Massine the perfect vehicle for incorporating Laban principles into a classical work. Dancing *en pointe*, Verchinina used "alternately tremulous, flowing movements or sharp, close-angled gestures."⁴⁹ The fusion spun a new kind of balletic freedom, *présaging* the direction of contemporary ballet.

The second movement's pas de deux was also trendsetting. In her 1989 review, Anna Kisselgoff believed that "Except for melodramatic hand-to-brow gestures, the pas de deux in the second movement is actually a neoclassic duet of superb invention and fluidity."⁵⁰ The pas de deux departed from both the traditional Petipa pas de deux (structured into four musical sections to display virtuosity) and from the Fokine model, where the pas de deux developed seamlessly from the score and emphasized the emotional unity of the couple. Massine's approach borrowed freely from both models. It was frankly virtuosic at points: P. W. Manchester recalls, "it was the first time we ever saw a man hold a girl above his head in a straight-arm lift, and drop her into a fish. Well, you can imagine the sensation that this caused."[51] However, the dazzling lift was not entirely gratuitous: it served both to visualize the introduction of Fate's musical theme and to underscore the lovers' fear of Fate.

Some of Massine's allegorical personifications were more successful than others. Over the years, many critics have concurred with Kisselgoff that "The weak point is the character of Destiny [Fate], whose conical hat and bat-like cape make him look like a green gnome. There is more than a touch of the ridiculous as he menaces the lovers or sets war in motion."[52]

Critical Survey

In Monte Carlo, Paris, and London, *Les Présages* was a triumph with the public and a bone of contention for the press. It was championed by England's foremost music critic, Ernest Newman, while the opposing view was led by composer Constant Lambert, who panned it in the *Sunday Referee*. Newman responded indignantly to a similarly scathing review by Richard Capell in the *Daily Telegraph*:

> The writer tells us that what he saw [in *Les Présages*] was "an encounter between the Demon Influenza and a mixed hockey team, and the consequent despair of the lady secretary impersonating Hygiene. Upon no other hypothesis could the actions be accounted for." To this monumental specimen of philistine fatuity, Mr. Capell adds the admiring comment, "This may be said to be the last word on "Les Présages."[53]

There were some criticisms in the dance world that Massine was selling out to modern dance, and several complaints about the costumes.[54] But, overall, it was considered a marvelous work by Europe's dance-going public. However, *Les Présages* fared very poorly in the United States: its reception was so lukewarm that it was quickly dropped from the repertoire. John Martin predicted the "early demise" of *Les Présages* and stated, "the direction of these romantic, nebulously emotional, philosophical, pseudo-profound creations is the one direction above all others which the ballet must avoid."[55]

In Retrospect

Les Présages remained in the repertory of de Basil's Original Ballet Russe until their disbandment in 1948. Massine revived the ballet in 1956 for the Teatro Municipal in Rio de Janeiro, where former de Basil dancer Tatiana Leskova had become ballet mistress. It was she who staged *Les Présages* for the Paris Opéra Ballet in 1989.

The Paris Opéra revival of *Les Présages* made a new audience aware of Massine's genius. The program was put together by Rudolf Nureyev to show examples of abstract dance ranging from pre–World War II through the present. For Anna Kisselgoff, this ballet looked dated "only in the sense that the historical period in which it was created is stylistically evident. This is not to say—and this is the surprise—that it cannot touch audiences today. In fact, the production is a complete triumph ... because the choreography has a dynamic invention that stands up on its own."[56]

The program notes for *Les Présages* state that the hero "restores peace" at the end of the ballet. It must have seemed so to past audiences, but with hindsight, a chilling subtext suggested itself to several contemporary critics. In 1933, Massine cannot have been unaware of the growing strength of the National Socialist Party in Germany (this was the year in which Hitler became Chancellor—by democratic vote). The very costuming of the fourth movement invited comparison to the familiar brown shirts worn by Nazi soldiers. Nor, for Percival, was this the only point of comparison:

> That pattern on the Hero's chest looks like a distorted swastika. His arm is raised in the Fascist salute—a motif that has occurred throughout the ballet, especially in a sequence for two men who entered goose-stepping for their solo passages ... there is a terrible implication here of how patriotic heroes were to tear Europe apart over the next few years. *Les Présages* means "The Omens," and in 1933, and all through the '30s, the times were ominous. Massine conveyed more than he knew about the times he lived in, and the afterglow of this, clearer to us than to his original audiences, gives the ballet a terrible tragic power.[57]

Likewise, Anna Kisselgoff believed, "*Les Présages* warned of war: Hitler came to power a month before its premiere. It is time to see *Les Présages* in a new light."[58]

LE BEAU DANUBE

Ballet in One Act and Two Scenes
Libretto: Léonide Massine
Music: Johann Strauss (II), orchestrated by Roger Désormière
Set Design: Vladimir Polunin, after Constantin Guys
Costume Design: Etienne de Beaumont
Première: Théâtre de Monte Carlo, April 15, 1933

ORIGINAL CAST

The Father: V. Psota   The Mother: A. Krassnova
The Eldest Daughter: Tatiana Riabouchinska
The Younger Daughters: Mlles Stepanova, Slavinska
The Hussar: Léonide Massine   The Artist: M. Ladré
The Street Dancer: Nina Tarakanova[59]
The Manager: J. Hoyer   The Athlete: E. Borovonsky
Dandies, Seamstresses, Needlewomen, Ladies of the Town, Salesmen

Synopsis

Scene One. The scene is a Viennese public garden of 1860, and a holiday throng begins to gather. The First Hand, a pretty little seamstress, attracts the attention of the Artist, who sketches her portrait. Now the King of the Dandies appears, and the First Hand abandons the Artist for the dashing newcomer.

The Hussar enters with a military stride and joins a family group, paying special attention to the eldest of the three daughters. They dance a mazurka together and stroll out of sight as the manager of a trio of itinerant entertainers enters. With a flourish, he introduces the Street Dancer, who is joined in the middle of her dance by her manager and an Athlete, the latter combining weightlifting with supported adagio.

The Hussar and the Eldest Daughter return from their walk. The Street Dancer recognizes in the handsome Hussar a former lover. She stages a jealous scene, whereupon the Eldest Daughter faints with true Victorian maidenliness and is taken away by her shocked and indignant parents. The Street Dancer, not to be outdone, also collapses into a handy chair. The intrigued bystanders begin to leave, making scornful gestures to the Hussar, who stands still and disdains to answer them.

The Hussar and the Street Dancer are left alone. At the first strains of "The Beautiful Blue Danube," he feels a stirring of old passion and embraces her. They dance together with mounting excitement and speed. They are interrupted by the Eldest Daughter who, revived, surprises the lovers in their embrace and challenges the Street Dancer. Touched by the young girl's courage and devotion, the Hussar repudiates the dancer, who accepts defeat and yields her ground. The girl's parents enter and are angry to find her with the Hussar, but when the two make clear that their love is genuine, the parents bestow their blessing on the young couple.

Scene Two. The park fills again with merry-makers who celebrate the reconciliation. The main characters each reappear for a solo turn, and next the entire ensemble forms a long chain, each holding the person in front. The group snakes around the stage and then whirls in four straight lines as the curtain descends.

Scenery and Costumes

Massine kept the original 1924 setting by Polunin based on a Constantin Guys watercolor. Guys left a memorable pictorial record of the swank Parisian scene during the Second Empire (1852–70) of Napoleon III, and Polunin's cream and sepia aquatint after Guys depicted a high carriage with two gentlemen riding in the park. The military drawings of Guys were also the inspiration for Massine's costume as the Hussar.[60]

Beaumont's delightful ballet costumes were designed in a muted color scheme that ranged from creamy white through beige to brown, with dark green, petunia and burgundy for contrast. When, as a result of litigation, Massine lost the original settings and costumes to Colonel de Basil, the replacement costumes of the Denham company were graceless and unattractive. Danilova recalls the night that she was given a shoddy yellow dress with a brown wig that "was impossible to fix, and I lost it in the middle of my waltz on my first appearance in America! What glamour!"[61]

Le Beau Danube was actually the joint inspiration of Polunin, Beaumont and Guys. Yet, the *Dancing Times* declared, "In spite of the fact that this decor has sprung from the minds of a team of three, one of them separated from the others by several decades, there can be no doubt that it is one of the most successful that Colonel de Basil has yet introduced."[62]

Music

Johann Strauss (II) was the eldest son of a father who was also an internationally famous Viennese composer. In 1844, when he was only nineteen, Strauss gave his first public concert, and his compositions were so successful that they established him as his father's most serious rival. Between 1856 and 1886 he toured Europe and Russia with his orchestra and was acclaimed everywhere as the "king of the waltz." When the growing popularity of the Offenbach *opéras bouffes* in Vienna prompted a craze for native Viennese operettas, Strauss composed *Die Fledermaus* (1874) and *Der Zigunerbaron* (1885), both of which have deservedly claimed a central place in the standard operetta repertory.

Strauss lived in and represented what was, on the surface, a brilliant and prosperous period of the Hapsburg monarchy. The vivacity and elegance of his music mirrored the glitter and *joie de vivre* of nineteenth-century imperial Vienna: "It is music that no longer breathes the air of country inns, city taverns and beer-gardens, as his father's still did, but reflects the hedonistic spirit of Vienna's high society."[63]

Le Beau Danube owed much of its popularity to the music of Strauss. It was uncharacteristic for Massine to turn to such familiar music, because Diaghilev had always conditioned him to look for the esoteric. Massine explained his facile musical choice by saying, "I very much liked the rhythm of the Strauss music. I liked the simplicity.... I felt it to be something that shouldn't be overlooked."[64]

Roger Désormière's orchestration for *Le Beau Danube*, drawn from many Strauss sources, made a judiciously sparing and, therefore, effective use of the waltz. If the "Blue Danube" was a musical cliché, it was at least reserved for the nostalgic pas de deux of the Street Dancer and Hussar. Elsewhere, to avoid the monotony of the waltz rhythm, Désormière turned to Strauss polkas, marches, and mazurkas.

Choreography

Le Beau Danube's narrative is almost entirely conveyed through its dances. The dancing is briefly interrupted for two short dramatic scenes—the Street Dancer's jealousy scene and the reconciliation of the Hussar and the Eldest Daughter. Elsewhere, the episodic plot supports a series of demonstration pieces for the soloists: the King of the Dandies' polka, the Street Dancer's jig, the Hussar and the Eldest Daughter's mazurka, and the Hussar and the Street Dancer's waltz.

Massine avoided straightforward mime to a much greater extent than he had in this work's original version: the gardener dances as he sweeps, the children dance as they skip rope, etc. Years later, Massine underscored the importance he placed upon the complete fusion of dance and mime: "every move and gesture must be treated as choreography. I would hate to see these roles treated realistically."[65]

To build to a balletic climax, Massine created a finale quite similar to that of a traditional Petipa ballet: each of the principals reappears to perform a final solo, and the finale culminates with the entire cast dancing in unison in straight lines across the stage. However, principals in *Le Beau Danube* intermingled with the ensemble to a greater extent in order to enhance the realism of the dramatic action.

Le Beau Danube's logical and uncluttered plot was a key to allowing it to work consistently in terms of dance, but its characters were deceptively complicated. The lovely yet vulgar Street Dancer, the dashing yet vulnerable Hussar, and the docile yet iron-willed Eldest Daughter were discernable both as stock characters and as unique individuals when performed by their original interpreters.

Alexandra Danilova and Léonide Massine as the Street Dancer and the Hussar in *Le Beau Danube*, 1933.

Critical Survey

Le Beau Danube became a staple for both the Denham and de Basil companies. Because it was so easy to understand, *Le Beau Danube* undoubtedly drew spectators who might otherwise have shied away from the ballet. Due to its traditional, uncontroversial nature, critics gave *Le Beau Danube* scant column space, but what remarks they made were almost always positive.

In Retrospect

The Street Dancer was one of Danilova's greatest roles. Passionate and brilliant in the duet that vainly attempts to recapture a love from the past, she then gave touching poignancy to the gestures with which she finally conceded defeat. Likewise, Massine's Hussar was unforgettable, and audiences were entranced with his charisma. On his first entrance, he strode to center stage, his shako supported under his crooked left arm. He clicked his heels briskly and "Then without a glance, without even a turn of the head, he threw the shako in a high arch off into the wings. What assurance, what arrogance, what panache!"[66] And when the Eldest Daughter fainted and the contemptuous crowd spurned him on their exit, in the words of P. W. Manchester,

> It was the tiny gesture that followed when he was finally alone, with only the Street Dancer still in her pretended faint, that makes the picture indelible for anyone who saw him. There was just that slight double wave of the upraised hand, the brushing away of the contempt and the acceptance that possibly he had lost the girl he loved. And then the Street Dancer rushed into his arms and they launched into the famous "Beautiful Blue Danube" waltz.[67]

For decades, *Le Beau Danube* was an ideal closing ballet, but the work lost its sheen over the years. By the 1940s, sans original cast and original décor, *Le Beau Danube* became for Grace Robert "a jewel in an inferior setting."[68] In his review for a 1960 production of *Le Beau Danube*, Richard Buckle went so far as to say, "Without Massine and Danilova the ballet is nothing."[69] A film of the original work from the Massine Film Collection preserves that "slight double wave of the upraised hand" described by Manchester. This tiny gesture unmasks the Hussar's bravado and reveals that he is actually very sensitive and in pain. It conveys a wealth of meaning that neither dance notation nor meticulous coaching can preserve, not only because it is so easy to miss, but also because no one but Massine could quite recapture it.

In 1924, during a Diaghilev-Massine rendezvous, Massine recalls that Diaghilev lambasted *Le Beau Danube* by saying "*Non parlons pas même, c'est de la crotte.*" Yet what this deeply loved ballet lacks in depth and originality is surely atoned for by the spirit of youth, joy and animation which delighted audiences worldwide. In 1971 Massine said, "I think a gay ballet of this kind is necessary, perhaps more now than when it was first created."[70] In its day, *Le Beau Danube* evoked nostalgia for a Vienna that never really existed except in some travelogue dream. In our own time, it evokes nostalgia for a charming ballet genre that really did exist once upon a time and has all but vanished today.

BEACH

Ballet in Two Scenes
Libretto: René Kerdyk
Music: Jean Françaix
Scenic Design: Raoul Dufy, executed by Prince A. Schervachidze
Costume Design: Raoul Dufy and Jeanne Lanvin, executed by Madame Karinska and Jeanne Lanvin
Première: Théâtre de Monte Carlo, April 19, 1933

ORIGINAL CAST
Nereus and The Swimmer: David Lichine
The Rose-White Maid: Irina Baronova
Cupid and The Messenger Boy: Tatiana Riabouchinska
American Sailors: Léonide Massine, Leon Woizikowsky

Synopsis

Nereus, the sea god, is bored to tears. To relieve his ennui, Cupid mischievously shoots a silver arrow which transforms him and his entourage into modern-day bathers at Monte Carlo. Young people parade on the beach, clothed in fantastic and modish beach attire. An oarsman shows off his skill to a crowd of bathing beauties as a splendid rajah and his consort inspect the wares of an obsequious carpet-seller. Into this motley crowd comes the Swimmer, and the heart of every fair bather on the beach is stirred by his splendid physique. They all hurriedly scrawl flattering invitations which are entrusted to Cupid (now transguised as a buttons-in-blue messenger boy). Pretending to be flustered by the ladies' demands for haste, he feigns a stumble and scatters the invitations in all directions. Retrieving them in the wrong order, the messenger boy makes good his escape.

There now arrives upon the scene a beautiful Rose-White Maid. The other ladies grow jealous as the handsome swimmer succumbs to her radiance. The swimmer, suddenly transformed into Nereus, returns to his kingdom with the Rose-White Maid, now a sea-sprite. When the messenger boy returns, he misdelivers his invitations to some American sailors, who are by no means reluctant to comply. The bathing beauties hesitate at first, but cheerfully reconcile themselves to their mates in the end. Twilight falls. The casino sheds its light and music upon the warm evening air.

Scenery and Costumes

Raoul Dufy was a French painter, printmaker and decorative artist. In 1910 Dufy's expressive woodcuts for Guillaume Apollinaire's *Bestiare ou cortège d'Orphée* marked the beginning of his work as a scenic artist. Dufy continued with stage designs for Jean Cocteau's *Le Boeuf sur le toit* in 1920 and *Beach* in 1933.

In the early 1920s, Dufy elaborated the style for which he remains best known: he created a poetic universe of fantastic nautical emblems, naïve sea creatures, and marine paraphernalia. The paintings feature randomly applied colors which are independent of line, creating an impression of verve and dynamism.[71] A series of English regatta paintings in the 1930s continued the theme of stylized nautical forms.

The first backdrop for *Beach*, used in the prologue and epilogue, was dominated by a large white shell, below which lay the kingdom of Nereus. It was bordered above and below with Dufy's ubiquitous marine gear and sea creatures, and the lighting was concentrated mainly on the enormous shell, leaving the dancers below in silhouette. The second backdrop depicted the Monte Carlo coastline. Boats with flags of many different nationalities were set off by the sea-blue background.

Like the 1924 *Le Train Bleu*, *Beach* had costumes by a famous designer and was in part a fashion show for chic summerwear. As the costumes of Coco Chanel had been the *dernier cri* in swim attire for *Le Train Bleu*, so Jeanne Lanvin's trendy swimsuits and evening gowns launched new fashions in 1933.

Music

Jean Françaix was a twenty-year-old protégé whose work was introduced in the salon of the Princesse de Polignac, the foremost musical hostess of Paris in the 1920s. He wrote his masterpiece, Piano Concertino (1932), while he was still a student. In an era when labored, dissonant music was in vogue, Françaix integrated new developments into a fresh, classically reserved and graceful style. For *Beach*, Françaix used a leitmotif for harps to depict the world of Nereus and jazz melodies for trombone in the contemporary beach scene. Ernest Newman complained that the score failed to link the two realms: "the music, that so concertedly accords with the pyjama-dom of the sands, cannot cross the frontier into an abstract world."⁷²

Choreography

Beach was a blend of sports gestures and various dance styles within a basic ballet structure. As the messenger boy, Riabouchinska did a simple tap solo which Massine created with ease, thanks to a year of cranking out dance routines at the Roxy. As the American sailors, Massine and Woizikowsky paired up in a humorous fox-trot to dramatize their neediness to the indifferent bathing beauties. The only purely classical number was the pas de deux of the Rose-White Maid and the Swimmer. All in all, the libretto was too slight to give Massine much material for choreography, and he himself dismissed the ballet as "an amusing trifle."⁷³

Critical Survey

Naturally, *Beach* was favorably reviewed in Monte Carlo since it was expressly designed to pay homage to that principality. Paris and London critics liked its frothy charm, but were generally condescending. *Beach* got its worst reviews in New York because audiences there were so far removed from the mores of Monte Carlo. John Martin wrote, "we do this sort of thing rather better in our musical comedies."⁷⁴

In Retrospect

Beach suffered from the same fault that has been the downfall of many a ballet. Striving to contrive deeper meanings for a jolly romp, Massine and Kerdyk complicated *Beach* by trying to equate the hedonism of Mediterranean gods with that of Monte Carlo's smart set. By 1935 the mythological characters had been omitted. Even so, the work was doomed to speedy extinction for a more important reason. Any production that interprets the latest in high life and fashion, no matter how successfully, runs the risk of dating quickly. G. E. Goodman advised, "Let the devisers of ballet take warning. Contemporary life may provide the material for an amazingly fine ballet, but it will be a ballet for the moment and not for all time."⁷⁵

SCUOLA DI BALLO

Ballet in One Act
Libretto: Léonide Massine after Carlo Goldoni
Music: Luigi Boccherini, orchestrated by Jean Françaix

Set Design: Etienne de Beaumont; executed by Prince A. Schervachidze
Costume Design: Etienne de Beaumont, costumes executed by Madame Karinska
Première: Théâtre de Monte Carlo, April 25, 1933

ORIGINAL CAST

Rigadon, the professor: Leon Woizikowsky
Ridolfo, his friend: Vania Psota
Fabrizio, an impresario: Edouard Borovansky
Count Anselmi: André Eglevsky
Josephina, the favorite pupil: Irina Baronova
Felicita, the bad pupil: Eugenia Delarova
Carlino: Léonide Massine   Philipino: Yurek Shabelevsky
Nicoletto: Marian Ladré
Lucrezia, mother of Rosina: Eleonora Marra
The Notary: Jean Hoyer

Synopsis

As the curtain rises, students are seen taking ballet class in the dancing school of Professor Rigadon. Lucrezia, an ambitious stage mother, arrives with her daughter Rosina and asks Professor Rigadon for an audition. He immediately sees her talent and signs an agent's contract with her mother. After they depart, the impresario Fabrizio enters in quest of a dancing "star." The dancing-master suggests Felicita, his most unpromising student and, by insisting that she is too important an artist to be subjected to an audition, tricks the impresario into signing a contract for her engagement. Josephina, the school's best student, enters and performs a pas de deux with her lover, Count Anselmi.

Later Fabrizio returns and desires Felicita to dance, after all. She performs an abysmally clumsy ballet variation, and the enraged Fabrizio sees that he has been duped. Rosina returns for a lesson and, impressed with her talent, Fabrizio demands a contract with Rosina in place of the ungifted Felicita. Rigadon refuses and kicks Fabrizio out, whereupon Fabrizio summons a notary and three policemen. There is a hearing, and the notary rules that the dancing master must return the commission paid to him by the impresario. As the ballet ends, the students dance mockingly around Rigadon and make their departure, leaving him in solitary misery.

Scenery and Costumes

Etienne de Beaumont's backcloth depicted a spacious Venetian room with two arches and an illuminated stage chandelier hung in the middle of the room. The costumes and wigs were ballet adaptations of eighteenth-century Venetian middle-class dress. Pastels predominated in "a lightsome colour-scheme: primrose, blushing to saffron and, rarely, crimson."[76]

Music

Luigi Boccherini was an Italian composer and cellist during the Viennese classical period of the late eighteenth century. His gifts lay in the direction of chamber music, primarily string quartets and quintets. While his taut, clear music has charm and grace, his essentially lyrical gift and feeling for melodic detail found less scope in more structurally demanding and heavily orchestrated symphonies. Often, a true sense of sustained momentum is lacking in his eighteen symphonies.

Because Boccherini's orchestration tends to sound simple and thin to modern listeners, Jean Françaix thickened the orchestral texture by adding extra notes to the chords. He also purposefully bent Boccherini's music here and there to reinforce the libretto's burlesque touches. The London *Mercury* critic approved this treatment: "The results ... are excellent: the rhythms are given point by interesting block thickening of the orchestration, and the various solo instruments are used with a fine sense of tone-contrast."[77]

Choreography

Part of Massine's genius for characterization lay in his superb musicality. As Newman noted, "once more one is astounded at Mr. Massine's genius for translating music into action. Only the musicians in the audience can fully appreciate what he does in this respect: there are a hundred subtleties in the way of capturing the very essence of a rhythm, of an accent, even of a splash of orchestral colour."[78]

One of the most vital characteristics of the commedia dell'arte style was spontaneity and improvisation. In keeping with a tradition in which the actors had some creative license to shape their parts, Massine placed his dancers in the roles that best suited them and then allowed them to establish their own unique trademarks. When the Ballets Russes danced *Scuola di ballo*, consummate character dancers with quick instincts kept recreating the ballet so that it stayed fresh. The ballet's choreographic highlight—Eugenia Delarova's droll performance as the clumsy pupil, Felicita— is a case in point. Newman wrote that "only a dancer up to all the tricks of the trade could pretend to dance so badly as Mme. Delarova does."[79]

Critical Survey

Scuola di ballo received highly favorable notices throughout Europe and the United States. In London, Newman wrote, "Over all the production there is that sense of 'nothing too much' ... never for a moment does the grotesquerie overshoot the mark."[80] In New York, John Martin concluded that *Scuola di ballo* had "style and taste and lusty good humor.... The story, as usual, doesn't matter, but somehow, in spite of all the bustle and brilliance, it manages to seep through."[81]

In Retrospect

Even though *Scuola di ballo* was well liked by press and public, it was rarely performed once *Les Femmes de bonne humeur* was revived in the late 1930s. If *Scuola* is less memorable than *Les Femmes*, it is primarily because of their librettos. Goldoni gave *Les Femmes de bonne humeur* a delicate subtext which lent pathos to such characters as the Marquise and penetrated the surface frivolity of the main storyline. *Scuola di ballo*'s broad humor gave little scope for the poetical and lacked the deeper implications which gave eloquence to *Les Femmes*.

CHOREARTIUM

Symphonic Ballet in Four Movements
Music: Johannes Brahms, Symphony No. 4 in E minor
Set Design: Constantin Terechkovitch and Eugène Lourié, executed by Elizabeth Polunin
Costume Design: Constantin Terechkovitch and Eugène Lourié
Curtain Design: Georges Annenkoff
Première: Alhambra Theatre, London, October 24, 1933

ORIGINAL CAST
The Ensemble

First Movement
Tamara Toumanova, David Lichine
Lubov Rostova   André Eglevsky

Second Movement
Nina Verchinina

Third Movement
Tatiana Riabouchinska, Leon Woizikowsky
Alexandra Danilova and Roman Jasinski

Fourth Movement
David Lichine, André Eglevsky
Tatiana Riabouchinska, Tamara Toumonova
Leon Woizikowsky   Alexandra Danilova, Nina Tarakanova

Synopsis

Because of its high degree of abstraction, recounting every entrance, exit, solo, trio, pattern, and formation in each of the four movements seems hardly necessary. However, a brief description of the fourth movement passacaglia does provide a sense of how Massine worked with the musical structure. As woodwinds and brass announce the passacaglia's subject with eight strong chords, six male figures in black move swiftly in to form a diagonal. At the opening chord of the first variation, they execute double *tours en l'air* one by one, downstage to upstage. As the second variation begins, Lichine and Eglevsky dance an opposing duo downstage, while the other four males perform patterns in counterpoint in the background. The third variation, an adagio, is danced by Toumanova and the six men. For the fourth, they encircle Toumanova while she performs a dazzling series of *fouettés* and streaks into the wings with *chaînés*, Lichine and Eglevsky exiting after.

As the music slows into a dialogue for strings and woodwinds, Riabouchinska enters and dances with the remaining men. Woizikowsky appears with four women, who pair off with the men. The leading couple perform a pas de deux to the flute passage as the four supporting couples repeat their movements in canon. The leads exit as the music climaxes with a direct restatement of the motif by the brass. The chorus forms in patterns all over the stage as Tarakanova dances in front. Toumanova and Riabouchinska join Tarakanova, and all the women exit with the conclusion of the twenty-third variation.

The men come to the front and form an "x" formation of four squares of four men each. On the first chord, the downstage square performs in unison double *tours en l'air*, followed at each succeeding chord by the three remaining groups. After the fourth group performs this feat, the first, in unison with the last, executes another set of double *tours* on the fifth chord. As these eight dancers land, the remaining eight complete the same step, and on their landing, all sixteen perform double *tours* on the seventh and penultimate chord. The men then greet the female dancers, pairing off for a passage of unison partnering. The leading female soloists enter and dance downstage.

As the final variation begins, the men and women exit to opposite wings. They emerge again to regroup in various patterns and formations. As the last chord unfolds, Lichine jumps onto the shoulders of a group of men as another group lifts Toumanova to face Lichine. Riabouchinska is lifted at a right angle to the pyramid formed by Toumanova. The chorus arranges itself in a serpentine design around the lifted figures. As the stage freezes in this final tableau, the curtain falls.

Scenery and Costumes

Constantin Terechkovitch, Eugène Lourié, and Georges Annenkoff were all Russian painters who were much involved with the Ecole de Paris. The first backdrop of Terechkovitch and Lourié was a vague landscape dominated by a rainbow; the second, a blue curtain gradually turned green by the lighting; the third, an abstraction of fruit and flower blossoms in yellows and beige; and the fourth, architectural slabs of doorways and arches against a light gray background.

G. E. Goodman found Annenkoff's front curtain to be "magnificent ... powerful, urgent and heroic." But he thought the four backcloths too soft-edged and anemic to support the bold, epic sweep of the music and choreography: "Once M. Annenkoff's fine curtain ascends to the flies the decor becomes one series of trifles.... All that remains for the ballet is a wishy-washy rainbow pinned to the realistic literariness of a flat landscape followed by a bare sheet of greenery-bluery." For him, the third backcloth was an improvement because it was "content to strike a mood," but the fourth was "pinned once more to earth" with its realistic slabs of architecture.[82]

As in *Les Présages*, the women's costumes were modeled after classical tunics. The men's costumes consisted of black bolero jackets and tights with low-heeled shoes instead of ballet slippers.

Music

Johannes Brahms, the composer of four symphonies and scores of concertos, songs, piano pieces, and chamber works, was one of the seminal musical figures of the second half of the nineteenth century. More than any other composer of this period, Brahms was responsible for reviving "absolute" music—compositions to be accepted on their own as interplays of sound rather than as programme music. A master of the compositional craft, Brahms often used established techniques such as counterpoint, but in such novel and refreshing ways that the listener first perceives the beauty and strength of the music and only later becomes aware of the composer's techniques.[83]

Brahms' Fourth Symphony was performed for the first time by the Neiningen Orchestra in October 1885. At forty-eight minutes, this quintessential Brahms symphony is formidably drawn out, monumental and agitated. (Stravinsky allegedly quipped that "all the Brahms symphonies sound like a pair of elephants failing to copulate."[84]) The first movement has an autumnal, elegiac quality. Quite early, a strident, "heroic" theme is introduced for contrast. The slow second movement is virtually an orchestral song, the tune of which has a quasi-archaic cadence in the

Phrygian mode. The verses are contrasted with an animated episode which, however, remains subordinate to the song. Musically, the third movement—the *allegro giocoso*—is perhaps the least successful. With its rattling of drums, uproar of trumpets and triangles ringing, its brawny humor serves more as a foil to the other movements.[85]

The Fourth Symphony is a good example of Brahms' genius for tying together a symphony so subtly that technical devices are perceived only subliminally, if at all, by the layperson. The opening eight bars—consisting of a chain of descending thirds followed by one of rising thirds—become the source-theme for the entire symphony. The source-theme is then subjected to numerous variations. Distant as the second-movement *andante moderato* may sound from the first, its Phrygian introduction in itself betrays a connection to the descending-third formula. The *allegro giocoso*'s opening statement seems to be composed of verticalized fragments of the source-theme in retrograde. The opening statement of the finale, combining fragmentary retrograde with modal transposition, is a "distant cousin" of the source-theme; other last-movement variations sound much closer to the source.[86]

The closing movement of the symphony is ranked by many musicians as Brahms' finest achievement. It is a passacaglia, a form which was originally a dance before musicians borrowed it and diverted it from its purpose. For musicians, the passacaglia came to designate a theme that remained unaltered throughout as the basis for contrapuntal invention. For the fourth movement's theme, Brahms went to the concluding chaconne of the Bach Cantata No. 150. This theme is exactly eight bars long and, having first stated it, Brahms proceeds to elaborate it in thirty variations, followed by a coda. There is amazing diversity in the treatment, but its strictness may be judged by the fact that to the end of the twenty-ninth variation there are exactly 240 bars—eight for the theme and eight each for the variations. The thirtieth variation was extended to twelve bars to allow the composer liberty to prepare for the final climax.[87] Brahms' passacaglia was described by Constant Lambert as "grimly intellectual" and "introspective."[88] Yet whatever objections musicians may have raised, Massine did indeed have a prior claim to the fourth movement on the grounds that a passacaglia is a dance. Moreover, Brahms shaped it in strict conformity with the metrics of the classical ballet, which is based on the eight-bar unit.

Choreography

The ballet's title probably derives from "chorea," an ancient Greek ceremonial dance, and "artium," a Latin word for art. This ballet's greatest historical significance lies in the fact that it was an unprecedented attempt to set serious dancing to serious music without reference to theme, era, characterization, plot or realistic set design. By comparison, Fokine's plotless ballet, *Les Sylphides* (1909), was not nearly so radical a departure, because its fairies and woodland setting still retained a traditional association with characters and milieu.

Massine's main objective was to interpret the design of the music—its themes, subjects, repetitions, balancings, tempos, orchestral color, etc.—in the lines, masses and movements of the dancers. As part of this approach, Massine used men for the more heavily orchestrated passages and women for the lighter phrases. His attempt to visualize the music went far beyond the merely coloristic, however, and resulted in an intricate parallel to the musical structure itself. In the passacaglia, Ernest Newman saw that Massine "designated the commanding main theme with six black figures who persist through the whole movement as the ground bass itself persists in the music," and he remarked, "I was more astonished than ever at the way in which Massine has solved most of the exceedingly difficult problems set him by the passacaglia form."[89]

As in *Les Présages*, Massine often used massed groups to approximate the architecture of the symphony itself. His concern with architectural design was even greater in *Choreartium*, however, because he was developing his dancers not as personifications but as structural building blocks for the erection of massed phalanxes, pyramids and friezes. In an effort to fill the entire stage space with maximum movement, Massine experimented with setting his mass constructions in motion. He wanted the spectators to follow formations in the saggital, frontal and transverse planes simultaneously—to look back to front, left and right, and up and down in a total sensing of space. Grace Robert gave a good example: "A great wave of dancers flashes past heralding a group that holds a figure aloft posed in arabesque [Lichine]. It is as though one had witnessed the passage of a god."[90]

As in *Les Présages*, Massine superseded the convention of placing the corps de ballet in symmetrical lines and patterns, and none of *Choreartium*'s dancers could truly be called "corps de ballet." As John Percival pointed out, "one important point about *Choreartium* is that it sets a stiff challenge even to its ensemble dancers, all of whom are picked out for individual attention, sometimes very prominently."[91] Since he jettisoned formal symmetry, Massine's use of the corps de ballet was undeniably more experimental than the Petipa-derived style of George Balanchine.

Once again, Massine used the fluid torso of German modern dance, particularly in the second movement; as in *Les Présages*, his muse for this style was Nina Verchinina. The second movement was, by all accounts, the most striking. A group of women in burgundy-red robes carried the leitmotif of the movement as they limped steadily in a human chain, came to rest in pyramidal patterns and then melted into the background to form an undulating series of tableaux. As the strings began the second theme, Verchinina entered, moving in sharp and stunning contrast to the ensemble, using her torso to suggest grief, despair, determination, and hope. Of her performance in *Choreartium*, P. W. Manchester said, "It was almost like some of the early Martha Graham. But not with that harshness that Graham had. It was always soft. But it was also very strong."[92] For a 1991 revival of *Choreartium*, Anna Kisselgoff perceived that "In the second movement, the woman seems to be weighted down by some terrible sadness. The implacability of the choreography implies that these women have been grieving since the dawn of creation and will continue doing so until the end of time."[93]

Although classical ballet was often fused with modern, unadulterated ballet gave *Choreartium* some of its most exciting moments. Manchester recalled that the audience was astonished when "sixteen male dancers all did double *tours en l'air* in the fourth movement of *Choreartium*. ... Nobody had ever seen that before."[94]

Massine's architectural designs were not uniformly successful. He never really solved the problem of how to build up architecturally on the stage what a composer can build up musically for a symphonic climax. In *Choreartium* one sees dancers running lickety-split to soar into tall pyramids, but the working down can involve some awkward transitions. In his review of a *Choreartium* revival, Richard Buckle noticed that "in attempting a visual equivalent to symphonic grandeur the choreographer tends to reveal his preparations for a big effect and his tidying up after it is over."[95]

Massine may also have tried too hard to tie the four movements of the symphony together. For the Birmingham Royal Ballet's revival, Allen Robertson noted that the four movements had no obvious emotional or stylistic links and that "the finale is most successful when it simply ignores what has gone before and gets on with its own business."[96]

Despite such imperfections, *Choreartium* remains a major milestone in the history of ballet. At the time, Fokine was widely quoted for his dismissal of *Choreartium* as "Wigman sur les pointes." But for Grace Robert, "This protest came rather oddly from one whose revolutionary ideas paved the way for modern dance movements. Ballet is a living art able to absorb the innovations of rebels and experimenters."[97]

Nina Verchinina in the second movement of *Choreartium*, 1933.

Critical Survey

Choreartium incited one of the most heated polemics in dance history. The use of Tchaikovsky for *Les Présages* was less offensive to conservative music critics because Tchaikovsky was already stigmatized as a ballet composer. But when Massine dared to lay hands on a symphony by Brahms—music's "sacred cow"—the offense was unforgivable. What was strange apropos the opposing view was the tone of moral disapproval invoked. It was not *right* to dance to this music. Exactly what made a ballet set to Brahms an act of blasphemy seems quite obscure today. *Choreartium* sent Constant Lambert into a tirade: "'Les Présages,' a brutal murder executed with a chopper, has the faintly forgivable quality of a *crime passionel*. 'Choreartium' is more like one of those premeditated family murders in which ground glass and arsenic do their lethal work over a course of weeks."[98]

Once again, Massine's chief advocate in the controversy was Ernest Newman, who declared, "Let the musicians say what they will ... the public has taken 'Choreartium' so closely to its heart that it is now one of the most popular pieces in the repertory of the Ballet Russe."[99] While Lambert's outrageous attacks were merely witty, Newman wrote some of the most serious and penetrating articles of his career while defending Massine.

The American première of *Choreartium* was postponed for almost two years until October 6, 1935, because of the poor reviews which had greeted the U.S. debut of *Les Présages*. *Choreartium*'s opening at the St. James Theatre, New York, was greeted with lukewarm notices, but it was popular with audiences and got a boost when Leopold Stokowski lent his approval by conducting the first two Philadelphia performances of *Choreartium* on November 12 and 15, 1935. *Choreartium* went to de Basil in the 1937 copyright litigation; it remained a valuable part of his repertoire until the company folded in 1947.

In Retrospect

Massine staged a revival of *Choreartium* for the Teatro Colón, Buenos Aires, in 1955 and again in 1960 for both the Nervi Festival in Italy and for the Ballets Européens in Edinburgh. In 1991 Tatiana Leskova, assisted by Nelly Laport, revived *Choreartium* for the Ballet Repertory Project at the Jacob's Pillow Dance Festival and for the Birmingham Royal Ballet at Covent Garden.

Sixty years later, critics are still divided in their assessment of this ballet. Writing of the Paris Opéra and Birmingham revivals of *Les Présages* and *Choreartium*, Alastair Macaulay decided that both "looked as portentous and ponderous as their opponents had claimed—but also, in comparison with their progeny, remarkably felicitous and well-crafted. They looked, in fact, like the best bad ballets ever made."[100] Anna Kisselgoff, however, was quite impressed with *Choreartium*: "the ballet is certainly a magnificent example of ensemble choreography.... It is a ballet of constant metamorphosis ... a treasure worthy of adorning the repertory of any company."[101] *Choreartium*'s great legacy—the principle that it is artistically permissible to use the work of any composer for dancing—spread, and it is now accepted without question throughout the Western world. The choreography in itself was an epic achievement:

> What can still amaze at the distance of nearly five decades ... is the sheer intellectual grasp which could assimilate and appreciate the complexities of Brahms's monumental score, contain it in the mind entire and project it, digested and transformed, on to the stage.... [Now] Massine is patronised as the purveyor of a few unimportant, if charming trifles; of no serious importance to the ballet scene in this century. Those of us with long memories who can clearly remember the "symphonic" ballets and *Choreartium* in particular, know better.[102]

Union Pacific

Ballet in One Act and Four Scenes
Libretto: Archibald MacLeish
Music: Nicholas Nabokov; based on nineteenth-century folk songs; orchestrated in collaboration with Edward Powell
Set Design: Albert Johnson
Costume Design: Irene Sharaff
Première: Forrest Theatre, Philadelphia, April 6, 1934

ORIGINAL CAST

Surveyor of the Irish Workmen: André Eglevsky
The Lady Gay: Eugenia Delarova
The Surveyor of the Chinese Workmen: David Lichine
The Barman: Léonide Massine
His Assistant: Sono Osato
The Mormon Missionary: V. Valentinov
The Mexican Girl: Tamara Toumanova
The Mexicans: Vania Psota, Edouard Borovansky
The Capitalists: Edouard Borovansky, Jean Hoyer, Vania Psota
The Cameraman: Roland Guérard
Irish Workmen, Chinese Workmen, Girls, Indians

Synopsis

The curtain rises to reveal a drop curtain representing a blueprint of the railroad construction plan. The Surveyor of the Irish Workmen dances a solo and then kneels on the floor, miming a telescope trained on the far horizon.

Scene One. The drop curtain rises to reveal the Irish workers' camp at the railroad east of Promontory Point. The hardy Irish Crew mimes the use of tap hammers as they drive in the spikes. The rails—rigid female dancers in brown sacks—are carried onto the stage to be laid on the tracks. A band of Indians appear, hopping between the rails in tribal fashion, and the blueprint drop descends.

Scene Two. The Chinese Surveyor dances a solo in front of the blueprint, which rises again to reveal the Chinese workers' camp at the railroad west of Promontory Point. (Massine emphasized the change of direction choreographically by presenting the Chinese crew's labors in reverse.) The Chinese workers scurry in and out like ants, performing quick, delicate movements in quasi–Oriental style. The curvaceous Lady Gay strolls out from the Big Tent, an itinerant saloon. She dances provocatively and lures the Chinese Surveyor to the tent as the Chinamen dance in imitation of a locomotor.

Scene Three. The scene is the Big Tent, where workmen and dance-hall girls spend their free time. A Mexican Girl and her two partners perform the Mexican Hat Dance while gamblers mime card playing. A sedate Mormon Missionary enters. He is easily distracted from his temperance mission when the Barman offers him a surreptitious drink. Lady Gay and the Chinese Surveyor arrive, and Lady Gay dances a jig with the Irish men. The Barman dances an eccentric solo, which at first bores and then amuses the customers. Next, Lady Gay and the Chinese Surveyor perform a flirtatious dance. The jealous Irish Surveyor then tries to come between them.

The strained relations that Lady Gay has caused between the two surveyors spreads to their crews. A general brawl breaks out as bottles, chairs, and tables are smashed upon the victims of the warring gangs. The scene ends in chaos.

Scene Four. A crowd has gathered at Promontory Point to celebrate the laying of the last rail, and the rival gangs work feverishly to be first at the meeting point. Two pasteboard engines puff in from opposite directions, bearing high officials in top hats. One official hammers in the golden spike, while the President makes a speech. A telegraph instrument beside the track ticks out the word "D-O-N-E." The Indian braves gaze on in wonderment as the camera man takes a picture of the historic event.

Finale from *Union Pacific* with Yurek Shabelevsky, Irina Baronova, Tamara Toumonova, and Léonide Massine in foreground, 1934.

Scenery and Costumes

Albert Johnson's first scene depicted a daytime workers' camp composed of makeshift dwellings, while the second used a moonlit drop with several white tents of different sizes. The third scene took place inside the Big Tent while the fourth scene was a daytime variation of the second.

The Irish workers, Lady Gay, Missionary and Capitalists were costumed in the period styles of the 1860s. The Chinese crew wore coolie hats; their Surveyor had the fringed buckskins of a frontiersman. As the Barman, Massine donned a ginger wig, white clownface makeup, thick fuzzy eyebrows and a moustache. The scenery and costumes provided a suitable, though unremarkable, background for the "Wild West" atmosphere.

Music

In *Union Pacific*, the themes of popular American music of the 1860s, such as "Pop Goes the Weasel," "Yankee Doodle," and "Oh! Susanna," were assimilated into Nabokov's own modern fantasia. Apparently, the score was not one of Nabokov's better efforts. Constant Lambert damned it with faint praise as "brazen, cheerful, and adequate," while Ernest Newman pronounced it "feeble and tiresome."[103]

Choreography

Only vaguely familiar with America's indigenous dances at first, Massine studied them at their source while on tour in New Orleans and New York. In New Orleans, Massine wrote that when he asked an elderly black man if he knew the cakewalk, "he gave me a broad grin and said nobody had mentioned that dance for years. Then he took off his coat and performed it for me with wonderful rhythm and verve." In New York, Massine went to a Harlem nightclub, where a youngster taught him the strut and the shuffle: "Wearing a brown derby and twirling a stick, he launched into his dance while I sat enthralled, drinking it in."[104] These two dances became the basis for Massine's Barman solo, which invariably stopped the show. The Barman's dance started with very slow jazz movements, emphasizing the shoulders, and ended with a loose-jointed strut around the stage. Intermittently, he sustained the assemblage by serving them drinks, with a few on the side for himself. Within the solo's limited span, Massine was able to create a fully rounded character which rivaled the popularity (though not the artistry) of his roles in *Le Tricorne* and *La Boutique fantasque*:

> At the first night of *Union Pacific* in London ... the audience simply stood and stamped and cheered and screamed until he gave a signal to the conductor and did it all over again. Perhaps the strangest thing of all is that, even as we all carried on like lunatics, I think a great many of us were very well aware that it was not a very good dance, nothing like his farruca or can-can. ... What we were actually doing was singling out this occasion—a première—to thank Massine for all the pleasure he had given us as both dancer and choreographer.[105]

One of the cleverest incidentals in Massine's choreography was the use of dancers to depict the wooden rails. Marlene Dietrich was greatly impressed with *Union Pacific* after seeing the work in Los Angeles and said that she wanted to appear in the production as one of the wooden sleepers. Massine said, "I had no idea she was serious, but in the next city we visited, there was Miss Dietrich at the theatre waiting for us, with several newspaper photographers."[106]

Critical Survey

This première was a critical one because it had been highly publicized as the Ballet Russe's first Americana ballet. Company nerves were doubly taut because right up until the night before the opening, it looked as if the company had a disaster on its hands. But the show went on, and the Philadelphia press reported twenty curtain calls the next morning. Nabokov recalled, "I sat among the public, more dead than alive, expecting a flop. But the applause went on rising, number after number, until Massine's Barman's Dance stopped the show."[107]

Some American critics claimed that despite its American librettist, subject and tunes, *Union Pacific* was an American ballet "à la Massine"— one still firmly rooted in the European tradition. At the time, a very strong nationalist sentiment was growing in the American dance community. There was a feeling of resentment against the Russians and their encroachment on the budding American ballet scene, exemplified in Lincoln Kirstein's comment that *Union Pacific* "was as authentically American as English jazz."[108] When the work was presented in Paris and London, audiences found it difficult to relate to. As Manchester pointed out, "A ballet about whoever built the Firth of Forth wouldn't be of any interest to anybody in America."[109]

Several critics objected to *Union Pacific*'s mixture of choreographic styles. Remarking that Massine might have treated the theme in the stylized constructivist manner of *Le Pas d'acier*, in the romantic-realist manner of Fokine or in the classical manner of a Petipa divertissement, Lambert noted that Massine "combined all three methods, sometimes in the same scene." In the opening, Lambert termed the mechanistic movements of the Irish workmen and the use of human forms for sleepers, rails, hammers and crowbars "a less exciting *Pas d'acier*." But for him, the entrance of the Indians "immediately switched us to the music-hall, and the second scene, with its 'me no likee vellee muchee' Chinamen, kept us there remorselessly." The Big Tent scene was successful for Lambert because it had a "full-blooded theatricality," but he was jarred by the return to constructivist stylization in the finale, especially when the saloon prostitutes mimed the rotary action of giant train wheels in the background:

> Now a ballerina can either pose as a prostitute or as a driving-wheel, but she can't do both in the same ballet.... It is evident that Massine had no very clear idea whether the ballet was going to be stylized or realistic, experimental or safe "theatre," and probably decided that the present-day ballet audience doesn't care a hoot.[110]

In Retrospect

Although *Union Pacific* provided an enjoyable half-hour's entertainment, it was not an artistic success. Like *Union Pacific*, Massine's *Parade* derived from a gutsy, "slice of life" premise—the seedy Sunday circuses of Paris. But its elements were thoroughly digested so that every production element cohered to a uniform style. Not so with *Union Pacific*.

Nevertheless, *Union Pacific* may have been criticized too harshly by those Americans who resented the invasion of the Russian ballet. In fairness, Massine was simply making a sincere attempt to fuse indigenous American dance with his own varied influences and to pay tribute to a country that provided him such eager audiences. Although it was subsequently outclassed by more coherent Americana classics such as Eugene Loring's *Billy the Kid* (1938), Agnes de Mille's *Rodeo* (1942), and Jerome Robbins' *Fancy Free* (1944), Massine set an important precedent for blending ballet with the dances of America.

Jardin Public

Ballet in One Act
Libretto: Vladimir Dukelsky and Léonide Massine; based on a fragment
  of *The Counterfeiters* by André Gide
Music: Vladimir Dukelsky
Set and Costume Design: Jean Lurcat (second version by Alice Halicka)
Première: Auditorium Theatre, Chicago, March 8, 1935

ORIGINAL CAST

The Statue: Roman Jasinski   Old Roué: Roland Guérard
The Poet: Yurek Shabelevsky
The One Who Commits Suicide: Marian Ladré
Old Couple: Pauline Stragova, Serge Bouslov
The Poor Couple: Tamara Toumonova, Léonide Massine
The Rich Couple: Alexandra Danilova, Paul Petrov
The Chair Vendor: Eugenia Delarova
The Vision: Vera Zorina, Roman Jasinski
Sweepers, Nurses, Schoolboys, Workmen

Synopsis

The scene is a public park in the early morning, and a drummer beats the tattoo which signals the opening. The first visitors to appear are the nurses with their charges; after them trails a lecherous roué. The next visitor is a Poet, who has come to ruminate on life's absurdities.

A man bent on suicide enters and hides from the passers-by. Two pairs of lovers next attract us—a Poor Couple and then a Rich Couple, who dance a rumba. A pas de six follows, engaging the two couples, the Suicide and the Poet. The Suicide argues with the Poet over the meaning of life and finally shoots himself.

Next an old couple appear to recall the days of their youth in this very park; gazing at a photograph, they relive in a vision their courtship. As they rise to leave, the old lady drops her handbag, and it is snatched by the poor lover, who empties the money from it and wantonly destroys her faded daguerreotype.

A shabby military orchestra heralds the gaiety of the park by night, and a Chair-Vendor hawks her wares and expresses her annoyance at the bad rhythm of the musicians. Throngs begin to gather. The old roué pursues a pretty nurse, schoolboys romp about, and workmen, together with the Poor Couple, menace the Rich Couple. Meanwhile, the Poor Couple return the stolen handbag to the old lady, spurning the reward which she offers. The workmen drive out the Rich Couple, then return to pay their homage to the poor lovers. The drummer beats the park's closing tattoo, and the Poet, life's keen observer, is thrilled by the spectacle.

Scenery and Costumes

Lurcat's main contribution to the arts was to promote the revival of tapestry in France and its international recognition as an art form. From 1937, he produced a series of outstanding tapestries at the Gobelins and Aubusson and at numerous international exhibitions. In 1935, however, Lurcat was still making the transition from painting to tapestry. The paintings of this period were influenced by Surrealism: his muted landscapes became increasingly nightmarish and desolate.

For *Jardin public*, Lurcat created an extremely somber park setting, composed of jagged human silhouettes and trees in purple hues. Constant Lambert believed that "No ballet in the world could 'get away' with the decor. One need only mention the primary colours of the costumes and coal-tar shades of the scenery."[111]

Music

Vladimir Dukelsky's score for *Jardin public* was unsuccessful. Lambert found it far inferior to Dukelsky's earlier ballet, *Zéphyr et Flore*: "This and the jazz music he has written under the name of Vernon Duke suggest that his talent is *au fond* simple and spontaneous. His new score, however, is very self-conscious." Ernest Newman was harsher: "The absurdity of this method of making discord the *mezza voce*, as it were, of your composition is that you have nothing in reserve for an emotional fortissimo; Dukelsky has tortured and twisted the basic musical speech so thoroughly for nothing more exciting than a dance of nurses or of schoolboys that no extra sophisticating of it is left him for the music of the Suicide."[112]

Choreography

The choreographic highlight of *Jardin public* was the dance of the Poor Couple, performed by Toumanova and Massine. This pas de deux served as the basis for the duet in Massine's 1938 *St. Francis*, in which he was to adopt the movements and even the costume style that he had devised for Toumanova and himself. Another highlight was Delarova's vigorous slapstick comedy scene as the Chair Vendor. Less effective was what one critic called "the ridiculous Rumba"[113] of Danilova and Petrov.

In his memoirs, Massine wrote, "I attempted to portray a series of rapidly contrasted moods and subjects, linked together by the unifying theme of the park."[114] His choreography was a mixture of broad farce (the buxom nurses and the Chair Vendor), philosophical reflection (the Poet), realistic scenes from everyday life (the Rich Couple and the Poor Couple), and a symbolization of the proletariat (the workmen). For the finale, Massine brought all of the characters into a final tableau, endeavoring to unite all the separate strands of the preceding scenes.

Critical Survey

Jardin public had a cool reception when it premièred in Chicago on March 8, 1935. It met with the same fate in New York and London. Newman found it to be a "disturbing mixture of comedy and tragedy and social philosophy." Lambert bluntly called it "a mess," mostly because of its "diffuseness."[115]

In 1936, Dukelsky and Massine reworked score, libretto and choreography, and commissioned Alice Halicka to design new sets and costumes. This version, which premièred in New York in April, remained an obstinate failure. Of the new version, *Dancing Times* wondered, "Exactly why he has taken the trouble to do this one does not know, for it was a poor ballet, always dull, and is no brighter today."[116]

In Retrospect

Massine's intent was to create a socially conscious work, following a trend already established in American modern dance. The contemporary masterpieces of Martha Graham, Anna Sokolow and Hanya Holm— *Heretic*, *Rooms* and *Trend*—also dealt with the theme of social alienation, but these were marked by a profound consistency of style and vision. Lambert wrote, "By all means blend symbolism and realism but don't put undigested slabs of both side by side. In *Jardin public* the process of artistic digestion, so to speak, is incomplete."[117]

What gave force and unity to Gide's novel was the strong feeling of estrangement shared by each of the diverse, yet psychically bonded, park visitors, resulting in the creation of a collective character representing the human condition. In the ballet adaptation, Massine mingled individual and archetype, broad farce and tragedy in an episodic procession of characters who took their turn onstage and were "united" in a contrived finale which was unmotivated by any essential vision which could tie them together convincingly.

SYMPHONIE FANTASTIQUE

Symphonic Ballet in Five Scenes
Music: Hector Berlioz, *Symphonie fantastique*
Libretto: Hector Berlioz
Set Design: Christian Bérard, executed by Prince A. Schervachidze
Costume Design: Christian Bérard, executed by Madame Karinska and Madame Larose
Première: Covent Garden, London, July 24, 1936

ORIGINAL CAST

First Movement

The Young Musician: Léonide Massine
The Beloved: Tamara Toumanova
Gaiety: Alexandra Danilova, Yurek Lazowski
Melancholy: MM. Jasinski, Zoritch, and Ozoline
Reverie: Tatiana Riabouchinska, Female Ensemble
Passion: Male Ensemble

Second Movement

The Beloved and the Musician   Guests

Third Movement

The Old Shepherd: Marc Platov
The Young Shepherd: George Zoritch
The Deer: Alexis Koslov   **The Winds:** MM. Petrov, Guérard, Bouslov
The Beloved and the Musician   Children, Picnickers

Fourth Movement

The Jailer: Yurek Shabelevsky
The Beloved and the Musician
Judges, Executioners, Crowd

Fifth Movement
Monsters: MM. Jasinski, Petrov
Witches: Mlles Danilova, Riabouchinska, Zorina, Toumonova, Verchinina
Ghosts, Spectres, Demons

Synopsis[118]

First Movement. Visions and Passions. A Young Musician, sitting alone in his room, poisons himself with opium in a paroxysm of lovesick despair. The dose he has taken is too weak to cause death but throws him into a state of hallucination. The walls of the room give way, revealing a dim background surmounted by a sphinx. Groups of dancers appear as personifications of the Musician's emotions: Gaiety, Melancholy, Reverie, and Passion. Next, the Beloved glides into the chamber. It is she who has caused the musician's despair, she who takes the form of a melody in his mind, like a fixed idea, which he hears everywhere. He tries to reach her, but she escapes.

Second Movement. The Ball. The scene changes to a ballroom, where the stage is taken by thirteen couples. The Musician arrives and searches for the Beloved amidst the confusion of this brilliant festival. She arrives to the strains of her *idée fixe*, seeming to float among the dancers. He dances with her ecstatically, but in a moment she is gone. Feverishly, he rejoins the crowd of waltzers.

Third Movement. In the Country. The Musician has taken refuge in pastoral surroundings on a summer evening. An old shepherd plays a nostalgic call on his pipe which is answered by a young shepherd. The Musician sits on a fallen shaft, at one with the countryside, yet strangely dreamy and removed. A tranquil band of women and children enter, and playful deer frolic among the classical ruins. As the *idée fixe* is heard, the Beloved flies above the scene. Painful forebodings fill his soul. A storm arises and the Winds, strange beings with wings, suddenly rush across the stage. The storm passes, and one of the girls attracts the young shepherd. The old shepherd plays his call, but the young shepherd does not answer—he has gone off with the maiden. The Musician stands up and gazes sorrowfully into the horizon... sunset... distant rolling of thunder... loneliness... silence.

Fourth Movement The March to the Scaffold. The Musician dreams that he has murdered his Beloved and, condemned to death, is being led to the stake. In a prison courtyard, a crowd enters gossiping and gloating over the punishment that is about to be meted out to him. The Musician is brought on by a sadistic jailer and four executioners. Behind come a phalanx of judges thumping their books of law. The executioners lift the

Tamara Toumonova and Léonide Massine as the Young Musician and the Beloved in the fourth movement of *Symphonie fantastique*, 1936.

prisoner by the arms and legs in opposite directions as if torturing him—first on an imaginary rack and then on an imaginary wheel. Then he is raised waist-high above the struggling throng. At last the *idée fixe* returns, but it is cut short by the death blow. To the rolling of drums, the corpse is tossed aside.

Fifth Movement. The Witches' Sabbath. The Musician dreams that he is in a dark cavern, where witches, ghosts, vampires, and devils have come to celebrate his funeral. The Beloved appears as the chief of all these fiendish creatures. Her melody has now become cheap and vulgar. The writhing body of the Musician is brought on, and the creatures dance around him, some crawling about the ground like an army of ants. The Beloved dances diabolically and leads her attendant fiends in a satanic round of increasing intensity. Amidst the mingled melodies of the *Dies irae* and the orgy, the curtain falls.

Scenery and Costumes

Bérard developed a reputation as a promising young realist painter in Paris during the 1920s. As a stage designer, Bérard was particularly gifted in his ability to create the illusion of endless space on a stage. For instance, the first scene of *Symphonie fantastique* depicts a bare room with only a table and chair, but when the Musician's delirium begins, the walls give way to a stark landscape of a limitless vista dominated by the statue of the Sphinx.

The second-movement ballroom had an imposing Renaissance décor with a backcloth of high red arches opening into a deep blue night and blackamoors holding candelabra between each arch. The deep reds and blues were in stunning contrast to the black and white costumes. The setting even caught the fancy of New York department store window designers, and the women's flowered headdresses also started a fashion.[119]

The third set suggested the Roman *compagna* with its broken columns, ruined aqueduct, and overall sense of brooding, endless space. In the London performances, the Beloved made her brief appearance suspended on wires, in the tradition of the nineteenth-century flying machines. In New York, though, the wires were scrapped because use of the same device in Balanchine's *Orpheus* had provoked gales of laughter from the audience. Instead, the return of the *idée fixe* was indicated only by the agitation of the Musician onstage.

The fourth scene was a prison courtyard. Backlights shining dolefully through prison bars upstage played on the duality of light and shadow. The fifth scene was set in a grim cavern. From a psychological as well as scenic point of view, the fourth and fifth scenes owed much to Honoré Daumier and Pieter Brueghel, respectively.

To contrast the real-life characters with those in the dream world, Bérard costumed the Musician and the Beloved in styles of the romantic era, while the visions wore costumes based on Greek tunics. Only in the waltz did the ensemble costuming replicate that of the Musician and the Beloved. While Bérard's sets were uniformly praised, the costumes were not. John Martin felt that the non-period costumes underplayed the florid, grandiose style of Romanticism and were "anemic," "arbitrary," and an "anachronism." Similarly, Ernest Newman said that the costumes "cut too violently across my Berliozian sensations."[120]

Music

Hector Berlioz was a pioneer in the field of orchestration: by his almost magical manipulation and understanding of individual instruments, he greatly increased the expressive capabilities of the orchestra. Other innovations, such as unorthodox musical structures and meters, superimposition of different rhythms and themes, and offstage use of music helped free composers from restrictive classical forms.

His life presents the archetypal tragic struggle of new ideas for acceptance, and his genius has only come to full recognition in the twentieth century. In Paris, he earned virtually nothing as a composer, received no official teaching appointments, and was compelled to earn a living in a profession which he abhorred—as a music critic.

It was the profound influence of Beethoven that in 1828 prompted the twenty-five-year-old Berlioz to go beyond the genres of opera and cantata and to explore the symphonic form. *Symphonie fantastique* (1830) can be seen as a deliberate attempt to work out literary ideas within the framework of a Beethoven symphony.[121] In its entwinement of music and literature, *Symphonie fantastique* stretched the traditional meaning of the word "symphony" to new limits. It is a five- rather than a four-movement symphony, and it is also an "Episode in an Artist's Life," set out in a detailed programme.

There is no mistaking the artist and the woman as Berlioz and Harriet Smithson. She was an Irish actress performing in Paris when Berlioz first saw her in the role of Juliet. In his memoirs, published in 1870, Berlioz wrote, "I cried out, 'I will marry that woman! and I will write my greatest symphony on that play!' I did both."[122] Berlioz pursued Smithson in vain from 1827 to 1829 until his swelling passion and frustration broke out in the *Symphonie fantastique*.[123] He composed it "furiously," his mind "boiling over." His symphony was to have "fire and tears within."[124]

The recurring *idée fixe* is the musical portrait of the courted actress. It appears in the guise of a flute solo at the end of the first movement's slow introduction. In the second movement, a fragment of the *idée fixe* is reshaped in the central section of the waltz. In the third movement, with its distant instrumentation, the return of the *idée fixe* portrays the loneliness of the artist. At the end of the fourth movement, the *idée fixe* is cut short by the executioner's blow. In the last movement, it becomes a symbol for the destruction of love as it degenerates into a music-hall tune played by a shrill clarinet.

Berlioz did not shrink from direct imitation. It is obvious that the play of English horn and offstage oboe is to represent two shepherds carrying on a dialogue and that the timpani are "distant sounds of thunder." One can hear, at the end of the *Marche au supplice*, the slam of the guillotine and the thump of a head falling into a basket: "We need not be embarrassed by these discoveries, for the effects are there to be discovered—conspiratorial winks of composer to listener."[125]

The guns were spiked for foes of the symphonic ballets, since Berlioz himself penned the scenario and had it distributed to nineteenth-century concert audiences so they might better understand the music. Moreover, a part of this symphony was actually assembled from theatrical sources. "The March to the Scaffold" is taken from Berlioz's opera *Les Francs-juges* (1826), and the "Witches' Sabbath" and portions of the second and third movements were derived from his ballet, *Faust* (1829).[126]

Choreography

Massine based his ballet on Berlioz's programme, although he created some illustrative details of his own at points where the action was thin (notably in the third scene). In accordance with the programme, Massine treated each movement of the symphony as though it were a separate ballet. Only the characters of the Musician and the Beloved, with the *idée fixe*, give continuity to the five scenes.

For the first movement, Massine wrote that he wanted to translate the Musician's emotions into "abstract ensemble movements."[127] Yet this "abstract" translation took the form of fairly obvious personification in the groups of dancers representing Gaiety, Melancholy, Reverie, and Passion. As Martin noted, the movements "are dictated by surface symbolism and lack markedly the romantic eloquence of the composer's material."[128] In his diaries, Lionel Bradley sensed that the first movement's architectural formations "hardly arise sufficiently from the flow of the dancing.... But perhaps the music moves, changes too often for anything else to be possible."[129]

The second movement captured the unreal glitter of the ballroom scene, matching the febrile whirling of the music to the mad waltzing of the corps de ballet. Using counterpoint and simultaneity, Massine gave each couple different steps and tempos within the same musical phrase. This served to enhance the ecstasy, dizziness and inner turmoil of the protagonist.

The third scene was the unlikely triumph of the ballet. The almost insuperable difficulty of interpreting this slow, contemplative music choreographically may explain why *Symphonie fantastique* was not treated in ballet form long before. Nor can the third movement be edited for the stage, because this long reflective adagio provides essential musical balance and relief between the dizzying waltz and the harshly realistic "March to the Scaffold." To this contemplative and mostly unkinetic pastorale, Massine somehow managed to realize a rustic dream world. For Grace Robert, the scene's "mesmerizing charm" lay in the way that Massine, "scarcely moving, managed to convey that all these events and people [the storm, the deer, the shepherds, and children] had no existence except as he thought of them—a miracle of theatrical projection."[130] Arnold Haskell deemed the third movement "the high-water mark of Massine's career,"[131] and Newman called it "as convincing a demonstration of his genius as he has ever given us."[132]

Though not so challenging, the fourth movement was nearly as successful. The inquisition, the imagery of the rack, the execution on a "gallows" of human forms were a rapid-fire series of chilling and vivid incidents, brilliantly conceived and imaginatively grouped. Particularly effective were the judges, moving in small staccato beats and thumping their law books in a parody on justice.

Like the first movement, the fifth movement was problematic. To be sure, it had memorable imagery, particularly the chilling illusion of four crosses at the corners of the stage: each "cross" was composed of two diabolical monks standing back to back, the one in front with arms overhead and the other with arms to the sides. Massine's difficulties arose from the fact that the fifth movement is the most inventive of the five orchestrally. At points, he found convincing visual parallels for the bizarre orchestration, as when he matched the lacerating sound of violins struck with the wooden backs of the bows to the slithering, squirming bodies of ghouls. In other places, Massine was less successful. Citing the preamble, where Berlioz set the woodwind line in octaves high above a "grisly chord" for bassoons and deep brass, Newman believed that the gnomes that crept onstage "have nothing, can have nothing, of the suggestion of horror that is in the music itself." At times, he concluded, "nothing that the choreographer can put before the eye can be anything but the faintest shadow of what Berlioz makes us visualize, so to speak, through the ear."[133]

Critical Survey

Symphonie fantastique was hailed at its première as one of the great modern ballets, even by the symphonic ballet's most trenchant foes. Constant Lambert, for instance, praised Massine for tackling an "impossible task" in his solution to the pastorale scene.[134] Describing this work as "the most complex production ever known to choreography," Haskell believed that Massine was "fully successful."[135] Russell Rhodes dubbed *Symphonie fantastique* Massine's "finest work as a choreographer."[136]

Symphonie fantastique received its North American première in New York on October 29, 1936. John Martin rather grudgingly judged *Symphonie fantastique* Massine's "most effective adventure in the turning of orchestral works into stage spectacles." But he felt that Massine "underplayed the tremendous emotionalism of these hectic days of the Romantic Revolution. He could have been more florid, more grandiose."[137]

In Retrospect

When Massine left the de Basil company, the Colonel won exclusive performance rights to *Symphonie fantastique* in the complicated copyright case of 1937. It would undoubtedly have become a popular favorite in the United States, but it was rarely seen here because of de Basil's extended overseas tours. De Basil continued to present this ballet right up until the company's last season in 1947. By this time, the ballet had suffered considerable attrition. P. W. Manchester said that by 1947 "there were sprinkled through the corps de ballet half a dozen who knew the ballet and the rest just followed."[138] In 1948, however, Massine staged two fine revivals for the Teatro Colón in Buenos Aires and for the Royal Danish Ballet.

Of all the symphonic ballets, *Symphonie fantastique* won, by far, the highest critical acclaim. Since *Les Présages* and *Choreartium* have both been given rave reviews in the recent Paris Opéra and Birmingham Royal Ballet revivals, it seems time for a fresh revival of the symphonic ballet that was deemed the best of them all.

6

August 1936–May 1939

By 1936 the professional relationship between de Basil and Massine had seriously deteriorated. The first quarrel began in 1933, when the two jointly acquired from Ray Goetz most of the scenery, costumes and props in the Diaghilev storehouse. However, in May 1934, a Ballet Russe press release asserted that de Basil was sole owner and proprietor of these assets. Massine took legal action and after months of litigation, de Basil agreed to purchase Massine's portion of the properties.[1]

Massine was also resentful that de Basil denied him the title of artistic director when he had undoubtedly earned the right to something more prestigious than his official title as ballet master. In the previous year, René Blum had severed his association with de Basil to form his own company, the Ballets de Monte Carlo. In March 1936 Massine secretly explored the possibility of leaving de Basil and joining forces with Blum.

The following year would mark Massine's definitive break with de Basil, culminating in an internationally publicized copyright case. Now determined to establish sole ownership of his ballets, he filed suit against de Basil when the Ballet Russe returned to London in the summer of 1937. Massine claimed to be the owner of the copyright in seventeen of his ballets that had been presented by Ballet Russe de Monte Carlo and sought a restraining order to prevent de Basil from presenting them.

When Massine and de Basil first became associated in 1932, it was admitted that Massine was the owner of the copyright in eight of these ballets. The remaining nine had not yet been brought into existence.

Between 1932 and 1934 Massine's contract with de Basil was rather vaguely defined in two letters, but after 1934 he was under a very detailed and specific contract. Judge Luxmoore, who tried the case, only dealt in detail with the last agreement of August 1934.

As the "author" of these seventeen ballets, Massine asserted that he could claim them under the provisions of the Copyright Act of 1911. Colonel de Basil's attorney, Mr. Henn Collins, K.C., countered that Massine was employed by the Colonel as a choreographer and that he was paid a salary to cover these services. He was therefore under a "contract of service" to de Basil within the meaning of Section Five of the 1911 Copyright Act, so the ballets rightfully belonged to de Basil. Sir Patrick Hastings, Massine's attorney, rebutted that an agreement could only be a "contract of service" if the employer was entitled to control the form and content of the work, and that the creative act of choreography could not be so controlled. He stated that a famous choreographer "would be fiercely indignant at being called a servant."[2]

To Massine's dismay, Judge Luxmoore's ruling centered on the commercial relationship between the antagonists. He did agree that it might theoretically be possible to claim copyright in choreography, especially when he learned that a ballet's succession of steps are usually notated. But he was not fully convinced in the last analysis, and he stated that any language pertaining to the copyright of choreography was *dicta*—loosely defined as an expression of the opinion of the court which is not necessary to support the reasoning of the actual ruling.[3]

Judge Luxmoore pointed out that a ballet is a composite entity comprising music, libretto, scenery and costumes, as well as choreography, and he doubted whether there could be copyright in the mere choreography divorced from these other elements. He held that the agreement between Massine and the Colonel was indeed a "contract of service" whether the employer could directly control the artistic work or not. Accordingly, in what would be considered a travesty of justice today, Luxmoore awarded the copyright of all nine ballets composed subsequent to January 1932 to Colonel de Basil.

Dealing with the eight pre–1932 ballets, Luxmoore said that it was admitted that in January 1932, the copyright in all of them was in the name of M. Massine. However, the contract of August 10, 1934 gave de Basil the option to buy Massine's rights to his ballets. Four of the pre–1932 ballets were presented before the agreement of 1934 and four afterwards. His Lordship denied de Basil the rights to the four presented prior to 1934, but he was free to exercise his right of purchasing the remaining four.[4]

Massine took his case to the Court of Appeals on February 22, 1938. Lord Justice Greer stated that he had "read Judge Luxmoore's judgment and agreed with every word of it." The appeal was dismissed.[5] It was not until the Copyright Revision Act of 1976 that choreography was expressly included in the subject matter protected by United States copyright legislation. P. W. Manchester stated, "It's really the difference between legal justice and moral right.... Like making sparkplugs—you don't own them if you are paid to make them."[6]

Massine now took decisive steps to negotiate the reorganizing of Rene Blum's Ballets de Monte Carlo with American financing. The necessary capital had already been found in the person of Cincinnati businessman Julius Fleischmann, heir to a family fortune from the Fleischmann Company, a yeast manufacturer. Fleischmann donated $250,000 to the new ballet's sponsoring company, Universal Art. On November 19, 1937, Blum sold the Ballets de Monte Carlo to Universal Art for $40,800.[7] Under the new arrangements, Fleischmann was to be president of the board, Blum the director of the Monte Carlo season only, and Massine the year-round artistic director of the company. A Russian-born banker who had changed his name to Serge Denham was appointed vice-president. Sol Hurok announced that as of March 1938, he would abandon further management of de Basil's company and become the American manager of Massine's.

There was a widespread feeling that to run two major Russian ballet companies in competition, splitting the repertoire and leading dancers, would be disastrous for all concerned. Massine was obviously unswayed, for he spent the fall of 1937 gathering a distinguished roster of dancers, many of them defectors from the de Basil company. Léonide gave his last performance with de Basil's troupe in January 1938 and returned to Europe. On February 10 Massine's new company began rehearsals in Monte Carlo for its spring debut. He had a company of experienced professionals, but one which had been gathered from a number of sources and which was not yet an artistic unit. Arnold Haskell predicted, "Massine's departure will not only damage the company as a whole, but Massine himself perhaps even more. It has taken all of five years' hard work and sacrifice to build up his magnificent ensemble.... It would take more than five years ... to create another such."[8]

In March there was a surprise development—a scheme to bury the hatchet and merge the Massine and de Basil companies. Hurok saw a chance to manage the largest and finest company the world had ever seen. (He had also hatched a plan to oust de Basil in the merger's process.[9]) John Martin spread the joyous tidings: "Congratulations are in order more or less all around over the healing of the breach in the Ballet Russe. ... With the signing of a treaty of peace last week, there comes into being an enormous new-old company with 110 productions in its repertoire, eighty dancers on its roster, and considerable American money to pay its bills."[10] "The Sitter Out" was staggered by the company-to-be's enormous pooled resources: "In fact," he mused, "it almost seems too good to be true."[11] He was quite right.

After lengthy debates, a verbal agreement with de Basil was reached in New York at the St. Regis Hotel. Afterwards, de Basil, whose English was quite poor, returned to Europe. From Europe, he cabled a power of attorney, who signed an agreement with Hurok and Denham on April 15, 1938. When he received a copy of the contract, de Basil burst into tears because it was so different from what he had understood.

What the contract contained was his agreement "to assign a contract to Universal Art which he claimed to have with the Covent Garden Theatre, London, which would have assured Universal Art of twelve-week performances for four years at a guaranteed payment." He relinquished in perpetuity the right to use the name "Ballet Russe." He agreed "that Universal Art might use for five years 125 ballets he owned upon payment of royalties."[12] On June 8, de Basil wrote a letter repudiating the contract, claiming that if he had known what the contract contained he would not have allowed it to be signed in his behalf. Any prayer for the merger of the two companies had now vanished: de Basil was not to be put out to pasture so easily.

In late June, the impassioned "Ballet War" hit London with a bang. De Basil's group, which temporarily rejoiced in the name of "Educational Ballets, Ltd.," and Massine's Ballet Russe de Monte Carlo had rival, concurrent seasons at Covent Garden and the Drury Lane, respectively. Balletomanes eager to see both groups found ways to cope: "It was at this period that a determined balletomane could see a couple of ballets at Drury Lane, and run like the wind to Covent Garden (passing a lot of his fellows performing the same exercise in reverse) and catch the last ballet there, and thus see almost every great dancer in the Western world on the same evening."[13] By 1939 the de Basil company would be renamed "Original Ballet Russe" and Massine's, the "One and Only Ballet Russe de Monte Carlo." The Original remained for most of the war in Latin America; the Monte Carlo settled down in the United States.

Of Massine's four new ballets, the first to première was *Gâité parisienne*. Etienne de Beaumont set the ballet at Tortoni's, a fashionable Parisian café of the Second Empire, and styled it after the contemporary court-and-society portrait painter, Franz Xavier Winterhalter. The

Second Empire—the period of Napoleon III—was also the period of Jacques Offenbach, whose music instantly evokes this era. Beaumont had obtained from Offenbach's nephew the manuscript scores of 105 operettas. From these, Beaumont and Massine finally chose enough music to last for about half an hour. *Gaîté parisienne*'s successful premières in Europe and New York gave the new company a powerful launch.

The theme of the second new ballet, *Seventh Symphony*, was nothing less than the creation and destruction of the world. Massine's ballet was not the first to take on this theme: Milhaud's *La Création du Monde* was choreographed by Jean Borlin in 1923 for the Ballet Suédois, and the same score was used by Ninette de Valois in a new version for the Vic-Wells Ballet in 1931. But Massine's *Seventh Symphony* was to be entirely different in its approach to the subject, involving a mixture of Greek mythology and the Bible. It also had a score of epic dimensions by Beethoven, causing Massine to acknowledge that "this was going to be a much more difficult task than my previous symphonic ballets."[14]

St. Francis was an ideal collaboration between composer and choreographer. Paul Hindemith's score for *St. Francis* was originally commissioned by Diaghilev, but the latter died before Hindemith had finished it.[15] A libretto for the unfinished score was worked out jointly after Hindemith suggested the subject during a chance meeting with Massine in Florence. For the next few months, Massine read everything he could find about St. Francis. Once he was certain that many episodes in the saint's life lent themselves to dramatic treatment, Massine and Hindemith worked in close unison—step by step, bar by bar. When rehearsals began in Monte Carlo, Hindemith joined the company. In a letter to Ernest R. Voigt he wrote, "We set quite a lot on its feet in Monte Carlo … and it promises to be gorgeous."[16] The ballet premièred in London with the title of *Nobilissima Visione*, but for the New York debut, it was retitled *St. Francis*.

Bogatyri was the last new Massine ballet to première. The Bogatyri were half-legendary, half-historic figures of the early Middle Ages who were the loyal servants of St. Vladimir (c. 956–1015), the first Christian ruler of Russia. Massine's libretto revolved around the Bogatyri legend about the abduction of Prince Vladimir's daughter by a snake-dragon and her rescue by the nobleman Dobryna Nikitisch.

Before Massine's new company left Europe for the United States, Massine finally divorced Eugenia Delarova. He wrote tersely that "It had for some time been apparent, both to Eugenia and to me, that because of our conflicting temperaments and the demands of our careers, our marriage was not a success."[17] Despite the breakup, Delarova continued to dance with the company for the next two years.

Following a six-week tour of Great Britain, Massine's Ballet Russe de Monte Carlo opened its inaugural American season at the Metropolitan in October of 1938. They were loved by the general public, but some critics were quite hostile. *Dance Observer*, for instance, found the repertoire to be irresponsibly escapist: "Today, world affairs, contemporary reality, the daily headlines are the subject matter which engross attention ... if it continues to devote itself to unreality, presented in a frivolous spirit and with no saving grace of technical excellence, we shall keep on saying what this review began with, 'The ballet is dead.'"[18] *The Daily Worker*, a Socialist paper, struck a similar note in its own review:

> All the audience gets is sugary anecdotes about princess loves pauper, warrior gets girl, brave Prince slays Ogre, man loves doll, bohemian life is the gay life, we'll die for good King Gargoyle, etc. from all and sundry of these settings.... Fortunately, the productions of such companies as the Jooss Ballet, the American Ballet, the Ballet Caravan and the Philadelphia Ballet give us reason to believe that the dance art still lives, and can contribute much to our cultural life.[19]

A major source of American resentment towards Massine's troupe was Julius Fleischmann's tremendous philanthropy to a foreign company. American companies were burning because it was so difficult to compete. Another thorn in their sides was the fact that major American companies all belonged to the American Guild of Musical Artists (AGMA), while the Ballet Russe did not have to pay union wages. AGMA was steadily pushing up union wages to the point where companies like Lincoln Kirstein's Ballet Caravan were having to cancel tours.[20]

Despite these objections, the general American public flocked to see the glamorous Ballet Russe de Monte Carlo and read eagerly of its endless backstage intrigues. Beyond his purely artistic duties, Massine had to deal with diva distemper on a daily basis. *Collier's* noted, "He has a weeping ballerina on his hands virtually every hour on the hour, and they weep in all languages and for any number of reasons."[21]

Massine's most sensational personnel problems occurred during the first season at the Metropolitan in October 1938. When the cast list went up, Toumanova was livid to discover that Alicia Markova, not she, was slated to dance Odette on *Swan Lake*'s opening night. By several newspaper accounts, Toumanova's father took revenge by storming backstage on opening night and landing a swarthy Russian fist on Massine's jaw. Massine responded by replacing Toumanova with Nathalie Krassovska as Odette Number Two. Krassovska and Massine rehearsed for two days and nights without sleep because "a sulking ballerina had to be taught a lesson."[22]

6. August 1936–May 1939

However, none of the tantrums of Massine's ballerinas could even remotely rival those of his premier danseur, Serge Lifar. By 1938 Lifar already had a worldwide reputation for being difficult—three years earlier, he had been temporarily suspended from the Paris Opéra for refusing to appear in a performance at which the President of France was present. He explained that he could not dance that night because he did not like the backdrop curtain for his variation.[23] During the 1938 Drury Lane season, Massine cast Lifar as Albrecht opposite Markova in the title role of *Giselle*. Leo Kersley recalled that "it came to blows in the gallery, since the Markova factions told the Lifar factions they wished Lifar would not carry on as if he thought the ballet ought to have been retitled 'Albrecht.' Lifar even went so far as to raise his head from Giselle's lifeless bosom, acknowledge applause, and return to his previous prostrate position, and he was booed with enthusiasm at curtain fall."[24] Lifar's conduct made the columns all the way across the Atlantic: the *New York Herald Tribune* reported, "Miss Markova, beloved by the Londoners, received twenty-four curtain calls, all of which M. Lifar insisted upon sharing. The English audience and the London press were quick to express their disapproval."[25] When the time came for *Giselle*'s New York première, a jealous Lifar demanded that Markova be replaced when he learned that he had been teamed up with her again. Sol Hurok said "no."

Furious with Markova's success and his own poor reviews for opening night, it is highly likely that Lifar took his revenge by deliberately dropping Markova from a lift "suddenly onto her delicately pointed toe. ... She was carried offstage and into an ambulance, to lie in bed with her foot in a plaster cast for the next three weeks."[26] In an interview for *Collier's*, Massine can only have been alluding to Lifar when he related the same tale: "A male dancer, jealous of his partner's success, threatens to drop her on the stage. And carries out his threat on the second night—cleverly, so that the audience never knows, but effectively ... and a wrenched foot keeps one of the company's three primas off the program for weeks."[27]

Lifar's final scrape with Hurok and Massine took place before his performance as Prince Siegfried in the company's second performance of *Swan Lake*. The *New York Herald Tribune* gave this account: "Before going on, Mr. Hurok said, M. Lifar came to him and demanded that a technical variation, danced by an American, Roland Guérard, and enthusiastically applauded, be eliminated. Mr. Hurok refused to delete it. So did M. Massine." Lifar retaliated by challenging Massine to a duel at dawn the next morning in the sheep meadow of Central Park. Massine responded, "Go take an aspirin, Serge." Lifar reacted to Massine's refusal to settle the dispute in the gallant tradition of pistols for two and coffee for one by threatening to quit. According to the *Tribune*, Sol Hurok replied, "The Champlain leaves for Paris on Saturday. Why don't you take it if you can't get along here?" Lifar sailed for Paris on October 22, 1938.[28]

Due partly to reams of publicity, the first American tour was a financial success. When the company returned to Europe, Massine married his third wife, Tatiana Orlova, in March 1939. Tatiana had joined the company in 1938 and met Léonide when she took some Spanish dance classes Massine was teaching at Egorova's studio in Paris.

The Monte Carlo spring season introduced two new works by Massine: *Capriccio espagnol* and *L'Etrange farandole*, later retitled *Rouge et noir*. *Capriccio* was conceived when Massine invited the great Spanish dancer and choreographer Argentinita to dance in a revival of *Le Tricorne* that he was staging in the summer of 1938. When Argentinita taught him such Spanish dances as the buleria, seguidilla and manchega, the zeal which had resulted in *Le Tricorne* was rekindled in Massine. He constructed the formal outline for a new Spanish ballet and collaborated with Argentinita on the choreography. She herself danced the Gypsy Girl at the ballet's first presentations in Monte Carlo and again in a single appearance on April 1, 1940, at the Metropolitan.

Massine's concept for *Rouge et noir* took definite form in 1938 when he visited the studio of Henri Matisse and was shown Matisse's current project, a series of painted panels. Massine noticed an affinity between the panels and his own work-in-progress to Shostakovich's First Symphony, which he visualized as a vast mural in motion. Matisse suggested that Shostakovich's music could be interpreted in five colors: white, black, blue, yellow and red. Massine decided that these same colors could correspond not only to the music but also to the ballet's theme, which was to be the conflict between the spiritual and the material world.

GAITE PARISIENNE

Ballet in One Act
Libretto: Count Etienne de Beaumont
Music: Jacques Offenbach; orchestrated by Manuel Rosenthal with the collaboration of Jacques Brindejonc-Offenbach
Set, Costume and Property Design: Count Etienne de Beaumont
Première: Théâtre de Monte Carlo, April 5, 1938

ORIGINAL CAST

Glove Seller: Nina Tarakanova[29]	**Flower Girl:** Eugenia Delarova
La Lionne: Lubov Rostova	**The Baron:** Frederic Franklin

The Duke: Casimir Kokitch   **The Peruvian:** Léonide Massine
Tortoni and Dance Master: Robert Irwin
Waiters, *Cocodettes*, Cancan Girls, Billiard-players, Dandies, Soldiers

Synposis

The setting is an elegant café of the Second Empire. Waiters tidy up the tables and take time off to join in a lively dance with the scrubwomen. Then a group of billiard players enter in company with several *cocodettes* (girls of easy virtue). An attractive Flower Girl and a fascinating Glove Seller enter and arrange their merchandise.

Next arrives a boisterous Peruvian, carrying two traveling bags full of riches. On the town, he is looking for conquests and is enthralled by the beauty of the Glove Seller. He goes to try on a pair of gloves, and the *cocodettes* seize this opportunity to run off with his bags. He chases frantically after them.

There now appears a young Austrian Baron whose friends have sung the praises of this fascinating vendor of gloves. The Baron falls head-over-heels in love with her, but his rapture is interrupted by the music of a march. Soldiers file in, led by a dashing officer. The remaining *cocodettes* flirt with the soldiers, who do an ultra-military strut for their benefit. La Lionne, gorgeously dressed in red and escorted by the Duke, makes an impressive entrance, and she lures the Officer from his dalliance with the Glove Seller. The Flower Girl, after making sporadic efforts to attract a man for the evening, tries her wiles on the Baron—a wasted effort.

At this point, the passions which have been gathering in the café boil over. The Peruvian, his bags recovered, has not forgotten the Glove Seller. When he tries to arrange a rendezvous with her, he becomes embroiled with the Baron. The Duke and the Officer start fighting over La Lionne, who plays one against the other. The scandal spreads, and blows are exchanged by everyone. The waiters drive the patrons out, leaving the café empty. In this deserted room, the Glove Seller and the Baron return and dance a romantic pas de deux. But the room is not deserted for long: a burst of clamorous music heralds the arrival of the cancan girls, and the patrons return.

Dawn approaches; the guests must leave. The soldiers pair off with the cancan girls, La Lionne leaves with the Officer, the Flower Girl exits with the Duke, and the Peruvian appears to make one last try for a rendezvous with the Glove Seller. He sees her in the arms of the Baron, and as the lovers wave him an ironic farewell, the Peruvian drops his bags in defeat and falls into a limp pose in the darkening cafe.

Scenery and Costumes

Beaumont's set for *Gaîté parisienne* was exactly what one would expect, but charming nonetheless. Though by no means pedantically accurate, the settings and costumes suggested the Second Empire. The cafe was dressed in creamy pastel colors to offset the loud stripes and multicolored petticoats of the cancan girls.

Music

The score, arranged and orchestrated by Manuel Rosenthal, is undoubtedly this ballet's greatest strength. For the most part, Rosenthal's score was tailored skillfully from bits and pieces of Offenbach's operettas, and all of the chosen music was supremely danceable. Robert Lawrence found Rosenthal's adaptation to be "Fresh, tuneful, and sophisticated," and the London *Times* called the arrangement "some of the most amusing and effective 'light music' ever composed."[30]

In 1855, Jacques Offenbach formed his own company, the Théâtre des Bouffes-parisiens. His *Orphée aux enfers* (1858), *La belle Hélène* (1864), *La vie parisienne* (1866), and *La Perichole* (1868) remain outstanding examples of the operetta genre. Offenbach's wit, his acute sense of social foibles and his hatred of pretentiousness were endemic in all of his operettas.

The *galop infernale* which concludes *Orphée aux enfers* is the famous cancan used as the main climax of Massine's ballet. Musically, it is in two-four meter with a fast, nonstop "oom-pah-pah" rhythm in the bass, and phrase endings usually have only a half-beat of repose. While this alone has a dizzying effect, the galop also goes on for a long time in relation to its own speed. The result is "a sensation of breathless, unremitting, mounting energy, with a pounding beat that frequently has the audience clapping and stamping in time to the music."[31]

For almost a century, the lack of a recognized international operetta tradition meant that revivals of Offenbach's operettas were infrequent. The best tunes, however, regained their lost popularity when used in *Gaîté parisienne*. More recently, the greater attention paid to the classical operetta since World War II has also made the best of Offenbach's complete operettas familiar again. Sacheverell Sitwell noted that Offenbach was able to produce "success after success with ease and assurance. This is not to suggest that the genius of Offenbach, for a genius he was within his limits, is ever of the first order; but Offenbach is one of those lesser men ... through whom more frequent delight is to be obtained than from their more austere betters."[32]

Choreography

Only a slender thread of a plot holds together the unrelated musical bits that comprise the ballet's score. Structurally speaking, *Gaîté parisienne* is essentially a string of entrées rather than an organic composition, but Massine used the divertissement form advantageously: he gave the audience a variety of ensemble sizes, pacing, and dynamics while simultaneously relating a narrative. This in itself is a task requiring masterful craftsmanship.

The work begins with an octet for four waiters and four scrubwomen, followed by the entrance of the Flower Girl. This is followed by three pas de trois for three billiard players and six *cocodettes* and two solos for the Glove Seller and the Peruvian. By the time that the Baron, seven soldiers, five dandies, and twelve cancan girls have entered, Massine has filled the stage with fifty dancers.

Massine's stage picture was not only well paced and dynamic in its general sweep, but it also provided vivid thumbnail sketches of every personality onstage. For instance, the affected waiters reveal their true dearth of social polish when they make the café brawl even worse by gleefully dumping buckets of water on the combatants; when they suddenly assume an air of genteel refinement as they expel the Peruvian with white handkerchiefs, their prissiness is all the funnier. Often the principal dancers are defined less by their solos than by witty stage action on the sidelines. For example, the sharp observer can bypass the main action and notice that the common Flower Girl prolongs the life of her flowers by spitting surreptitiously into the bouquets.

Massine provided himself with one of the wittiest roles of his career as the Peruvian. In his boundless zeal to conquer Paris, the Peruvian was absurd yet sympathetic. Conveying his idiosyncrasies required Chaplinesque precision, for Massine made his variations so detailed that almost every note of the music was described with a step. No less Chaplinesque was the Peruvian's conviction of his own poetic nature and irresistible sex appeal. The contrast between belief and actuality in this characterization gave it a touch of poignancy.

The chief flaw of the choreography was put succinctly by P. W. Manchester: "There is no construction at all. Somebody comes on and does a dance.... And all the way through, either a lot of people come on and do a dance or one person or two people. But there is no actual development of a real story."[33] Grace Robert observed that "the pas de deux is not too glorified ballroom dancing," and that "the cancan has been lifted straight from a Paris *boîte de nuit* in contrast to the truly balletic treatment of the

Léonide Massine, Milada Mladova, and Frederic Franklin as the Peruvian, Glove Seller and Baron in "The Gay Parisian" (Warner Bros. movie short of *Gaîté parisienne*), 1941.

'Cancan' of *La Boutique fantasque.*"³⁴ Yet despite its shortcomings, *Gaîté parisienne* recaptured the period with great wit and flair and displayed Massine's genius for comic characterization and superb deployment of the ensemble.

Critical Survey

The ballet was a huge popular success throughout Europe and America and was also received kindly by the critics. John Martin's review was quite typical: "It is, to be sure, pure foolishness and may have little or nothing to do with Art with a large A. It is nevertheless fresh as a daisy, extraordinarily skillful and inventive."³⁵

In Retrospect

Gaîté parisienne became the perennial closing ballet and the signature work of the Ballet Russe de Monte Carlo. It was especially popular with less sophisticated members of the audience who went to the ballet for light entertainment. The company kept *Gaîté parisienne* in the repertory until its last season in 1962, maintaining the original vestiges of scenery and costumes by Etienne de Beaumont.

In 1941, Warner Bros. made an abysmal movie short of this ballet called "The Gay Parisian." Frenetic editing butchered the choreography and, with true Hollywood ineptitude, a younger and prettier girl from the corps de ballet replaced Alexandra Danilova as the Glove Seller. Milada Mladova may have been more photogenic, but she lacked the technique, depth, and elegance of the senior ballerina. Balletomanes deplored the lost opportunity to preserve one of Danilova's greatest interpretations.

No Massine ballet has ever been revived more extensively. Among the more important revivals, Léonide and Tatiana Massine restaged *Gaîté parisienne* for American Ballet Theatre (ABT) in April 1970, and ABT subsequently did a more controversial revival in 1988, staged by Lorca Massine and Susanna della Pietra. The furor revolved around the wacky costumes of trendy fashion designer Christian Lacroix. Lacroix clothed the dancers in zesty cartoon couture which was actually a thinly disguised reworking of his 1987 collection.³⁶ Massine was never one to shun fussy designs and loud colors, but Lacroix's relentless ruffles, flounces, garters, plumes and baubles obscured the choreographic line and made a travesty of the ballet by emphasizing the characters' vulgarity. Ann Barzel was not alone in decrying "the atrocious spectacle to which ABT has reduced this ballet."³⁷ John Percival noted that it was not easy for the ABT dancers to capture *Gaîté*'s demi-caractère style (especially in an era when Baryshnikov's policy was to turn away from this style in favor of Petipa and

Balanchine classics). He wrote, "Add the dreadfully misconceived new designs ... and you have a recipe for disaster."[38]

Unfortunately, *Gaîté parisienne* is vulnerable to the cartoonist approach because it is crisp, hard-edged, and, at several points, unabashedly slapstick. Undeniably, it has less of the subtlety that gave three dimensions to the Hussar and Street Dancer of *Beau Danube*. But for that same reason, it can be revived more successfully than *Beau Danube* because it does not, on the whole, demand such sensitive characterizations. In regional ballet companies throughout the world, *Gaîté parisienne* has been an excellent vehicle for young dancers who are getting their first experience in the genre of demi-caractère. In her review of Boston Ballet's 1979 revival of *Gaîté*, Debra Cash cut to the heart of this ballet's enduring appeal for dancers as well as audiences: "The corps de ballet was having a wonderful time: waiters trying to douse the melée that erupts over the Glove Seller with buckets of water; ladies swooning; and the cancan girls shrieking as they fell into splits ... if a hard-working corps can't let go during Massine's broad comedy and have some fun, when else will they have the opportunity?"[39]

SEVENTH SYMPHONY

Symphonic Ballet in Four Movements
Libretto: Léonide Massine
Music: Ludwig van Beethoven, Symphony No. 7 in A major
Set and Costume Design: Christian Bérard
Première: Théâtre de Monte Carlo, May 5, 1938

ORIGINAL CAST

First Movement

The Spirit of Creation: Frederic Franklin
The Sky: Mia Slavenska   **The Stream:** Nini Theilade
The Plant: Nathalie Krassovska
The Deer: Marina Franca, Yura Skibine
The Bird: Tania Grantzeva   **The Serpent:** T. Robert Irwin
The Sun: Casimir Kokitch   **The Fish:** Rosella Hightower
The Woman: Jeanette Lauret   **The Man:** George Zoritch

Second Movement

The Adolescent: Charles Dickson   **The Innocent:** Max Kirbos
The Woman: Nini Theilade

Third Movement

The Gods: Mia Slavenska,[40] Igor Youskevitch

Fourth Movement
Bacchanale: Nini Theilade, Lubov Rostova, Frederic Franklin
The Fire: Igor Youskevitch   The Ensemble

Synopsis[41]

Seventh Symphony has no actual plot but is based on a biblical theme: the creation of the world and humanity which, forgetting the words of God, is plunged into sin and consumed by fire.

First Movement. The Creation. This movement represents chaos, which gradually takes on form under the command of the Spirit of Creation.

The curtain rises to reveal formless chaos as the introductory theme is heard. But as the score intensifies rhythmically, the groupings on stage gradually acquire focus and animation. All living things are assembled by the Spirit of Creation, a commanding figure in white. First, He bids recumbent green forms, suggestive of plant life, to arise. The sky appears above the water and, as the lights come up, the arches of ancient Greece are seen. Two deer gambol across the stage, followed by birds and fish. The sinister serpent makes his slithering entrance. Finally man and woman are created, and the world has progressed from a formless mass to civilization.

Second Movement. The Earth. Humanity is plunged into the depths of despair after the first crime has been committed.

To the somber strains of the second movement's principal theme, a procession of three trios of mourners appears. As the main theme crests, six men enter from upstage left bearing the body of a slain youth, designated "The Adolescent." The ensemble women move in counterpoint to one another, first singly and then in three groups. The entire ensemble, except for the bearers, form a long diagonal as the body is raised one last time and borne off downstage right. Here we see death and grief, the murdered Abel and the martyred Christ, brought together in a striking image.

Third Movement. The Sky. An Olympian interlude, far from the earth and its cares, amidst the ether where reign the mythological Gods.

The carefree gods are frolicking on Olympus. A small group enters festively with the opening measures of the scherzo and, in contrast, the Sky Goddess and her mate glide in to the lyrical strains of the movement's second theme and dance a serene pas de deux. There follows a pas de quatre for Markova and three males, two solos for Eglevsky and Markova, and then dancing for the entire ensemble.

Fourth Movement. The Bacchanale and the Destruction.[42] *This movement brings us back once more to the Earth, where Humanity is abandoning itself to an orgy. The ire of God puts an end to this downfall.*

To the opening of the finale, a mass of bacchantes enter, led by

Krassovska, Theilade and Franklin. They are equipped with long trumpets, bowls of flowers, grapes, wine and other requisite accouterments for conducting orgies in ancient Greece. Cupid appears and shoots his arrows, bringing the orgy to a fever pitch. Towards the end, the Fire appears (fourteen women and six men in flame-colored costumes with streamers). They trap the revelers and consume them. When the last reveler has been felled, the Flames form a pyramid at upstage right.

Scenery and Costumes[43]

After *Symphonie fantastique*, this was Bérard's second design for a symphonic ballet. Given the epic scale of both theme and music, Bérard wisely chose simplicity as his keynote. Shortly into the first movement, a gauze scrim was lifted to reveal, against a practically plain backcloth, a crosspiece of stone supported at each end by a pair of tall caryatid columns. These archaic columns gave an ironic note to the first movement, "The Creation," suggesting that an old world was now being remade. The second backcloth depicted a Palestinian landscape dominated by a hill (perhaps Golgotha) with a red cloth draped over the crosspiece of stone from the previous movement. The third-movement backcloth was an Olympian skyscape, and the last backdrop showed a ruined castle. The slender caryatid columns (which appeared in front of all four backcloths) appeared to have suffered some destruction in the fourth movement and now had only one figure at each side instead of a pair.

Costume colors followed the mood of the symphony. As the Spirit of Creation, Franklin wore a short white Grecian tunic and white shoes with putties on the calves. The other first-movement costumes for the sky, rocks, plants and water suggested their natural colors. The serpent was actually a prone dancer in a tube of mustard stretch jersey. Dancers in the second movement wore long robes with cowls in rich, full-bodied colors of brown, citron, blue, olive-green and purple. The costumes were balanced and blended to intensify the counterbalanced groupings of the mourners.[44] In the third movement, the males were bare-chested with tights of deep rose; the females wore sky-blue chiffon costumes marked with a thin red band. The fourth movement's bacchantes were clad in black and mustard, while the symbols of fire, of course, wore red and carried scarlet streamers.

Even the archenemies of Massine's symphonic ballets took pains to acknowledge the merits of Bérard's decor. One of them, Lincoln Kirstein, said, "As for the 'Seventh Symphony,' it had to be sure, far better clothes than the symphonies Bérard doesn't dress, but it is scarcely a comment on Beethoven."[45]

Music

Ludwig van Beethoven is probably the most admired composer in the history of Western music. He was born in the provincial court city of Bonn, where three generations of the Beethoven family found employment as musicians at the court of the Electorate of Cologne. In 1792 Beethoven moved permanently to Vienna. He never held an official position in Vienna but supported himself through the patronage of the Viennese aristocracy, through concerts, and, increasingly, through the sale of his works. Beethoven's thirty-five years in Vienna were shaped by a series of personal afflictions. The first was the onset of deafness, and the second was his subsequent inability to find happy personal relationships.

The early symptoms of deafness sent him through the stages of despair, resignation and, finally defiance. In an 1802 document addressed to his brothers, now known as the "Heiligenstadt Testament," he resolved to "seize fate by the throat," and he emerged from the crisis by his usual means—hard work. His next series of triumphant works indicate a firm repudiation of any notion that his deafness would handicap him professionally.

Traditionally, Beethoven's works are grouped into early, middle, and late periods. The early works, up to about 1802, are written primarily for the piano and chamber ensembles. Beethoven approached the less familiar symphonic genre with caution: his first two symphonies of 1800 and 1801–02 are still decidedly conservative. A general growth in the proportions and power of Beethoven's works culminates in the highly dramatic compositions that mark the beginning of the middle period in 1803. The earliest of these—the Third Symphony, or the "Eroica"—was only one of many Beethoven works from this period that appear to embody extra-musical ideas of heroism. The music of the sub-period 1809–12 follows the same stylistic impetus, but becomes a bit less radical and turbulent as it grows more and more effortless in technique. The Seventh Symphony (1812) is a good example—here, the heroic character alternates with an Olympian serenity.

Beethoven's music became generally less monumental and more introspective and personal in the works from 1817 until his death in 1827. Occasionally he reverted to elements of the heroic middle-period style, as in the Ninth (Choral) Symphony, completed in 1823. Even this work, however, is colored by a new immediacy of expression.

The forcefulness, expanded range, and evident radical intent of the Third, Fifth, Sixth, Seventh and Ninth symphonies created a new symphonic ideal. All contrive to create the impression of a spiritual journey or growth process. This illusion of arriving, triumphing or transcending is enhanced by evolving themes, actual thematic recurrences from one movement to another, and, often, by the involvement of extra-musical ideas, as in the "Eroica."[46] Because of their powerful dynamics, concertgoers of the nineteenth century gladly attached programmatic ideas to these symphonies: to the Fifth, Beethoven's remark about fate knocking at the door; and to the Seventh, Wagner's evocation of an apotheosis of the dance.

Beethoven's single-minded devotion to his art and his ability to transform lonely adversity into a series of affirmative artistic visions give him a mythical stature as the prototype of the modern artist-hero. At the same time, his use of large-scale structure rather than local thematic events to achieve his most profound effects has influenced nearly every significant composer and theorist since his time.[47]

The Seventh Symphony is most celebrated for its second-movement allegretto. For its main theme, Beethoven used a motif from his String Quartet op. 59 no. 3. The allegretto's rhythm is the principal cause of its profound impact. It consists exclusively of a dactyl followed by a spondee, which recur without ceasing, and it appears first for the lower strings of the violas, cellos and double basses. From there it passes to the second violins, rising from octave to octave, until it arrives at the pitch of the first violins. These, by a crescendo, transmit it to the wind instruments, where it then bursts forth in all its force. At this point, wrote Hector Berlioz, the melody assumes the character of a "convulsive lamentation ... the expression of a grief without limit."[48] This agonizing section is succeeded by a simple melody in D major derived from an old Protestant song, "The Pilgrim's Hymn." It is soft and resigned, "like patience smiling at grief." At the conclusion, individual instruments enter in a fugato on fragments of the main theme. Afterwards, "the wind instruments exhale a profound sigh upon an indecisive harmony, and all is silence." The unrealized harmony of the concluding notes increases the feeling of sadness engendered by the whole. This allegretto gave Franz Liszt the famous image of mourners processing "as though they were burying the most precious thing in the world,"[49] a comment that may well have inspired Massine's own interpretation.

The first movement is best known for the principal theme of its allegro. It has a marked rhythm which is passed to the harmony and reproduced in a multitude of aspects without stopping its cadenced march until the end. The first movement's employment of a rhythmic form in ostinato, said Berlioz, "has never been attempted with so much success." The novelty of the third-movement Scherzo is that its subject is in F major, and instead of concluding its first section on a more predictable key, it modulates to A major.

It was the fourth movement which inspired Wagner to designate the Seventh "the apotheosis of the dance."[49] This driving, muscular finale is noteworthy not only for its sheer power but also for its elegance. Here, Berlioz stated, "Beethoven has drawn effects as graceful as they are unforeseen," citing the sudden transition from the key of C-sharp minor to that of D major as an example.[50] The Seventh Symphony is less obvious in its emotional rhetoric than are the "Eroica" and the Fifth, but its graceful control over musical structure can make these earlier works seem hectic by comparison.

Choreography

In the first movement, Massine worked with an acute sense of structure, tailoring each entry to coincide with the evolving musical patterns. Each entity was also given a movement style suited to its nature. Thus, Sky's traveling *fouettés* conveyed a quality different from Water's long, low leaps. The most distinctive movement style was reserved for the slithering serpent, especially when it returned at the end, crawling over a pyramid of rocks at stage left. Massine found a way to unite the different groups coherently through the grand, controlling gestures of the Spirit of Creation.

The allegretto was composed in the style of the second-movement andante in *Choreartium*, with its balletic variations on German expressionist modern dance. Massine wrote that he saw this movement "as the story of man's guilt and despair, symbolized by Cain and Abel."[51] But the pictorial implications of its tableaux bore a clear resemblance to numerous Renaissance paintings of the Descent from the Cross. As a matter of taste, the presence of Christ on the stage of a theatre—even if the word "Jesus" did not appear in program notes—was disturbing to some viewers in an era which predated *Jesus Christ Superstar* by three decades. From the standpoint of pure logic, some viewers were also troubled by Massine's juxtaposition of biblical myth on a background of ancient Greek pediments.

However, the theme of some great religious lamentation fit the music like a glove and had a profound emotional impact on most viewers. Robert Lawrence lauded the exquisite dance patterns Massine arranged for the female mourners. He found them "musical in the extreme, particularly toward the end of the scene, when—as the individual voices of the orchestra enter in a fugato on the main theme—the women follow Beethoven's structural design at first singly, then in groups."[52]

Certainly, the third movement had the least controversial choreography. It served to introduce two superb ballet dancers, Igor Youskevitch and Alicia Markova, to New York audiences in a purely classical style. For Lawrence, the third movement had the best choreography because the classicism was most "in tune with the spirit of Beethoven's score." But Ernest Newman found this movement's choreography to be the "weak spot," because the repetitions of the same material in the same terms "that are well enough in the concert room, where we listen with other cares, sorely hamper the choreographer."[53]

Lionel Bradley's account of the fourth movement indicates that Massine relied almost entirely on ensemble movement without soloists. They also suggest that motivations for Massine's mass designs were pallid, ineffectual, and bogged down. Moreover, the destruction by fire was too naïve and cliché-ridden to be taken seriously. The Metropolitan Opera House provided a smoke screen to give some realism to the infernos of many a spectacular opera, but in Massine's version, the blazing apocalypse was represented by twenty dancers in red who carried streamers on sticks. They dashed furiously from stage left to stage right in order to immolate their dissipated colleagues and then made equally furious backstage crossovers to provide the holocaust a steady fuel supply. In the dénouement, according to Grace Robert, the world's end is symbolized when these agents of the apocalypse mass together and "flutter their hands like flames." She added that "Many uneven dramatic presentations have been saved by a thrilling last act. The *Seventh Symphony* cannot be counted among that number."[54]

Critical Survey

Needless to say, there were the usual sermons on the crime of using a symphony for a ballet. Leonid Sabaneev wrote, "It is nauseating to see him [Beethoven] and his symphonies squeezed into the skin of the ballet."[55] In contrast, Ernest Newman marveled at the "astonishing" extent to which Beethoven's symphony lent itself to Massine's conceptions, and Anatole Vitak saw the *Seventh Symphony* as proof that "Massine is really progressing and bettering his 'symphonic style' with each successive attempt."[56] But even the most positive reviews noted that the fourth movement was ineffectual.

Much of the critical controversy revolved around the second movement. At the time, many viewers shared Lawrence's belief that "the presence of the Deity on the stage of a theatre—even though otherwise designated in the program—is most questionable." Other critics sided with Arnold Haskell that the "one positive result" of the ballet was a second movement of "extraordinary plastic beauty, one of the greatest frescoes in Massine's vast museum."[57]

In Retrospect

Despite the sublime beauty of its second movement, some reviews of *Seventh Symphony* indicate a degree of weariness with the genre itself, as is evident in *Dancing Times'* comment that "there are many moments when one feels that Massine has done this before in one of his other symphonic ballets." For the *Modern Music* critic, *Seventh Symphony* was merely a string of unmotivated effects: "I could see a kaleidoscopic succession of clever arrangements, but there was no thrill in the order in which they came. There was no sequence in the movement that awakened some kind of special feeling, some kind of urgency. It all occupied the eye as long as it lasted, and left no reality, no secret emotion behind." The author subsequently characterized *Seventh Symphony* as "showmanship with a vengeance" which "leaves behind a feeling of cheapness."[58] By 1938, the symphonic ballets looked formulaic to the cognoscenti, and one is reminded of the old adage, "familiarity breeds contempt."

ST. FRANCIS (Nobilissima Visione)

Ballet in One Act and Five Scenes
Libretto: Paul Hindemith and Léonide Massine
Music: Paul Hindemith
Scenic and Costume Design: Pavel Tchelitchew
Première: Drury Lane Theatre, London, July 21, 1938

ORIGINAL CAST
St. Francis: Léonide Massine
Three Companions: Marcel Fenchel, Roland Guérard, Michel Panaiev
St. Francis' Father: Simon Semenov
The Knight and the Wolf: Frederic Franklin
The Poor Man: Nicolas Ivangin
Poverty: Nini Theilade   **Chastity:** Lubov Roudenko
Obedience: Jeanette Lauret
Purchasers, Travelers, Soldiers, Minor Brothers, Minor Sisters

Synopsis

Scene One. The shop of Pietro Bernadone. Francis and his three companions are gossiping in the fabric shop belonging to Francis's father. Purchasers from all parts of the world call to inspect his father's wares. Francis is captivated by the news of foreign countries and longs for travel and adventure. Next arrives the Knight, who is anxious to replenish his wardrobe. Francis is mesmerized by the Knight's splendor, and the Knight invites him to join his train. Francis puts on helm, breastplate, and gauntlets and takes service with the Knight.

Scene Two. A country road. An officer initiates Francis into the techniques of war as an unarmed band of travelers approach. The Knight orders his men to rob the party. The male travelers are struck down, the loot seized, and the women carried off. Francis, horrified at this injustice, refuses to obey the Knight's command to resume the march. He takes off his military gear and, kneeling, prays for guidance. Three allegorical figures—Poverty, Obedience, and Chastity—appear to assist him.

Scene Three. The house of Pietro Bernadone. The house is splendidly decorated for a feast to celebrate the return of Francis. The guests, including Francis's three companions, are drinking and dancing around a great table, but Francis is troubled and moody. A band of beggars steals in, hoping to be given crusts of bread. Francis, overcome by their wretchedness, impulsively gives them the golden vessels from the table. Francis's father is furious at this high-handed disposal of his costly possessions, and he strikes his son. Francis accepts his father's anger with meekness. In token of his decision to renounce riches, he takes off his fine clothes and lays them at his father's feet. He leaves the house.

Scene Four. A country hillside. Francis, clad in rags, now lives as a hermit. He dances to express his intense religious ecstasy, waving two leafy olive branches which he later places together to form a cross. He is interrupted by a group of peasants who are fleeing from a savage Wolf of evil fame. Among the fugitives are Francis's three companions, who have also renounced materialism to devote themselves to a life of austerity. The Wolf springs out to attack the villagers, but he is unable to withstand the saint's mystic power. The creature allows himself to be tamed and led away by the country folk. Poverty appears, and Francis welcomes her as his bride. They exchange girdles and, with the three companions, celebrate a marriage feast of bread and water.

Scene Five. A landscape with a great rock in the distance. Monks and nuns file in stately procession about Francis. Poverty takes Francis by the hand and slowly leads him up the side of the rock to its peak. When they reach the summit, the monks and nuns turn to face the rock and raise their hands in farewell as the sky blazes with light.

Scenery and Costumes

Pavel Tchelitchew explained in an interview that the period for *St. Francis* was a transitional one between the decay of Rome in the Dark

Ages and the pre–Renaissance era of pretentious opulence.[59] The décor for the first and third scenes was dominated by a Romanesque arch decorated with richly swagged and colored curtains at stage left. The second-scene backcloth depicted a late medieval stone wall topped by a rugged landscape; the fourth showed a country hillside. The fifth, by far the most memorable, showed a landscape with a great eminence in the distance. Above this precipice appeared six hands with fingers held in obviously symbolic positions. Each hand was actually a visual "letter" in the sign language for the deaf and, together, they spelled out "G-L-O-R-I-A."[60]

Tchelitchew's costumes came in for some criticism. Lady Poverty had some gaping rips in her costume, many of them in suggestive areas. Some critics claimed that the designs were carried out in unsuitable materials. John Martin, for instance, felt "a slight uneasiness that Assisi is perhaps a bit farther away than Schiaparelli."[61]

In 1938 Tchelitchew completed his celebrated oil-on-canvas *Phenomena*, now in the collection of the Tretyakoff State Gallery in Moscow. This enormous painting uses rocks and stone walls as universal symbols for poverty and hardship. Parker Tyler believes that *St. Francis* clearly shows the influence of *Phenomena*. He notes that similar walls flank the second-scene set of *St. Francis* and that the Knight's suit of chain mail is a *trompe l'oeil* stone wall. He remarks, "The very condition of humanity and poverty which in *Phenomena* wears so hard, bleak and sinister a look is sublimated in *St. Francis* by theatrical means and the nature of the theme."[62]

Music

The foremost German composer of his generation, Paul Hindemith was a figure central to the music and philosophies of the interwar years. In 1935 his music was banned by the Nazi government on the charge of "musical opportunism." He made his first visit to the United States in 1937 and became an American citizen in 1946.

From about 1924 until 1933, Hindemith developed an antiromantic, neo–Baroque style—marked by chromaticism, strict forms, and harmonic asperity. Afterwards, he adapted this new and explicitly atonal style to classical sonata forms and conventional genres, resulting in a more melodious mode of expression.[63]

Hindemith's best-known works, the opera *Mathis der Maler* (1934) and its attendant symphony, exemplify Hindemith's new, more lyrical style. *Mathis der Maler* concerns painter Matthias Grünewald's decision to renounce his art and commit himself to a life of political action and his ensuing discovery that such action is futile and that he must return to his art. *St. Francis* is a counterpart to *Mathis der Maler* in which the idea of renunciation is played out on a more spiritual plane.[64]

Hindemith's score for this ballet is of symphonic breadth and is composed of eleven separate numbers: Introduction and March of the Troubadours, Buyers and Beggars, the Knight, March, the Three Apparitions, Festal Music, Close of the Feast, Meditation, the Wolf, Wedding to Poverty and Finale. Its style is an evocation of the Middle Ages, especially in the composer's use of old troubadour melodies. The troubadour ballad "Ce fut en Mai" was used as Hindemith's main theme: it weaves itself through the score like the thread of a tapestry.

Critics were almost unanimous in citing Hindemith's score as the greatest artistic achievement of this ballet. They were divided, however, on its suitability to the purpose at hand: Hindemith's music is intensely contrapuntal, and ordinarily the mating of polyphony and dancing is thought to be akin to mixing oil and water. Yet even without a driving rhythm, the score did rise and fall in intensity and texture in exact correspondence to the dramatic action, and it had a mood and dignity well suited to the subject matter. For John Martin, the marriage of movement and music was "utterly and completely right."[65] Walter Terry wrote that the score "was almost uncanny in its unbroken communion with the texture and the tempo of the dancing."[66] Cyril Beaumont, however, felt that the music "does not readily lend itself to interpretation in terms of dancing," and Grace Robert said that the score "lacks the dramatic climaxes necessary to support the action of the ballet."[67]

Hindemith's letters provide a fascinating glimpse into the fierce rivalries of the ballet world during the 1930s. By 1939 he had agreed to compose a work for George Balanchine. According to Hindemith, when he broke the news to Ballet Russe manager Serge Denham, "he nearly broke into tears. He yowled and yammered and tried every trick to get me to give it up.... Denham telephoned Massine in Portland, Oregon as soon as he could, and the dancer became furious."[68] It is fortunate that Hindemith was unswayed by any claims on his allegiance; his liason with Balanchine eventually resulted in his 1946 masterpiece, *The Four Temperaments*.

Choreography

Both Massine and Hindemith were inspired scholars whose research enabled them to recreate the spirit of a period in modern terms. The choreography for much of *St. Francis* was based on a profound study of Byzantine and Italian primitive artists such as Giotto. For Martin, Massine "evoked a masterly picture of the Middle Ages in which he [St.

Studio portrait of Nini Theilade and Léonide Massine as Lady Poverty and St. Francis in *St. Francis*, 1938. *(MAURICE SEYMOUR)*

Francis] moved ... only a complete absorption in his material could possibly have enabled him to accomplish it."[69]

To recapture the spirit of medieval illuminations, Massine employed a flat, angular style vitalized by percussive, brittle movements. The stylized movements of the hands and arms were also an evocation of the thirteenth century. Particularly beautiful is the scene where St. Francis, after giving his rich clothes to his father, is protected from nakedness by the hands of the beggars he has fed.

Massine did give himself the freedom to stray from this Byzantine style where another movement quality would best convey his meaning. As the Knight, Frederic Franklin's solo in the first scene is athletic and vigorous, but still flat and angular. Franklin's Wolf, introduced as comic relief after the meditation episode, departs from the ballet's signature style with crouches and raucous leaps.

In the fourth scene the movements are free and plastic, owing much to modern dance. The long solo for St. Francis which opens this scene is very *terre-à-terre* as he whirls, kneels and throws himself forward on the floor, arms extended in the sign of the cross. As Lady Poverty, Nini Theilade employed the gentle, flowing movements appropriate to her character. The duet for Lady Poverty and Francis is notable for the way in which their hands intertwine chastely over their heads with very little other touching. There is a return to the primary style at the end of the fourth movement, when the three companions and Poverty, Obedience and Chastity form a succession of beautiful Italian primitive and Byzantine tableaux as they comfort and protect Francis.

The apotheosis is true to the signature style throughout, and it conveys a powerful sense of religious fervor. The massed corps forms and reforms striking architectural formations to create a living Byzantine fresco. In the last moments, as Poverty and Francis ascend to the summit of the rocky upstage peak, the ensemble below forms a large pyramidal tableau, crossing, flipping and quivering their wrists. They appear like the wings of angels and cherubim or perhaps like the wings of the soaring birds so well loved by St. Francis.

Critical Survey

St. Francis was almost the twin of *Gaîté parisienne* in date of birth; as Robert Lawrence pointed out, "Few men in the history of the theatre have turned out two prime works, so dissimilar, in the space of four months."[70] Many balletgoers, attracted to surface glitter and fairy tales, were simply puzzled by the asceticism of *St. Francis*. "There was little," noted Martin, "for your dyed-in-the-wool balletomane to get his teeth into." It was not an unqualified success with the critics, either. American critics, better accustomed to the stark and serious work of such artists as Martha Graham, were generally more receptive to *St. Francis* than were European critics. In his rave review, Martin called it "one of the most memorable and beautiful dance works of our time. Unorthodox in subject matter, elevated in tone, and revolutionary in its choreographic procedure, it is one of those creations which, like Bronislava Nijinska's 'Les Noces,' grow out of boldness of conception without regard for precedent."[71]

In London, the verdict of *Dancing Times* was that "Massine has here conceived a work in the grand manner ... but somehow failed to carry it out entirely satisfactorily." *The Bystander* was blunt: "Unfortunately, it suffers from the one unforgivable sin: it is dull."[72] Perhaps the most thought-provoking objection to the ballet was that the story of St. Francis was good literary material, but contained too much soul-searching for expression in pure movement, which cannot alone project all the subtle stages in the process of spiritual enlightenment. For Walter Terry, Massine was able to project the conflicting elements of St. Francis's nature successfully in the first three scenes because of the differences between him and his shallow-spirited associates. But by the fourth scene, with the glitter and contrasting personalities gone, Terry saw difficulties: "Massine had to project himself the shining beauty of his emotional discoveries and to delineate himself the contrasting moods of his transitional stage ... he never quite achieved a union of these discoveries, a knowing, humble fulfillment of his deep emotional searchings."[73]

In Retrospect

Unfortunately, *St. Francis* was taken out of the repertory when Massine left the company in 1942. The management took no long-range steps to preserve the work, and all that remains today is a 1938 rehearsal film, danced in practice clothes. Modern viewers are apt to think that its blend of severe Byzantine angularity with early modern dance looks naïve and quaint and, yes, they may also find it to be "dull."

St. Francis may look dated, but this in no way negates its historical importance. It was passionately conceived and masterfully crafted. It commanded respect for its courageous attempt to analyze the process of religious discovery in the language of dance. In the words of Walter Terry, "For this more than for anything else he deserves unending praise—in this 'Saint Francis' Massine has added his proof to that of other dancers, that profundity and the theatrical dance can be mated and that this union fosters an unending wealth of stimulating experiences for beholder and creator alike."[74]

BOGATYRI *(Russian Heroes)*

Ballet in Prologue and Three Scenes
Libretto: Léonide Massine
Music: Alexander Borodin; Symphony No. 2 in B minor; Symphony
    No. 3 in A minor (Unfinished); String Quartet in D major
Set and Costume Design: Nathalie Gontcharova
Première: Metropolitan Opera House, New York, October 20, 1938

ORIGINAL CAST

Princess Anastachiuska: Mia Slavenska
Alyosha Popovitch: Igor Youskevitch
Dobryna Nikitisch: Frederic Franklin   Khanja: Nathalie Krassovska
Mouromitz: Marc Platov   Tartar Prince: George Zoritch

Synopsis

Prologue. The Princess Anastachiuska is asleep in her apartments. She dreams of a terrifying ogre, succeeded by the vision of a handsome Tartar prince. She awakens and recounts the strange dream to her ladies-in-waiting as she is garbed in ceremonial robes. Handmaidens style her hair, weaving in and out of a dance themselves as they braid the plaits.

Scene One. Before the walls of Kiev stand the Bogatyri, Russian heroes who are starting an expedition against the Tartars. They are joined by the Princess Anastachiuska, who gives her blessings. But suddenly the sky darkens, and the monstrous ogre of Anastachiuska's dream now appears. While the assembly recoils, the ogre grasps the princess in its claws and flies away with her. The Bogatyri prepare to go to her rescue, and an angel appears in the sky to bless their venture.

Scene Two. The second movement is divided into three sections.

A. The Tartar's Camp. The great Khan, recognizable as the Tartar Prince of Anastachiuska's dream, takes his ease as the Tartar warriors dance ferociously.

B. A Forest Glade. Nearby the camp, Khanja, the wife of the Tartar Prince, dances seductively with the Tartar women. To this clearing come the Bogatyri, who fall under the spell of the Tartar women and forget the object of their long journey.

C. The Ogre's Enchanted Garden. The Ogre's attendants stand guard over Anastachiuska as the princess is suddenly discovered by the Bogatyri. Their leader, Dobryna Nikitisch, challenges the ogre to single combat, from which Dobryna emerges victorious. Anastachiuska is rescued, and the party returns joyfully to Kiev.

Scene Three. Back in Kiev, the Princess Anastachiuska marries her brave rescuer. In celebration, jesters and acrobats cavort, followed by the dance of Khanja, whom the Bogatyri have brought back as a captive. At last the princess and Dobryna Nikitisch descend to lead the dance, and the hall is filled with joyous whirling figures.

Scenery and Costumes

With her lifetime companion and partner Mikhail Larionov, Nathalie Gontcharova was a prime mover in the outburst of activity in the Moscow art world that occurred in the decade before the Revolution. Beginning in 1908, both artists were on the organizing committee of the Golden Fleece Salon. Its exhibitions of avant-garde French art influenced Gontcharova to use more distortion in her subsequent paintings. However, this never took the form of direct imitation; it was instead a search for new forms of expression inspired by Russian ancient and folk art. Gontcharova, in her own words, "shook off the dust of the West"[73] from her feet.

The use of strong colors, applied with the Fauve's breadth and freedom, and a transition from descriptive detail to broad simplification can be found in her paintings of this period. By 1909, a series of paintings depicting her favorite theme of Russian peasants working the land already revealed her new style—Neo-Primitivism.

Her first neo-primitive set design for Diaghilev was the 1914 *Le Coq d'or* at the Paris Opéra, and it took Paris by storm. In 1915 Gontcharova and Larionov joined Diaghilev in Switzerland and followed the Diaghilev company to Spain and Italy during the war years. In 1919 the couple settled permanently in Paris.

Gontcharova became known among her colleagues in the Ecole de Paris as one of the most vivacious artists of her day. From 1921 to 1923, she had important exhibitions in London, New York, Tokyo and Brussels. In 1923, she produced one of her finest set designs for the Ballets Russes production of *Les Noces*, danced to Stravinsky's ballet cantata and choreographed by Bronislava Nijinska.

Gontcharova never worked exclusively for Diaghilev, but her finest creations were for the Ballets Russes. Following Diaghilev's death in 1929, her creative vitality declined. She painted a number of flower pieces, the most saleable type of picture in the difficult years of the Depression, but no imaginative works. Although financial conditions became almost unbearably hard, both Gontcharova and Larionov were upheld by the growing interest in their early paintings. The Tate Gallery acquired two Gontcharovas and one Larionov in 1953. The important exhibition entitled "Le Rayonnisme, 1909–14," held at the Galerie des Deux Iles in Paris in 1948, reestablished Gontcharova and Larionov as the first masters of Russian abstraction.[76]

For *Bogatyri*, Gontcharova created six dance tapestries in the fantastic style of Russian fairy-tale illustrations. They employed Gontcharova's typical color scheme—blindingly bright, with violent contrasts. The most memorable scenic effect was the entrance of the ogre in the first scene: he first appeared in the form of a curtain, lowered to a point just above the amazed Bogatyri's heads. The head and claws of the monster were cut out so that a stagehand could seize the princess and carry her offstage. What little praise this ballet received went to Gontcharova; however, her grandiose sets engulfed and overpowered the dancing.

Music

As originally produced, *Bogatyri* used Alexander Borodin's Symphony No. 2 in B minor, the two movements of his unfinished Symphony No. 3 in A minor, and the Nocturne from his String Quartet No. 2 in D major. In the revised 1941 version of *Bogatyri*, the latter two works were cut and the Second Symphony alone was used.

Alexander Borodin was a renowned Russian composer who was also a distinguished professor of chemistry at the Medico-Surgical Academy in St. Petersburg. In 1862, he met Mily Balakirev and joined the Mighty Five. Preoccupied with chemistry, Borodin had precious little time for composing; nevertheless, his first symphony was completed in 1867. It is hard to exaggerate the boldness of Borodin's decision to embark on a full-length symphony at a time when he had so little experience with extended forms and none at all with orchestration. Yet this symphony's technical shortcomings were mitigated by its freshness, charm and exuberance.

In 1876 Borodin completed his greatest symphony, the Symphony No. 2 in B minor. Its scherzo in particular is a marvel of orchestral dexterity and syncopation, while the trio introduces the note of orientalism that was to become one of Borodin's most appealing characteristics. Above all, the Second Symphony has one of the hallmarks of a great symphony: four movements of contrasting mood, color and tempo that nevertheless form a whole with an underlying unity.[77]

Choreography

For most critics, the only exciting choreography to be found was in the second scene, where ferocious Tartars flourished their scimitars and Tartar maidens danced with oriental sinuousness in harem suits with transparent veils. But this choreography is so indebted to Fokine's *Polovtsian Dances* (1909) that it could scarcely be called imaginative. Equally derivative was the ritualistic dance performed by the handmaidens as they braided Anastachiuska's hair. This "idea" was almost certainly lifted straight out of Bronislava Nijinska's *Les Noces*. Put simply, the choreography did not come up to Massine's usual standards.

Critical Survey

Of all the works created for the Ballet Russe de Monte Carlo's first season, only *Bogatyri* could be counted a failure. Its complicated story proved difficult to follow, and the names of its characters were tongue-twisters. The consensus was, "The choreography is thin and the dancing, as such, seems quite insignificant against the background of settings and costumes which utterly dwarfed it." Or, put less delicately, "This shining bore was longer than one imagined, with little dancing and wads of splashy canvas in the taste of 1915."[78]

Surprisingly, Massine seemed to be quite attached to this ballet, as he revived and simplified it in 1941. The score was cut, the prologue was dropped altogether, and the first two sections of the second scene were consolidated. But even with editing, the ballet was still a flop. For the second version, John Martin could see little improvement in *Bogatyri*'s plot "or what might euphemistically be called its form."[79]

In Retrospect

Diaghilev's creed that the scenic element in ballet could, in some cases, be even more important than the dancing was now coming into serious question. Lincoln Kirstein wrote, "How fierce to think that an advance-guard movement such as Diaghilev's Russian Ballet can so quickly become an academic and philistine standard. Gontcharova's tomato-sauce and a general color-blind confusion [in *Bogatyri*] induced a deep coma."[80]

Looking at the Massine company's first season as a whole, it would appear that things were going well. In his essay on Massine's 1938 ballets, George Dorris wrote that all excepting *Bogatyri* "show Massine expanding his scope in works that can be related to important genres he had already explored, but in no way was he merely repeating himself ... what we have here, I believe, is a great choreographer in fullest control of his materials and with the inestimable advantage of working with a company devoted to the realization of his artistic vision."[81]

CAPRICCIO ESPAGNOL

Ballet in One Act
Libretto: Léonide Massine

Choreography: Léonide Massine, in collaboration with Mlle Argentinita
Music: Nikolai Rimsky-Korsakov
Scenery and Costumes: Mariano Andreù
Première: Théâtre de Monte Carlo, May 4, 1939

ORIGINAL CAST

The Gypsy Girl: Mlle Argentinita[82] **A Gypsy Youth**: Léonide Massine
A Peasant Girl: Alexandra Danilova **A Peasant Youth**: Michael Panaiev
Peasant Girls and Youths

Synopsis

It is a festival day in a small Iberian town and a crowd has gathered for the *Romeria*. A group of boys armed with sticks move with short, energetic steps followed by the girls of the town, who join the older men in a more languid dance. For a moment, the boys resume their prancing dance. Then to a flourish of trumpets, the two Gypsy Youths enter, and their savage natures find vent in their dances. The dancing of the two gypsies enkindles the townspeople, who join in a frenzied jota.

Scenery and Costumes

The setting and costumes of Mariano Andreù were originally designed for Fokine's ballet *Jota Aragonesa*. This ballet premièred at the Maryinsky in 1916 and was revived with new décor by Andreù for René Blum's Les Ballets de Monte Carlo in 1937. Andreù produced a skillful evocation of nineteenth-century Spanish dress and architecture for *Jota Aragonesa*. Part of the action for this Fokine ballet was given on a forestage masked by large curtains which were pulled back to reveal the main setting of an Andalusian village. For *Capriccio*, the curtains were retained, but pulled back throughout the ballet.

Music

The purely orchestral works for which Rimsky-Korsakov is best known—*Scheherazade* (1888), *Capriccio espagnol* (1887) and the *Easter Festival Overture* (1888)—are traditionally regarded by music critics as brightly colored mosaics whose thematic ideas, while striking and piquant, lack organic cohesion. At its première, critics hailed the *Capriccio* solely for its brilliant instrumentation; however, it is also a fine work structurally. Rimsky-Korsakov did not hesitate to point this out: "The opinion formed by both critics and the public, that the *Capriccio* is a magnificently orchestrated piece—is wrong. The *Capriccio* is a brilliant composition."[83]

Capriccio espagnol was written before the era in which composers like Ravel and Falla introduced the concept of understated, thoroughly modern reworkings of nationalist themes. Once they had, *Capriccio espagnol* was long taken for granted as a dated tone poem. Fortunately, its architectural and rhythmic virtues were rediscovered when united to the sensitive choreography of Massine and Argentinita.

The musical design falls into five compact, connected movements and lasts about twenty minutes. It begins with a loud and blaring *alborada*. The second section, "Variation," begins quietly with a languid theme, occasionally bursting into crescendos on its variations. The third movement is a return to the more turbulent *alborada*. The fourth section, "*scena e canto gitano*," consists of five successive cadenzas for brass, violin, flute, clarinet, and harp with a gypsylike melody between each. The gypsy tune rises in dynamics until it spills over into the colorful finale, "Asturian fandango," which leads to a concluding jota.

Choreography

The ballet had no particular story to tell; instead, it created through a series of skillfully related dances the atmosphere of a village square on festival day. The *alborada* was performed with wild abandon by boys using capes and sticks as props. In the second movement, the girls rebuffed the boys by choosing the elders (*mahas*) of the village for their partners in a slow-paced *seguidilla*. After the boys repeated the *alborada*, the fourth movement began with a dramatic solo entrance for the Gypsy Girl. The entrance of the Gypsy Youth was anticipated by the sound of staccato flamenco heelwork coming from the wings. Then, "At last Massine emerged: slim, dark, slightly sinister with his broad-brimmed hat pulled down over his face, whip in hand. From the moment of his entrance until the fall of the curtain, it was he who dominated the ballet." As the music built to a climax, the ensemble joined the two gypsies in their rapid stampings, quick whirls, and persistent rhythms. Next, in "a supreme touch of theatre,"[84] the audience was surprised by the introduction of the two second leads very late in the ballet, at the moment that the fourth movement plunged into the closing fandango. The Peasant Girl and Peasant Youth came leaping forward and were soon joined by the Gypsy Girl and Gypsy Youth. This fifth movement concluded with a group jota, as the four principals led the revel to a frenzied conclusion.

Even though Argentinita was not associated with classical ballet, the jump was probably not as great as it might seem. She was an expert in the ethnological aspects of her native dances, but she was also a concert artist who was well accustomed to blending regional styles to suit her

Studio portrait of Mia Slavinska and Léonide Massine as the Gypsy Girl and the Gypsy Youth in *Capriccio espagnol*, 1939. *(MAURICE SEYMOUR)*

purposes. Since Massine had used exactly the same approach in *Le Tricorne*, the two artists probably worked very well together.

Critical Survey

To no one's surprise, this colorful work was a popular success: it had all the requisite crowd-pleasing ingredients of beautiful costumes, lively action, and infectious, familiar music. Critical response was rather bland, but basically favorable: John Martin termed it "a graceful and eye-filling suite of dances," and Edwin Denby wrote, "Most of it is pleasant to watch." He added that Massine "makes the other men look like little boys. The showmanship, the bite of his stage presence is superlative."[85]

In Retrospect

Warner Bros. made a film short of this ballet entitled "Spanish Fiesta," and in 1951, Massine revived the stage version of *Capriccio* for Ballet Theatre, La Scala, and the Ballet Russe de Monte Carlo. For years, it provided ballet companies with a very effective closing number. Because it didn't give critics much to sink their teeth into, it got only a fraction of the column space accorded to more controversial ballets. Yet, like the score to which it was danced, there was more to the form and structure of this work than met the eye. The co-choreographers added fresh value to familiar, underrated music by pointing up its architectural and rhythmical interests and showed their mastery of Iberian style by using that idiom as the material for a highly theatrical ballet.

ROUGE ET NOIR

Symphonic Ballet in Four Movements
Libretto: Léonide Massine, Henri Matisse
Music: Dmitri Shostakovich, Symphony No. 1
Scenic and Costume Design: Henri Matisse
Première: Théâtre de Monte Carlo, May 11, 1939

ORIGINAL CAST

Woman: Alicia Markova **Man:** Igor Youskevitch
Leader of the Red Group: Frederic Franklin
Leader of the Black Group: Marc Platov
Leader of the Yellow Group: Nathalie Krassovska
Eleanora Marra, Rosella Hightower,
and Lubov Rostova performed solo roles
throughout the four movements.
The Ensemble

Synopsis[86]

First Movement (Aggression). Man, symbolizing the poetic spirit, is pursued and overtaken by brutal forces. The forces of Yellow, Red, Blue and Black appear to the first musical theme. The poetic forces of White (Markova, Youskevitch) appear from upstage left and dance a pas de deux to the movement's lyrical second theme. The forces of White are engulfed, harried and split by the forces of Red, Blue, Black and Yellow. Youskevitch staggers off upstage right, slumped over, hands bound. Blue and Yellow *bourrée* to Markova and gesture urgently towards upstage right.

Second Movement (Field and City). The men of the city encounter the men of the field and bear them off. The forces of Red (similar to Black but more impish than evil) race across the stage and make mischief to a brittle staccato subject in the orchestra. The leader of the Red group performs a solo in the foreground as the ensemble moves in intricate counterpoint. White and two trios of Blue and Yellow enter to a contrasting lyrical theme, but Blue and Yellow are overpowered and carried off by Red. The forces of Red return to form a high pyramid, separating Markova and Youskevitch. The lovers reach for one another on either side.

Third Movement (Solitude). Woman, parted from man, is tormented in her solitude by an evil spirit. Markova dances mournfully to a sorrowful oboe theme. The evil leader of Black appears and throws her into acrobatic backovers and strained lifts indicative of torture and suffering. Blue, Red, and Yellow enter and briefly overpower the leader of the Black. He withdraws into the shadows, and Markova rises as Blue and Yellow exit.

Fourth Movement (Destiny). Man eludes the brutal forces and finds woman again. But joy is shortlived, for in freeing himself from his worldly enemies he is conquered by destiny. To the first theme of the fourth movement, Youskevitch enters and is pursued furiously by the forces of Black, Blue, Yellow and Red. All of the colors battle until they are stilled by a bolt from above which chases them off the stage. Left alone, the couple in white are briefly reunited to a new musical motif, but the struggle recommences. The forces of Black return; they lift Youskevitch overhead, spin him around, and push him to the floor. Youskevitch tries vainly to escape, but he is lifted to the top of a mass pyramid upstage right, thrown to the floor by Red, Yellow, Blue and Black and brought to the front, now utterly lifeless. The leader of the Black emerges to the pounding of the timpani. Markova falls dead across the back of the Black leader in a final tableau of the triumph of materialism.

Scenery and Costumes

In 1930–32 Matisse planned and completed his famous large mural, *The Dance*, for the Barnes Foundation in Merion, Pennsylvania. In the Merion gallery where *The Dance* was installed, the intersection of the small transverse vaults over the windows with the main vault of the ceiling had created an effect of pointed arches when seen in flat projection. Matisse used the broad flat planes of pure color between the arches of the gallery as backgrounds for the dancing figures in the mural. The parallels between *The Dance* and Matisse's design for *Rouge et noir* are remarkable.[87] For the backdrop of *Rouge et noir*, Matisse now adapted not only a version of the three pointed arches of the gallery in Merion, but also the broad flat planes of pure color that existed between them.

Matisse devised a vaulted hall with a canary yellow roof and three white pillars at stage left, center, and right. In the center of the backcloth was an enormous blue isosceles triangle. The wings framing the backcloth were scarlet on one side and black on the other.[88] The effect resembles an imposing Gothic arcade. For critics, the great strength of Matisse's razor-edged design was "its sharp and uncompromising architectural lines."[89] Lighting effects enhanced the set's dramatic impact: shadowy sequences alternated with sections that punched the colors into brilliant illumination. Together with the Barnes mural, the designs for *Rouge et noir* are considered among the finest Matisse works of the 1930s.

All the dancers wore hooded unitards in their assigned colors, enlivened by short flame like strips which wound around their figures. While Lincoln Kirstein noted that the unitards did allow one to see the dancers' lines better than any other option excepting nudity, he also found them distracting: "Union-suit tights are hard to make look neat, but the line of undergarments shining through continually destroyed the line."[90] Nonetheless, the costumes afforded complete freedom of movement, and they were well suited to the spirit and energy of both choreography and music.

Music

In 1939 Dmitri Shostakovich was a newcomer to the Western ballet world and as yet scarcely even known in Western concert halls. His First Symphony was completed in 1925, and it was a remarkable achievement on the part of a young man of nineteen. As a composer, Shostakovich can be described as an eclectic progressive, rooted in tradition and tonality, yet using dissonance and occasional atonality without adhering to a specific school. One salient characteristic of his First Symphony, and of the composer's style in general, is the manner in which themes grow organically from one another. Their relationship is not always immediately obvious, but it produces a remarkable effect of unity and cohesion.

The First Symphony uses the piano extensively, indicating that the composer is still a student of orchestration, relying on what he knows best, but still quite comfortable to work masterfully within his own limitations. The economy of orchestration does not detract from the power of the score: in the First Symphony, Shostakovich relies on the value and balance of his structural material to create something of high artistic merit.[91]

The most celebrated section of the First Symphony is the third movement, the lento in B-flat minor. It begins with a melody for the solo cello and a distant quasi-military harmony in the horns. The passion and intensity of the harmony increase, and the fanfare rapidly assumes prime importance. It passes from instrument to instrument as the music blackens. Solo oboe suggests a second melody, but harsh brass chords harden its texture. Eventually a solo violin introduces a moment of peace and stillness, only to be contradicted by the unyielding rhythm of the fanfare motif. Muted trumpet takes up the oboe's second melody as the strings divide themselves into sixteen voices, bringing this profoundly troubled movement to its conclusion.[92] Although the composer did not avow any programme for this symphony, it is the intensely dramatic third movement which suggests the existence of some underlying story or allegory. For Massine, the striking contrast between the sorrowful oboe theme and the strident rhythm of the march suggested a struggle between fragile White and evil Black.

Like Prokofiev, Shostakovich was subjected to stringent musico-political pressures. In 1948, Andrey Zhadanov, an uncultured bureaucrat and a leading member of the Central Committee, issued the Zhadanov Decree, which compelled Shostakovich and many other musicians to appear before the committee to hear the formal charges against them. Facing the ruination of their careers, most musicians apologized for their erroneous adventures. Shostakovich confessed, "I again deviated in the direction of formalism, and began to speak in a language incomprehensible to the people. ... I know that the Party is right. ... I am deeply grateful."[93]

And yet, through the strength of his genius, Shostakovich eventually attained a plateau beyond such parochial ideological criticism. His great *tour de force*, the Tenth Symphony (1953), was composed in the very year of Stalin's death. He eventually came back into favor with the Communist Party and is now unanimously regarded as the greatest symphonist of the mid-twentieth century.

Choreography

Leonid Sabaneev noted that the music has "a rather unexpected old-fashioned flavour, a precocious academicism, despite its sufficiently modernistic external features."[94] Accordingly, modern dance was not incorporated to the extent seen in previous symphonic ballets. Walter Terry observed, "The technique is always that of the pure ballet, and the precision, the clarity of line and the crispness of this highly stylized technique is admirably suited to the parallel qualities of the music."

From the standpoint of pure movement invention, *Rouge et noir* may well be among Massine's finest ballets. Terry wrote that the movement was "so coldly abstract that it resolves itself into a study of design, a brilliant kaleidoscope that fascinates the eye."[95] Massine made great progress in solving one of the chief difficulties encountered in earlier symphonic ballets: the awkward juggling of dancers on their way into and out of his signature architectural tableaux. Critics had groused about the problem frequently in the past, but Grace Robert felt that "he answered it superbly in *Rouge et noir*, where the groups (many and fascinating) click into position as though placed there by a gigantic hand working a jigsaw puzzle."[96]

The choreographic highlights included the second-movement solo for Frederic Franklin, the emotional, acrobatic pas de deux for Markova and Platov in the third movement, and the exquisite solo for Markova which began the third movement.

Massine's choreographic intent was to create an abstract interpretation of the score in a mobile and fluctuating color scheme and to provide a thematic interpretation of the score as the conflict between the material and spiritual world via color symbolism. The concept got even more involved when Massine opted to give each movement program notes which gave the audience a plot that simply didn't seem to be occurring onstage.

Critical Survey

For the most part, *Rouge et noir* was favorably received. A. E. Twysden: "I am convinced that it is his greatest work since *Choreartium*"; Robert Lawrence: "one of Massine's finest"; Walter Terry: "new and stimulating each time that it is on view."[97]

The chief objection to the ballet was that it was a mistake to append a story line to a work that was virtually abstract, save for the fact that it tied the changing moods of the symphony to a fluctuating color scheme. The program notes gave the ballet a false emotional framework, and thus left Massine wide open to the usual charges that symphonic ballets were histrionic and hackneyed: for instance, the *Ballet* critic wrote that *Rouge et noir* "is full of clichés which become increasingly noticeable with repeated performances."[98]

In Retrospect

Rouge et noir remained in the repertoire from 1939 to 1942 and was revived in 1948 at the Metropolitan Opera and in 1949 at New York City Center. *Rouge et noir* was a superbly crafted ballet, and one wonders why Massine felt the need to cling to a literary smokescreen six full years after his successful *Choreartium*. When viewed today, *Rouge et noir* does not *look* as dated as the misleading program notes imply. This ballet is now an underrated museum piece. Even so, we are left with Terry's testimony that *Rouge et Noir* "stands as a monument in pure dance to the physical beauty of the human body and to man's complete mastery of that body."[99]

7

June 1939–February 1943

After the 1939 Paris season ended in late June, the members of the Ballet Russe went on vacation, then returned to work for a Covent Garden booking scheduled to begin on September 4. Already, Londoners were mobilizing and building air-raid shelters. The company rehearsed daily in a London armory: all day long the British reserves were bringing in loads of machine guns, grenades, and ammunition. After a while painters began daubing the windows of the building with black paint, an air-raid precaution, and the paint spattered on the floor. "Move over here," said Massine. "Here's a clear space." One of the dancers collapsed in laughter on the sticky floor. "Léonide Fedorovitch," he gasped, "if a bomb were to fall and wreck the building, you would say, 'Move over here people, here's a clear space!'" Massine admitted that he probably would.[1]

The scheduled opening at Covent Garden never took place. On September 1, Nazi troops marched into Warsaw and bombarded the Polish capitol. On September 3 England and France declared war on Germany. Léonide and his dancers found themselves stranded in Europe, unable to reach the United States.

The first transatlantic passage that Massine was able to book was chivalrously given over to Delarova, now quite alone after their divorce. Fortunately, Massine and Tatiana were also able to cross the Atlantic soon afterwards, arriving in America on September 14. However, Massine had no dancers. Visas caused complications, because many of the dancers, being Russian refugees, traveled on Nansen passports. These were actually travel documents, not official citizenship passports, and they compounded the difficulties of arranging passages across the Atlantic. To make matters worse, the U.S. government ruled in October that American citizens must have first precedence in passages from Europe to America.

In New York, panic and despair held sway at the offices of Universal Art, but cooler heads prevailed in the end. It was largely through the innumerable transatlantic cables and telephone calls of Sol Hurok that the Ballet Russe was able to reach this country at all. Thanks to Hurok, in less than two months, and only two weeks behind the scheduled departure date, practically the entire company was reassembled in Europe and set sail from France on the *Rotterdam*.

Arriving on the very day of their Metropolitan première on October 27, the dancers were rushed away from the docks to the opera house. Lillian Moore reports that a "chattering and laughing horde" burst through the stage door at the Met, but within five minutes, Massine had whisked them all off to their dressing rooms to prepare for their one and only rehearsal before the opening.[2] John Martin applauded the company for its pluckiness: "The chief news this morning about the opening of the Ballet Russe de Monte Carlo at the Met last night is to be found in the mere fact that it actually did open.... The famous slogan that 'the show must go on' was never more courageously exemplified."[3]

The first world première of the Ballet Russe de Monte Carlo took place on November 9 with *Bacchanale*, a Salvador Dalí/Massine collaboration. It was a curious and controversial bringing together of Sigmund Freud, Richard Wagner and King Ludwig of Bavaria. Both Diaghilev and de Basil had employed surrealist artists (Ernst, Miró, Chirico), but Dalí was the first to have provided a scenario.

After the fall Metropolitan season, the Ballet Russe spent the winter on a coast-to-coast tour. Meanwhile, American companies and the American Guild of Musical Artists turned up the heat on Universal Art to unionize.

When AGMA started unionizing ballet companies at the beginning of 1939, it was warmly received by such company heads as Lincoln Kirstein (Ballet Caravan), Catherine Littlefield (Littlefield Ballet), and Richard Pleasant (Ballet Theatre). All companies, though, when signing, demanded assurances that Ballet Russe would be lined up, too. AGMA gave its promise and contacted Serge Denham before the fall 1939 season. At several points, the contract seemed as good as signed, but at the last moment, Denham always managed to find new causes for delay. Pressure from AGMA increased when it was learned that Massine had "hired" several young girls who were willing to work gratis and pay their own traveling expenses.⁴ Now, despite furious resentment, the company had left on tour without signing.

Kirstein and Pleasant led the fight to force the unionization of their foreign rival. The campaign reached the boiling point with an angry protest in the *New York Herald Tribune* upon the Ballet Russe's return to New York:

> Mr. Pleasant said that the Ballet Russe pays a minimum salary of $22.50 a week, while the Ballet Theater pays a minimum of $45 a week. He added that the backers of the Ballet Theater had refused to finance any more performances unless there was reasonable assurance that they would at least break even and not be forced out of business by lower-priced competition.... [Mr. Kirstein] said that if the Ballet Russe had not signed by Tuesday, he and his dancers would picket the Metropolitan Opera House "in white tights if necessary."⁵

The main holdup was that Denham wanted AGMA to grant a number of concessions, particularly an increase in the maximum number of rehearsal hours. But during the third week of March, the Ballet Russe dancers voted to strike if the AGMA contract was not signed. Subsequently, the musician, stagehand and theatre manager unions advised Universal Art that their members would not cross the dancers' picket lines in the event of a strike. Backed up to the wall, Universal Art finally settled with AGMA. The new contract provided $45 weekly performance minimums. Furthermore, AGMA withdrew from Universal Art all previously granted concessions. *Dance* reported that the "contract bristles with restrictions on rehearsal time, and is far stiffer than the contract AGMA almost signed with Universal Art last fall."⁶

While the AGMA dispute did nothing for the Ballet Russe's public relations in America, it should also be remembered that the company did indeed make a few sincere efforts to provide, rather than thwart, opportunities for American artists. Universal Art formed a subsidiary body known as the Ballet Guild. In February 1940 the Ballet Guild announced a national competition, open to Americans only, for a new ballet on American subject matter. Three cash prizes for the winning score, décor and libretto would be awarded by Massine and other judges on the panel. The scenario division was won by Glen Westcott, and David Diamond won first prize for the score. But a problem arose when the Ballet Guild wanted to award the prize for décor to a young, nonunion designer, while United Scenic Artists' Union rules decreed that its members could work with union designers only.⁷ Ultimately, the entire project was scrapped, but it was still a commendable effort.

Following their spring season in New York, the Ballet Russe embarked on a South American tour in the summer of 1940 and returned to New York in the fall for a season at the Fifty-first Street Theatre. Two new and unsuccessful Massine works premièred: *The New Yorker* and *Vienna—1814*. It was writer and caricaturist Rea Irwin of the *New Yorker* staff who suggested to Massine a ballet based on the cartoon characters who appeared regularly in this magazine. Massine chose the music of George Gershwin and, assisted by Gershwin's brother, Ira, Léonide assembled the score from a number of Gershwin's popular songs and concert works.[8]

Massine had long admired the music of Carl Maria von Weber. In 1937 he had discussed plans for a Weber ballet on a German theme with Count Etienne de Beaumont, but Hitler's subsequent aggression made this unthinkable. In 1940 Massine gave his postponed Weber ballet the new premise of a ball given by Count Metternich to celebrate the downfall of Napoleon and entitled it *Vienna—1814*. By the time rehearsals began, Beaumont was in occupied France, so the scenic and costume designs were entrusted to Stewart Chaney.

After a two-year absence from the United States, de Basil's Original Ballet Russe succeeded the Massine/Denham company, opening at the same theatre in November, one week after Massine's departure. John Martin believed that the auspices for de Basil's company were quite fortunate "because it comes on the heels of what has been undoubtedly the least distinguished season Massine's company has given. The new works were in no case unqualified successes, and the general staging and lighting of the whole repertoire have been shockingly inadequate."[10] Like Martin, Walter Terry also noted sloppiness on the part of everyone from the dancers to the stage technicians: "On the debit side, one finds a lighting system which seems to be left entirely in the hands of pixies, and a corps de ballet which sends you streaking for the Music Hall Rockettes."[11] Sir Lionel Bradley caught word of the companies' rival seasons, even during the dark days of the London Blitz: "The De Basil Co. has had an extraordinary success (14 weeks in New York) and Massine's company seems to be in a bad way."[12]

With the Fifty-first Street Theatre season behind them, the Denham company departed on a long tour of the United States and Canada and did not return to New York until the fall of 1941. Relations between Massine and Denham, always strained, now began to erode rapidly. During the company's first season, Massine was almost invincible—he had no rival in international prestige or in his ability to attract investors on both sides of the Atlantic. But Massine was inevitably weakened by the facts that he was cut off from his main power base in Europe and that America's ballet pioneers were eager to get rid of him. Denham was quick to perceive his vulnerability, and he began chipping away at Massine's status from 1939 onwards.

He started by giving Massine unsolicited advice on artistic decisions, which prompted angry retorts from Massine. Massine bristled when Denham commissioned Balanchine to mount *Poker Game* and *Le Baiser de la fée* for the Ballet Russe. *Dance* magazine reported rumors about the Massine/Denham standoff and alluded to another rumor that Denham had "discussed with George Balanchine the possibility of the latter's replacing Massine as director."[13]

Denham was also trying to prevent Massine from choreographing any more symphonic ballets, suggesting in a letter to Fleischmann that they were box-office poison.[14] Since Massine had just told *Dance* magazine that this genre "is what most of all interests me,"[15] one can imagine his frustration. Massine also complained that his title of artistic director was omitted from posters, that his salary was often late, and that he was receiving neither royalties nor traveling expenses.[16]

The fact that Ballet Russe dancers were up in arms over Massine's casting decisions only increased his demoralization. The dressing-room scuttlebutt revolved around charges that Massine's wife, Tatiana, was being cast in leading roles which she did not deserve. They may have been right: as Zobedie in *Scheherazade*, Walter Terry wrote that her characterization "seems to be limited to unfortunate posturings, and her supposedly enticing walk is dangerously reminiscent of an American Indian stalking his prey."[17] Many dancers, among them Igor Youskevitch, threatened to strike if such blatant nepotism continued. But according to Jack Anderson, Youskevitch would never have been so obstinate on the casting issue had he realized the degree of tension between Massine and Denham.[18] Youskevitch found much to admire in Massine but had little, if any, respect for ex-banker Denham. He claimed that the "wily" Denham was "a penny-pinching scoundrel. ... Financially, he knew his business. Artistically, it was a different story."[19]

In the midst of all this intrigue, Léonide must have found it a godsend to escape once more into the fantastic world of Salvador Dalí. Dalí spent the entirety of World War II in the United States, where his eccentric appearance—flowing capes, handlebar moustache, and pop eyes—made him an instant photo celebrity. Dalí approached Massine early in 1941 with an idea for a second ballet collaboration. He wanted to use Schubert's Symphony No. 7 for a modern rendering of the story of Theseus and Ariadne.

Once he was drawn into the project, Massine related that he was "both amused and revolted" by some of Dalí's bizarre ideas. For instance, Massine "drew the line" when Dalí suggested that, as a symbol of destruction, the stagehands should drop a Steinway piano onto the stage from the catwalks. Dalí also wanted to use a real calf's head for the episode in which Theseus kills the Minotaur, to be followed by a scene in which the dancers would ceremoniously cut off chunks from the carnage and eat them raw. In his most sporting mood, Massine accompanied Dalí on a taxi ride to Sixth Avenue where he reported, "we visited one restaurant after another in search of a calf's head. The waiters were stunned, but polite; the best they could do was offer us a veal sandwich!"[20] Thus began the second Dalí-Massine collaboration. It may have been a fiasco, but no one could ever say that it was dull.

Massine's last ballet of 1941, *Saratoga*, had no chance of success from the get-go because exceedingly poor material was foisted upon him as a fait accompli. To reduce the financial risks of touring a large company and a full orchestra, Universal Art announced that from the fall of 1941 onward, they would produce only ballets directly sponsored by individual backers. Massine "sensed that this would mean lowering our standards," and wrote that "It was therefore no surprise to me to be asked to produce *Saratoga*, a contrived story about the American racing resort."[21] This wretched ballet prompted the harshest invectives yet heard against Massine.

In January of 1942 Massine attempted to prove his continuing artistic vitality by sending Denham a list of twenty ballets he was prepared to undertake over the next few years. But by then, Massine's unbroken series of four failures in a row had put Denham in the driver's seat. In a letter to Fleischmann, Denham spoke of a need to curb Massine's artistic activities and to commission more works from Balanchine.[22]

Calling Denham a "mere tyro at ballet direction" and an "amateur," Sol Hurok came to Massine's defence: "Massine had given of his best to create and maintain a fine organization. He had been a shining example to the others. The company had started on a high plane of accomplishments; but it was impossible for Massine to continue under conditions that daily became less and less bearable."[23] It was Hurok who actually dominated the ballet world by 1940. In addition to his far-reaching booking apparatus, he alone held the exclusive lease for ballet productions at the Metropolitan Opera. Thus, he held the fate of any company he sponsored in his powerful hands. In 1941 Hurok dropped his exclusive contract with Denham's company and signed on as manager for the up-and-coming Ballet Theatre. Hurok wanted to secure Massine's services for Ballet Theatre. He was shrewdly aware that to the general American

Family portrait of Massine, Tatiana Orlova and Tatiana Massine, 1941. *(MAURICE SEYMOUR)*

public, "ballet" still meant Russian ballet, which, outside the cognoscenti, still meant Massine. His management policy was to embrace "Russianization" to ensure good box-office for Ballet Theatre.

Almost undoubtedly in an effort to further his plans, Hurok selected two dismal failures—*Labyrinth* and *Saratoga*—for the 1942 opening night at the Metropolitan. This doomsday program was characterized by Walter Terry as "ballet at its nadir." He added, "The current weakness of the Ballet Russe de Monte Carlo is not a sudden occurrence. The process of enervation commenced months, perhaps years ago, and a good share of the blame must be laid to its artistic director. ... [E]very creator needs a rest and Massine has needed one for two years."[24] The suggestion that he needed a "rest" could only have goaded Massine to follow Hurok's suggestion of obtaining a leave of absence from Ballet Russe in order to create two new works for Ballet Theatre in the summer of 1942.

In May, Ballet Theatre went to Mexico City for five months as the guest of the Mexican government. Massine's two new ballets—*Aleko* and

Don Domingo de Don Blas—were created that summer. *Aleko* was inspired by Pushkin's 1826 poem "Gypsies," a long narrative saga in the romantic tradition about a disillusioned young aristocrat who leaves society to live with a band of Bessarabian gypsies. *Don Domingo* had as its *raison d'être* Ballet Theatre's desire to thank the Mexican government for its hospitality. Massine wrote the libretto, which he based on a play of the same name by the seventeenth-century dramatist, Juan Ruiz de Alarcon y Mendoza. He kept the basic story of the love rivalry between the rich Don Domingo and the poor young adventurer Don Juan, but transferred the action from Spain to Mexico.

When Massine returned to the Ballet Russe in the fall of 1942, his connections with the company were severed. His contract as artistic director (due to expire in 1948) was annulled in November of 1942. Massine wrote: "After working for them for three years, I was summarily dismissed. It was a bitter blow, which left me feeling bereft and disillusioned. Although I protested vehemently, there was nothing I could do."[25]

Once again Massine had to face a courtroom battle for the ownership of his ballets. The case was heard by the American Arbitration Association, and arbitrator James Gifford ruled that the scenic properties and costumes for most of Massine's ballets, including *Le Tricorne*, *La Boutique* and *Capriccio*, should be assigned to him without fail. When Massine thanked Gifford for his decision, he replied, "Just remember that bankers must not have the right to dismiss artists so easily."[26]

Massine continued to be proactive for choreographers' legal rights in the decades which followed. He was one of the first to make it a policy to film 16-mm. rehearsal copies of his ballets as a means of securing copyright,[27] and in 1966, he took the Nice Opera Ballet to court in a case which had far-reaching implications. This company had commissioned new choreography from Françoise Adret for *Le Tricorne*. Massine charged that the ballet was a joint collaboration and that his choreography was therefore inseparable from Falla's score. The court agreed, ruling that music and choreography "were born of a common will and constitute an indivisible work."[28]

On November 10, Massine officially joined Ballet Theatre. From the moment of their permanent arrival in the United States in 1939, Massine and his third wife had constantly been on tour. Finally, the couple could say farewell to their nomadic trailer existence. Tatiana and Léonide now had a child named after her mother, and they purchased a house on Long Island. Massine built a large dance studio onto the house and began work on Ballet Theatre revivals of *La Boutique*, *Le Tricorne*, *Capriccio espagnol*, and his third Ballet Theatre world première, *Mademoiselle Angot*.

Many American critics were unhappy over Massine's association with Ballet Theatre, and their remarks took on a distinct nationalist tone:

> Massine would seem to be a singularly inappropriate choreographer for the Ballet Theater.... Somebody seems to have got the idea that it is a Ballet Russe, or should be, and is apparently determined to force the standard Ballet repertory and procedure down its throat, whether or no. Sooner or later, choked with dancers, choreographers and repertory which are not its native diet, it is likely one day suddenly to expire, leaving nothing behind but a sad memory."[29]

BACCHANALE

The First Paranoiac Performance[30]
Libretto: Salvador Dalí
Music: Richard Wagner, the Venusberg music from *Tannhäuser*
Set Design: Salvador Dalí, executed by Prince A. Schervachidze
Costume Design: Salvador Dalí, executed by Mme Karinska
Première: Metropolitan Opera House, New York, November 9, 1939

ORIGINAL CAST
Ludwig II: Casimir Kokitch
Two Cupids: Mlles Pourmel, Etheridge
Venus: Nini Theilade
Her Companions: Mlles Rklitzka, Williams, Godkin
The Three Graces: Mlles Rostova, Kelepovska, Geleznova
Lola Montez: Milada Mladova
The Nymph: Nathalie Krassovska   **The Faun**: André Eglevsky
Two Bacchantes: Mlles Lvova, Rosson
The Satyrs: MM. Armour, Katcharov
Sacher Masoch: Marc Platov   **His Wife**: Jeanette Laurel
Knight of Death: Chris Volkov
Assistant Nymphs and Fauns

Synopsis

Bacchanale brings together King Ludwig II of Bavaria and Richard Wagner in a scenario based upon the Venusberg scene from Wagner's *Tannhäuser*. Ludwig (known to history as "The Mad King") is the central character, and the perceptions of his demented brain are the only reality for everything that transpires in this ballet.

The curtain rises on a landscape dominated by a huge swan. Lola Montez emerges from the swan, clad in harem trousers and a hoop skirt. A parade of weird bacchantes from the pages of psychological casebooks succeed her onstage and wander across its length: a fish-headed woman,

Graces with strange protuberances, psychopathic nymphs, and fauns with enormous genitalia. Periodically, Sacher Masoch and his spouse make appearances in which Masoch gleefully subjects himself to fierce whippings by his wife. In the midst of this confusion wanders Ludwig, seeking some kind of relief from his scary hallucinations.

All the while, a satyr and his dwarf companion, seated in a downstage corner, are imperturbably wool-winding and knitting a red sock. But as Nymphs and Fauns begin to roll around on the floor with sensual abandon, the Satyr packs up his knitting in disgust and leaves, his petite friend clinging to his leg. After the orgy, Venus enters in a nude-colored unitard. Imagining himself to be Tannhäuser, Ludwig approaches Venus, but she becomes a dragon and, as Lohengrin, Ludwig kills her. In his last vision before death, Leda appears and performs a pas de deux with the swan as her static partner.

The Knight of Death enters in the form of an anthropomorphic umbrella, attended by two men wrapped in opposite ends of a winding sheet. As Ludwig falls dead, four large black umbrellas, planted at the corners, open with stately dignity. Lola Montez emerges once more from the belly of the swan.

Concept

Dalí brings Freud to bear on King Ludwig II, who came to the Bavarian throne in 1864. He is remembered for his patronage of Richard Wagner, for his lavish palaces and, mainly, for his insanity. History records how this monarch, despising people in general, abandoned politics and immersed himself in a fantasy world of his own creation and in his homosexual love life.

It is a well-known historical fact that King Ludwig actually "lived" all of Wagner's myths, identifying himself with their legendary heroes to the point of profound visual hyperesthesia. Thus, in honor of Wagner's visit to his castle of Hohenschwangau, he appeared as Lohengrin, Knight of the Holy Grail, clad in golden armor and borne on a boat which floated gently across the lake.[31] In 1864, Ludwig gave Wagner a pension to complete his opera-cycle, *Der Ring des Nibelungen*. "Embodiment of my happiness ... Exalted, divine friend ... Lord of my life ... O Holy One, I worship you!" wrote Ludwig to Wagner on January 5, 1865.[32] Although public hostility soon forced Ludwig to renounce his intimacy with Wagner, he continued his financial support of a friend whom he adored to the point of obsession. Pronounced insane in 1886, Ludwig committed suicide by drowning himself in the Starnberger See on June 13 of the same year.

Music

The most controversial musical figure of the nineteenth century, Wagner greatly expanded the expressive powers of the operatic genre with *Der fliegende Holländer* (1843), *Tannhäuser* (1845), *Lohengrin* (1848), his vast tetralogy *Der Ring des Nibelungen* (1853-74), *Tristan und Isolde* (1857-59), *Die Meistersinger von Nürnberg* (1862-67) and *Parsifal* (1877-82). Wagner's distinctive style began to emerge in the first three operas above and in the treatises written around 1850. The guiding principles of his theory were naturalism and dramatic truth, which he felt had been compromised by the artificial conventions of Italian and French opera. He advocated a new synthesis of music, verse, and staging based on the principles of Greek tragedy—what he called a *Gesamtkunstwerk*.

Ensemble singing was to be avoided. The verse was to dispense with the end-rhyme that led to closed musical structures. The music, played by a greatly augmented orchestra, would weave a dense network of relationships extending over the entire work from the repetition, variation and regrouping of motifs. By their direct association with characters, events, or ideas, the motifs were to reinforce the dramatic action.

The 1521 *Tannhäuser* ballad tells of the knight Tannhäuser's visit to the Venusberg—a subterranean grotto in Germany to which the goddess Venus has been banished by Christian theology. Here, she entertains Tannhäuser and other renegade knights with endless bacchanales. Tannhäuser spends a year living with the Lady Venus until longing and remorse drive him out of his mountain retreat. He goes to Rome and implores the pope's forgiveness, but Pope Urban IV will not absolve him. Just as the bishop's staff which he holds in his hand will never again put forth leaves, he says, so Tannhäuser can never hope to attain God's grace. With heavy heart, Tannhäuser returns to the Venusberg. On the third day, Pope Urban's staff puts forth leaves. He sends out messengers in search of Tannhäuser, but he is never found. As a result the pope, like Tannhäuser, will be damned for all eternity.

The opening scene in the Venusberg, Wagner insisted, was not to be a typical ballet divertissement but an expressive mime scene with minimal formal dancing. Here, Wagner was already carrying out his maxim for truth and naturalism in the opera. In 1859 Emperor Napoleon III commanded a revival of *Tannhäuser* at the Paris Opéra. In his first meeting with Wagner, Opéra director Alphonse Royer stated adamantly that the most important precondition for a successful production was a large-scale ballet in the second act. This was imperative because the aristocratic members of the Jockey Club, all of whom were immensely influential season-ticket holders, were not in the habit of attending the opera until after they had dined. It was then—at the beginning of the second act—that they expected their ballet and the sport of ogling fair young dancers through their opera glasses. Wagner was vigorously opposed to a second-act ballet; he compromised only to the extent of agreeing to revamp the Act One Venusberg scene into an elaborate ballet sequence.

Wagner and choreographer Lucien Petipa created an allegory of rampant sexuality. The curtain rises on Venus, lying on her couch with Tannhäuser's head in her lap. The stage is replete with Cupids, Naiads, Satyrs and Fauns who dance with increasing abandon as "the general frenzy gives way to maenadic fury."[33] At this point, the three Graces order the Cupids to aim their darts into the midst of the tumult, and the Graces advise Venus of their victory over her dissolute subjects. *Tableaux vivants* appear as visions at the back of the stage, including Leda and the swan.

The Paris première took place on March 13, 1861, in the presence of the court, and the rowdies of the Jockey Club staged a famous demonstration of shouts, jeers and laughter, which was mostly an assault on Wagner for denying them their Act Two ballet. On the second night, the Jockey Club came to the theater equipped with dog whistles, and the din reached unimaginable proportions.[34] After this performance, Wagner withdrew *Tannhäuser* from the Opéra.

Most opera-goers thus missed the chance to see a spectacular new Venusberg scene. Ernst Bloch termed it "an abyss of satyriasis ... brothel splendor of the highest order."[35] Today, the Venusberg scene is regarded as one of Wagner's greatest and most quintessential compositions—stridently Germanic, perpetually punctuated with cymbal and drums.

When the Massine/Dalí *Bacchanale* premièred, many Wagnerites fumed, but they forgot that the Venusberg had degenerated over the years into an often ponderous operatic cliché. It was Massine and Dalí who realized that the Venusberg music itself was glorious and could never be out of date: "it was its presentation which had become standardized and therefore boring, and this was an opportunity for us to rescue it."[36] The Venusberg music was a perfect choice for *Bacchanale*. Its very solemnity and its associations with other meanings gave the dancers ideal ingredients for creating a mood of ultimate lunacy onstage.

Scenery and Costumes

The Spanish painter Salvador Dalí was a leader of Surrealism: his paintings became part of the definitive record of twentieth-century art. In 1929 Dalí made the film *Un Chien andalou* with Luis Buñuel. The film simulated the conditions of the dream and used montage to achieve a transformation of objects, which was to become the most salient physical characteristic of Dalí's version of Surrealism. *Un Chien andalou* brought Dalí to the attention of André Breton, and he was officially accepted into the surrealist movement in the same year.

Dalí's principal theoretical contribution to Surrealism was his "paranoiac-critical method." What distinguishes the disease of paranoia from other forms of delirium is a perfect and coherent systematization, the accession of a state of omnipotence which often leads to megalomania, a persecution mania, or both. It is accompanied by hallucination: far from submitting to life's necessary compromises, the paranoiac models life to suit his own desires.

According to Dalí, paranoia-criticism is a method based on "systematic objectification of delirious associations and interpretations.... In the painting it would be merely the hand-made color photograph of concrete irrationality and of the imaginative world in general."[37] Dalí saw the paranoiac-critical method as a means of destabilizing the world, believing everything the viewer saw was potentially something else. This accounts for the famous double images of his mature technique.

In its dependence on associations and hidden meanings, the method owed much to Sigmund Freud's understanding of the dream as an expression of unconscious desire, in which one object may signify another. Asserting that the instinctual, subconscious part of our thought processes has been suppressed under the pretense of civilization and progress, Dalí thanked Sigmund Freud for forming a current of opinion "by means of which the human explorer will be able to carry his investigation much further, authorized as he will henceforth be not to confine himself solely to the most summary realities. The imagination is perhaps on the point of reasserting itself, of reclaiming its rights."[38]

Bacchanale, Dalí's first theatrical venture, is a fine example of his paranoiac-critical method, relying as it does on the dreamlike association of seemingly incongruous images. Dalí's stunning backdrop was dominated by a gigantic swan with outspread wings and a skull-shaped opening in its breast. In the background was a landscape depicting Mount Venus. The composition was flanked with stacks of bureau drawers and a few burning carcasses.[39]

Those in the audience who had read a little Freud could see that there were few deviations from the clichés of standard Freudian symbolism. The double row of teeth adorning the hoopskirt of Lola Montez not only reinforced the skull imagery, but also encircled her pubic area. Other costume grotesqueries included a woman with a huge rose-colored fish head, Graces who had an astounding number of "graces" attached to their anatomies, Nymphs in schizophrenic costumes (one-half frilly organdy

Studio portrait of Chris Volkov as the Knight of Death in *Bacchanale*, 1939. Costume design by Salvador Dalí. *(MAURICE SEYMOUR)*

party frocks, one-half men's underwear), and hyperbolically virile Fauns who wore nothing but neckties and sassy red lobsters stitched to their loincloths.[40]

Some of the props were references to King Ludwig, such as the image of Death as a large, black umbrella decorated with a luminous skull.[41]

Dalí also provided stray allusions to the original Venusberg scene with the duet for Leda and the swan, along with the requisite quota of nymphs and fauns. Throughout, the symbolism was less to be pursued to the depth of psycho-sexual import than to simply be taken in the spirit of zany fun. For John Martin, only the recurrent theme of Masoch's masochism, "a theme couched in neither symbolic nor surrealistic terms," bordered on the offensive. "Elsewhere," he quipped, "Dalí's concern with the libido is likely to go safely over the heads of Little Willie and Grandma alike."[42]

Choreography

In *Bacchanale*, the choreography was essentially an underlying mechanism supporting the set design and the literary concept. Although Massine worked avidly with Dalí on the motivating idea, he seems to have been content to function as a surrealist sideshow coordinator, merely contributing mobile accessories to Dalí's décor. The most frequent criticism of his choreography, as articulated by Albertina Vitak, was that Massine failed to invent "some distinctly peculiar style of movements, whether serious or frivolous, for this psychoanalytic Ballet." Similarly, Martin asked, "If the surrealist approach is to be made, why not make it wholeheartedly, in movement as well as in idea and visual design? The cool, clear, eminently objective manner of the classic ballet is many light years away from super-realism."[43]

Critical Survey

Not surprisingly, *Bacchanale* got mixed reviews. Vitak wrote that it "doesn't warrant repeated showings." Pitt Sanborn disagreed: "It is something to watch alertly, and is not simply a soporific for a source of titillation. ... [T]he effect does not miss, but asserts itself insidiously under the skin, and for a long time stimulates and troubles the mind."[44] Martin's November 19 review was mixed, yet he took the work so seriously that he devoted two full columns to it.

Bacchanale's notoriety ensured its return to the Met for the company's 1940 season. But once the novelty began to fade, Martin decided that it was "inclined to lack edge," and Robert noted that it "faded from the repertoire" after 1940.[45]

In Retrospect

The idea behind *Bacchanale*—putting a Freudian interpretation on Mad Ludwig's attempts to "live" the roles in Wagner's operas—is ingenious. Martin made a pertinent remark when he wrote that *Bacchanale* was "extremely well done within its own limitations."[46] Massine and Dalí could only actualize their concept up to a point, reined in as they were by the boundaries of the stage and the relatively primitive state of technical theatre in 1939. Wagner, Ludwig and Freud exert a timeless fascination, and the Dalí/Massine concept deserves to be rescued from the dustbins of time. In the hands of a gifted videographer, it could take wings and fly.

THE NEW YORKER

Ballet in Three Scenes
Libretto: Rea Irwin and Léonide Massine
Music: George Gershwin, orchestrated by David Raskin
Scenic and Costume Design: Carl Kent, after Rea Irwin and Nathalie Crothers
Première: Fifty-first Street Theatre, New York, October 18, 1940

ORIGINAL CAST

Scene One

Hokinson Lady: Tatiana Chamié
Timid Man: Léonide Massine
The Dowager: Jean Yazvinsky   **Eustace Tilley:** George Zoritch
Chauffeur: Nicholas Beriozov   **The Colonel:** Vladimir Kostenko
Columnist: Frederic Franklin

Scene Two

Maitre d'Hotel: Casimir Kokitch   **Drunkard:** Georges Tomin
Debutante: Nathalie Krassovska
Her Three Boyfriends: André Eglevsky, Roland Guérard, Igor Youskevitch
Small Fry: Lubov Roudenko, Ian Gibson
The Girl: Alexandra Danilova   **The Little King:** Michel Katcharov

Scene Three

Drunkard, Gossip Columnist, Guests

Synopsis[47]

A dioramic view of New York's café society in three scenes presents a nocturnal adventure of the animated drawings made famous by Peter Arno, Helen E. Hokinson, William Steig, James Thurber and other artists' creations whose habitudes are the pages of the *New Yorker* magazine. To Central Park's Plaza come Arno's Colonel, the Dowager and the Timid Man, Hokinson's Clubwoman, boys and girls, each intent on hot-spotting. Venal headwaiters, baby-faced debutantes, keyhole columnists, Steig's "small-fry," gullible gangsters, Thurber's introverts, all these with gentle madness people the parade of New York after dark. The thread of the story is incidental to the portrayal of characters whose lives begin when the city goes to bed.

Scenery and Costumes

In consultation with Rea Irwin, Carl Kent modeled the costumes after *New Yorker* cartoon illustrations, supplemented with variations on contemporary tuxedos and ball gowns. The first set was the exterior of a nightclub with a view of the Manhattan skyline, and the second was the interior of the nightclub itself. Both sets were unremarkable, and Irving Kolodin's remark that "Rea Irwin's imaginative costumes rather shamed the settings"[48] suggests that even the costumes were more to the credit of Irwin than to Kent.

Music

From an impoverished childhood, George Gershwin quickly achieved renown as one of America's most gifted composers of popular songs and musicals. While he briefly studied theory, harmony, counterpoint and orchestration, he acquired only a limited knowledge of these subjects and never became proficient at reading music.

In 1914 he became a pianist and song-plugger at Remick's, a Tin Pan Alley publisher. In 1919, at the age of twenty-three, he wrote the song that made him famous. His lyricist, Irving Caesar, claims that "we wrote 'Swanee' in about 12 or 13 minutes."[49] "Swanee" became a worldwide hit, and during the 1920s and 1930s, Gershwin continued to turn out a steady stream of pleasing, memorable songs for a series of successful musicals and four film scores.

Gershwin's aspirations as a serious composer advanced when he wrote *Rhapsody in Blue* (1924) and *An American in Paris* (1928). While Gershwin's songs thrive in their brief format, his serious works are sometimes structurally hampered because of his limited experience in developing musical material. The development in *Rhapsody in Blue*, for instance, was confined mainly to ideas in a sequence.[50] Many music critics tended to treat Gershwin's concert works with contempt. Typical was the debut of Gershwin's *Cuban Overture* on August 16, 1932. Howard Taubman wrote that "if he had any pretensions to being considered a truly gifted composer, the almost unvarying sameness and formlessness of this body of music did not help him."[51] Yet others maintain that Gershwin's melodic materials are attractive enough in themselves to compensate for their structural deficiencies and have accepted his music as the embodiment of musical Americana.

Studio portrait of Léonide Massine as the Timid Man in *The New Yorker*, 1940.
(MAURICE SEYMOUR)

Gershwin selections for *The New Yorker* included excerpts from his *Cuban Overture*, Rhapsody No. 2, Piano Concerto No. 1, and *An American in Paris*. These were spliced in with the popular songs "Strike Up the Band," "The Man I Love," "I Got Rhythm," "Somebody Loves Me," "Swanee," "Fascinating Rhythm," "Love Is Sweeping the Country," "Let's Call the Whole Thing Off," and one more: Among Massine's favorite songs was an unfamiliar Gershwin tune called "Walking the Dog."[52]

Kolodin praised Raskin's deft and painstaking orchestration, but Robert Lawrence faulted him for excerpting "dribs and drabs" of Gershwin's serious, more extended works. For him, this only accentuated Gershwin's main weakness: "the lack of architectural merit which plagued Gershwin's larger works at their best was even more apparent in this loosely arranged version."[53]

Choreography

The choreographic climax occurred in the opening section with the anticipation aroused by the rowdy playing of "Strike Up the Band" and the introduction of the main characters to that choice bit of Gershwinia, "Walking the Dog." But from there, the stage action took a nosedive. Albertina Vitak stated, "There just wasn't anything for them to do once they were assembled on the stage except many, too many, numbers of a sort of ring-around-the-rosy." As put by Walter Terry, "Massine didn't seem to realize that a Hokinson woman and an Arno old man with a white mustache are not funny in themselves, but funny when they get caught up in a predicament foreign to their characters."[54]

The ensuing nightclub divertissement was overlong, and most of its dances fell flat. For Kolodin, "the venom of Steig was absent from the hoydenish pair [Small Fry] who danced 'Let's Call the Whole Thing Off,'" and the burlesque on adagio acts performed by the Debutante and her Boyfriends "was not sufficiently pointed to make its intent apparent." In the next number, Vitak was aghast when "Danilova was dragged in and performed a sort of pseudo tap dance sur les pointes."[55]

Throughout the three scenes, the corps de ballet was used in theatrical versions of popular social dances like the Suzie-Q, conga, and lindy hop. But trained ballet dancers were out of their element compared to bona fide Harlem "rug-cutters." They were not as good as the real thing, nor did they satirize the real thing.

Constant revision of the ballet continued throughout the New York engagement; Massine even tried to save the ballet by changing his merely incidental role as a house painter into a principal role. His new character—the pasty, washed-out Timid Man—is set loose in the nightclub and coerced into dancing with a steamy siren. John Martin called Massine's new role "funny, inventive and completely off the beaten track for this dancer of countless character roles."[56]

Critical Survey

The New Yorker had no real libretto or even a sustained satiric mood. Terry wrote that the characters' "aimless wandering is hardly funny." His verdict that it was "one of the worst ballets that it has been my misfortune to see in a long time," and Vitak's that "it really would be best if it were just quietly forgotten" were representative.

The slams of some American critics became increasingly chauvinistic. Vitak: "they do things better in my country"; Kolodin: "Massine's good intentions and wit did not compensate for the orientation that might have been supplied by an American choreographer"; and Terry: "This is the third time that the Russian ballet has tried to use an American theme ... and in each case it has failed to capture the spirit of the people it was trying to represent."[57]

In Retrospect

The New Yorker had some fatal flaws, but it was also the victim of bad timing. First, the music of Gershwin was actually a very awkward choice for the year 1940. As Massine admitted, the Gershwin era was recent enough so that the older viewers could not easily suspend their personal associations with the tunes, while the music was also just dated enough to sound "corny" to the younger viewers.[58] Second, a 1940 Americana work by a Russian ballet company was a vulnerable target indeed.

VIENNA—1814

Ballet in One Act
Libretto: Léonide Massine
Music: Carl Marlo von Weber, orchestrated by Robert Russell Bennett
Scenic and Costume Design: Stewart Chaney
Première: Fifty-first Street Theatre, New York, October 28, 1940

ORIGINAL CAST
Characters
Prince Metternich: Marc Platov
Princess Lieven: Mia Slavenska
Secretaries: Igor Youskevitch, Roland Guérard, Ian Gibson,
Frederic Franklin, George Zoritch, André Eglevsky

Divertissement
Saxon Dance: Nathalie Krassovska   **Sicilienne:** Chris Volkov
Theme Russe: Mia Slavenska, Marc Platov
Princess Turandot: Alicia Markova
Unknown Prince: Léonide Massine
Pas de Deux: Alexandra Danilova, Igor Youskevitch
Mazurka: Katia Geleznova, Frederic Franklin
Barons and Baronesses, Lords and Ladies, Ambassadors and Wives,
Dutch and Tyrolean Legations

Synopsis[59]

The scene represents the gala peace ball tendered by Prince Metternich to celebrate the defeat of Napoleon. With the arrival of the Ambassadors comes the Princess Lieven, with whom Metternich falls in love. A brilliant polonaise opens the ball, followed by a grand divertissement. The sudden news of Napoleon's escape from the island of Elba causes a panic among the celebrants, though Metternich calms them, prevailing upon the men to exhibit courage, and upon the women, to follow their example. Prince Metternich takes tender leave of Princess Lieven.

Scenery and Costumes

Stewart Chaney, an American designer, lived for a long time in the Austrian capital, where he fell in love with its beautiful Baroque buildings. For this ballet, Chaney designed a ballroom in the style of the Bibienas, the great family of eighteenth-century Northern Italian stage architects. However, unlike Bakst's heavy and ornate set for *The Sleeping Princess*, which was also in the style of the Bibienas, Chaney's setting was light in key, painted simply and delicately.[60] His period costumes were ideal for dancing, executed in fabrics that would sail with the movement. Rich in color and beautiful in line, both sets and costumes created a radiant stage picture and won top honors in this ballet.

Music

At the time Carl Maria von Weber was born, Prussia dominated a loose confederation of some three hundred independent sovereignties. Germany, as a single political unit, was still eighty-five years away from realization. At no time was the longing for unity deeper or more widespread than at the turn of the nineteenth century. As John Warrack notes, "no study of the Romantics and their most representative composer has proper meaning unless seen against the background of this aspiration."[61]

The time was ripe for music which was nationalist, emotional, and in touch with the ambitions of the rising middle class. With his inherent love for Germany's scenery, legends, and heroes, Weber could not have been born at a more advantageous time.

Around 1803, Weber moved to Vienna where he studied all aspects of music and developed his fine vocal talent. In 1803 he was appointed to the post of Kapellmeister at Breslau, but his position came to an untimely end. Arriving at Weber's quarters one evening, a colleague found young Carl passed out on the floor—he had absentmindedly drunk from a wine bottle which his father had filled with engraving acid! Carl was ill for two months, and he never recovered his singing voice.[62]

In 1816 Weber was appointed Royal Saxon Kapellmeister of Dresden, with the charge of developing a German opera. Weber did so with *Der Freischütz* (1821), a fresh kind of opera based on German folklore, folk song, and country life. In this new romantic opera, Germany found its true voice. *Der Freischütz* became popular throughout Europe: no other German opera has ever been adopted so rapidly.[63]

In addition to his role as the champion of German opera, Weber was a brilliant pianist who wrote a number of virtuoso keyboard works for himself to play, of which the most famous by far is the *Aufforderung zum Tanze* (1819).[64] Massine turned principally to Weber's piano pieces for *Vienna—1814*, supplemented by his overture for Schiller's *Turandot* (1821).

From the 1920s to the 1960s, Robert Russell Bennett orchestrated some three hundred Broadway musicals and greatly enhanced the status of the orchestrator. In his arrangement of Weber, Robert Lawrence praised Bennett's avoidance of "lush harmonies" and "soapy glissandi for the strings," but he found the musical choices themselves to be "lacking the necessary élan" and "not the best of Weber."[65]

Choreography

Both *Vienna—1814* and the company's 1940 production of *Nutcracker* were attempts to fill a need for a classical divertissement in the Petipa tradition. The plot of *Vienna* was nothing more than a pretext for a stock-style suite of ballet variations. Choreographically, the most exciting variations were a dazzling dance for the six Legation Secretaries (perhaps because the six were Youskevitch, Eglevsky, Franklin, Zoritch, Guérard and Gibson), the Sicilian Dance arranged for Chris Volkov, and a pas de deux for Danilova and Youskevitch. Massine's duet with Markova as the Chinese princess and her unknown prince failed to make an impression. For Albertina Vitak, Massine's new role was too derivative of his Peruvian and barman.[66]

Critical Survey

Robert Sabin observed that Massine "leaned heavily on the Petipa tradition" and that "the ballet does not measure up to its predecessors in the same vein." Most critics were puzzled by the ballet's "plot." The title suggested undercurrents of political intrigue that were rampant in the Napoleonic era, but which were seldom in evidence on stage. Russell Rhodes remarked that *Vienna—1814* came to "a confused close, as if the choreographer suddenly remembered that he was dealing with an historical episode and recalled himself from a lapse into mere entertainment dancing."[67]

In Retrospect

In 1940, Massine was the most celebrated choreographer in the world. Referring to the twin failures of *The New Yorker* and *Vienna—1814*, Terry wrote, "this seems to be an off year for the great man."[68] Sadly, this year would be only the first of a very difficult decade for Massine, a development which would have surprised Terry when he penned those words.

LABYRINTH

Ballet in Four Scenes
Libretto: Salvador Dalí, based on the classic myth of Theseus and Ariadne
Music: Franz Schubert, Symphony No. 7 in C major
Set and Costume Design: Salvador Dalí
Première: Metropolitan Opera House, New York, October 8, 1941

ORIGINAL CAST
Theseus: Andre Eglevsky   Castor: George Zoritch
Pollux: Chris Volkov   Ariadne: Tamara Toumanova
The Minotaur: Frederic Franklin
The Roosters: Nicholas Beriosov, Alexis Koslov
The People

Synopsis[69]

In *Labyrinth* one revives the eternal myth of the aesthetic and ideologic confusion which characterizes romanticism, and especially, in the highest degree that of our epoch. The "thread of Ariadne," thanks to which Theseus succeeds in finding the exit from the labyrinth, symbolizes the tradition, the continuity, the thread of classicism, the saviour. All romanticism merely searches more or less dramatically its "thread of Ariadne," of classicism.

Lord Byron, the most integrated of the romantics, died romantically in the classicism of his beloved Greece, and Schubert, in his Seventh

Symphony, finds, by the uninterrupted continuity, the "thread of Ariadne," of his melody the exit from the musical labyrinth.

The three Fates, who symbolize destiny, attempt to prevent Theseus (symbol of History) from entering the labyrinth. But Theseus overpowers his destiny, enters the labyrinth, saves the couples of virgins (the people), kills the Minotaur (symbol of revolution) and, thanks to the thread of Ariadne (tradition), finds the exit from that abode of Death.

After the festival which celebrates the liberation of the people, the romantic symbols of the Orient are seen. Theseus abandons Ariadne on the shore and departs for new adventures, triumphantly borne by the apotheosis of the Sea which symbolizes the merciless march of History and which, in its heroic and blind course, alternately revives classicism and romanticism through the eternal sacrifice of the people.

Scenery and Costumes

In the decade of the 1940s, Dalí turned more and more towards classicism. *Labyrinth*'s theme—the triumph of classicism over romanticism—suggests that Dalí was already on the pathway toward a more traditional style in 1941. His vehement distaste for the *dernier cri* in art is unmistakable by the time of his 1942 essay, "Tradition vs. Modern Times": "Inescapably, there must be a return to tradition in painting.... The empty and pseudo-philosophic gossip of café tables was increasingly encroaching upon honest work in studio and workshop.... All this was hostile to me and [I] did not cease to work like a dog!"[70]

In a pre-première press release for *Labyrinth*, Walter Terry warned readers, "Don't be frightened, but here is a recipe that calls for twelve stuffed pigeons, one head of fresh veal, one eye three feet in diameter, one hundred and ten human skulls and bones, one horse's head, fishing nets, tackle, anchors and other marine paraphernalia."[71] It is true that *Labyrinth* abounded in the same surrealist props that had adorned *Bacchanale*, but there was no levity in *Labyrinth*'s visual imagery.

Dalí's opening scene revealed a tremendous cracked skull and a chest carved out by a tall doorway which gave the effect of archaic grandeur. The second scene was highlighted by a throne for the Minotaur composed of human skulls. The third scene, a corridor of the labyrinth, was memorable mainly for Dalí's ingenious costume designs for the Roosters. They were designed to be worn backwards and took advantage of the natural bend of the human knee to simulate the posterior flexion of a rooster's knee; this reverse orientation also allowed the arms to function more plausibly as wings. For the fourth scene, Dalí designed a boreal seascape with cavorting dolphins riding the waves. The corps de ballet wore pale green

Studio portrait of Tamara Toumonova, unidentified male and Casimir Kokitch as Ariadne, Rooster, and the Minotaur in *Labyrinth*, 1941. Costume designs by Salvador Dalí. *(MAURICE SEYMOUR)*

unitards with frothy headdresses of white bows; gathered in a clump, they formed a white crest. Walter Terry claimed that the sets "are more magnificent than any that ballet has disclosed before," and John Martin termed it "very fine surrealist painting."[72]

Music

Franz Schubert was one of the last great classical composers of the early nineteenth century and is widely regarded as the world's premier composer of lieder. In 1808, at the age of eleven, he began studies with Antonio Salieri, archrival of Mozart. He had already composed over two hundred songs, three masses, and three symphonies before his nineteenth birthday, and he continued to be an immensely prolific composer in all musical genres until his death.

Schubert depended for his existence on the support of his middle-class friends, plus the sporadic sales of his compositions. During his lifetime, his musical achievements went practically unnoticed while hosts of other lesser composers were readily accepted and published. At the time, fame as a concert performer or conductor was the key to publication, not merit as a composer.

Schubert's first six symphonies are apprentice works and heavily indebted at times to Mozart, Haydn and Beethoven. During the years 1818–22, he strove to evolve a more individual, subjective conception of the symphony, and his struggles are revealed by the fact that none of the symphonies attempted during this period were completed. They were followed by the famous "Unfinished" Symphony, composed in the autumn of 1822. This highly original composition is marked by intense lyricism, chromatic modulation within an inherent tonal system, and unusual changes of key.[73]

Having failed to complete four successive symphonies, Schubert might have given up on the genre, but his travels in Upper Austria in 1825 seem to have unleashed an abundant creative energy that resulted in the "Great" C-major Symphony. It has an insistent rhythmic vitality, from the opening horn call to the brisk pace of the marchlike *Andante con moto*, from the joyous dance of the scherzo to the swelling triplets of the epic finale.[74] Biographer John Reed believes that the "Great" Symphony No. 7 and the "Unfinished" encapsulate the contrast between the private and public sides of Schubert's personality. The latter, in a minor key, is intensely personal, its somber tone constantly interrupted by turbulent explosions of emotion. Symphony No. 7, in a major key, is markedly extroverted, aiming at celebration and sublimity. The "Great" Symphony is now seen as a culmination of Schubert's long quest for a grand symphony and is his greatest public work.[75]

The "Unfinished" Symphony and Symphony No. 7 forced the nineteenth-century musical world to acknowledge that in this songwriter there was also a purely instrumental master of the first rank. Many theories have evolved to explain why Schubert never completed the "Unfinished." The reason may be that Schubert contracted syphilis in 1822. To such a sensitive man, the association of the "Unfinished" with the events which led to his illness might have made a return to it repugnant. Schubert died from syphilis at the age of only thirty-one. On his monument in the Währing cemetery is inscribed this epitaph: "The art of music here entombed a rich possession, but even fairer hopes."

One difference between *Bacchanale* and *Labyrinth* is that Wagner's Venusberg music was expressly written for stage action, while Schubert's symphony is what Linton Martin termed an "emphatically unkinetic"[76] composition. Consequently, the Dalí-Massine interpretation of Symphony

No. 7 stirred up the same old controversy that arose when the Tchaikovsky Fifth, Brahms Fourth, and Beethoven Seventh were literally "put on their feet" by Massine. Unlike these, however, Symphony No. 7 was insuperably difficult to interpret through dance and a most unhappy choice.

Choreography

Massine must have sensed from the start that *Labyrinth* would be seen mainly as another Dalí art exhibit, and the unfortunate musical choice was Dalí's as well. Add to this the problem that Schubert and Dalí are worlds apart stylistically, and there are several reasons to explain why Massine simply abdicated from wholehearted participation. Several reviews used the word "listless" to describe his choreography for *Labyrinth*. He did not, for instance, take advantage of the invaluable resource that he had in Toumanova. As Ariadne, she did more passive observing than real dancing. In the second tableau, trussed on a narrow overhead platform, she represented a spool of thread, slowly revolving to unwind the thread of deliverance. At the conclusion she was simply left in static abandonment on the beach as Theseus left for fresh adventures. The dance patterns for the corps de ballet were equally devitalized. Walter Terry wisecracked that the ensemble dancing of *Labyrinth* was "just about on a par with activities captured in the annual Greek play by a girl's finishing school."[77] Yet here and there, Massine rallied and did some imaginative work. The jovial cockfight and the pas de deux for Castor and Pollux,[78] an electrifying blend of ballet and virile athleticism, provided two interludes when the dancing actually upstaged the décor.

Critical Survey

In his analysis of *Labyrinth* Cyril Beaumont dispensed with his normally detailed critique and said only, "The consensus of opinion of American critics is that the scenery and costumes have been allowed to dominate instead of contribute to the ballet, to the detriment of the production as a whole."[79] Critics also pounced upon the pretentious, "labyrinthine" program notes with glee. After reprinting the notes in their entirety, Linton Martin quipped, "Wouldn't Schubert be surprised!" Grace Robert stated that *Labyrinth* was "remarkable chiefly for the silly misuse of the magnificent music, by the same man who had given *Choreartium* to the world."[80]

In Retrospect

In a press release for *Labyrinth*, Terry stated, "The surrealism of a Salvador Dalí stands for novelty, but whether or not it represents actual progress in dance development is a moot question."[81] Terry sensed which way the wind was blowing—within a decade, Balanchine would revolutionize ballet by "costuming" his dancers in practice clothes and sending them out onto a bare stage. The days of top-heavy décor were coming to an end.

Ironically, this ballet trapped Léonide in a labyrinth of his own. And, unlike Ariadne, neither Schubert nor Dalí gave him a thread to guide him out of his maze.

SARATOGA

Ballet in One Act
Libretto: Jaromír Weinberger
Music: Jaromír Weinberger
Scenic Design: Oliver Smith
Costume Design: Alvin Colt
Première: Metropolitan Opera House, New York, October 19, 1941

ORIGINAL CAST

Young Girl: Alexandra Danilova   **Jockey**: Frederic Franklin
Mother: Tatiana Chamié   **Rich Man**: Nicholas Beriozov
Dandies: Tamara Toumanova, Léonide Massine
Jockeys, Spectators, Gamblers

Synopsis

It is the height of the racing season in turn-of-the-century Saratoga, and throngs of elegant patrons parade the streets. A widowed dowager enters with her beautiful young daughter. Mama is determined to marry her daughter off and has made arrangements for a rendezvous with a wealthy suitor. This rich gentleman arrives with a floral bouquet, and the daughter's face falls in dismay—he is rotund, crude and ugly.

A young Jockey enters and mimes his racing skills with imaginary reins and a riding crop. Eight more jockeys and a group of debutantes join him in the dance. When the young Jockey invites the daughter to dance, their romantic duet is too much for the wealthy suitor: he snatches the young upstart's hat and stamps on it. Mama pulls her daughter off by the ear for a private talking-to, and the crowd disperses. A pair of Dandies enter and dance a spirited cakewalk.

Bugles sound; the race is about to begin. The crowd gathers excitedly, facing the grandstand at the back of the stage. Whistles blow, and the horses are off. In a successive wave, the jockeys leap high above the grandstand. At the home stretch, the young Jockey surges ahead to win by a nose-length.

Now the owner of a handsome purse, the Jockey approaches Mama and begs to become her son-in-law. Mama looks down at his bulging nugget pouch and consents immediately. Not to be left out, the wealthy suitor proposes to Mama—a double wedding! Borne on the shoulders of the cheering throng, the couples and the ensemble frolic in blissful anticipation of the nuptial rites.

Scenery and Costumes

A great deal of money was lavished on the costumes and scenery of Alvin Colt and Oliver Smith. Colt's colorful turn-of-the-century costumes were the sole features of this ballet to win praise. Smith's set design consisted of a downstage pavilion with a grandstand and racetrack in the background. For Robert Sabin and others, it was not convincing: "there was not a trace of the American 'nineties in the whole ballet."[82]

Music

When Jaromír Weinberger, a Czechoslovakian-born, naturalized American composer, died in Florida in 1967 of a sedative overdose, the world paid little heed. Obituaries were few and invariably mentioned his one great achievement—the 1927 opera *Schwanda the Bagpiper*. Its success was overwhelming and shows Weinberger's gifts for tuneful melody, effective treatment of Czech and Slovak folklore, dance rhythm and orchestration. *Schwanda* became the first Czech opera since Smetana's *The Bartered Bride* to be widely performed internationally.

Weinberger was only thirty-one when *Schwanda* was first produced. Christopher Palmer feels that Weinberger's fine talent "fulfilled itself conclusively in *Schwanda*, and having once delivered this topic ... the composer found himself left with nothing more to say that the world cared to hear."[83] In 1938, Hitler's anti–Semitic persecutions forced Weinberger to flee his homeland. He moved to St. Petersburg, Florida, where he applied himself to American folk material in such works as *Legend of Sleepy Hollow*, *Prelude and Fugue on Dixie*, and *Mississippi Rhapsody*.

Weinberger's score for *Saratoga* was in the style of a potpourri of Gay Nineties tunes. However, the similarity of the tunes began to pall after a while. For Robert Sabin the score was "written in the style of a third-rate musical comedy of ten or fifteen years ago."[84]

Choreography

Saddled with a dull score and a sophomoric libretto (both written by Weinberger), Massine again did his work halfheartedly, for the dancing was minimal and often aimless. *Musical America* noted that Massine "simply let the dancers wander about the stage waving hands and dashing off into the wings."[85]

Saratoga's intended climax was to have been the race proper. Léonide concocted a clever way to visualize the race by having the jockeys perform *grand jetés* in canon across the back of the stage. They were hidden from the waist down by guard rails, so that each was only fully visible at the height of his leap. Unfortunately, the audience's view of the race was obscured by race patrons in the foreground who cluttered up the action with superfluous dancing. Like *Gaîté parisienne*, *Saratoga* was designed to simmer up to a "potboiler" finale—one in which Massine gradually filled the stage with progressive waves of dancers and then raised the energy to a fever pitch in a whirlwind climax. But this normally reliable device failed in *Saratoga*, not only because the stage picture was poorly focused, but also because the preceding scenes fell far too flat to empower an exciting climax.

The only spirited choreography to be found was in Massine and Toumanova's cakewalk,[86] inserted as a feature spot two weeks after the première. Although it was charming, the cakewalk was still a contrived interpolation in an already contrived ballet, a brief respite from the ennui that prevailed on both sides of the footlights.

Critical Survey

Reviews were disastrous. Sabin: "an all time low"; Walter Terry: "pretty tragic"; Henry Simon: "'Saratoga' Misses the Spittoon"—and so on.[87]

In Retrospect

Massine believed that he was being forced against his will to choreograph for a lemon at a point in his career when he had earned the right to choose his own composers, painters, and librettists. *Saratoga*'s American subject matter only compounded his sense of futility. When Terry called *Saratoga* "a Russian's Frenchified version of an American locale,"[88] Massine can hardly have been surprised.

It borders on the tragic that this ballet was dumped in Massine's lap at the very time when he most desperately needed a hit. *Saratoga*'s failure was seen as final confirmation of a serious artistic slump. He would spend the better part of the next thirty-eight years trying to prove his continuing vitality, but without the benefit of his own ballet company. The scene now shifts to Ballet Theatre.

ALEKO

Ballet in Four Scenes
Libretto: Léonide Massine and Marc Chagall, inspired by Pushkin's poem "Gypsies"
Music: Peter Illych Tchaikovsky, Trio in A minor, orchestrated by Erno Rapée
Scenic and Costume Design: Marc Chagall
Première: Palacio de Bellas Artes, Mexico City, September 8, 1942

ORIGINAL CAST

Zemphira: Alicia Markova   Aleko: Yura Skibine
Young Gypsy: Hugh Laing   Zemphira's Father: Anthony Tudor
Fortune Teller: Lucia Chase   Butterfly: Annabelle Lyon
Pan: Ian Gibson   Bathers: Jean Hunt, Marie Karnilova, Nina Popova
Gypsies: Margaret Banks, Muriel Bentley, Jean Davidson, Barbara Fallia, Miriam Golden
Gypsy Boys: Hubert Bland, Charles Dickson, John Kriza, Jerome Robbins
Clown, Bondura Player, Horse, Bear, Peasants, Society Lady, Duke, Poet, His Beloved, Socialites

Synopsis

Scene One. Into the midst of a gypsy camp in the vast Russian wasteland wanders a city youth named Aleko. Self-exiled from his community, he turns to the nomads for sympathy and acceptance. Aleko is instantly attracted to Zemphira, daughter of the chieftain. At the bidding of her father, Zemphira and Aleko dance a passionate pas de deux, but they are interrupted by a dark-skinned youth of the tribe. He attracts Zemphira, who turns to him and ignores Aleko. Zemphira's father and the younger nomads try to console Aleko and drag him off to share their adventures.

Scene Two. The scene changes; the gypsies have become part of a traveling circus. An acrobat, a street dancer, a clown and a dancing bear go through their paces. Aleko sees Zemphira with her new lover on the fringe of the circus ground and sinks into melancholy. Dusk arrives; the customers dissolve.

Scene Three. Peasant men and women revel on the edge of a wheat field in the bright summer sun. Two soloists—"Butterfly and Pan"—perform a pas de deux, and then the whole ensemble dances lustily before dashing off. Zemphira enters with her gypsy lover, and they are confronted by Aleko who, for the first time, threatens them. Zemphira and the Young Gypsy defy him scornfully. Heartbroken, Aleko goes away.

Studio portrait of Léonide Massine in the title role of *Aleko*, 1942. *(MAURICE SEYMOUR)*

Scene Four. Aleko is having a nightmare in which he sees the phantoms of his past from St. Petersburg. He sees a poet in love with a city girl who rejects him for a handsome duke. Identifying himself with the poet, Aleko dreams he challenges the duke to a duel. The poet is slain, yet the frolic of nobles, flunkies and monsters goes on. Aleko's mind whirls with delirious images. He awakens, and there before him—as in his nightmare—stand Zemphira and the Young Gypsy.

Their happiness, contrasted with his own misery, is too much for him. Raising his knife, Aleko plunges it into the body of his rival. Zemphira thrusts herself on Aleko's knife and dies as well. As Aleko stands in shock, the father confronts him. Scorning revenge, he sentences the youth not to death, but to banishment. Aleko must now live as an outcast. He drops senseless to the ground amid the mourning throng.

Scenery and Costumes

Chagall was recognized as a major figure of the Ecole de Paris in the 1920s and 1930s. His work is noted for its consistent use of folkloric imagery, its sense of Jewish identity, and its expressive color. In the 1920s, Chagall refused an invitation to join the surrealists; nevertheless, a surrealistic strain of dreamlike imagery can be said to run through all of his works.

Aleko was Chagall's first ballet. He accompanied Ballet Theatre to Mexico City and plunged happily into the make-believe world of an art form which he had always loved. Chagall worked closely with Massine and even painted the backdrops with his own hand.

Chagall's four magnificent backdrops—each forty-eight feet in length and thirty feet high—contained many of his familiar motifs and symbols. The first backcloth, "Aleko and Zemphira by Moonlight," is dominated by a cobalt-blue sky lit by the moon. A brilliant red cockerel (whose symbolism is obvious) flies to reach the moon's reflection while two lovers embrace in a cluster of clouds. The second backcloth, "The Carnival," shows a fiddle-playing bear floating over a slanted village, another couple set afloat in space, and a monkey dangling from a lilac tree. Scene Three, "A Wheatfield on a Summer's Afternoon," is a golden field of ripe wheat below a large sun which is a bull's eye encompassed in rings. The whole backdrop is flooded with hot, brilliant yellow. Loveliest of all was the Scene Four backdrop—"A Fantasy of St. Petersburg." Clearly silhouetted against the lowering gray sky, Chagall shows the statue of the Bronze Horseman, the inspiration for Pushkin's famous poem of the same name. Up in the sky is a white horse whose nose touches the light from a candelabra and whose flanks merge into the wheels of a carriage.

While he depicted *Aleko*'s locale, period and social classes authentically, Chagall was also deeply concerned with the psychological implications of each costume, and he hand-painted many of the motifs on their bodices.[89] For instance, Zemphira's first-scene bodice was painted with a bright red rooster identical to that painted on the backdrop. The costumes of the gypsies were whimsically decorated with disembodied hands and faces, animals, and images from playing cards.

The Mexico première of *Aleko* was a triumph for Chagall. Since he had been consulted on every detail of the dance, music and lighting, there was a Chagallian unity to it all. Less than a month after the Mexico City triumph, *Aleko* opened at the Met. John Martin wrote that the sets were "not actually good stage settings at all, but are wonderful works of art.... So exciting are they in their own right that more than once one wishes all those people would quit getting in front of them."[90] Since all the *gouache* studies remain, we can easily project the effect they must have had when unfurled as huge backdrops.

Music

Tchaikovsky's Trio in A minor (1881) is a forty-eight-minute work for violin, cello, and piano. It consists of an elegiac first movement in sonata form, a theme with eleven shorter variations, and a final variation which has a much more extended and elaborate development and culminates in a recapitulation of the opening theme.

Sergei Rachmaninoff composed an opera based specifically on Pushkin's "Gypsies" for the Bolshoi Theatre in 1893. Since Rachmaninoff's incidental music was created for stage action, some critics wondered why Massine turned to Tchaikovsky's more cerebral trio instead of the opera. Critics also pointed out that Tchaikovsky's last variation, even as orchestrated by Erno Rapée, was a poor match for the anguished drama onstage.

Although the music was not always a good fit to the drama, the action was at least tailored sensitively to Tchaikovsky's musical transitions. The second backdrop was lowered at the musical transition to a major key in the second scene. The third canvas was lowered for the theme and variations, and the backdrop representing *Aleko*'s nightmare was offered for the last variation and coda.[91]

Choreography

Grace Robert recognized the ballet as "a brilliant montage of gypsy life that never existed out of the realm of poetry. When a realistic touch appears, it is only for the purposes of pointing up the fantasy."[92] To achieve this ambience, Massine utilized methods and means from both his symphonic and his character ballets. Realistic touches included expert stylization of local color, clearly conceived characterizations, and a stirring, melodramatic finale. After his third viewing, Robert Lawrence said, "for the writer, the double murder of the gypsy girl and her lover by Aleko is one of the most shattering experiences, not only in the dance, but in the whole world of the theatre."[93]

In assigning the role of Zemphira to Alicia Markova, Massine was extending the range of a dancer who preferred the pristine, ethereal roles of the romantic ballets. As Zemphira, Markova seemed like a "priestess of evil" to Carl van Vechten. George Skibine claimed that "Hugh Laing was better in *Aleko* than he was in the Tudor ballets, and Tudor—he was magnificent in it."[94]

In the second scene, Aleko and Zemphira were depicted as itinerant entertainers and had short passages of gypsy character dancing. The third scene's pastorale episode had a typical character ballet divertissement. Elsewhere, for *Aleko*'s surrealist episodes, Massine used the typical sweep and hectic activity of his symphonic ballets.

Robert found the choreography to be in "Massine's best symphonic manner."[95] Other critics disagreed. John Martin saw *Aleko* as representing Massine "in his most centrifugal mood"; Edwin Denby deplored "an agitation that seems senseless, a piling up of scraps of movement and bits of character like so much junk from Woolworth's"; and Winthrop Palmer believed that Massine "strangled his theme with a multiplicity of detail," particularly in the nightmare scene, where the factors which drive the hero from the city "get lost in the choreographic clutter."[96]

Critical Survey

At the Mexico City première, *Aleko* got nineteen curtain calls, and the painter and choreographer won vociferous praise.[97] Reviews for the New York première in October were mixed. Chagall's decor was unanimously seen as the ballet's supreme triumph—Massine's choreography was either lauded or torn to shreds, as noted above.

In Retrospect

Aleko remained in Ballet Theatre's active repertory until the 1948 season and had a major restoration in 1953 for ABT performances abroad. It had its last ABT revival at the new Metropolitan Opera House in 1968. Sadly, ABT's sale of the Chagall backdrops in 1977 consigned the ballet to oblivion.

According to Sol Hurok, the 1953 *Aleko* became "the outstanding hit of the London season, both with the press and public."[98] An avid Massine constituency still existed in London, but for American audiences, *Aleko* revivals served mainly as curtain raisers for ballets by trendier choreographers.

ABT's 1968 revival, personally supervised by Massine, was seen by a new generation of critics. Arlene Croce described the ballet as "an unsortable series of choreographic 'scenes'" with dancers "trailing clouds of kitsch surrealism."[99] However, Jack Anderson and George Jackson—two critics with a strong interest in dance history—enjoyed certain aspects of the revival. Anderson admired "the rhapsodic sweep of the thing!" Jackson saw *Aleko* as a work "so outside the current choreographic mainstream that it is an exercise in seeing.... What Massine has done in the best scenes is to bring the Chagall canvases not to life, but into dream."[100]

This lushly romantic ballet premièred in the same year as Anthony Tudor's *Pillar of Fire*. The Tudor ballet heralded a new genre of realistic psychological ballets which boldly challenged Massine's point of view. In his excellent article on *Aleko*, Leland Windreich wrote, "*Aleko* was the final product of a romantic revolution initiated early in this century by Michel Fokine, and like most of the ballets in this genre, its fascination continues to outlive its usefulness."[101]

DON DOMINGO DE DON BLAS

Ballet in One Act
Libretto: Léonide Massine, based on a play by Juan Ruiz de Alarcon y Mendoza
Music: Silvestre Revueltas
Scenic and Costume Design: Julio Castellanos
Première: Palacio de Bellas Artes, Mexico City, September 16, 1942

ORIGINAL CAST

Don Domingo de Don Blas: Anton Dolin
Leonor Ramiro: Alicia Markova   **Don Juan**: Dimitri Romanov
Don Ramiro: Simon Semonov   **Viceroy**: Anthony Tudor
Constanza, Leonor's Companion: Lucia Chase

Don Juan's Dream
Mayan Goddess: Alicia Markova   **Mayan Warrior**: George Skibine

Finale
The Virgin: Jean Hunt   **The Death**: Hubert Bland
Peasants and Indians: All the Company

Synopsis[102]

Impecunious Don Juan, to win the hand of Leonor from wealthy Don Domingo, presents a dance festival for her amusement, only to be driven off by her father, Don Ramiro, who prefers Domingo's lavish gifts. Old Ramiro hates the Viceroy and conspires against his life. Don Domingo overhears the plot and is imprisoned in Ramiro's house. Meanwhile, Don Juan, yearning for Leonor, dreams of himself as a Mayan warrior in a love dance with Leonor as a Mayan princess. Waking, he tries to enter Leonor's house, finds Domingo a prisoner there, learns of the Viceroy's danger, and foils the assassins. The Viceroy pardons Don Ramiro with the provision that Don Juan be rewarded with the hand of Leonor. Don Domingo accepts this decision and asks Leonor's friend, Constanza, to be his wife. A double wedding ensues.

Scenery and Costumes

Julio Castellanos studied at the Academia de San Carlos in Mexico City and then moved to Paris, where he was exposed to the sources of great Western art. His works of the 1930s, following his return to Mexico, show a departure from his earlier Mexican influences. At a time when grandiloquent, politically motivated paintings were the trend in Mexican art, Castellanos captured simple, everyday themes that also form an essential part of Mexican culture and consciousness.[103]

Castellanos' designs for *Don Domingo* were keyed to project the Spanish colonial period with somber authenticity. The setting was a Mexican street with a Spanish hacienda at stage right. The backdrop depicted a Mayan ruin at stage left and, in the middle, a massive stone archway spanning a huge cactus plant. Castellanos' costumes were appropriately opulent and colorful. For Robert Lawrence, the costumes were "dazzling"; and for Anthony Fay, they "evoked Denishawn and presaged the Ballet Folklorico of Mexico."[104]

Music

Silvestre Revueltas's mature works weave folk melodies and the street music of modern Mexico into a gaudy instrumental fabric, typically ending *fortissimo*. In rhythm, he wove uneven meters into the hemiola (three-four alternating with six-eight) rhythm endemic to Hispanic-American popular music. For *Don Domingo*'s score, Revueltas took six of his previously written piano pieces and arranged them for orchestra. The music was supposed to project the Spanish colonial period, but for Massine, "it lacked the real inspiration and the somber accuracy of Castellanos' sets, and seemed to keep the production at a rather pedestrian level."[105] John Martin snapped that the "loud" music was "one of the most consistently annoying ballet scores on record."[106]

Choreography

During his free evenings in Mexico, Massine went to local cafés, where he studied the native dancers. He was struck by their "rollicking vulgarizations of the flamenco." He used this native material as the partial basis for the opening divertissement. For the Mayan and Aztec dances,

Massine's research was assisted by the Mexican Ministry of Education. The Indian dances in the divertissement included a Yaqui deer dance, the sun dance of Oaxaca, and a native depiction of the Spanish Crusades called *Los Mors y Los Christianos*.

Massine's intent was to blend Mexico's folk and native dances with Spanish dances and ballet, but the Indian dances were stubbornly resistant to such fusions. He "was disappointed to find how few native dances there were that I could use."[107] So Massine relied heavily upon straight classical ballet or a balletization of Spanish folk dances. But this resulted in such garbled cultural references that they pushed credulity to the limits. For instance, Don Juan (Romanov) dreams of himself as a Mayan warrior (Skibine). He is joined by a Mayan goddess (Markova), who wears an odd combination of Yucatan beads, floating chiffon, and pointe shoes. The two Mayans then proceed to dance a strictly classical pas de deux.

Critical Survey

Following the Mexican world première, *Don Domingo* had its New York opening on October 9, 1942.[108] Audience response was demonstratively negative. All critics were quick to see that the ballet suffered from a lack of basic clarity due to the unsuitable score and Massine's failure to create a successful synthesis from the dance forms on his palette. Yet Robert Lawrence did at least admire its "blazing color."[109]

In Retrospect

Don Domingo received a few performances at the Met, but it was quickly dropped. Still, it should at least be remembered that *Don Domingo* was a gracious gesture to the Mexican government and a showcase for Mexican art.

MADEMOISELLE ANGOT *(Mam'zelle Angot)*

Ballet in Three Scenes
Libretto: Léonide Massine, based upon an *opera-bouffé* by Alexandre Lecocq
Music: Alexandre Lecocq, reorchestrated by Richard Mohaupt and Gordon Jacob
Scenery and Costumes: Mastislav Dobujinsky (New York) and André Derain (London)
Premières: Metropolitan Opera House, New York, October 10, 1943; Covent Garden Opera, London, November 26, 1947

ORIGINAL CASTS

Mademoiselle Angot: Nora Kaye (New York)   Margot Fonteyn (London)
The Barber: Léonide Massine (New York)   Alexander Grant (London)
The Caricaturist: Andre Eglevsky (New York)   Michael Somes (London)
The Aristocrat: Rosella Hightower (New York)   Moira Shearer (London)

Synopsis

Scene One. The curtain rises on a bustling French marketplace. In its midst is Mademoiselle Angot, who is betrothed against her will to the Barber. So when a handsome Caricaturist arrives and flirts with her, she is delighted to join him in a passionate pas de deux. But as they dance, the desolate little Barber sobs and protests so violently that he has to be restrained by his friends. Then a government official enters with his aristocratic mistress, and the Caricaturist draws a picture mocking the official. Soon, he becomes so entranced with the Aristocrat that he forgets Mademoiselle Angot. She is jealous and insults the Aristocrat in public. In no time, she is being hauled off to prison by two gendarmes. But Mademoiselle exercises all her feminine wiles and at last manages to make her escape.

Scene Two. A reception is in progress in the salon of the Aristocrat's house. The Caricaturist and Mademoiselle Angot enter—Mademoiselle has been sent for by the offended Aristocrat to explain her behavior, but the meeting reveals that they are old school friends. The Caricaturist is fleeing from the soldiers sent to arrest him for his damaging drawings. The two women think quickly and decide that the Caricaturist should pose behind a pedestal in the salon on which a bust has been standing. The bust is removed, and the head and shoulders of the Caricaturist take its place. Soldiers and the chief of police arrive in search of the Caricaturist. They search high and low, beginning with a thorough inspection of the salon, but return to the salon empty-handed. However, the Caricaturist cannot resist the temptation to make faces at the chief of police, and his clever disguise is exposed! He is arrested, but the Aristocrat intercedes for him successfully. Mademoiselle discovers that the lovelorn Barber has also come to the house in search of her, and she decides to forget her disdain for him.

Scene Three. It is Carnival, and the scene begins with dancers dressed as pirates, blackface minstrels and savages. Mademoiselle has plotted a meeting between the Aristocrat and Caricaturist. With the help of her market friends, she exposes the Aristocrat in the arms of the Caricaturist to the duped government official. The official realizes that the Aristocrat loves another and gives up the chase. Mademoiselle decides to marry her faithful little Barber after all, much to his delight.

Scenery and Costumes

Three backdrops and over one hundred costumes were required for *Mademoiselle Angot*. For both the New York and London productions, the first scene was a provincial marketplace; the second, a mansion; and the third, a street carnival. According to Massine, Dobujinsky's was a "witty, beautifully detailed setting."[110]

Mademoiselle Angot was put in a worthier setting, though, with the designs of André Derain for Sadler's Wells. Décor by an artist of Derain's stature added immeasurably to the prestige of the British production. In 1948 Mary Clarke wrote that the sets and costumes had all "the charm and beauty of Boutique."[111]

Music

French composer Alexandre Lecocq is remembered for his light, gay, sparkling melodies. The international popular acclaim accorded his operettas *Fleur de thé* (1871), *Les cent vierges* (1872), *La fille de Madame Angot* (1872) and *Giroflé-Girofla* (1874) established him as a natural successor to Offenbach. Lecocq's delightful madcap opera *La fille de Madame Angot* was his greatest popular triumph and a fine choice for a ballet adaptation.

Richard Mohaupt was a German composer who emigrated to New York in 1939. There, he was highly successful as a composer for the cinema, broadcasting and musical theatre. Gordon Jacob, a British composer, taught at the Royal Conservatory of Music from 1926 to 1966. Both Mohaupt and Jacob did a fairly straightforward reorchestration which simply added body to the instrumentation in order to compensate for the loss of the human voice.

Choreography

Massine stuck with his typical formula for comedy ballets, fusing classical, character, and demi-caractère styles to sustain interest and distinguish characters. G. B. L. Wilson termed the choreography "a masterpiece of characterization" and noted that all four of the leading roles defied stereotypes.[112] Peter Williams defined the character of Mademoiselle as "damned common."[113] For this reason, many critics found Margot Fonteyn to be too intractably sweet to convey Massine's conception of a lovely but conniving fishmonger—Nora Kaye was far better suited to the role. Michael Somes was more convincing than Eglevsky because the Caricaturist is not the typical leading man, but more accurately, a young lecher. The Barber is a tragi-comic character. Alexander Grant, who

Léonide Massine as the Barber in *Mademoiselle Angot* (Ballet Theatre production), 1943.

inherited the role from Massine, was outstanding not only for his sharp comedic timing but also because he was not afraid to be pathetic. Massine also filled the background with rewarding small parts for those dancers who could animate them, from the market people to the two gendarmes.

Critical Survey

For the New York première, the reactions of the American press and public were so tepid that the ballet was soon withdrawn. Yet the Sadler's Wells revival was a resounding triumph. Mary Clarke analyzed the reason for the drastically different responses to this ballet on either side of the Atlantic. She surmised that American dancers were much more at ease simply being themselves in the clean modern lines of an abstract Balanchine ballet than in assuming disguises of nationality or period and that the different approach required by Massine left American dancers "baffled." By contrast, Clarke believed that the Sadler's Wells dancers took happily to Massine's style because of their previous experience in the ballets of Ninette de Valois. Like Massine's, her works were often period pieces which sparkled with vigorous character dancing and emphasized acting.

In Retrospect

Mademoiselle Angot has been in and out of the active repertory of the Royal Ballet since Massine first staged it for them. The most recent revival by the Royal was in 1980. Of this production, Clarke wrote, "And what a good ballet it is! A silly, terribly complicated story and yet it works marvelously well in the theatre."[114] In his memoirs, Massine called *Mademoiselle Angot* "an amusing and satirical trifle,"[115] but he may have underestimated a ballet which contained some of his sharpest characterizations.

8

March 1943–October 1954

After the 1943 American première of *Mademoiselle Angot*, Massine produced only two new works over the next three years—*Mad Tristan* and *Moonlight Sonata*, both of which he created in 1944. *Moonlight Sonata* opened at the Chicago Opera House on November 24. Massine and Toumanova were both appearing as guest artists with Ballet Theatre, and *Moonlight Sonata* was an occasion for them to pair up in a sentimental pas de deux after a long separation. Dalí and Massine collaborated for a third time in *Mad Tristan* for the Marquis de Cuevas' Ballet International.

With the appointment of Lucia Chase and Oliver Smith in 1944, Ballet Theatre began a campaign of de–Russianization. Gone were the days when Hurok could promote this company as "The Greatest in Russian Ballet by Ballet Theatre." With the new policy, Massine became persona non grata, and there followed a long hiatus in his dealings with Ballet Theatre. Once again, Léonide faced an unstable professional life. The 1944 birth of his second child, Lorca, made it even more imperative to find a steady source of income.

Accordingly, in 1945 Massine organized a ballet troupe called the Ballet Russe Highlights under the management of impresario Fortune Gallo. There were only six principal dancers, but since they could capitalize both on their own name recognition and on the reputation of the Ballet Russe de Monte Carlo, they drew huge crowds. Ballet Russe Highlights had its opening performance in June of 1945 at New York's

Lewisholm Stadium with an estimated attendance of over 25,000 for two performances. In Philadelphia's Robin Hood Dell they danced to an audience of 15,000 at a single performance.[1] From nineteen other cities throughout the United States came similar reports of enormous, sold-out houses. A second national tour, also spectacularly well attended, took place in 1946. Even so, Massine claimed that the operating expenses, especially those of hiring orchestras, eventually outweighed the box-office profits, and the venture was discontinued.

In the summer of 1946 Massine went to Central America to work on Twentieth Century Fox's *Carnival in Costa Rica*. He choreographed three Costa Rican dance sequences and played the role of a coffee picker who dances with Vera Ellen. Another offer in the summer of 1946 gave Massine a chance to work in Europe for the first time since the war. The play *A Bullet in the Ballet* revolved around a backstage murder mystery of a ballet company where every dancer cast in the role of Petrouchka is killed. It included Fokine's *Petrouchka*, staged by Massine, excerpts from *Gaîté parisienne* and a new ballet blanc, *Reverie classique*. The musical had a successful provincial tour, but it closed in Liverpool when backing for a London booking could not be found.

Massine's presence in England was in itself of great interest to the ballet community. Ninette de Valois, artistic director of the Sadler's Wells, was a great Massine admirer, and she wanted to hire Massine as the company's first guest choreographer. Massine still had a strong British following and meant good box-office for her company. He revived *Le Tricorne* and *La Boutique* for the Sadler's Wells along with a new version of *Mademoiselle Angot*, now shortened to *Mam'zelle Angot*.

As the 1947 Sadler's Wells ballet season drew to a close, Massine was approached by British film director Michael Powell to participate in the film *The Red Shoes*. The team of Powell and writer Emeric Pressburger had already achieved international acclaim for their films *Stairway to Heaven* (1946) and *Black Narcissus* (1947). Because of his love and knowledge of ballet, Powell wanted *The Red Shoes* to be an authentic depiction of the art, with a real ballerina in the leading role and an unbroken twenty-minute ballet as the film's highlight.

Pressburger's screenplay revolved around a ballet company and its impresario, Lermontov, a character obviously modeled after Diaghilev. The impresario demands nothing less than utter devotion to the ballet from his artists. When his prima ballerina, Victoria Page, falls in love with the company's musical director, Lermontov forces Victoria to choose between her career and her fiancée and inadvertently causes her death. The film's plot is an extended parable of the theme of the Hans Christian

Andersen fairy tale used for the ballet sequence. "The Red Shoes" are magic ballet slippers which an evil magician sells to a young girl; the shoes drive her to dance on relentlessly, all over the world, until they finally dance her to death. The ballet is thus woven ingeniously and inextricably into the context of Victoria's agonizing choice between love and art.

Powell's choice of choreographer and leading male dancer for the film was Robert Helpmann, and the leading female role was given to the stunning redhead Moira Shearer, both from the Sadler's Wells. The dual role of the company's choreographer, Ljubov, and the sinister Shoemaker in the ballet sequence was given to Massine. Massine agreed to appear in the film only if he could create the part of the Shoemaker himself and get credit in the film titles for doing so.[2]

Shooting began on location in France in June 1947. In an electronic, two-dimensional medium with which he had only limited experience, Massine quickly discovered that film choreography was "infinitely more complex than working in a theatre.... While I was dancing I was always acutely aware of the camera, picking up and magnifying the most minute detail."[3] His meticulous efforts to adapt to this new medium paid off splendidly:

> Again and again through the ballet, Massine furnishes the film with some of its most striking visual effects.... Massine contemplating his victim, Massine leaping forward to pour ink over a little bit of rag and so turn day into night, Massine crouching forward upon the church steps quite indifferent to the threat of the knife upheld in the girl's hands, all these moments are unforgettable.[4]

When Michael Powell screened the film for Eagle Lion Classics, Inc. executives Bob Benjamin and Arthur Krim, he claims that both of them "were scared shitless. This was an art film with a vengeance! And everybody knew art and money were two different things."[5] Most Eagle Lion executives believed that the film would simply have to be written off. But one board member disagreed: his name was Benjamin Heineman, and his wife and daughters were all ballet dancers. After dogged lobbying, he was finally given permission to see if he could actually make this ballet film turn a profit in New York.

Heineman chose the Bijou Cinema on Forty-fifth Street and guaranteed its managers a run of six months. After it had run a year, Heineman was crowing "I told you so." On December 19, 1950, the *New York Herald Tribune* reported: "A new record in Broadway movie history was established last week when that hard perennial, 'The Red Shoes,' played

Léonide Massine as the Shoemaker in the motion picture *The Red Shoes*, 1948.

its 108th consecutive week at the Bijou Theater."[6] According to an interoffice Eagle Lion memo, *The Red Shoes* also had record-breaking runs in Los Angeles, Chicago, Miami Beach, San Francisco, Boston and Philadelphia.[7]

By 1948 Massine's most popular works were in great demand, and he was operating on an extensive international circuit. During the next few years he restaged his ballets for La Scala, the Teatro Colón, the Opéra-

Comique, the London Festival Ballet, Marquis de Cuevas's Ballet International, the Rome Opera Ballet, the Royal Swedish Ballet, the Paris Opéra, and many other companies. Massine's wife acted as his assistant, bustling all over the world to supervise opening rehearsals while he worked elsewhere before joining her for the final touch-ups.

Massine did two new works in 1948. *Capriccio* premièred at La Scala on May 24, 1948. It was a minor work for a gala Stravinsky program whose main event was Massine's revival of his 1921 *Le Sacre du printemps*. The second new work, *Clock Symphony*, was for Sadler's Wells. He wrote that the "persistent rhythm of the 'Clock' Symphony had reminded me of the revolving figures in delicate porcelain often found on baroque clocks, and I conceived the new ballet as an animation of these."[8]

Massine's *Quattro stagione* ("The Four Seasons") premièred on February 19, 1949, at La Scala. Unfortunately, no film of Massine's *Quattro stagione* survives, but we do know from its review that Massine followed the musical architecture and programme of these concertos very closely, but altered the traditional order, starting with "Winter" and ending with "Autumn." There was precious little critical response to *Quattro stagione* except the uninformative account of an anonymous Italian critic who wrote, "In the choreography, imaginative, noble and comic scenes alternate with one another."[9]

By 1949 the Massines had settled in Paris in a house on Neuilly-sur-Seine. From the beginning of their relationship, Diaghilev had generously made a practice of acquiring contemporary paintings for Massine. Later, Massine began to buy for himself, and the walls of his new house in Paris were hung resplendently with the works of Bakst, Braque, de Chirico, Derain, Gontcharova, Larionov and Picasso. Pride of place, though, was given to a large photograph of Diaghilev.

Now that he was back in Europe, Massine's summer residence was once again the Isole dei Galli. He returned in 1947, for the first time since the war, to find that the caretakers had kept everything in the best possible condition under the circumstances. In the years which followed, Massine's building and landscaping on Galli took on epic dimensions. Working against the deteriorating effects of salt, storms and harsh winter winds, he poured unflagging energy and a huge portion of his income into transforming these craggy islands into a palatial retreat. Isola Lunga was eventually equipped with a private radio station, four manmade beaches, an electrical generating plant, a boathouse port, a terraced garden, a lighthouse, and a two-story villa with a magnificent view of Capri.[10] Massine also built a large open-air theatre on Isola Lunga, but it was destroyed by a mid-1960s storm. The fourteenth-century tower on

Brigante was restored and became Massine's favorite residence in his last years.

During a 1962 Mediterranean vacation, First Lady Jacqueline Bouvier Kennedy accepted Massine's invitation to spend a day exploring the islands.[11] When actress Elizabeth Taylor saw Galli in 1964, she was so keen to buy them that she offered Massine a million dollars. "He said no politely—not at any price."[12]

The winter, spring and summer of 1949 were occupied with several revivals and ballet scenes for operas at La Scala. In the fall, Léonide returned to Paris to choreograph a new pas de deux for Boris Kochno's Ballets des Champs-Elysées. *Le Peintre et son modèle* was based on Kochno's intriguing concept of a model who succeeds in possessing and destroying the artist who is painting her. This short, minor work premièred at the Théâtre des Champs-Elysées on November 15, 1949, and was danced by Irene Skorik and Youly Algeroff to a score by Georges Auric. In this erotic pas de deux, the artist's palette, a frame and the easel become involved. The work's sustained, clean lines and essential lyricism were a dramatic departure from Massine's typical staccato style.[13]

In April 1950, Massine created two new works for *Les Fêtes d'Avènement* in Monaco. *Concertino* and *Platée* were both single-performance *pièces d'occasion*, performed in the presence of Prince Rainier III. The ballets were staged in the palace courtyard, where twin marble staircases, descending in two graceful arcs from the first balcony to ground level, provided a stunning setting. Both ballets used six couples. *Concertino* was danced to Jean Françaix's Piano Concertino and *Platée* was danced to Jean-Philippe Rameau's opera-ballet of the same name. In both ballets, Massine added a strong vertical element by skillfully incorporating the staircases.[14]

From Monaco, Massine went to Paris and created a minor new work for the Opéra-Comique. *Le Bal du Pont du Nord* had a libretto by Hubert Deviellez based on a dramatic Flemish tale. In the ballet, Adele, daughter of the town's bellringer, steals away during her father's appointed watch to meet her lover at Carnival, where she finds her swain kissing her best friend, Marion. Adele commits suicide by throwing herself from the Pont du Nord. To recreate the story's local color, André Masson designed the ballet in the style of a rustic Flemish painting by Brueghel. The score by young pianist and composer Jacques Dupont was pronounced "rather dull" by critic Pierre Tugal, but Massine did an interesting second-act divertissement based on French proverbs hailed by Tugal as "a magnificent ballabillé."[15] *Le Bal du Pont du Nord* and the more important ballet, *Donald of the Burthens*, were both created in the same year, and there are definite similarities. Both combine a romantic-realist approach with a Petipa-style divertissement in the second act which is not dramatically in keeping with the tragic ending.

Massine's next commission was a new work for the appearance of the de Cuevas company at the Bordeaux International Music Festival of 1951. *Les Saisons* was danced to Henri Sauguet's four-movement *Symphonie Allégorique* (1949). No film exists, and the ballet received only one performance on May 20.

Michael Powell decided to direct a second dance film based on Offenbach's *The Tales of Hoffmann*. This 1951 London film reunited Powell, Pressburger, Shearer, Helpmann and Massine. Frederick Ashton was the choreographer but, once again, Léonide insisted upon choreographing his own sequences.

Massine played a different role in each of the three acts. In the first, his Spalanzani was a foppish dandy, "a perfumed creature, taking immense pride in his own showmanship." As Schlemil in the second act, Massine portrayed a battered, cruelly maligned old soldier. Monk Gibbon wrote, "His face expresses a profound sadness ... but it is the stoicism of despair rather than its desperation." Massine's portrayal of the simple and sprightly old peasant Franz was judged to be the best of them all. Gibbon found Massine's characterization to be "unforgettable." In Franz's dance solo, "the old man liberates all his repressed aspirations and ambitions.... Massine has taken the rather obvious burlesque which Offenbach probably had in mind and turned it into something much more subtle, human and universal."[16] Fernau Hall thought that Massine's work far outclassed Ashton's: "At no point in the film did Ashton create dance images expressive of the characters and moods of the personages involved. ... Massine's superb acting ... and complete grasp of the film medium, showed very clearly what was wrong with Ashton's choreography."[17]

Overall, the chief criticism of the film was that it was extremely fractured and disjointed. In 1968 Thomas Elsaesser noted that Powell's camera techniques were way ahead of his time.[18] Although it was never a popular success, *The Tales of Hoffmann* was awarded the Special Jury Prize at the 1951 Cannes Film Festival, and it is now viewed by some film historians as a masterpiece.

Massine's next project was *Donald of the Burthens*, his last ballet for the Sadler's Wells. Léonide studied Scottish folklore for an appropriate tale and chose a variation on the Faust legend about the adventures of a young woodsman. The ballet adaptation became an all–Caledonian affair with music and décor by Scottish artists.

In 1952, Massine was hired by the Maggio Musicale Fiorentino to stage the dances for three operas. While there, Francesco Siciliani, the artistic director of the festival, introduced Massine to the *Laudes Dramaticae Umbriae*, a medieval Italian version of a Latin liturgical play on the life of Christ. Thirty-two years after his abandoned *Liturgie*, Massine now saw a chance to resurrect it. He wrote, "it seemed almost as if Diaghilev himself were giving me back my lost opportunity."[19]

Siciliani received ecclesiastical permission from the Archbishop of Perugia to have the new ballet—*Laudes Evangelii*—staged in the fourteenth-century church of Santo Domenico in Perugia. Once Massine had acquired a number of thirteenth-century Umbrian chants, work on this splendid ballet began in earnest. Never—so far as Vatican authorities could remember—had any Roman Catholic church been used for a ballet performance.[20]

In 1953, Massine choreographed for operas at La Scala and the Rome Opera and made his third film—*Carosello Napolitano*. The latter was a collaboration with the gifted writer and director Ettore Giannini. Giannini knew that Massine already had a fine track record for his work in *The Red Shoes* and *Hoffmann*, that he was a master of the commedia dell'arte style and that his international prestige would help Giannini to secure financial backing. Massine was to stage several pantomime scenes and choreograph four dance episodes.

Carosello Napolitano is a five-episode allegory of the spirit of the Neapolitan people and their courage in adversity. *Carosello* has no linear story or consistent characters to follow: its only theme is the streets of Naples through the ages. The idea is simple, but its execution is fantastically complex, using the most esoteric methods and techniques of the avant-garde cinema of the day. Narrative continuity is replaced with brilliant touches of optical and acoustical continuity. Visual metaphors abound: dance is used to carry one action through vast reaches of time and space.

The best example occurs in the last episode, when an Italian Renaissance prince hands a deed to a merchant and receives a bag of gold in exchange. The movement is choreographed to a nursery-rhyme tune with the words, "I give you, you give me." The camera then pans right, catching the merchant handing the deed to another and receiving some goods in exchange. As the camera keeps panning further to the right, it moves from the seventeenth century to the present. By the time the shot is over, the viewer is in a plaza filled with almost a thousand dancers and extras, each of them exchanging commodities, and the sound swells up from that of a single voice to a huge choir. The scene has traveled in time to the end of World War II. The Americans have liberated Napoli. The last transaction is an exchange of a machine gun for a Coca-Cola bottle—"I give you, you give me."

Appearing in the heyday of neo-realist cinema, *Carosello* sparked a great deal of controversy. Some critics missed the film's point altogether. Laura Clandon, for example, complained that "the many disparate elements and moods fail to fuse into a consistently entertaining pageant."[21] More perceptive reviewers raved about this film, and its critical success was international. For Ernest Borneman it was "a cinematic freak" but a "fascinating, ingenious, provocative film." He continued: "This is Massine at his best.... It's beautifully done, taking bits from commedia dell'arte, bits from Neapolitan folk dances, bits from the damndest places and blending them all with an astounding degree of style ... no other dance film, made in Hollywood or anywhere else, has come closer to pointing the lesson of cinematic choreography."[22]

At its première, *Carosello Napolitano* was applauded continuously throughout the screening and was awarded the Grand Prix at the Cannes Film Festival. Why is the film now shrouded in obscurity? Like *The Tales of Hoffmann*, it was ahead of its time, but *Carosello* is even more richly deserving of rediscovery.

On January 12, 1954, Léonide created a *pièce d'occasion* for guest artist Yvette Chauviré for the Rome Opera Ballet. *Les Dryades* was styled after Fokine's *Les Sylphides* and, like the earlier ballet, was danced to Chopin piano pieces.

The tremendous success of *Laudes Evangelii* led the philanthropist Count Vittorio Cini and Francesco Siciliani to invite Massine to produce another religious spectacle on the life of Christ. *Resurrezione e Vita* took place on the island of San Giorgio Maggiore. Until the end of the 1940s, this island had belonged to the Italian army; then, under the supervision of Count Cini, it was converted into an international artistic center with a fully equipped and beautifully landscaped outdoor theatre, the Teatro Verde. *Resurrezione e Vita* inaugurated the Teatro Verde on July 13, 1954.

Because it is a spin-off of *Laudes Evangelii* and received few performances, *Resurrezione* is not included for separate analysis. The title is taken from Christ's words, "I am the Resurrection and the Life," and it took the form of a sixteenth-century pageant depicting the life of Christ in fifteen episodes. Designer Virgilio Marchi created an impressive spectacle involving three revolving levels. On each level were Renaissance arches, columns and pediments, which allowed the action to unfold as if the dancers were figures on frescoes.

Resurrezione was danced to the music of Claudio Monteverdi, Andrea and Giovanni Gabrieli, and Biagio Marini, orchestrated by Virgilio

Mortari. Since he was now using Italian Renaissance music, Massine turned to the painterly sources of Titian, Veronese, and Tintoretto to recapture the imposing High Renaissance style. Although this called for a "broader, more animated approach" than he had used in *Laudes*, it was still a succession of choreographic tableaux. Tatiana Massine (who danced the Angel of the Annunciation) confirms that *Resurrezione* was "plastically staged, there was no real dancing."[23]

Resurrezione e Vita received laudatory reviews from *Musical America*, *Le Monde* and *Dance News*.[24] Massine was able to take the same subject matter used in *Laudes Evangelii* and restate it eloquently in the entirely different ethos of the High Renaissance. Few, if any, other choreographers in history have been able to bring to their interpretations the same depth and breadth of knowledge of the entire historical gamut of the visual and performing arts. In his review of *Laudes Evangelii*, Arnold Haskell wrote, "Massine alone could have created it."[25] The same can be said of *Resurrezione e Vita*.

After fulfilling his commitment to Count Cini, Massine returned to Galli to prepare himself for his return to the United States. He was to choreograph a new work for the Ballet Russe; after almost fifteen years, he and Denham had negotiated a peace treaty, and Denham actually approved a new symphonic ballet despite his former distaste for them. While choreographing his *Symphonie fantastique* in 1936, Léonide had also made notes for a possible ballet on Berlioz's *Harold en Italie*. Rehearsals for *Harold* began in the late summer and autumn of 1954.

MAD TRISTAN (Tristan Fou)

Ballet in Two Scenes
Libretto: Salvador Dalí
Music: Richard Wagner, excerpts from *Tristan und Isolde*, orchestrated
   by Ivan Boutnikov
Scenic and Costume Design: Salvador Dalí; costumes executed by
   Mme Berthe, supervised by Nathalie Crothers
Première: International Theatre, New York, December 15, 1944

ORIGINAL CAST

Tristan: Francisco Monicion   Isolde: Marjorie Tallchief
The Chimera of Isolde: Lisa Maslov
Hallucination of Ship: Jean Guelis
King Mark: David Adhar   **Brangäne:** Zoya Leporska
Flute Player: Robert Armstrong
Spirits of Love, Spirits of Death, Ceremonial of Death, Soldiers

Synopsis[26]

The First Paranoiac Ballet Based on the Eternal Myth of Love in Death
Scene 1—Forest of Idylls. Spring.
Scene 2—Isle of Death. Autumn.

Tristan, in Dalí's conception, has been driven insane with love, and in this state he sees himself slowly devoured by Isolde's Chimera, a horrible and awesome transformation of his beloved. Thus, in the sublimity of the human being, are reincarnated the perverse and tragic nuptial rites of the praying mantis, wherein the female devours the male as the consummation of their union.

Dalí sees the whole romantic philosophy of Wagner as an uninterrupted complex of impotence, an exasperating procession of wheelbarrows, heavy with the earth of reality, struggling up toward the inaccessible heaven of the ecstasy of love, at the summit of which there is only a precipice—love in death and death in love.

The curtain rises to reveal an insect-like woman lying on her back on an altar, her head upstage so that only her raised V-shaped legs are visible. Isolde circles and crawls up onto the altar, followed by Tristan. The sprawling, grotesque creatures on the periphery come to life, encircling the altar in a spastic, twitchy fashion. Wheelbarrows are dragged across the stage by figures in death shrouds. The Spirits of Love step forward and dance, and the female on the altar alights, revealing herself as Isolde's Chimera. Her legs are imprisoned in a tutu which Tristan cuts off with his sword so that she can dance. Everyone exits, leaving Tristan utterly alone.

Scene Two finds Tristan lying on a bed of leaves, attended by an anthropomorphic female cat. The Flute Player sounds a melody in his ear and clings to him like a leech until Tristan finally wrests himself from his grip. Isolde and her Chimera enter and dance with two shovels; next, the Hallucination of Ship comes on with threatening movements and chases Tristan offstage. The backcloth parts to reveal a grave into which the shrouded corpse of Tristan is lowered inch by inch. From the tomb, one sees white arms, whose waving fingers gradually envelop the slowly descending body and guide it to its final resting place.

Concept

Early reports on the ballet that eventually became *Bacchanale* had it that the title would be "Tristan Fou" or "The Praying Mantis." The score would blend selections from Wagner's *Tristan und Isolde* with Cole Porter tunes and some never-performed music by Friedrich Wilhelm Nietzsche, composed when he was in an asylum. The role of Tristan, to be patterned after Harpo Marx, would be mimed by Massine in a tousled blonde wig. In a *New York Herald Tribune* interview, Massine explained that Tristan would emerge from a completely paralytic state "and go into paroxysms of the most frenetic choreographical delirium."[27] A ballet only faintly fitting that description finally materialized in 1944 when Massine and Dalí created *Tristan Fou* ("Mad Tristan") for the Marquis de Cuevas.

Dalí's obsession with a pastoral religious painting by Jean-François Millet, the *Angelus* (1857–59), helps to clarify his concept for *Mad Tristan*. Dalí had used a paranoiac resemblance between the pose of the female figure in *Angelus* and that of a post-copulatory female praying mantis about to devour her mate in order to trigger a rereading of the Millet religious image as one of sexual aggression. *Atavism of Twilight* (1933; Berne, Kstmus) was the most celebrated of a number of paintings that developed the *Angelus* theme.

In 1933 Dalí published in *Minotaure* his "Paranoiac-Critical Interpretation of the Obsessive Image of the *Angelus* by Millet." It was subtitled "A Chance Encounter of an Umbrella and a Sewing Machine on a Dissecting Table":

> The umbrella ... as a result of its flagrant and well-known phenomenon of erection, would be none other than the masculine figure in the *Angelus* which in the picture, as the reader will do me the favour of remembering, is trying to hide his state of erection—and thereby merely succeeding in drawing attention to it—by the shameful and compromising position of his own hat. Opposite him, the sewing machine ... goes so far as to invoke the mortal and cannibal virtue of her sewing needle, the activity of which may be identified with that super fine perforation of the praying mantis "emptying" her male.[28]

In a 1944 interview for *Cue* magazine, Dalí explained that his protagonist, Tristan, becomes so acutely *fou de l'amour* that he sees Isolde as a praying mantis preparing to devour him. The well-known view of Wagner's opera is "presented from the angle of love in death and death in love—the great theme of life."[29] Dalí entwined the forces of love and self-destruction in a gruesome affinity, letting them evolve into and out of each other.

Scenery and Costumes

Grace Robert noticed that some of the symbolism employed in *Mad Tristan* was startlingly original—"less related to the textbooks of abnormal psychology than in the two former ballets."[30] Here, wheelbarrows

Salvador Dalí's backdrop for *Mad Tristan*, 1944.

carted by hooded figures became symbols of earthly oppression and mortality. The faceless Spirits of Love wore white tutus with huge globe-shaped headpieces symbolizing fertility. The vessel which bears Tristan and Isolde to Cornwall was represented by a male dancer with a large ship around his waist. Tristan wore the winged helmet of the Valkyrie, a waist-length blonde wig, and Cupid's diapers. Isolde was garbed like the conventional operatic heroine, while her Chimera wore red gloves and a ragged, filthy version of her dress.

Dalí's set depicted a fantastic island with three jutting masonried horses' heads rising from the sea. On the periphery were a car flung out on a rampart, *fleur-de-lis* sprouting from human eyes, crumbling balustrades and stairs winding up to nowhere. The ballet's highlight was the fantastic final section, when the large horses' heads on the backcloth parted for the death and transfiguration of Tristan. Dismembered arms outstretched in a grave slowly received and lowered his corpse. Overall, Robert Bagar found Dalí's work "superb, painted with Mr. Dalí's wonted mastery." John Martin, however, groused that Dalí's stage picture was "patchy, painty, without unity and as cluttered as a bargain basement."[31]

Music

The score was a pastiche of excerpts from Wagner's *Tristan und Isolde*. The final concept for *Mad Tristan* must be contextualized not only as a stage expression of Dalí's *Angelus* series, but also as a literary reference to the themes of the 1865 opera itself. Isolde is being brought from Ireland to Cornwall by Tristan, the murderer of Morold, Isolde's betrothed. She is now to become the bride of Tristan's uncle, King Mark. Isolde has only vengeance in mind and selects the draught of death. She hands Tristan one of two cups, and both drink in their turn; however, Brangäne, Isolde's maid, has substituted the love potion for the death potion. The protagonists embrace ecstatically and express their mutual passion. Once in Cornwall, the lovers meet secretly in a garden in King Mark's castle, but they are discovered by King Mark and Melot, a courtier. Melot draws his sword; Tristan also draws, but allows himself to be wounded. Tristan returns to his castle in Brittany, where he lies near death. In his fevered imagination, Tristan imagines that he sees the ship bearing Isolde approaching. Later, Isolde finally does arrive, but Tristan expires in her arms. Isolde sinks lifeless onto his body.

Tristan und Isolde was strongly influenced by the German philosopher Arthur Schopenhauer, who taught a pessimistic view of existence that cedes control to the ultimately destructive human will rather than to the human intellect. For Schopenhauer, the only road to liberation is the sheer extinction of the will. In Schopenhauer, Wagner found a confirmation of his own world of ideas, and he was stunned by this recognition. On December 16, 1854, Wagner wrote to Franz Liszt: "His main idea, the ultimate denial of the will to live, is of terrible seriousness, but it is the only thing that can redeem us."[32] Of *Tristan und Isolde*'s tragic ending Wagner wrote, "What fate kept apart in life is now revived in death, in transfigured form. ... [T]he dying Isolde perceives the most blissful fulfillment of her fervent longing to be joined together with Tristan for all eternity."[33] Thus, the protagonists' deaths are actually celebrated: the material realm of phenomena is transcended and the lovers' salvation is attained in the noumenal.[34] The influence of Schopenhauerian philosophy on *Tristan und Isolde* has made the opera a favorite subject for psychological analysis and experimental productions. The history of reactions to *Tristan und Isolde* has been called a "a history of fascination," with only a few critical minds speaking of the suicidal tendencies inherent in such fascination. Among the French intelligentsia around the turn of the century, one could speak not only of *Wagnérisme* but of a quite specific *tristanisme*.[35]

Because the score for *Mad Tristan* was a pastiche, it could not possibly do justice to the cumulative surge of the opera. Moreover, Ivan Boutnikov's arrangement sounded very thin as played by a small orchestra. Edwin Denby realized that the score should be taken merely "as an effigy of a masterpiece, a literary reference."[36]

Choreography

In a sense, it is almost a misnomer to refer to Massine's inventions for *Mad Tristan* as choreography. There was very little organized ensemble dancing. Where it occurred, as in the dance of the Spirits of Love, most critics faulted Massine again for failing to devise appropriately surrealist choreography. The *New Statesman* critic, perhaps shortsightedly, referred to Massine's choreography as "hackwork."[37]

But Denby was sharp enough to see that "As the score isn't music, so the ballet isn't dancing. Its best effects are properly stage effects." Denby's assessment explains why so much of Massine's work was purely sculptural. He created several arresting visual images, such as the Chimera's opening pose, the hooded figures who twitch with the tics of spastic paralysis as they cling to their wheelbarrows, and the Flute Player who signifies death's triumph by clinging to Tristan like a leech. It was in these sculptural effects that Massine's creativity was at its height. The choreographic highlight was the prolonged descent of the limp figure in the closing death and transfiguration scene. For Cyril Beaumont, this image had a "rare, haunting beauty."[38]

Critical Survey

Verdicts on the ballet as a whole were quite mixed. A. V. Coton: "merely a bore"; Arthur Berger: "rather abject"; and John Martin: "a twenty-five minute yawn."[39] However, Carl Brahms was "moved and stimulated" by the ballet and called the sets "the strangest form of beauty this theatre can ever have seen." For Edwin Denby, the ballet was "a first-class mental carnival."[40]

In Retrospect

Ballet International revived *Mad Tristan* only once, for its Covent Garden season in the summer of 1949. With their rich visual imagery, Dalí and Massine conveyed an aching sense of human affliction and mortal struggle that now lives on only in the illustrated textbooks of the ballet. Bagar grasped its true significance when he saw in this ballet "a pitiful sense of yearning, a frustration so tragic that it approaches the maudlin. And over it all—struggle and struggle of perpetual forces."[41] With *Mad Tristan*, Dalí and Massine completed their last surrealist collaboration.

BALLET RUSSE HIGHLIGHTS

A Collection of New and Classical Dances from the Ballet Repertoire
Première: Lewisohn Stadium, June 30, 1945

ORIGINAL CAST
Irina Baronova, André Eglevsky, Anna Istomina,
Yurek Lazowsky, Kathryn Lee, and Léonide Massine

1946 CAST
André Eglevsky, Jean Guelis, Rosella Hightower,
Anna Istomina, Helen Komarova, Yurek Lazowsky,
Léonide Massine, Bettina Rosay and Igor Youskevitch

Choreography

The unapologetic philosophy of Ballet Russe Highlights was to prove that ballet could be popular with the masses. The project was geared to what John Martin termed "the not too discriminating box-office."[42] For this balletic "Reader's Digest," Massine and his ballet stars gave between thirty and forty highlights from both nineteenth- and twentieth-century ballets.

The repertoire included several pas de deux by Petipa, a number of excerpts from Fokine and Massine ballets, and a great variety of original compositions choreographed for the occasion by Massine. John Martin helped his readers to sort out the baffling array of Massine's new dances: "They fall at once into categories. There is the folk and national group, the department of butterflies and bees, the division of low comedy, the 'interpretative' and symphonic, and that other department which can only be described as cutie-pie."[43]

Interspersed among the new dances, though, were at least two with some redeeming virtues. *Leningrad Symphony*—danced to the first movement of Shostakovich's Seventh Symphony—was a war piece in which Massine paid tribute to the Russians' resistance to the German invasion. The music has three allegretto themes representing the peoples' sorrow at war, their determination to overcome the Germans, and their increasing militancy as the twenty-minute movement builds to a climax. Martin liked the *Leningrad Symphony*'s "exciting drive" and felt that "the choreography of the two Nazi soldiers has considerable dramatic effectiveness."[44]

Ann Barzel felt that "Strange Sarabande" was the only exception to this troupe's otherwise "expendable offerings. A line of blind beggars danced in, secure in the companionship assured by their clasped hands. But as they lost contact, they showed the frightened desperation of isolation. One by one, they found a friendly hand again. Reassured, they resumed the farandole on their exit."[45]

Critical Survey

The Ballet Russe Highlights received favorable press notices in many cities west of New York. In these, critics praised Massine for packing large theatres and stadiums and proving that ballet was an art that was accessible to all. Not surprisingly, the New York reviews were utterly scathing. Martin gave the most cogent summary of the program's artistic weakness: "The trouble apparently lies in the fact that the program was not organized but merely agglomerated.... They [the numbers] bear no conceivable relation to each other, but are shot out in rapid succession, one virtually on the heels of the other, in traditional vaudeville tempo, and the dancers work like Trojans to keep up the pace."[46] Robert Hague's pitiless review—"Ballet Borscht at the Stadium"—made sport of Massine's new dances:

> The so-called new ones—which Massine has inflicted on the members of the company, shouldn't happen to a dog.... In "Contredanses" (Beethoven), pert Miss Lee, between dashes backstage to alter her costume, is required to be in turn a soldierette, a chop-suey Ming-Toy Chinese and a tightrope-walker; later in the evening, dressed as a bumble bee, she spins and turns busily to—you guessed it—Rimsky-Korsakoff.... For himself, Massine has provided a dish of spinach

called "Vision," paced out to the inevitable Bach "Air for the G-string." Dressed in tattered overalls, he re-plays his favorite role — the dreaming, yearning artist plagued by a beautiful vision (Miss Lee). In this particular version he also seems to be plagued by a Bachache and does a great deal of lying down on the stage. That took him out of my own line of vision, fortunately ... the most distinguished feature of the evening was the scenery. There wasn't any.[47]

In Retrospect

An interesting question is raised by Martin's concluding remarks on the Ballet Russe Highlights: "It is manifest that the whole project has been conceived with the 'popular' trade as its goal, but there is something rather discouraging (almost cynical, in fact) about such a conception of popular taste."[48] Cynical or not, huge and enthusiastic crowds in cities all across the nation prove that Massine's conception of popular taste in mid-century America was, in fact, correct. Ballet Russe Highlights gave tens of thousands of people their first exposure to ballet and an evening of pleasure. In turn, New York critics gave the troupe the smart spanking it deserved for its artistic iniquities. All's well that ends well.

CLOCK SYMPHONY

Ballet in Four Scenes
Libretto: Léonide Massine
Music: Franz Joseph Haydn (Symphony No. 101 in D major, "The Clock")
Scenery and Costumes: Christian Bérard
Première: Covent Garden, London, June 25, 1948

ORIGINAL CAST
The Princess: Moira Shearer
The Clockmaker: Alexander Grant   The Mandarin: Franklin White
The Genie of the Lightning: Michael Somes
King, Insect Suitors, Figurines

Synopsis

The King, ruler of the Kingdom of Insects, announces that he is looking for suitors for his daughter. A poor young Clockmaker brings him an elaborate, intricate clock. The insect suitors, seeing that the Princess is attracted to the Clockmaker, secretly hide one of their pages inside the clock case to dislocate its mechanism. The hands of the clock begin to go in reverse, but when the page has been extracted, the suitors are banished from the kingdom. The Clockmaker is able to repair his masterpiece and so wins the Princess's hand.

Scenery and Costumes

Clock Symphony was a huge production with a large cast. Christian Bérard's décor for this ballet featured a giant clock upstage center that opened up to allow the many dancing figures to emerge from it. For the dazzling opening, the curtain rose on Shearer, in a black and night-blue tutu, seated commandingly on a throne under a white canopy.[49] Arnold Haskell noted that "this is essentially a work in which the fantasy of the decorative artist counts for at least half the effect."[50]

Music

Franz Joseph Haydn played a central role in the establishment of the classical style, and its subsequent growth can be seen in the development of his own music. His lifelong labors brought the symphony and string quartet to real life. Haydn entered the service of the Austrian princes Esterházy at Eisenstadt in 1761. His duties included daily music performances and thus constant composition of new works. Of special interest are the works of the period 1768–74, often referred to as Haydn's *Sturm und Drang* ("Storm and Stress") period, in which he was particularly inventive in his search for new styles and forms. The *Sturm und Drang* symphonies still impress with their remarkable sincerity, directness, and passion, reflected in popular names like *La passione* (No. 49). The most important stylistic features are a strong rhythmic drive, a new stressing of harmonic tension, and a new preference for minor keys.[51] In their own time, these symphonies must have been quite controversial.

In 1790 Haydn's life changed radically; Prince Anton, who succeeded Prince Nicolaus in that year, cared little for music and required almost nothing of Haydn. Thus Haydn was free to compose and travel as he wished. He was invited by London impresario Johann Peter Salomon to do two sets of concert series in that city in 1791 and 1794. The twelve symphonies that Haydn composed for London (Nos. 93–104, usually called the London symphonies) represent the pinnacle of his symphonic work.

The London symphonies were often given popular nicknames like "Surprise," "Clock," "Military," and "Drumroll." While they don't show any new stylistic evolutions, they are known for their use of simple and memorable themes. For the "Military" Symphony, Haydn's clear intention was to evoke the terrifying sounds of battle via triangle, cymbal, bass drum and an actual army call, the Austrian General Salute.[52]

The slow second movement of the "Clock" Symphony, also pictorially conceived, is another example of Haydn's use of simple, compelling motifs. A rondo with variations in duple time, its theme imitates the steady tick of a clock. It is the steadfast rhythm of this movement which inspired Massine's concept of revolving Meissen clock figurines. At its March 3, 1794, première, the "Clock" Symphony was received with jubilation: "This was HAYDN: what can we, what need we say more?" said the *Morning Chronicle*.[53]

In the summer of 1795, Haydn returned to Vienna, where he lived for the rest of his life. Rather unexpectedly, oratorio was to be the last phase of Haydn's career and the most brilliantly successful one. No works better reveal his mastery as an oratorio composer than *The Creation* (1798) and *The Seasons* (1801).

Choreography

Massine's concept was to contrast "elegant, flowing" movements for the clock figures with the "rapid contorted movements and stiff jerky postures of the insects."[54] The first scene introduces the insects, the Clockmaker, and the Princess. The second scene is by far the most imaginative and is danced to the famous "tick-tock" of the slow rondo. Here, the porcelain-white clock figures come to life and revolve rhythmically around the clock, each one performing solos in character. In the third scene, the Princess rises from her throne and leaps into action with a quick allegro solo of jumps and *batterie*. The fourth scene is a happy wedding celebration.

Although Massine's fairy tale used a symphony, it was not in any sense a symphonic ballet. Rather than attempting a visualization of the "Clock" Symphony's other musical features, Massine focused almost solely on its rhythm. Noting the more distant connection between music and movement, Haskell remarked, "This is not to say that the music has been abused, but that one could imagine the use of other music."[55]

Even though this was Massine's fourth staging for Sadler's Wells, the choreography presented dancers with a new degree of difficulty. It was extremely intricate, involving quick, staccato isolations of the legs, arms, torso, and head. In his earlier works, Moira Shearer recalled that Massine's choreography had more lyricism and flow. But in *Clock Symphony*, she believed that "all the work he did was quite fussy. ... He would put perhaps one step too many into each phrase of music."[56] Alexander Grant described the movement as "exhausting ... a type of technique that demands an extensive quick allegro footwork."[57]

Critical Survey

Clock Symphony was not a success. "The Sitter Out" complained that the story was too complicated and the choreography too busy: "Massine appears to have so overloaded his choreography with exceedingly intricate dances that in many instances there is no clear pattern ... the huge clock serves mostly as an excuse for some elaborate and rather long drawn-out 'chinoiserie.' Moira Shearer as the Princess is charming to the eye and dances delightfully, but has been given no opportunity to build up the character."[58]

In Retrospect

In his book review of Vincente García-Márquez's biography on Massine, Alastair Macaulay was quite critical of Massine's musicality, charging that "his ballets failed to see the music for the notes. How deep did music run in him?"[59] Certainly there are stretches of supreme musicality in Massine's best works, but this was not the case in *Clock Symphony*. Massine's choreography for the *Les Femmes de bonne humeur* (1917) had also been extremely busy, but this could be justified because Goldoni's characters were such fussy and overstimulated individuals. While insects also tend to be fussy and overstimulated, the uniformly frenetic choreography sorely hampered the human characters. They were "given no opportunity to build up the character," with the result that the ballet suffered from a lack of warmth and charm.

DONALD OF THE BURTHENS

Ballet in Two Scenes
Libretto: Léonide Massine, based on a Scottish folk legend
Music: Ian Whyte
Scenic and Costume Design: Robert Colquhoun and Robert MacBryde
Première: Covent Garden, London, December 12, 1951

ORIGINAL CAST
Donald of the Burthens: Alexander Grant
Death: Beryl Grey   **King:** Leslie Edwards
Leader of the Sword Dancers: Brian Shaw

Synopsis[60]

Scene One. A Forest Glade in Scotland. A group of young girls are dancing together in the forest when Donald the Woodcutter comes to the clearing. The girls taunt him for his humble occupation. When they leave, a mysterious tall woman in scarlet clothes appears before Donald, and he is terrified to learn that she is Death herself. She advises him that she has come to help him, and Donald confesses that his dearest wish is to become a doctor. Death tells him that she will indeed help him to become a doctor, but only on the condition that he worship her exclusively. If he ever prays to another god, then she will kill him. Donald next asks Death how he can become a doctor without schooling. She replies that if Donald sees her standing at the head of the patient's bed, he will know that the patient will die and that he should not waste time trying to cure him. But if he sees her standing at the foot of anyone's bed, then the patient will recover. Donald accepts Death's offer and immediately encounters a trio of epileptics. Death stands at their feet, and Donald cures them. A lady comes on with a sick baby and Donald brings the baby back to health. As word spreads, Donald soon becomes the most famous doctor in Scotland. He always knows whether a patient will die or not, and everyone regards him as a genius.

Scene Two. The King's Bedchamber. The King of Scotland lies on his deathbed. There is only one last hope: the courtiers have sent for Donald. Donald enters the room, and to his despair, sees the figure of Death standing at the head of the bed. Desperate to save his king, Donald turns the bed completely around, and in this way, Death finds herself standing at its foot. Death will not be duped so easily though, and she returns at once to the head of the bed. Donald, in his turn, spins the bed around once more. Death realizes that his love for his king is stronger than his loyalty to her. She leaves in a rage.

Now the king is fully recovered, and a celebration is arranged. The young men of the court perform a traditional sword dance, and the divertissement continues with a suite of Scottish dances. The children of the court approach Donald and ask for a recitation of a prayer which they have forgotten. Without thinking, Donald recites it, having forgotten that Death has told him never to pray to another. Death appears, sinister and unforgiving, and stands at his head; Donald collapses and expires. The king and his court are overwhelmed with sorrow, but Death cuts short their mourning: she orders everyone to dance with her as a sign that they accept her ultimate power.

Scenery and Costumes

The painters Robert Colquhoun and Robert MacBryde were lifetime associates whose essential art and lifestyle can best be understood in the context of Scottish nationalism. For the first scene of *Donald*, Colquhoun and MacBryde devised a misty pastoral landscape and for the second, a vast medieval hall. The latter set thus placed the action in the archaic past, with beams, massive monoliths and costumes from the preplaid age of Scotland. Many viewers—Alexander Bland among them—missed the theatricality of "genuine highland dress in its full eighteenth-century splendour" and found that the sets and costumes were "just as easily reminiscent of Ireland."[61]

Music

Ian Whyte was a staunch nationalist composer. Whyte's desire that Scotland should originate its own music broadcasts and the determination with which he went about achieving this had its most important outcome in the founding of the Scottish Symphony Orchestra in 1935. His compositional output was large and consistently inspired by his deep love for his homeland, as is evident in his numerous arrangements of Scottish madrigals, choral pieces and music for strings. His original works, though they have a distinct personality, can seem backward-looking: "Their utter fidelity to Scott qualities suggest that, in loving his country, Whyte was also its prisoner."[62]

Whyte's score for *Donald of the Burthens* made the innovation of incorporating the bagpipes into an otherwise conventional orchestra. However, the music lacked sustaining power for the very reason that it was so unremittingly Scottish. Bland found that "The quick twittery rhythms become wearisome after a time and often seem too trivial for the situation."[63]

Choreography

For *Donald*, Massine diligently researched authentic Scottish dances such as the sword dance, reel, *seann triubhas*, and *gillie calum*. "The Sitter Out" judged that the best first-scene choreography included the sword dance led by Brian Shaw and a "brilliant solo" for Alexander Grant, involving capers, high-cuts and pirouettes, interspersed with comical slapstick. Throughout, Massine arranged excellent dances for the ensemble. In the second scene, *Ballet Annual* praised their "superb ground patterns"; Clive Barnes admired their "ingenious use of obliquely-placed blocks of dancers."[64]

Only Beryl Grey's allegorical role of Death was strictly classical, and she alone danced en pointe. For Bland, the ballet's essential Scottish authenticity was its downfall because folk dancing is meant for doing, not watching. In particular, he believed that Scottish dancing's rigid torso, nimble footwork and intricate small-scale patterns "are as sexually ambivalent as a kilt. It is a staccato art, well adapted for indications of wit and gaiety but unsuitable for expressing tenderness, majesty or grief." He joked, "Massine seems determined we shall take our Scotch unadulterated; but now and then one longs for a dash of bourbon or vodka—even a splash of classical soda."[65]

Fernau Hall suggested that the work's main flaw was that Massine tried to impose the format of a Petipa ballet on a work which should have been treated expressionistically, resulting in a "puzzling cheerful climax."[66] Massine now faced an era in which pure expressionism had lost its appeal to the public, whereas the Petipa ballets, in London at least, were reliable box-office attractions. Massine may well have tried to ensure the success of *Donald* by giving it the shape of a Petipa ballet—even though this shape was an aberration to his chosen theme.

Critical Survey

The main criticisms of *Donald* are cited above in the comments of Bland and Hall. Critics also bemoaned *Donald*'s poor libretto whose climax was a "quibble enacted in a ludicrous manner by means of a kind of whirling bedstead." Thereafter, Alexander Bland could not take the ballet seriously on any level, so that Death's dancing in the finale, "toeing and heeling with the rest, fails to evoke any surprise."

Uncharacteristically, Massine's characters in *Donald* were murky rather than sharply focused. As Donald, Alexander Grant made his first entrance with a bright and quirky solo reminiscent of Massine's Peruvian. But Grant's role of hero compelled him "to wobble between the serious and the comic," with the result that his personality never coalesced. Massine's movement for Beryl Grey as Death was equally unconvincing for Bland because her sexy scarlet unitard and "sharply sinuous twists and niggly jumps and beats" failed to convey the concept of a "horrific figure who telescopes the attributes of Death and the Devil."[67]

In Retrospect

In his 1953 *Anatomy of Ballet*, Hall maintained that ballet audiences of the 1950s favored either abstract neoclassicism or classical nineteenth-century staples and that a short folk ballet with a complicated story was bound to look old-fashioned.[68] Those who believed that Massine's adaptation of Scottish dances needed the same degree of fusion with ballet that had been the glory of *Le Tricorne* also hit the mark. One year later, George Balanchine did a far more successful and enduring ballet with a Scottish inspiration. *Scotch Symphony* (1952) sparked the imagination by merely alluding to the folk dances which inspired it.

LAUDES EVANGELII

Choreographic Pageant in Seven Scenes
Libretto: Giorgio Signorini, based on the Latin liturgical play, *Laudes Dramaticae Umbriae*

8. March 1943–October 1954

Music: Thirteenth-century Umbrian chants, orchestrated by Valentino Bucchi
Scenic and Costume Design: Ezio Rossi
Première: Church of Santo Domenico, Perugia, Italy, September 20, 1952

ORIGINAL CAST
Christ: Angelo Pietri
Mary: Geneviève Lespagnol   Joseph: Carlo Faraboni
St. John: Alberto Moro   Veronica: Bianca Sampideccia
Judas: Alberto Testa
Vocal Soloists: Antonietta Stella, Rina Corsi,
Renato Cappecchi, Silvio Maionica

Synopsis

This spectacle of mime, dance and song depicts, in the course of two hours, the Life and Passion of Christ. *Laudes Evangelii* has seven scenes: the Annunciation and the Visitation; the Nativity and the Flight into Egypt; the Entrance into Jerusalem; the Garden of Olives (Gethsemane); the Flagellation and the *Via Crucis*; the Crucifixion and Deposition; and the Resurrection and the Ascension.

Scenic and Costume Design

Designer Ezio Rossi set his stage at the head of the central nave of the church of Santo Domenico. The stage had three levels and two sections. While one section was being used, the other was flown out to allow for uninterrupted changes of scene. The first three scenes took place at stage level. The next two took place on the winding ramp that connected the first level to the second. The Crucifixion and Deposition were staged on the second level, while the Resurrection and the Ascension were enacted on the highest.[69]

Since the Church of Santo Domenico was breathtakingly beautiful in its own right, Rossi's decoration was tastefully restrained and mostly limited to a gold mosaic backdrop which was hung beneath the church's seventy-five-foot stained glass rose window. The sparse scenery consisted of a chapel in the first scene, a grotto in the second, a palm tree and fountain at the entrance to Jerusalem in the third, and a crucifix in the sixth, which was cross-lit from behind to create a haunting shadow. Spotlights for the scenes were concealed in the organ and pulpit.

Music

Laudes Evangelii is arranged to what is possibly the oldest existing score in Europe, a collection of airs and recitatives (*laudi*) by Jacopone da Todi and other anonymous thirteenth-century composers which was discovered in a library at Cortona. Orchestrator Valentino Bucchi wrote, "we followed, with very few exceptions, the old *laudi*, remaining faithful, as far as language went, to the original harmonized melody."[70] His essential conservatism was apparent to *Time* magazine's critic, who observed that Bucchi's "measured music was a careful reflection of medieval modes."[71]

Choreography

In order to keep his choreography in harmony with the pre–Giotto *laudi*, Massine used an approach quite similar to that of his earlier *St. Francis*. It was based "on the attitudes depicted in Byzantine mosaics, and on the paintings of the primitive Lucca and Pisa school."[72] As in *St. Francis*, however, Massine wanted to avoid merely imitating his sources. He was striving, said Signorini, "to create a contemporary vision of that language."[73]

Few ballets in history have had a more unusual rehearsal period. Massine assembled a fifty-member company, using dancers from La Scala and the Maggio Musicale. He settled the company in a large villa on a hilltop in Positano, an arrangement which enabled him to commute back and forth each day from Galli. The first publicity photographs of Massine's rehearsals showed French ballerina Geneviève Lespagnol practicing her role of the Virgin Mary in a lowcut leotard and pink ballet tights. The photos aroused such a storm of protest that a deputation of five Dominicans was sent to keep an eye on rehearsals. However, reports have it that the Dominicans' anxieties were soothed over in a wink: "Before rehearsals were over, the monks had begun serving coffee and wine to the artists and technicians."[74]

Once rehearsals were moved to the church itself, Massine recounts, "I was confronted with a number of technical problems, as the church was not really suitable for such a large-scale production." The final rehearsal lasted twenty-four hours: "When it was over my nervous system was so overstrained that in the middle of the night I woke up and found myself on the floor."[75]

Critical Survey

With a vocal chorus of ninety-six and a fifty-five-piece orchestra, *Laudes* was a grand production. A ramp running the length of the church accommodated the audience, which numbered over two thousand. Italian and international critics hailed *Laudes Evangelii* as a work of rare beauty. *Dance and Dancers* called it "unforgettable. ... With the greatest discretion, a sense of time and a poetic beauty, Massine has succeeded in recapturing the simplicity of the Florentine Quattrocento." Arnold Haskell termed it a "masterwork: it is religious in feeling and scholarly in its understanding of liturgy and of the spirit and movement of the period."[76]

The show got only one bad notice—but it came from a very ominous source. The Vatican had not been officially informed of Perugia's plans and was taken aback to learn of the performances after the fact: "Churches," announced a Vatican spokesman, "are meant to be places of worship in the most absolute sense of the word. ... For the time being, the Archbishop of Perugia will be requested to handle the matter in such a way that it will not repeat itself."[77]

In Retrospect

The success of *Laudes Evangelii* at Perugia prompted other churches to request the production, and it was restaged in several Italian and French cities. In Nantes, from May 5 to 18, 1954, it was the most important feature of the *Fêtes du Mai Musicale*. During this same run, Bishop Villepet opened the doors of Nôtre Dame du Bon Port to this ballet.[78] In Italy, *Laudes* had revivals in the churches of Perugia and Palermo in 1954 and was given a stage revival at La Scala in 1959.

Laudes Evangelii was filmed by London's Associated-Rediffusion Television in 1961. It was broadcast throughout England, Holland, Denmark, Canada, and Italy; on April 8, 1962, it was rebroadcast in the United States. *USA* critic Jack Iams pronounced the television production "splendid." Jack Gould found it to be "stunning" and added, "'Laudes Evangelii' surely will stand as one of television's lasting accomplishments, a work of breathtaking reverence and beauty that has enriched the home screen as much as any single program in recent years."[79]

Laudes Evangelii was one of Massine's most important postwar achievements and a project that was deeply fulfilling to him, artistically and spiritually. When first performed in Perugia, he wrote, "When I saw that many of the spectators and even some of the performers were in tears throughout, I felt far more gratified than I would have been by any amount of applause."[80]

A 16-millimeter film of the 1961 telecast of *Laudes Evangelii* now slumbers peacefully in the archives of the Jerome Robbins Dance Division, Lincoln Center. It is well worth studying, especially for those with an interest in liturgical dance. *Laudes Evangelii* richly deserves a new revival, preferably in the setting for which it was intended.

HAROLD IN ITALY

Ballet in Four Movements
Libretto: Léonide Massine, based on *Childe Harold's Pilgrimage*, by
  Lord George Gordon Byron
Music: Hector Berlioz, *Harold en Italie*, op. 16, orchestrated by Ivan
  Boutnikoff
Scenic and Costume Design: Bernard Lamotte
Première: Opera House, Boston, October 14, 1954

ORIGINAL CAST

First Movement
Harold: Leon Danielia   Happy Couple: Irina Baronova and Ian Howard

Second Movement
Leader of the Pilgrims: Yvonne Chouteau   Simpleton: Terry de Mare

Third Movement
Young Shepherds: Nina Novak and Deni Lamont

Fourth Movement
Leader of the Brigands: Victor Moreno   Lead Captive: Gertrude Tyven

Synopsis

The story is that of a poet (the "Childe Harold" of Byron's poem) who travels in Italy in the early part of the nineteenth century. He comments on and reacts to what he sees, while remaining a comparatively static figure.

First Movement. Harold in the Mountains. A quartet of leaves are blown about by the wind as Harold enters. The Happy Couple come onstage and perform a pas de deux with high lifts and dramatic sweeps to the floor. A woman enters and dances briefly with Harold. They are joined by nine couples and then by the reappearance of the Happy Couple. After the leaves blow across the stage a second time, the entire ensemble does a lengthy sweeping sequence to both sides of the stage.

Second Movement. Harold Meets the Pilgrims. A group of pilgrims in a three-tiered formation are seen upstage left. The Simpleton leaves the group with a summersault, and the pilgrims resume their trek—slumped over, linked by the shoulders, rocking backwards at intervals in their labored walking pattern. As Harold enters from stage left, there are four movement patterns in counterpoint for Harold, the Simpleton, the male quartet and the female pilgrims. Gradually, all the pilgrims resolve into a line again. The Simpleton pulls Harold's hand in the direction of the pilgrimage, but Harold declines and follows their long, slow march with his gaze.

Third Movement. Pastoral Scene. The Young Shepherds perform a pas de deux, supported in the background by three peasant couples. Looking lost, Harold enters from stage right and circles the eight dancers who encircle him in turn and then exit. Harold watches their retreat and forlornly continues on his solitary journey.

Fourth Movement. Orgy of the Brigands. A towering pyramid of ten brigands and their Leader chase a band of maidens. All of the females from the three previous movements are dragged on to form a semicircle, each sequestered by a brigand. The soloists are molested with arm locks, swings into *chaînés* and precarious tossing lifts, while the ensemble maidens are thrown to the floor. Harold and the male soloists appear in the nick of time, and they banish the brigands. The ballet ends with Harold atop a high pyramid, flanked by the Happy Couple and the Young Shepherds.

Scenery and Costumes

Bernard Lamotte designed five backdrops for *Harold in Italy*. The five drops are indistinguishable in the 1954 rehearsal film of this work: the figures are too diminutive for the scale of a theatre. P. W. Manchester observed that the drops were "a little too much of an easel painting." For Baird Hastings, "The designs by Lamotte were the weakest of Massine's symphonic ballets."[81]

Music

In 1830 Berlioz was awarded the Paris Conservatoire's annual Prix de Rome, which permitted a sojourn in Rome at government expense. He was supposed to draw inspiration from the relics of classical antiquity, but they made little impression on him. However, his acute perceptions of Italy, its people, and their customs inspired him powerfully. Henceforth, there was a new color, glow, vivacity and sensuality in his music. Byronism—engendered by the craze for Lord George Gordon's verse-tales in romantic Eastern settings—was at its height, and in Italy, Byronism became a reality for Berlioz as he encountered brigands, corsairs, revolutionaries, and storms at sea.[82]

Harold en Italie (1834) entwines picturesque echoes of his Italian journey with Lord Byron's verse-tale, *Childe Harold's Pilgrimage*. *Harold en Italie* is the most conservative of Berlioz's symphonies. It is the only one to have but four movements, and they are cast in traditional modes: a sonata, a slow march, a scherzo-like movement and a finale that begins

Léonide Massine and unidentified dancers in rehearsal for *Harold in Italy*, 1954.

with thematic material from the earlier movements. The *idée fixe*—the solo viola which impersonates the character of Harold—recurs unchanged in each movement, and the drama is more episodic and less cogent than in the *Symphonie fantastique*. Still, *Harold* is noteworthy for its clarity, rhythmic articulation, tone design and phrasing.

The nineteenth-century public admired the Pilgrims' March most of all. It was Berlioz's first rigorous experiment with the use of space and distance as compositional variables. D. Kern Holoman likens the great crescendo and diminuendo of the approaching and receding pilgrimage to a musical version of the Doppler effect.[83]

Choreography

For P. W. Manchester, the choreographic highlights included the Happy Couple pas de deux, characterized by unusual lifts, the Pilgrim's March, and the duet for the Young Shepherds, who express their love with "an awestruck, simple wonderment which Massine transcribes beautifully into a folk dance idiom." She found the ensemble choreography to be "masterly."

However, she spotted some "outdated" touches, such as the "blowing leaves" and "that ubiquitous pair of deer" that Massine seemed to find indispensable in his symphonic ballets. He also noted "a considerable falling off" in the last movement. This was due to the length of the movement and to Massine's desire to "resolve" a four-movement symphony. The movement thus "could not be sustained satisfactorily in one mood, and the intrusions of the leading figures of the previous movements ... seem out of key."

Critical Survey

Reactions were mixed. Manchester believed that the work revealed "a master choreographer who has not lost his touch."[84] Ann Barzel found the first three movements to be "epic in poetry and grandeur" but noted that it lacked "a worthy concluding movement."[85] Doris Hering, however, called *Harold* "a hopelessly outdated ordeal of plushy plastique."[86]

In Retrospect

Harold in Italy disappeared from the Denham repertory after only one season. A company touring one-night stands could not afford the union-labor costs of hanging five backdrops for just one ballet. In her article "Ballets Down the Drain," Barzel wrote, "The greatest loss is 'Harold in Italy.' ... It was seen the least, although it was the summation of Massine's symphonic style."[87]

9

July 1955–July 1960

In 1955 Massine traveled to South America to serve as guest choreographer for the Teatro Colón in Buenos Aires and the Teatro Municipal in Rio de Janeiro. Massine had already revived eight works for the Colón, but *Usher* was Léonide's first original production for them. He began work on this ballet in June of 1955 and choreographed the entire forty-minute work in less than a month.

From Buenos Aires Massine went to Rio de Janeiro, where he revived six works with an impressive roster of guest stars (Franklin, Chauviré, Eglevsky, Maria Tallchief, Lupe Serrano, and Michael Lland). His only original work for Rio's Teatro Municipal was the minor and unimpressive *Hymne à la Beauté*, danced to a score by the Brazilian composer and conductor, Francisco Mignone.

Hymne à la Beauté premièred on November 18, 1955, and was based on a poem of the same name by Charles Baudelaire. Baudelaire's 1857 *Les Fleurs du mal* ("Flowers of Evil") probed humankind's depravity and lonely suffering in a bleak and boring world. He perversely selected morbid subjects, yet he cast his ideas in exquisitely wrought classical form, extracting from them a strange beauty.

Massine's ballet adaptation of the Baudelaire poem "Hymn to Beauty" takes the form of three episodes portraying "Faith," "Murder," and "First Love." Dancers symbolizing faith are pitted against twelve figures personifying murder. However, in Baudelaire's poem, beauty and evil are so closely intertwined that he embodies them in one and the same alluring woman—a "soft-eyed sprite" who is also an "artless monster wreaking endless pain."[1] Massine's segregation of beauty and evil therefore seems to be at odds with the poem; moreover, the movement is unimaginative. The symbols of beauty (or faith) perform conventional ballet steps; the symbols of evil (or murder) move with the same spastic twitches that Massine used earlier, and more convincingly, in *Mad Tristan*.[2]

During the second half of the 1950s, Massine did only one original ballet—*Don Juan*—and the dance sequences for *Mario e il Mago*. The gestation of *Mario* dates back to August 27, 1951, when theatre and film director Luchino Visconti met the great German author Thomas Mann in Rome. Mann agreed to cede Visconti the rights to his novella *Mario und der Zauberer* ("Mario and the Magician"). Visconti was to write the libretto and to direct the "choreographical action"—a phrase coined by Visconti and Mann to describe a mixture of dance, mime, music, song and speech— while Massine would choreograph the discrete dance sequences.[3] *Mario e il Mago* cannot, strictly speaking, be classified as a "Massine ballet," since Visconti was the real mastermind behind much of the action.

Mann's novella was an unmistakable parable of the Fascist dictatorship. In Act Three, the hunchback conjuror Cipolla—a clear allusion to Mussolini—begins his magic act by conducting a séance, summoning forth exotic characters from India, China, and Arabia. Next he tells the audience, "Freedom exists and also the will exists; but freedom of the will does not exist." There follows one long series of attacks on the volition of every spectator/victim in the crowd as Cipolla compels them to perform humiliating, puppet-like acts. His last victim is a waiter named Mario, who is hopelessly in love with Silvestra. Cipolla deludes Mario into believing that he is Silvestra. "Kiss me!" says the hunchback, and Mario bends down and kisses Cipolla. When the spell is broken, the jeers and mockery of the audience are too much for Mario: he takes out a pistol and kills Cipolla. It is "an end of horror, a fatal end. And yet, a liberation."[4]

Mario e il Mago was performed to a score by Franco Mannino, and set designer Lila de Nobilii created a grandiose series of stage spectacles. The work premièred at La Scala on February 25, 1956, to favorable reviews: Gianni Caradente wrote, "The nightmare quality of Mann's story has been wonderfully translated into stage terms."[5] *Mario e il Mago* won the 1956 Diaghilev Award, given by La Scala for the best production of the year, but it was never performed again after the 1956 season.

Jean Babilée, who played the role of Mario, recalled that the "choreographic action" was such a unique fusion of gesture, cinematographic techniques and dance that it was often hard to tell where Visconti's work ended and Massine's began. The only exceptions were the discrete dance numbers and for these Babliée admired Massine's originality and richness of gesture.[6]

Between *Mario e il Mago* and *Don Juan*, Massine gave a remarkable performance in *Le Tricorne* at the 1958 Holland Festival. Now sixty-three, Léonide danced opposite his sixteen-year-old daughter, Tatiana. Janet Sinclair reported, "he still dances with incredible vitality. ... [H]is powers of projection are still quite the most remarkable to be seen."[7]

In late 1958, Michael Powell asked Massine to collaborate on an English-Spanish co-production, *Luna de miel* ("Honeymoon"). This colorful travelogue was shot in Spain and starred Ludmilla Tcherina and Antonio as a honeymoon couple. The two main dance sequences were an excerpt from Falla's *El Amor Brujo* and a pas de deux for Tcherina and Antonio. The film was awarded the Special Prize of the *Commission Supérieure* at the 1959 Cannes Film Festival.

In 1959 Massine returned to La Scala to stage *Laudes Evangelii* and his new version of *Don Juan*. This Gluck ballet was first presented in Vienna in 1761 with libretto and choreography by Gasparo Angiolini. The ballet was lost for 150 years until it was recreated by Michel Fokine at the Alhambra Theatre on June 25, 1936. Massine's third version was by all accounts a vast improvement over Fokine's.

In 1959 Massine was appointed by industrialist Ariodante Borelli to act as artistic director of the Fifth International Festival of Ballet at Nervi, an old Roman town lying just outside Genoa. Previously, the festival had used an assortment of guest companies, but this year Massine was asked to put together a single resident ballet company from scratch, with full artistic control over roster and repertory. After holding auditions all over Europe, Massine hired fifty-five dancers. He finally had his own company again, for the first time since 1941.

At a press conference held at Maxim's in Paris, Massine declared that the Nervi Festival was nothing less than a "resurrection of the Diaghilev era." Vicente García-Márquez notes that "Massine believed himself to be the last bastion of a form of theater he feared was on the brink of extinction, and Nervi was to be a reiteration of his own aesthetic."[8] With good financial backing from the Festival, the municipality of Genoa and corporate sponsors, Massine could afford to resurrect Diaghilev on a truly opulent scale. Besides a large ballet company, Massine was granted a full orchestra, a chorus from the Genoa opera, and principals from La Scala for his leading vocalists. He brought designers and composers to work at Nervi *in situ*. Madame Karinska, for instance, settled at Nervi for three months to execute costumes for the ballets.

For the Nervi Festival's repertory, Massine selected revivals of

Fokine's *Scheherazade*, Maurice Béjart's *Alta tensione*, and Jack Carter's *Señor Manara*. Massine would present three new works—*La commedia umana*, *Le Bal des voleurs*, and *Il barbiere di Siviglia*—plus revivals of *Choreartium* and *Le Beau Danube*. With the revivals, three lengthy new ballets and the responsibility for directing the entire enterprise, Massine was setting astoundingly ambitious goals for himself.

Rehearsals began in March, and the dancers' schedules were grueling. Company class began at 8:45 A.M., and rehearsals continued until midnight. G. B. L. Wilson remarked that Massine "offered his troops nothing but 'blood, tears, toil and sweat' and set the example himself." Wilson paints a vivid picture of the rehearsal ambience:

> In the school rehearsal room, a corner was partitioned off and a camp bed made up. Here Massine slept, in short shifts of a few hours at a time (as Napoleon and Churchill did during their campaigns)—and sometimes in the middle of a rehearsal of *Choreartium* taken by Madame Leskova, the classroom would be electrified by a ghostly but compelling voice shouting, "Uno, due, tre." The Maestro had woken up.... I found myself fascinated by him, squinting over the top of his Schubert spectacles (my own similar ones were in constant demand in his absence for the dancers to work off their emotions by imitating him), and saying, "Ecco, ecco—tikky-tikky-tak."[9]

La commedia umana was born when Francesco Siciliani introduced Massine to Vittore Branca, editor of the definitive edition of Giovanni Boccaccio's *Decameron*. Branca selected several stories which he thought would adapt to ballet, and Massine used a collection of fourteenth-century Italian music, the *Squarcialupi Codex*, as the source for the score. The second première of the June 8–30 Festival was *Le Bal des voleurs*, based on a 1938 comedy of the same name by Jean Anouilh. Massine was "delighted by the iridescent wit of the dialogue." Anouilh was quite amenable to a ballet adaptation and discussed each character at length.[10] The last world première, *Il barbiere de Siviglia*, expanded upon Diaghilev's concept for the staging of the opera *Le astuzie femminili*. *Il barbiere* was danced on stage while the vocalists sang in the orchestra pit.

Unfortunately, the 1960 Nervi Festival was an out-and-out disaster. Barnes had "hoped that this new company would have done much to have restored Massine to his rightful position among the top choreographers of the world, but for a variety of reasons, I cannot honestly believe that this has been the case. Indeed, if anything, Massine's reputation appears to be more crumpled now than before."[11] What made the Festival's failure all the more painful was its costliness. Massine paid scant heed to keeping costs down, and his productions were so expensive that the Nervi Festival went into bankruptcy and had to cancel its 1961 season. Even if Massine's new works had been artistically successful, their massive sets and huge casts of dancers, musicians and choruses made them prohibitively impractical to revive for another company. Massine was branded as extravagant, self-indulgent, and out-of-touch. Nervi was an all-time career low from which Léonide never recovered.

USHER *(The Fall of the House of Usher)*

Based on a story by Edgar Allan Poe
Music: Roberto García Morillo
Scenery: Armando Chisea
Costumes: Alvaro Durañona
Première: Teatro Colón, Buenos Aires, July 1, 1955

ORIGINAL CAST
Roderick: José Neglia[12]   Madeline: Maria Ruanova
The Poet: Jorge Tomin

Synopsis[13]

On a dark autumn day, the Poet finds himself within view of the gloomy House of Usher. From its "rank sedges" and "trunks of decayed trees" there reeks up a foul atmosphere. The poet notes the building's antiquity and a barely perceptible fissure which zigzags down the wall. He has come to Usher in response to an urgent letter from the mansion's proprietor, Roderick Usher. Usher was one of the Poet's boon companions in boyhood, and his letter tells of acute physical and mental illness.

The Poet dismounts and is led by a valet through the dark and cryptic manor to Roderick's chamber. He is stricken with Roderick's terribly altered appearance. Roderick's malady causes him to be terrified of food, flowers, and light. He is a slave not only to his fears, but to the house itself, a building which he has not dared to leave for many years. He is also distressed by the lengthy and mysterious illness of his twin sister, the Lady Madeline. Her eminent death will leave Roderick the last living descendant of the ancient race of the Ushers.

For the next few days, the Poet tries in vain to alleviate the melancholy of his friend. One day Roderick shows the Poet his phantasmagoric painting. It presents the interior of a luminous vault lying far below the surface of the earth. He tells the poet of his conviction that rocks, fungi and trees are capable of sensing, feeling, and exerting their evil will. Their sentience at Usher is due to their long undisturbed presence. Roderick believes that the result has been a gradual, yet cumulative, condensation of a Satanic atmosphere residing actively in the supposedly inanimate things that compose and surround the house.

Several nights later, Roderick announces that the Lady Madeline is "no more"; he plans to store her body in the mansion's vault prior to her burial. They place her in the coffin, nail down its lid securely and leave it in a dark vault lying far below the main floor. The vault's massive iron door causes a "sharp grating sound" as it closes.

Usher now changes appreciably, wandering feverishly from one chamber to another, as though listening to some faint sound. On the eighth night after the entombment of Madeline, a raging windstorm occurs, and all objects glow in the huge masses of agitated vapor enshrouding Usher. To calm their nerves, the Poet reads aloud from Sir Launcelot Canning's *Mad Trist*. When he arrives at the point where Ethelred rips up the planks of the hermit's door, the Poet himself hears the very cracking and ripping sound described by Sir Launcelot. Shaken, the Poet reads next of Ethelred's slaying of the dragon, who expires with a "horrid and harsh" shriek. The Poet himself then hears a "harsh, protracted and most unusual screaming." Anxious not to alarm Roderick, the Poet manages to continue. Arriving at the part where Ethelred's shield flies over the castle to land at his feet with "a terrible ringing sound," the Poet himself hears metallic reverberations. Now completely unnerved, the Poet looks at Roderick and drinks in the hideous import of Usher's words: "Not hear it?—yes, I hear it, and *have* heard it....*We have put her living in the tomb!*"

Roderick now has heard the rending of the coffin and Madeline's dying screams, and then her groaning struggle with the great iron door and now she is on the stairs and now so close that Roderick can hear "the heavy and horrible beating of her heart." At this moment, with superhuman strength, the antique doors are thrown open and there is revealed the Lady Madeline. Her white shrouds are covered with blood—evidence of a fierce and desperate struggle. With the last drop of her energy, she falls heavily upon her twin brother and in her "violent and now final death-agonies," she bears Roderick down to the floor a corpse himself.

As the Poet flees in terror from the mansion, a wild light shines through the mansion's slight zigzag fissure. While he gazes, this fissure widens rapidly and the mighty walls crumble with the din "of a thousand waters." The dank swamp closes "sullenly and silently over the fragments of the House of Usher."

Scenery and Costumes

Armando Chisea painted a front curtain showing a landscape of the House of Usher for the opening scene, in which the Poet mimes a horseback ride to the mansion. The front curtain lifts to reveal the interior of Roderick's chamber. The two side walls of the chamber converge to upstage center, stopping about eight feet apart, where they are bridged by a high Gothic vault. The gap is filled by a curtain which lifts at several points in the ballet to create a second setting for events which occur in the minds of the main characters.

Victoria García wrote, "The ballet could definitely be improved with better scenery and costumes."[14] Observation of the 16-millimeter film supports her conclusion. Early in the ballet, Roderick has a "vision scene," where the upstage center curtain is flown to reveal a corps de ballet of twelve females clad in handkerchief skirts and long trailing bandeaus of chiffon. Their soft, floating costumes (not to mention the conventional choreography) bring to a halt the sense of tension engendered thus far. Likewise, the next batch of specters are six females in white robes with angel wings, who would look quite at home in a Christmas pageant, and six horned male "bats" whose huge spiked wings evoke more laughter than dread.

In the final demolition scene, Massine claimed that he and Chisea created "a truly horrific effect."[15] But the destruction of the House of Usher does not really look "horrific" on film. It is represented by the impact of a single papier-mâché boulder dropped from the catwalks. It would have been easy enough to drop dozens of stones instead of only one, and the scene called for every fog machine in Buenos Aires.[16]

Music

Roberto García Morillo's score was well received by critics. The *New York Times* hailed him as "one of Argentina's most creative composers," and *Dancing Times* found the music "eminently theatrical." *Dance News* attributed much of *Usher*'s success to "Morillo's excellent score, which seemed to emerge from Poe's story, creating the exact atmosphere."[17]

Choreography

Poe's short story provided Massine with a superb libretto. As he said in an interview, "It is extremely dynamic writing, with quite a few indications for movement by Poe himself."[18] *Usher* centered on the psychological implications of three clearly defined principals—Roderick, Madeline and the Poet. The most riveting choreography occurs in the long solos and pas de deux of the three principals, who remain onstage for most of the ballet.

Less impressive was the choreography for the ensemble. The corps de ballet entered through the upstage center opening as three very unfrightening hallucinations in Roderick's mind. The first, mentioned above, is an ensemble number for twelve chiffon-clad ladies who dance prettily in symmetrical formations. The second vision is danced by angels who perform traditional ballet steps with their hands in prayer position. The bats enter next with grotesque leaps and then line up neatly behind the angels to partner them in standard supported adagio steps, culminating in a lift onto the rodents' shoulders. All the partnering had to be strictly frontal: had the bats turned with respect to their partners, they would have impaled the angels on their wing spikes. From the standpoint of logic, one wonders why celestial and Satanic beings should be dancing together so amicably.

The final vision scene shows Ethelred miming the ripping of the planks, the slaying of the dragon, and the flinging of the shield. This is very effectively choreographed; the upstage curtain parts to reveal a sculpted dragon who flips its tail menacingly and drops the shield from its own claws on its demise. This scene might have had more horror, though, if it were done in tandem with Madeline's gruesome struggle in the vault—a vision which is omitted altogether in the ballet.

Critics had nothing but praise for the choreography and performances of the principals—Neglia, Ruanova and Tomin. Fernando Emery wrote, "Massine gives us moments of great pathetic intensity: Roderick's first three poses as he lies on his bed, his body tensed up like a bow that is being violently stretched."[19] The male pas de deux for Roderick and the Poet was quite novel for its day. Using principles akin to contact improvisation, Massine gave the men a striking sequence of counterbalances and lifts without making them look the least bit effeminate. Roderick and Madeline have two lengthy, acrobatic pas de deux which strike a superb balance between virtuosity and dramatic expression. They are also rather erotic and open to the interpretation that Roderick and Madeline are incestuous lovers. Certainly, Massine took some risks with his choreography for the principals; the scenes involving them and them alone are arresting in their beauty and intensity.

Critical Survey

Usher was a tremendous hit on opening night, receiving ten curtain calls. The *New York Times* reported that Massine "scored a critical and popular triumph"; *Dance News* called it "a work of great dramatic force."[20]

Usher was also highly praised by the local Argentinian press, although some critics were disturbed by the incestuous implications of the duet for Roderick and Madeline.

In Retrospect

The only essentially negative review of *Usher* came from Hans Ehrmann-Ewart. He observed, "What is lacking in the ballet is not Poe's plot, but the romantic spirit of the supernatural, of growing terror."[21] In his literary analysis of "Usher," James L. Roberts wrote:

> Late in the story, Roderick Usher says: "I feel that the period will sooner or later arrive when I must abandon life and reason together, in some struggle with the grim phantasm, FEAR." Clearly, Poe has chosen the "grim phantasm, FEAR" for his prime effect to be achieved in this story. As a result, every word, every image, and every description in the story is chosen with the central idea in mind of creating a sense of abject terror.[22]

Choreographically, "every word, every image, and every description" of the principal dancers was right on the mark, but the ensemble numbers eased the viewer back down into the comfort zone and killed the momentum towards terror. *Usher* is an excellent revival prospect, but not in its original state. Leaving Morillo's score and Massine's choreography for the principals completely intact, but with better scenery, costumes, technical effects and a whole new concept for the ensemble, a modern-day choreographer could create a work of considerable power, majesty, and suspense.

Don Juan

Ballet in Four Scenes
Based on the Molière play *Don Juan ou le Festin de Pierre*
Music: Christoph Willibald Gluck
Scenery and Costumes: Georges Wakhevitch
Première: La Scala, Milan, March 7, 1959

ORIGINAL CAST
Don Juan: Mario Pistoni   Elvira: Carla Fracci

Synopsis

Scene One. The Streets. Musicians, directed by Sganarelle (Don Juan's valet), are serenading Elvira when Don Juan appears and gazes upon Elvira at her bedroom window. He slips into the house unobserved and whispers love-confidences to her. But Elvira's father, the Commendatore, appears on the scene. He challenges Don Juan to a duel, which is fought forthwith, the Commendatore the loser. Don Juan departs, and Elvira kneels beside her dead father in horror.

Scene Two. The Fields. Here, Don Juan has a fleeting episode with two country girls, saves a nobleman from robbers, and generously gives a *louis-d'or* to a beggar.

Scene Three. The Ballroom. Don Juan is holding a banquet for his friends. At the banquet's height, the ghost of the Commendatore appears briefly and then disappears. Sganarelle brings in a veiled figure. The guests are asked to retire, and Don Juan withdraws the veil, revealing Elvira. She tries unsuccessfully to reform him, and when the guests return, Don Juan has the audacity to present her to them as his mistress. The ghost of the Commendatore appears once more. He invites Don Juan to visit him that night in the cemetery. In a spirit of bravado, Don Juan accepts and, accompanied by Sganarelle, departs with firm step.

Scene Four. The Cemetery. As Don Juan enters the gloomy cemetery, he boldly challenges the statue of the Commendatore, which nods its head in greeting. The valet, terrified, takes to his heels. A wraith bearing a human skull hovers about him, hopeful that he will reform. The Commendatore calls up the spirits of Don Juan's dead mistresses. They entreat him to mend his dissolute ways, but the libertine only derides them. As he goes towards the statue, he is caught up by its stone arm. The Commendatore, seeing him to be past salvation, looses the furies upon him. In they burst, an eager, writhing mass. Don Juan is tossed from one to another until, nearly torn to pieces, he expires. The dance of the infernal spirits fades away, and the wraith dances in sorrow over the felled Don Juan.

Scenery and Costumes

The scenery and costumes of Georges Wakhevitch were probably standard, unremarkable period designs since no mention is made of them, either in reviews or Massine's memoirs.

Music

Christoph Willibald Gluck, a German composer, was one of opera's profoundest reformers. Interestingly, in renouncing the conventions of Viennese opera, he began with ballets. Between 1761 and 1765 Gluck produced five self-contained ballet pantomimes, the first of which was *Don Juan*, a landmark of dramatic orchestration.

Jean Georges Noverre had published his *Letters on Dancing and Ballets* in 1760, and there is certainly a close relationship between this publication and the *Don Juan* of Gluck and choreographer Gasparo Angiolini. Noverre's main principle was that technical virtuosity was not an end in itself but that dance should serve instead to express human passions in the truest possible fashion. To attain such ends, however, the subject matter must be likely to move an audience and the music could no longer be composed as a string of interchangeable numbers—every note must be wedded to the storyline. It was in the spirit of Noverre's reforms, which chimed in so well with their own ideas, that Gluck and Angiolini set to work.[23]

Gluck's operas *Orpheo ed Eurydice* (1762), *Alceste* (1767) and *Paride ed Elena* (1770) renounced cold formalities and are known collectively as the "reform operas."[24] Although it was no part of Gluck's reform to exclude the castrato hero, all three concentrate on a single dramatic issue of crucial significance, omitting all subplots. *Iphigenia en Aulis* (1774) and *Iphigenia en Tauris* (1779) represent the summit of Gluck's achievement. The musical forms are calculated to develop the drama and all of the characters are intensely vivid, combining the monumental grandeur of the Greek myths with the humanity of the Enlightenment.

Gluck's historical importance rests not only on his establishment of a new equilibrium between music and drama, but on the clarity with which he projected this vision. Gluck simplified both drama and music, but not artlessly. He had the rare gift, shared by Mozart, of achieving intense emotional poignancy by means of simple melody and harmony in the major mode.[25]

Choreography

In discussing his concept Massine wrote, "I wanted to present Don Juan not simply as a romantic adventurer, but as a man in conflict with himself."[26] This was exactly the impression made on critic Robert Lawrence: "The pathos of the girl, the tragic conflict in the soul of Don Juan, have here been projected incandescently.... I had thought this kind of enkindling emotion lost forever to theatrical dance; but there it was, burning up the stage and the audience."

Lawrence believed that Michel Fokine's 1936 revival lost intensity because Fokine did not use all of the music from the original score. While Massine did use the full score, he took a liberty by reprising *Don Juan*'s opening serenade, the "Siciliana," at the end of the ballet. The melody's return as a coda to the entire drama had for Lawrence "the most wonderfully poetic result. Don Juan has been torn to pieces by the Furies.... Suddenly, out of this rises the Siciliana ... and on stage, the wraith with the skull dances compassionately above the fallen Don."[27]

Critical Survey

Lawrence's remarks were representative: "One had forgotten, after not having seen a major work by this master for many years, the impact of his balletic statement, his profound grasp of music. ... [T]he new 'Don Juan' is a work of high importance."[28]

In Retrospect

Massine did only three original ballets between 1955 and 1960. His name could still bring prestige to a ballet company, but the demand was for revivals. A revival of *Le Tricorne* offered not only the name of Massine but those of Picasso and Falla as well. However, press reaction to *Usher* and *Don Juan* indicates that Massine, although uneven, was still capable of superb choreography.

LA COMMEDIA UMANA

Ballet in Epilogue, Three Acts, and Prologue
Based on Stories from Giovanni Boccaccio's *Decameron*
Literary Supervision: Vittore Branca
Music: Fourteenth-Century Compositions; orchestrated by Claude Arrieu
Scenery and Costumes: Alfred Manessier
Première: Nervi Park Theatre, Genoa, July 7, 1960

ORIGINAL CAST

Prologue

Plague and Pestilence: Claude Darnet   **Death**: Nicholas Petrov

Act One

I. **Young Man**: Enrico Sportiella   **Fiordaliso**: Yvonne Meyer
II. **Barnabo**: Alfredo Kollner   **Ginerva**: Duska Sinfios
Ambrigiolo: Wassili Sulich

Act Two

I. **Solimonda**: Carla Fracci   **Guardistagno**: Aldolfo Andrade
Rossiglione: Alfredo Koline
II. **Nastagio**: Milorad Miskovitch   **Woman in Torment**: Yvonne Meyer
Traversari: Nicole Nogaret

Act Three[29]

I. **Peronella**: Vjera Markovic   **Her Husband**: Enrico Sportiella
Her Lover: Ivan Dragakze
II. **Elena**: Duska Sinfinos   **Her Neglected Lover**: Pado Bortoluzze
His Wife: Tania Ouspenska

Epilogue
Griselda: Tatiana Massine   **The Prince**: Milorad Miskovitch

Synopsis

This choreographic interpretation of the *Decameron* takes as its basis the idea that the lives of humans are largely governed by three forces: Fortune, Love and Ingenuity. Yet the power of Virtue is greater than these three even when put together.

Act One: The Triumph of Fortune

Prologue. It is the fourteenth century and in Florence, plague and pestilence rage. Death walks unchecked in the city and those who can, flee to the country. A group of these refugees meet in a villa, where to pass the time they tell stories.

Andreuccio. A young man who goes to Naples to buy horses meets Fiordaliso who robs him and then throws him into an unusual underground exit. However, he has not been deserted by Fortune, and presently he is released from his tomb by a group of robbers. All ends happily as he is reunited with his friends.

Ginerva. Ginerva's husband Barnabo makes a wager that his wife is faithful to him. Ambrogiolo accepts the wager and soon furnishes Barnabo with proof of her infidelity. Barnabo orders his servants to kill her, but instead they help her to escape to Alexandria, where in the guise of a man, she becomes a great power in the land.

Act Two: The Triumph of Love

Amore e Morte. Solimonda and Guardistagno are illicit lovers. The husband of Solimonda discovers their love and takes his revenge by serving the heart of his rival at a banquet.

Nastagio. Nastagio is haunted by a vision of a woman who is beset by devils. He is finally united to his beloved Traversari after she too has shared the vision.

Act Three: The Triumph of Ingenuity

Peronella. Peronella tells her husband that the man who has been found alone in the house with her and hiding in a barrel has merely come to buy it.

Elena. Elena is persuaded by a neglected lover that when she wishes to return to him, she must first sing naked from a tall tower (from which he removes the means of egress and where she is attacked by mosquitoes).

Calandrino. Calandrino is fully convinced that he is invisible. He is relieved of this delusion only to imagine that he is pregnant, for which state his friends arrange a "cure," knowing that he will give them a grand repast in gratitude.

Epilogue: The Triumph of Virtue

Griselda personifies virtue. A Prince marries a shepherdess, but after some time exiles her and her children from the palace. More years pass, and she is recalled to the palace to serve a mysterious new princess, who is finally revealed to be her own daughter. Griselda is reunited to the Prince and all celebrate, including the Narrators.

Concept

In the year 1345, Giovanni Boccaccio wrote one hundred short stories in his little medieval room in Florence. There are a number of interesting points about these stories. They were the first short stories ever written. They were called *novella*, from which we get our word "novel," and all of the millions of novels that have been written ever since are the lineal descendants of these one hundred ancestors. They were so popular that hundreds of authors plagiarized them. Their influence might not be so remarkable if only mediocre authors had stolen their plots from *The Decameron*. But when Shakespeare, Chaucer, Dryden, Keats, Tennyson and the like borrowed liberally from Boccaccio,[30] it becomes obvious that Giovanni had some good stuff. Boccaccio titled his collection "Decameron" because it contains a group of one hundred stories told ten a day for ten days by a company of ten people.

His accounts of the hovels and the palaces, the morals and customs of Italy in the fourteenth century give the reader a picture of how people lived back then that no history book has ever equaled. Boccaccio begins his hundred stories with a preface describing the terrible 1348 scourge of bubonic plague in Florence. His account of the plague is chilling and gruesome in its graphic detail. Just why a volume of short stories should open so morbidly might seem puzzling, but Boccaccio did it deliberately, so to enhance the lightness and gaiety of some of the stories which follow.

During this preface, he tells of a group of young people, survivors of the plague, who were so affected by the death and gore in the streets that they left Florence and went out into the country. There in order to forget, if they could, they agreed to tell stories. Then follows the first tale which lifts the reader, as it may have lifted the fictitious Florentines, out of their stricken city and into a world of humor and hope.

Scenery and Costumes

Alfred Manessier was a French painter and decorative artist. From 1948 to 1957, he designed and executed several renowned stained-glass windows for churches in France and abroad. A devout Catholic, Manessier is rare among twentieth-century painters in his concentration on religious themes.

For *La commedia umana*, Manessier executed dozens of sets and well over two hundred costumes. He created a series of multileveled tableaux for depth and perspective, opening up a vista of Italian streets and courtyards painted in vivid colors. Lillian Moore wrote that Manessier's décor was "excellent and overcame all the difficulties of an open-air stage." But she noted that it could be seen only in Nervi, "for it would be too costly to transfer it." Clive Barnes praised sets and costumes for "conveying an appropriate sense of period while being in themselves quite modern."[31]

Music

The score was based on authentic fourteenth-century medieval airs from a wide assortment of composers, the best known of whom were the Flemish pioneer contrapuntist Guillaume Dufay and the blind Italian composer Francesco Landini. Orchestrator Claude Arrieu retained in her own music the ease of flow and elegance of structure that typifies Parisian Neoclassicism.[32] However, Richard Buckle decreed that her orchestration was "boring"; Clive Barnes found it "monotonous and unsuitable for choreographic purposes."[33]

Choreography

La commedia umana was two hours long, the Festival's magnum opus. The stories called for choreography ranging from solos to huge ensembles, from moods of darkest tragedy to burlesque. Structurally, Massine and his literary collaborator, Vittore Branca, tried to impose a form upon these tales by grouping them under the headings of "Fortune," "Love," "Ingenuity," and "Virtue."

Massine used many of his signature choreographic devices, such as ensemble counterpoint, simultaneity, and fast-paced mime. García-Márquez characterized Massine's movement invention as "a reaffirmation of his choreographic 'baroquism.'"[34] At a time in dance history when the choreographic line had been simplified, understanding Massine's overwhelmingly rich choreography required hyper-alertness from the audience for a long stretch of time. Clive Barnes felt that the *Decameron* stories "could never have been made into a ballet, as their narratives are far too complex for the narrative power of dancing ... it was so full of padding, so loaded down with triviality, so lacking in any real inspiration or originality that the effect was crushingly dispiriting."[35] The reviewer for *Le Figaro* found that "The principal fault of the choreography is, without doubt, a relative disproportion among the various episodes."[36] The preponderant tone of the prologue and first two acts was one of grim medieval horror, and the transition to slapstick, raucous humor in Act Three was far too abrupt and disconcerting. Had the ballet sustained a single tone it would have been easier to fathom and would also have shortened a ballet which badly needed editing.

Critical Survey

Among major reviews, only *Le Figaro*'s said anything positive. It included some praise for Massine's "innate theatrical sense" and "very sure taste." Barnes' sour response to this ballet is certainly clear, as is Buckle's, who nicknamed this "shapeless" and "unintelligible" ballet "1,001 stories from Boccaccio."[37]

In Retrospect

La commedia umana had only one revival. Robert Ponsonby attended some of the Nervi performances and subsequently invited Massine to take *La commedia umana* to the 1960 Edinburgh Festival of which he was artistic director.

LE BAL DES VOLEURS (The Ball of Thieves)

Ballet in One Act
Libretto: Based on Jean Anouilh's play of the same name
Music: Georges Auric
Scenery and Costumes: Jean-Denis Malclès
Première: Nervi Park Theatre, Genoa, July 16, 1960 (Covent Garden, London, May 17, 1963)

COVENT GARDEN CAST

Lady Hurf: Lorna Mossford   **Juliet:** Carla Fracci
Eva: Shirley Graham   **Lord Edgar:** Bryan Ashbridge
Dupont-Dufort Senior: Alexander Bennet
Dupont-Dufort Junior: Alan Beale
Peterborne, leader of the thieves: Harry Hawthorne
Proctor, his assistant: Ian Hamilton
Gustiva, his apprentice: Jelko Yuresh
Town Official, Tennis Couple, Photographer and Girl,
Elegant Couple, Valets, Policemen, Sandwichboard Men

Synopsis

The scene is a spa where two wealthy English visitors, Lady Hurf and Lord Edgar, are on holiday with their pretty nieces Juliet and Eva.

Two shady financiers, the Dupont-Dufort father and son, are also there, in search of illicit fortunes. The town is invaded by a band of robbers who seduce Lady Hurf in the guise of Spanish noblemen in order to steal her pearls. But Lady Hurf plays their game, pretending to recognize in Peterborne an old friend, the Duke of Miraflor. She invites the gang to stay in her house. Juliet falls in love with Gustiva, the apprentice thief.

Lord Edgar reads a letter to the effect that the Duke of Miraflor has died some years before. Horrified by this discovery he faints, and Juliet picks up the letter to read the news. Meanwhile, Lady Hurf, who has purposely misread an announcement, disguises her guests as thieves and sets off with them to a masked ball (in reality a *"Bal des fleurs"* and not a *"Bal des voleurs"*). Gustiva decides to escape, but not before robbing the drawing room. Juliet, who now realizes that he is nothing but a thief, is determined to escape with him anyway, and they elope.

On returning to the house the Dupont-Duforts discover the robbery and accuse Peterborne and Hector. Father and son call the police, but the officers fail to grasp the situation. Since the Dupont-Duforts are still dressed as thieves, they are arrested themselves. Lady Hurf, who has tired of the comedy, removes her stolen pearls from Peterborne's pocket. Gustiva brings Juliet back home again, convinced that they could never be happy together. Lord Edgar appears and, pretending to recognize in Gustiva a disinherited son of his, allows them to marry. The two less fortunate thieves remain to play out the comedy.

Scenery and Costumes

Jean-Denis Malclès fared poorly with the critics. Mary Clarke remarked that the set "might have been used for a Ruth Page ballet fifteen years ago."[38] Peter Williams likened the sets to "a 'twenties musical on its number three tour" and added, "it is hard to determine why the ballet calls for female costumes in the 'twenties and males dressed Victorian and Edwardian."[39]

Music

Georges Auric tried hard to match the ebullience that he had achieved in earlier ballets, but he was daunted by *Le Bal*'s length. For *Ballet Today*, "Auric's gaiety remained laboured, and the score had much too little vitality and variety to sustain a ballet lasting nearly an hour."[40]

Choreography

Massine himself admitted that the libretto was too literary to facilitate "a really free and inventive choreographic interpretation."[41] It is the hilarity of the vacuous remarks made by Anouilh's shallow, flippant characters which gives the play its wit and charm. In her review of this "interminable" ballet, Mary Clarke wrote, "The plot is a real Anouilh tangle of disguises and counter-disguises and after sitting through the ballet twice, I still haven't grasped it. Massine tries to convey in mime past history, reported speech, and all kinds of things that can't be so conveyed."[42] Massine tried to compensate for the missing words by piling on movement details, causing the characters to become puppet-like and robotic.

Critical Survey

Just why the Royal Ballet decided to revive this ballet is a mystery. In 1968, Peter Williams reflected that "*Le Bal des voleurs* was a tragic mistake that should never have been permitted."[43] His 1963 review of the revival read as follows:

> **Production**
> Anouilh; Ennui, Fooey.
> **Choreography**
> R.I.P.
> **Dancing**
> Everyone did their best. The Show must go on. It did. Why?[44]

In Retrospect

It is hard for any artist to consign the product of strenuous personal labor to the dumpster and move on to something else. There is always that powerful urge to take out the tool kit and make repairs, even on materials that are wrong to begin with. Mary Clarke praised the Royal Ballet for doing their "valiant best," but said that "they were all trying to make bricks without straw."[45]

IL BARBIERE DI SIVIGLIA

Ballet in Two Acts
Based on the Eighteenth-Century Play by Pierre Augustin Beaumarchais
Music: Gioacchino Rossini
Scenery and Costumes: André Beaurepaire
Première: Nervi Park Theatre, Genoa, July 21, 1960

ORIGINAL CAST

Figaro: René Bon   Rosina: Tessa Beaumont
Count Almaviva: Gerald Ohn
Don Bartolo: Enrico Sportiella

Synopsis

Act One. Scene One. A square in Seville. Dr. Bartolo is determined to marry his wealthy young ward, Rosina, but she has already attracted the attention of Count Almaviva. He has followed her from Madrid, disguised as the student Lindoro, for if Rosina is ever to be the Countess of Almaviva, it must not be only for his money.

When Almaviva encounters the barber Figaro, he is overjoyed to learn that Figaro is the handyman of the Bartolo household. Figaro formulates a plot to get Almaviva inside the house. A regiment is due in town that day and, posing as a drunk soldier, the Count will ask at the house for a "billet," a military demand for lodging.

Act One. Scene Two. A room in Dr. Bartolo's house. Figaro has meanwhile snatched a brief meeting with Rosina. Bartolo is suspicious of Figaro's busybodying and when the musician-marriage broker Don Basilio arrives, Bartolo confides in him and is persuaded that Almaviva is his rival.

The first act ends with Almaviva's appearance in Bartolo's house disguised as the drunken officer. Almaviva responds violently when Bartolo unearths his exemption from the military billet. Mayhem ensues. The arrival of Don Basilio, Figaro and the local militia adds to the confusion and builds to a crazed *vivace*.

Act Two. A music room in Dr. Bartolo's house with a balcony nearby. Almaviva presents himself to Dr. Bartolo in a new disguise—as Don Alonso, music-teacher and pupil of the indisposed Don Basilio. Bartolo falls for the ruse and hurries off to fetch Rosina. While Bartolo dozes she and the man she supposes to be Lindoro express their love.

Figaro now arrives to shave Bartolo and steals the key to the balcony. Rosina and Figaro conspire, but Bartolo overhears them, and the lovers are foiled again. Dr. Bartolo determines to marry Rosina straight away and leaves to summon soldiers. Almaviva reveals his true identity, which Rosina accepts with very good grace indeed. Time now being of the essence, Figaro becomes increasingly frustrated as the lovers bill and coo at length. When they finally try to leave, the ladder is gone. But the situation is saved when Don Basilio arrives with a notary. Threatened with a few bullets through his brain, Don Basilio consents to stand witness to the marriage of Rosina and Almaviva. Bartolo arrives with the soldiers, but he is too late. The ballet ends with a jaunty finale.

Scenery and Costumes

André Beaurepaire created a luxurious eighteenth-century spectacle to satisfy Massine's concept for an "apotheosis of the opera buffa."[46] The elaborate costumes were executed by Lydia Douboujinsky.

Music

During the last years of the eighteenth century many factors combined to bring the *opera seria* and *buffa* genres closer together. Due partly to the influence of Gluck, *opera seria* began to use a simpler, more direct manner of expression than before. Texts were revised to vary the round of solo arias with choruses, duets and trios. In Naples, Gluck's use of the full orchestra to accompany recitative marked a small but important step towards that integration of the lyrical and the declamatory which would finally be achieved by 1800. The all-powerful castrato was now giving way to the female contralto. The new variety and flexibility afforded by the partial merging of the *opera buffa* and *opera seria* resulted, however, in a certain amorphousness.

Rossini codified a new form and accompanying style that dominated Italian opera for half a century. Under the "code Rossini," gratuitous displays of vocal virtuosity were curbed, and the basic formal unit was no longer the separate vocal number but the scene (the period when the same number of people remain on stage); each scene had one or more formal numbers within it. Rossini's finales are a good illustration of his consistent structure. The last four movements are always the same. There is a rapid movement consisting of declamation against an orchestral motif, during which the plot advances. Suddenly the action halts and the music builds to complex multiple part-writing for the singers, often in canon. Next, the first movement is resumed and with it, the action. The final movement is again a purely vocal *tour de force*. *Il Barbiere*'s bawdy first-act finale exemplifies this architecture.

The compositions in *Il Barbiere* are gems of rhythmic exhilaration, superb ensemble writing, striking orchestration and marvelous wit. Take the delightful incongruity of form and content in the trio "Ai! qual dolce inaspettato!" where the Count and Rosina go through obligatory operatic conventions, including a strict cabaletta (final fast-movement repeat). In the meantime, their escape ladder is disappearing while Figaro frantically goads them to hurry up and finish.

The first version of this opera, *Le Barbier de Séville*, was written by Giovanni Paisiello in 1782. It premièred in St. Petersburg and was a huge success when Paisiello returned to Italy. When Rossini decided to try his hand at a new version of *Il Barbiere*, he was faced with a ticklish problem. Not only was Paisiello's work still extant, but so was the composer, backed by a vociferous and mischievous claque of supporters. For the Rome première, the nervous Teatro Argentini management printed a lengthy notice in the program notes, stating that the new adaptation had been made out of "respect and veneration" for the "greatly celebrated Paisiello."[47] So much effusiveness can only have added fuel to the fire of the Paisiellisti, who sensed the management's uneasiness and made ready to pounce.

A good deal has been written about the fiasco of *Il Barbiere*'s Rome première on February 20, 1816. It is from the Rome Rosina, Gertrude Righetti-Giorgi, that we learn what happened. The singer playing Dr. Bartolo tripped over the trap door as he entered, and spent the whole of his first aria trying to ignore the blood which was streaming profusely from his nose. As if this was not enough, a cat appeared onstage during the first-act finale, trotting friskily amongst the performers. Figaro chased it off stage right, but the feline made a fast crossover, reentered noisily from stage left and hurled herself, howling, into the arms of the bleeding Bartolo. The audience went into hysterics, shrieked "meows," and by howls and yowls, encouraged the kitty to complete her cavatina. There are few audiences, now or then, who could maintain proper decorum in the face of such mishaps, but this audience never intended to.[48]

Il Barbiere di Siviglia (1816) was eventually accepted by contemporary audiences, and its fame spread rapidly. It soon reached London, Paris, Berlin and St. Petersburg; in 1825, at New York's Park Theatre, it became the first opera in American history to be sung in Italian.

Choreography

Massine felt that much of Beaumarchais' wit and humor evaporated in the opera because the physical demands of the singing required the singers to be still where the text obviously demanded movement. With the singers in the orchestra pit, Massine "was free to create movements and gestures which fully explored the comic situations inherent in the dialogue."[49]

Critical Survey

Il Barbiere was ill-received for the simple reason that viewers wanted to see as well as hear the singers in their roles. After all, the essence of opera is singing, and it can be both a visual and kinetic pleasure to watch a fine virtuoso delivering a physically taxing aria. Many critics felt that Massine violated both the letter and the spirit of opera in general, and Rossini in particular.

In Retrospect

The failure of *Il Barbiere*, following on the heels of those of *La commedia umana* and *Le Bal des voleurs*, set the seal on Massine's slump in reputation.

10

The Final Years

One bright spot in this discouraging period was a 1961 offer from the Soviet Export Film Company to produce some of Massine's ballets for distribution to American television. After an absence of forty-seven years, Massine returned to Russia in June. A "flood of memories"[1] came back to him, and the Massines stayed at the Metropole Hotel, the very place where the young Léonide had first met Diaghilev. The trip's highlight was Massine's reunion with his remaining family at the old family house in Zvenigorod-Moskovsky. From the garden there he could still see the lovely monastery of St. Saavo, and he put flowers on the graves of his parents and his brother Konstantin.

From the business standpoint, the trip was unsuccessful: a contract to make the ballet films did not materialize. Massine returned to Moscow again in 1963, hoping to revive interest in the filming project, but this trip was equally unsuccessful. Massine was now sixty-eight, and he showed no signs of slowing down. He returned to Europe and a punishing work schedule, mounting revivals for the Cologne and Vienna Operas, the Royal Ballet and Ballet du XXI Siècle.

In 1963, while in Cologne, Massine met Hannelore Holtwick, a Bayer Aspirin employee who offered to be his German interpreter. She soon became his personal assistant and lover. Their child, Peter, was born in 1964, followed a year later by the birth of a second son, Theodor. Massine bought a house in Weseke, Germany, where he lived with Holtwick and the children in between engagements. In 1968 he and Tatiana

Massine in Palm Beach attending the 1977 première of Dennis Wayne's Dancers. *(ROBERT SCHULENBERG)*

Orlova were divorced, yet he did not marry Holtwick until just before his death.

In spite of numerous revival commitments, Massine still found time to work assiduously on two books. His autobiography, *My Life in Ballet*, was published in 1968. It is a generally informative chronology which pays the customary "thank-you" to everyone he ever worked with, but unfortunately for history, it is badly edited, and Massine's narrative style is impersonal and fails to convey his passionate personality. Interestingly, Alexandra Danilova was hailed as the ultimate Massine dancer, but Massine ignores her in his autobiography. He gives Tarakanova sole credit for the Glove Seller in *Gaîté parisienne*, when this part was immediately taken over by Danilova and became her most famous role. Danilova is listed three times, by last name only, in his memoirs. However, when one turns to the index, the only Danilova to be found is a "Marie Danilova," an obscure Russian dancer who died in 1801!

Massine on Choreography (1976) is based on the theories of Iva Stepanov, inventor of a system of dance notation in the 1890s. Massine's textbook was both a means of notating dance and also an aid to dance composition. When he died, he was working on a sequel, *Elaborations and Variants*.[2] In an interview he explained that it is "not just that it is a recording system—it is a system that permits you vertically to compose and see what you have in every bar. It has a magic effect. By that, you see at once what the time signature is, you see at once whether it fits contrapuntally or not, and you see if in your body you get something to look at."[3]

In the late 1960s, Léonide was invited to teach his theory of choreography at the Royal Ballet School in London and at Pittsburgh's Point Park College. By the 1970s his teaching and lecture-demonstrations included several summer workshops in Europe and the United States. However, certified movement analysts generally found Massine's system to be far more complicated and less precise than Labanotation, leaving critical gaps in notation of the dimensional aspects of a movement. When he taught his system at the Royal Ballet School in 1969, Ann Hutchinson expressed serious reservations in her course evaluation: "There is a fear among several top people here that Massine has too long been isolated from the mainstream of the dance and that, indeed, he may have become a crank, working on some pet ideas that have no practical application. ... [T]he Laban system could suit him just as well and be much more worthwhile studying than the Stepanov."[4]

Most of *Massine on Choreography* was written on Galli in the renovated fourteenth-century tower where he now lived. In the last decade of his life, Massine's great passion was to convert Galli into an international art center which would be a tribute to Diaghilev. Increasingly, Diaghilev became a near deity in Massine's memory and preserving his legacy, a sacred crusade. In a 1972 interview with John Gruen, he said that in 1921 he was "too young to understand the value of this great man. I should have listened to every word he would say because he was so right."[5] Five years later, he told *Dance*, "his principles and the way he conducted his artistic life are ... not to be deviated from."[6]

By 1970, Massine was plagued with financial obligations that were quite beyond his means, including caretakers' salaries on Galli, tuition for his illegitimate children in Germany, and taxes on his Swiss and Paris residences. Starting with gifts from Diaghilev and continuing with his own acquisitions, Massine had built up an awe-inspiring twentieth-century art collection. In July of 1971 he was forced to auction off works by Braque, Miró, Matisse and Picasso.[7]

An important renaissance of American Massine revivals began in 1969 when Massine staged *Le Tricorne* for the Joffrey Ballet. During the next five years, the Joffrey revived three more Massine ballets, and the 1970s also saw revivals for American Ballet Theatre, the Australian Ballet, London Festival Ballet, Royal Ballet, the Sadler's Wells, La Scala, and the Vienna State Opera Ballet. In 1976, Léonide went to Palm Beach for the première of Dennis Wayne's new company, Dancers. While there, he met two local dancers, Ariane Csonka and Susan Gieliotti-Ford. Both became Léonide's personal assistants who alternately accompanied the eighty-one-year-old on his travels.

There was no slow-down in 1977. In the spring, Massine returned to the Bay Area to conduct another series of workshops in choreography and to revive *Le Beau Danube* for the Marin Ballet. In the summer Massine invited Csonka, Gieliotti-Ford and his son Lorca to join him on Galli. He used the trio to work on *Parisina*, based on a poem about infidelity by Lord Byron. This ballet had been commissioned by ballerina Natalia Makarova, and the scenes involving Makarova were staged on Gieliotti-Ford. When Massine began working with Natalia in San Francisco that autumn, plans for *Parisina* were scrapped, partly because Makarova was incensed that her character was initially created on another dancer.[8]

However, being in the Bay Area again allowed Massine to renew ties with the Marin Ballet. That fall, Maria Vegh and Norbert Vesak announced Massine's appointment as choreographer-in-residence until the end of 1977.[9] Although he immediately began work on two new ballets, he had scant rehearsal time because it was *Nutcracker* season. Neither ballet was ever performed outside the studio.

Massine spent Christmas with Hannelore and their children. In January 1978 he retuned to the Bay Area, which he now considered his working base. On this visit, he met a twenty-five-year-old named Mary Ann de Vlieg, who worked at the Holiday Inn where Massine stayed when he was in town. She quit her job and dropped out of college to work as Massine's new personal assistant. Her hours, she claimed, ran from 8 A.M. until midnight.[10]

In conversations with García-Márquez, de Vlieg related that she was amazed with the octogenarian's disciplined daily regime. He rose early every morning to do his Cecchetti barre, took long walks, swam twice, spent the rest of his day working on new artistic projects, and retired early. While riding in de Vlieg's car, he did not permit any radio-playing and allowed only work or emergency-related conversation—a rule he claimed to have inherited from Diaghilev.[11]

In 1978 Massine worked with Fred Maroth, a National Public Radio producer, on a television documentary on Diaghilev and revived *La Boutique fantasque* for the Oakland Ballet. A third project for 1978 was a ballet version of Handel's *Messiah*, commissioned by Igor Youskevitch from the dance department of the University of Texas at Austin. Massine began work on this project in the Bay Area.

The summer of 1979 was spent on Galli with Hannelore and the children. Léonide became seriously ill during a storm at sea, making it hard to get medical assistance to the island. Once the crisis had passed, he prepared a handwritten will. His last projects were revivals of *La*

Boutique fantasque for the Sadler's Wells touring company and *Le Soleil de nuit* for the Oakland Ballet. In December, he returned to Germany for the Christmas holidays. De Vlieg drove him to the airport and before he got on the plane, he told her, "You'll never see me again."[12]

Massine was suffering from prostate cancer, and his condition deteriorated rapidly in the first months of 1979. He was hospitalized at Borken, and his body failed before his children could reach Germany to be with him. Only de Vlieg and Hannelore were with him when he died. It was March 15, 1979.

Epilogue

The days when Massine was the single most important figure in all of ballet—when his adulators wrote panegyrics while his detractors hissed in the gallery—are gone, but not entirely forgotten. As a dancer, Massine was unique. He was not a virtuoso, but he has no peer in the creation of certain character roles. He invented a kind of dancing that was exactly right for himself, and that, with his blazing personality, made him almost impossible to follow.

As a choreographer, Massine's versatility made him perhaps the most representative choreographer of the twentieth century. He used a vast range of subjects and rarely treated them superficially. His character ballets dealt with vivid, unforgettable individuals, not stereotypes. His symphonic ballets revolutionized choreography and the relation of dance to music.

Any assessment of Massine's true historic significance must emphasize the devastating effect of his isolation in America during World War II. With the 1930s and the Great Depression came a renaissance of Americanism in the arts. Lincoln Kirstein epitomized the zeal of the American dance community. He foresaw:

> a real national ballet by, with, and for American dancers, designers, and musicians. Its symbol is a screaming eagle. Not the Janus-headed stuffed bird of the mythical Romanovs, looking two ways at once—if neither forward—but rather the eagle of the Rockies, Old Baldy, with

lightning flashing from one talon, laurel quivering in the other, a rising dawn gilding its spreading pinions, and its steel eyes fixed in the dancing of our own present and future.[1]

With the coming of war, nationalism reached an apogee, inevitably leading to the triumph of American ballet and modern dance. As the icon of the Russian ballet, Massine was the perfect scapegoat. George Amberg wondered "why none of Massine's contacts with American life and art show in his work, since his art had so thoroughly and easily assimilated the indigenous qualities of other peoples."[2] Of course, those "indigenous qualities" were, all of them, Russo-European qualities. Physically and spiritually uprooted from his true headquarters in Europe, domiciled in a country whose aesthetics were so different from his own, Massine only added fuel to the fire with such Americana offerings as *Union Pacific* and *The New Yorker*. Both were rightly accused of being phony, but Massine was congenitally incapable of creating an Americana ballet that rang true.

George Amberg writes that Massine's years in America "did little to further the growth of a native tradition."[3] But his crucial role in introducing the art of ballet to millions of Americans in thousands of one-night stands across the length and breadth of this country has never been properly acknowledged. That "native tradition" might have been delayed for many years were it not for the excitement generated by Massine and the Ballet Russe de Monte Carlo.

Massine's contemporary relevance has been the subject of much controversy. P. W. Manchester noted, "It's the same with a great many artists, that they belong in their time.... Who knows what of Balanchine's will survive?"[4] New stagings of Massine's character ballets raise the question of how to evaluate revivals in the first place. Naturally, our ideas of satisfying form, musicality, characterization, etc., shift with time. The passage of time has other effects. The first time that anything is done in art with great flair, it naturally has impact because of its novelty. This impact has no guaranteed staying power. For both of these reasons, it is easy to understand why some critics view Massine's character ballets as hopelessly dated. Others approach them with strict historic sensibility and would maintain that *Le Tricorne* remains a masterpiece whether today's audience watches it on the edge of their seats or not.

One of the most encouraging developments for admirers of Massine has occurred quite recently—within the past decade. After a half-century of neglect, Massine's symphonic ballets are not only being revived by major ballet companies, but garnering rave reviews from world-renowned critics. Three reviews in particular reveal these works' importance. Anna

Kisselgoff: "The revival in France of 'Les Présages' ... is of major historic importance. ... The time may be ripe for a Massine renaissance"; Clement Crisp: "The restoration of *Choreartium* to the repertory brings back to life a work that should retain an honoured place in any assessment of this century's ballet"; Jack Anderson: "*Choreartium* is a vast mural in motion that makes much recent choreography seem puny by comparison.... The Birmingham Royal Ballet has uncovered a treasure."[5] These remarks lend credence to García-Márquez's assertion that "Now at last the reconsideration and re-evaluation of Massine's oeuvre are irreversibly on the ascent. He has been re-established as one of the century's most influential and innovative choreographers."[6]

One cannot decipher Massine's enigmatic personality without framing it in the deeply enmeshed contexts of his credo of art as religion and his idolization of Diaghilev. Massine's mystical experiences at St. Saavo and the Florentine galleries were early signs of the blossoming spirituality that would lead him towards an almost martyr-like devotion towards art. García-Márquez surmised that the young Massine's "idealism was total. He believed that his efforts, if solemnly undertaken, should lead to moments of divine exaltation and religious ecstasy."

Certainly, Massine's asceticism carried over into his personal life, and his stormy relationship with Diaghilev only fed his evolving creed of art-as-religion: "any distress his personal situation may have caused him was justified in his mind by the work that grew out of their affiliation. In the creative process he could insist upon an alternative reality, sublimating his private needs to his work and its realization."[7] The dark side of this bargain was that as the years went on, art increasingly became for Massine a substitute for and a refuge from close personal relationships.

From 1921 onwards, Massine certainly never lacked for sexual relationships with women. But his four marriages and innumerable affairs can only lead one towards the conclusion that he was afraid of intimacy in its truest and most demanding sense. Short vignettes, little scraps of correspondence from those who lived and worked with Massine, sketch an often poignant portrait of this man.

Tamara Karsavina: "We walked together one day [in 1921] before rehearsal. In the passage by Saint Martin's in the Fields, an organ grinder played and several little girls danced around. The organ grinder beamed at them. I thought it was a pretty sight, and I said so. Massine suddenly broke out, 'I can hate you for that—spending your love on children—your art should be your only love.'"[8]

Massine with rehearsal notes, 1960. *(OTTO HESS)*

Tatiana Massine Weinbaum: "It was an enormous effort just to get him to see a movie or do something outside his normal schedule.... The only thing that mattered to him was the work.... It was difficult to grow up as children that way. I've always thought of him as someone with no pity for himself. He can be aching and ill, and he'll continue to work in an obsessive manner.... And I think he suffers from it."[9]

Agnes de Mille: "He was not gracious; neither was he unpleasant. He was totally unattainably withdrawn from casual contact, and you could place on his attitude any interpretation you chose. He was Massine and a very impressive figure."[10]

Dance: "He has cultivated a repose which insulates him from unnecessary nervous tension. He reserves his energy for the stage. In an ordinary room, he almost seems to sit without personality, like a polite electric battery, recharging itself."[11]

Massine was a legendary presence in the rehearsal studio—absorbed, indefatigable, relentlessly demanding. Yet if his dancers thought him a tyrant, they had only to remind themselves of how hard Massine worked himself. His contemporaries have startlingly contradictory, though vivid, memories of his working methods:

Diane Menuhin: "He was always well-prepared, extremely musical and easy to follow, changing little."[12]

Keith Lester: "[Massine] frightened one with his unending inventions, often to the same piece of music.... Massine, volatile and fluid in mind, almost recreates the steps a dozen times till dancer and steps are as near to what he wants as is possible."[13]

Charles Dickson: "[Massine] seldom changed choreography. If you could do it fine, and if you couldn't do it, you damned well had to learn how to do it."[14]

G. B. L. Wilson: "[Massine was] always looking down at scraps of paper held in his left hand. At first, I thought that they were the steps for the ballet which he had written down—but no, for sometimes he held them *upside down* and still stared at them. At last I could restrain myself no longer and I asked him. He was charming about it; they were photostats of pages from Feuillet's *Receuil de Danses* of 1704. He told me that he had always used them, they were like a vocabulary of steps for him.... 'But you often hold them upside down,' I persisted. 'I believe they are really like a talisman to you—something you can look at when you are concentrating.' Yes, that was it! With Feuillet in his hand, he had something to look at (or appear to) and so was able to withdraw himself from the turmoil of the rehearsal and think."[15]

Massine once told Robert Sabin, "I am very much against teaching human beings merely as instruments.... Proceed on this basis and you are likely to get sterile results. The cultural background of a dancer is decisive.... It is what a dancer knows about sculpture, painting, literature, finance, history that determine how far he can go."[16] Twenty-three years later, in an interview for *Dance* magazine, he stated: "I do not understand Balanchine's point of view that the body is an instrument. I say, yes, it is an instrument, but it has a soul, a heart, and nerves.... Don't get away from your country, your people, from their legends, from their meat. They are your strengths, they give you the power to create."[17] If Massine was the last of a dying breed, these words may tell us much about our own time as well.

When Massine went to Moscow in 1961 and reminisced at the Metropole Hotel, he found that "for some reason, I found myself thinking of Galli, of my first view of it in 1917, of my decision to buy it. It seemed to me that it had always been more than just a place of refuge; it represented something in my life which I had yet to discover." What was it? Massine never answers this question directly, but the last few pages of his memoirs lend us powerful clues. "Galli," he said, "has been a source of inspiration, and brought me closer to a life of simplicity, offering a kind of spiritual peace and serenity which I have never found anywhere else." Galli was also to be the site where he intended "to establish a foundation which will maintain the island as an artistic centre, and in this way I hope to carry on Diaghilev's tradition."[18] Perhaps what Galli ultimately represented was the great bringing together of the two driving forces in Massine's life—his sanctification of art and his abiding love for Diaghilev, a love fully realized only after Diaghilev's death.

Sadly, Massine's amphitheatre on Galli was demolished when a 1964 storm sent its columns crashing into the sea, but he never abandoned plans for this eternal monument. In the very last line of his memoirs, Massine reiterated that his plans for Galli were meant to "carry on the traditions and high standards set by Diaghilev." In this way, he could thank and pay homage to "this great man who brought so much beauty into the world."[19] Massine had already honored his mentor by doing just this, giving so much to make us laugh, so much to make us cry. The wealth of sublime, transcendent moments he offered his world awaits our rediscovery.

Notes

1. July 1895–May 1917

1. Léonide Massine, *My Life in Ballet* (London: Macmillan, 1968), 16.
2. *Ibid.*, 20.
3. Alexander Demidov, *The Russian Ballet*, trans. Guy Daniels (Garden City, N.Y.: Doubleday, 1977), 122.
4. Massine, *My Life in Ballet*, 34.
5. *Ibid.*, 42.
6. *Ibid.*, 43.
7. *Ibid.*, 47.
8. *Ibid.*, 49.
9. Tamara Karsavina, "Diaghileff—and Other Partners," *Dancing Times* (Jan. 1967): 197.
10. Massine, *My Life in Ballet*, 53–54.
11. *Ibid.*, 60.
12. Charles Ricketts, *Self-Portrait*, ed. Cecil Lewis (London: Peter Davies, 1939), 237.
13. Massine, *My Life in Ballet*, 69.
14. *Ibid.*, 70.
15. *New York Sun*, 16 January 1916; cited in Nesta Macdonald, *Diaghilev Observed* (New York: Dance Horizons, 1975), 144.
16. *New York Herald Tribune*, 27 January 1916; cited in *ibid.*, 147.
17. *New York Times*, 26 January 1916; cited in *ibid.*, 144.
18. Ashton Stevens, "'Faun' Dance Startles Ballets Russes Spectators," *Chicago Examiner*, 17 February 1916.
19. *Kansas City Star*, 4 March 1916; cited in Macdonald, 162.
20. Massine, *My Life in Ballet*, 82.
21. Lydia Sokolova, *Dancing for Diaghilev* (London: John Murray, 1960), 76.
22. *Ibid.*
23. Macdonald, 358.
24. Massine, *My Life in Ballet*, 90.
25. *Ibid.*, 106.
26. Misia Sert, *Two or Three Muses* (London: Museum Press, 1953), 118.
27. Mary Chamot, *Gontcharova: Stage Designs and Paintings* (London: Oresko Books, 1979), 12.
28. Virginia Spate, *Orphism: The Evolution of Non-Figurative Painting in Paris, 1910–1914* (Oxford: Clarendon Press, 1979), 11.
29. Sokolova, 71.
30. Sir Lionel Bradley, unpublished diaries, 21–25 June 1938, Bequest of the Theatre Museum at Covent Garden, London.
31. Robert C. Ridenour, *Nationalism, Modernism, and Personal Rivalry in Nineteenth-Century Russian Music* (Bloomington: UNI Research Press, 1981), 32.
32. Nikolai Rimsky-Korsakov, *My Musical Life*, ed. Carl van Vechten, trans. Judah A. Jofee (New York: Knopf, 1923), 193.
33. *Ibid.*, 199–201.
34. Massine, *My Life in Ballet*, 20.
35. *Ibid.*, 75–77.
36. *Ibid.*, 76.

Notes—Chapter 1

37. Serge Grigoriev, *The Diaghilev Ballet: 1909–1929*, trans. and ed. Vera Bowen (London: Constable, 1953), 117.
38. Arthur Gold and Robert Fizdale, *Misia* (New York: Knopf, 1980), 173.
39. *Journal de Genève*, 22 December 1915; cited in Vicente García-Márquez, *Massine: A Biography* (New York: Alfred A. Knopf, 1995), 58.
40. Reviews of *Le Soleil de nuit* (Century Theatre, New York, 18 January 1916); quoted in Macdonald, 138, 139.
41. Sokolova, 84.
42. Edwin Evans, *Dancing Times* (Aug. 1928): 488.
43. *Grove Dictionary of Music and Musicians*, 1980, s.v. "Gabriel Fauré," by Jean-Michel Nectoux, 423.
44. Jean-Michel Nectoux, *Gabriel Fauré: A Musical Life*, trans. Roger Nichols (Cambridge: Cambridge University Press, 1991), 109.
45. M. D. Calvocoressi, *Musician's Gallery* (London: Faber, 1933), 136.
46. Massine, *My Life in Ballet*, 90.
47. Alfredo Salazar, "Algo Más sobre los Bailes Rusos," *Revista Musical Hispano-Americana* (Aug. 1916); cited in García-Márquez, *Massine*, 77.
48. Grigoriev, 132.
49. Review of *Las Meninas* (Les Ballets Russes, Teatro de San Carlo), *Il Giorno*, 22 April 1917; cited in Richard Buckle, *Diaghilev* (New York: Atheneum, 1984), 328.
50. 7 March 1928; cited in Macdonald, 358.
51. Quoted passages from Cyril Beaumont, *Complete Book of Ballets* (London: Putnam, 1951), 843–49.
52. Josefin Peladan, *Les Arts du Theatre*; cited in Charles Spencer, *Léon Bakst* (New York: Rizzoli, 1973), 73.
53. George Amberg, *Art in Modern Ballet* (New York: Pantheon, 1946), 19–20.
54. Serge Lifar, *A History of the Russian Ballet* (London: Hutchinsons, 1954), 241.
55. Valerian Svetloff with Louis Reau, Denis Roche and A. Tessier, *Unedited Works of Bakst* (New York: Brentano's, 1927), n.p.
56. Grigoriev, 129.
57. Beaumont, *Complete Book of Ballets*, 843–44.
58. *Grove Dictionary of Music and Musicians*, 1980, s.v. "Domenico Scarlatti," by Joel Scheveloff, 572.
59. Malcolm Boyd, *Domenico Scarlatti—Master of Music* (New York: Schirmer, 1986), 222–23.
60. *Les Femmes de bonne humeur* (Motion Picture), Royal Ballet, 1962, 24 min., sd. b&cw, 16mm., Jerome Robbins Dance Division, New York Public Library at Lincoln Center.
61. Quoted in Lynn Garafola, *Diaghilev's Ballets Russes* (New York: Oxford University Press, 1989), 87.
62. W. A. Propert, *The Russian Ballet in Western Europe: 1909–1929* (London: John Lane the Bodley Head, 1921), 41.
63. Massine, *My Life in Ballet*, 95.
64. 11 September 1918; cited in Macdonald, 216.
65. Beaumont, *Complete Book of Ballets*, 850.
66. P. W. Manchester, "A Conversation with P. W. Manchester," interview by David Vaughan and Dale Harris, *Ballet Review* 6:3 (Fall 1977–Winter 1978): 111.
67. Dynely Hussey, "The Good-Humoured Ladies," *Dancing Times* (Sept. 1949): 687–88; Peter Williams, "The Case for Massine," *Dance and Dancers* (March 1968): 16.
68. Hussey, "The Good-Humoured Ladies."
69. Quoted passages taken from Cyril Beaumont, *Complete Book of Ballets*, 850–58.
70. *Ibid.*, 858.
71. *Ibid.*, 861.
72. Unpublished essay, Diaghilev Scrapbooks, Vol. 5, Theatre Museum at Covent Garden, London.
73. *Grove Dictionary of Music and Musicians*, 1980, s.v. "Anatol Lyadov," by Jennifer Spencer, 384.
74. Rimsky-Korsakov, 170.
75. Massine, *My Life in Ballet*, 98.
76. Karsavina, "Diaghileff—and Other Partners," 197.
77. Massine, *My Life in Ballet*, 101.
78. 24 December 1918; cited in Macdonald, 221.
79. Cyril Beaumont, *The Diaghilev Ballet in London* (London: Putnam, 1949), 125.
80. Quoted in Hugh Honour and John Fleming, *The Visual Arts: A History* (New Jersey: Prentice-Hall, 1982), 606.
81. *Ibid.*, 608.
82. Filippo Marinetti, "The Futurist Dance," trans. Elizabeth Delza, reprinted in *Dance Observer* (Oct. 1935): 76.
83. Francis Steegmuller, *Cocteau* (London: Macmillan, 1970), 146.
84. Massine, *My Life in Ballet*, 102.
85. *Ibid.*
86. Quoted in Lifar, 215.

87. *Grolier's Encyclopedia*, 1983, s.v. "Pablo Picasso," by Roland Elzea.
88. Roland Penrose, *Picasso: His Life and Work* (New York: Harper & Row, 1971), 222.
89. Massine, *My Life in Ballet*, 604.
90. Alfred H. Barr, Jr., *Picasso: Fifty Years of His Art* (New York: The Museum of Modern Art & Arno Press, 1966), 99.
91. Macdonald, 238–41.
92. Quoted in *ibid.*, 239.
93. James Harding, *Erik Satie* (New York: Praeger Publishers, 1975), 31.
94. *Ibid.*, 32.
95. *Ibid.*, 159–61.
96. *Ibid.*, 161.
97. Massine, *My Life in Ballet*, 103.
98. Penrose, 220.
99. *Ibid.*
100. *Parade* (Motion Picture), 1964 rehearsal film of Maurice Bejart's Ballet du XXI Siècle, 22 min., si. b&w, 16 mm., Jerome Robbins Dance Division, New York Public Library at Lincoln Center.
101. James Monahan, "Parade in 1974," *Dancing Times* (July 1974): 568.
102. Massine, *My Life in Ballet*, 104.
103. Jean Cocteau, "Parade: Ballet Realiste," *Vanity Fair* (Sept. 1917): 105.
104. Quoted in Harding, 158.
105. Ornella Volta, ed., *Satie Seen Through His Letters*, trans. Michael Bullock (London: Marion Boyars, 1989), 132.
106. *Ibid.*, 132–33.
107. *Ibid.*, 140.
108. Massine, *My Life in Ballet*, 111.
109. Macdonald, 238.
110. Monahan, 566, 568.
111. Nancy Goldner, "Reviews," *Dance News* (May 1973): 428.
112. Jack Anderson, "New York Newsletter," *Dancing Times* (May 1973): 428.
113. Massine, *My Life in Ballet*, 105.
114. Monahan, 568.

2. June 1917–June 1920

1. Michel Kirby, *Futurist Performance* (New York: Dutton, 1971), 204.
2. Sokolova, 113.
3. Massine, *My Life in Ballet*, 117.
4. *Ibid.*, 127.
5. Sokolova, 114, 134.
6. Massine, *My Life in Ballet*, 143.
7. Sokolova, 137.
8. Massine, *My Life in Ballet*, 132–33.
9. Peter Lieven, *The Birth of the Ballets Russes*, trans. L. Zarine (New York: Dover, 1973), 307.
10. Tamara Karsavina, *Theatre Street* (London: Dance Books, 1981), 298.
11. Lifar, 214.
12. Sokolova, 137.
13. Clive Bell, "The New Ballet," *The New Republic* (30 July 1919): 416.
14. T. S. Eliot, "Dramatis Personae," *Criterion* (April 1923): 303.
15. Massine, *My Life in Ballet*, 145.
16. Grigoriev, 161.
17. Quoted passages taken from Beaumont, *Complete Book of Ballets*, 868–78.
18. Macdonald, 228.
19. Constant Lambert, *Sunday Referee*, 22 July 1935.
20. Massine, *My Life in Ballet*, 121.
21. P. W. Manchester, "Massine the Dancer," *Dance Chronicle* 3:1 (1979): 88.
22. *Sunday Times*, 22 June 1919; cited in Macdonald, 227.
23. Valerian Svetloff, "The Diaghileff Ballet in Paris: Part II," *Dancing Times* (Jan. 1930): 480.
24. Peter Williams, "The Case for Massine," *Dance and Dancers* (March 1968): 13.
25. Mary Clarke, "Massine Revivals at Stratford," *Dancing Times* (Feb. 1967): 294.
26. Vladimir Polunin, *The Continental Method of Scene Painting* (London: Beaumont, 1927), 53.
27. Penrose, 235.
28. Tomás Marco, *Spanish Music in the Twentieth Century*, trans. Cola Franzen (Cambridge: Harvard University Press, 1993), 20.
29. *Grove Dictionary of Music and Musicians*, 1980, s.v. "Manuel de Falla," by Enrique Franco, 372.
30. *Ibid.*
31. Marco, 23.
32. Massine, *My Life in Ballet*, 141.
33. *Ibid.*, 122.
34. 27 July 1919; cited in Macdonald, 232.
35. Léonide Massine, interview by John Gruen, 26 September 1972, transcript, Jerome Robbins Dance Division, New York Public Library at Lincoln Center.
36. Clive Barnes, "Past—and Future—of a Spanish Hat," *New York Times*, 5 October 1969.
37. *Ibid.*
38. Jack Anderson, "Legends in the Flesh," *Ballet Review* 3:2 (1969): 37.
39. Arlene Croce, "The Three-Cornered Hat," *New Yorker* (Nov. 1969). Reprinted in

Arlene Croce, *Afterimages* (New York: Knopf, 1978), 273–75.
40. *Grove Dictionary of Music and Musicians*, 1980, s.v. "Henri Matisse," by Nicholas Watkins, 825.
41. Alfred H. Barr, Jr., *Matisse: His Art and His Public* (New York: Museum of Modern Art, 1951), 207.
42. Polunin, 61–62.
43. Sokolova, 146–48.
44. *Ibid.*, and Massine, *My Life in Ballet*, 147.
45. *Commoedia*, 4 February 1920; cited in García-Márquez, *Massine*, 146.
46. Valerian Svetloff, "The Diaghilev Ballet in Paris," *Dancing Times* (Dec. 1929): 274.
47. Polunin, 62.
48. Vera Stravinsky and Robert Craft, *Stravinsky in Pictures and Documents* (New York: Simon and Schuster, 1978), 60–61.
49. See Massine's 1920 revival of this ballet.
50. *Grove Dictionary of Music and Musicians*, 1980, s.v. "Igor Stravinsky," by Eric Walter White, 247.
51. Igor Stravinsky and Robert Craft, *Conversations with Igor Stravinsky* (London: Faber, 1959), 61.
52. Quoted in Igor Stravinsky and Robert Craft, *Memories and Commentaries* (Garden City, N.Y.: Doubleday, 1960), 123.
53. Laloy, *Commoedia*, 4 February 1920; cited in García-Márquez, *Massine*, 146.
54. The [London] *Times*, 17 July 1920; cited in Macdonald, 253.
55. Ernest Newman, *Sunday Times*, 18 July 1920; cited in *ibid.*
56. Robert Lawrence, *Victor Book of Ballets and Ballet Music* (New York: Simon and Schuster, 1950), 172.
57. Laloy, *Commoedia*, 4 February 1920; quoted in Nancy van Norman Baer, *The Art of Enchantment: Diaghilev's Ballets Russes, 1909–1929*, exhibition catalog, Fine Arts Museum of San Francisco (1989), 75; cited in García-Márquez, *Massine*, 146.
58. Quoted in Boris Kochno, *Diaghilev and the Ballets Russes* (New York: Harper and Row, 1960), 138.
59. Tamara Karsavina, "Dancers of the Twenties," *Dancing Times* (Feb. 1967): 253.
60. Grigoriev, 160.
61. Svetloff, "Diaghilev Ballet in Paris" (Dec. 1929), 274.
62. The [London] *Times*, 7 July 1920; cited in Macdonald, 253.
63. Percy Scholes, *Observer*, 18 July 1920; cited in *ibid.*

64. *Daily Herald*, 17 July 1920; cited in *ibid.*
65. Bernard Taper, *Balanchine* (New York: Harper and Row, 1960), 85.
66. Penrose, 238.
67. *Grove Dictionary of Music and Musicians*, 1980, s.v. "Giovanni Battista Pergolesi," by Helmet Heicke, 396.
68. Igor Stravinsky and Robert Craft, *Expositions and Developments* (Berkeley: University of California Press, 1981), 111–12.
69. Stravinsky and Craft, *Conversations*, 85.
70. Mary Meeker, "Putting Punch in Pulcinella," *Dance* (April 1981): 80.
71. Massine, *My Life in Ballet*, 150.
72. Stravinsky and Craft, *Memories and Commentaries*, 41.
73. Igor Stravinsky, *Chronicle of My Life* (London: Gollancz, 1936), 139.
74. *Observer*, 13 June 1920; cited in Macdonald, 248.
75. *Sunday Times*, 13 June 1920; cited in *ibid.*
76. Edward Dent, *Athaneum*, 18 June 1920; cited in *ibid.*

3. July 1920–April 1926

1. Kochno, 89.
2. Sokolova, 161.
3. *Ibid.*, 163.
4. Sokolova and Vera Stravinsky; cited in Buckle, *Diaghilev*, 371.
5. Grigoriev, 169.
6. Sokolova, 171.
7. Lifar, 208.
8. Massine, *My Life in Ballet*, 154.
9. Macdonald, 284.
10. Quoted in Ninette de Valois, *Come Dance with Me* (London: Hamish Hamilton, 1957), 49.
11. *Ibid.*
12. Quoted in Kochno, 256.
13. Polly Hill and Richard Keynes, *Lydia and Maynard: The Letters of L.L. and J.M.K.* (New York: Charles Scribner's Sons, 1989), 197, 219.
14. See Massine's 1933 revival of *Le Beau Danube* for Ballet Russe de Monte Carlo.
15. Harding, *Erik Satie*, 211.
16. Jean Hugo, *Avant d'Oublier* (Paris: Fayard, 1976), 177.
17. Grigoriev, 210.
18. Massine, *My Life in Ballet*, 162.
19. Sokolova, 229.

20. Vernon Duke, *Passport to Paris* (Boston: Little, Brown, 1955), 135.
21. Garafola, *Diaghilev's Ballets Russes*, 115–18.
22. *Ibid.*, 250.
23. Grigoriev, 215.
24. *Observer*, 3 July 1921; cited in Macdonald, 266.
25. E. Walter White, *Stravinsky: The Composer and His Works* (Berkeley: University of California Press, 1966), 174–75.
26. Buckle, *Diaghilev*, 254.
27. *Grove Dictionary*, "Igor Stravinsky," 247.
28. *Observer*, 3 July 1921; cited in Vera Stravinsky and Craft, *Stravinsky in Pictures and Documents*, 511.
29. Shelley Berg, *Le Sacre du Printemps: Seven Productions from Nijinsky to Martha Graham* (Ann Arbor: UMI Press, 1988), 73.
30. *Commoedia*, 11 December 1920; cited in Vera Stravinsky and Craft, *Stravinsky in Pictures and Documents*, 512.
31. Sokolova, 166.
32. *Ibid.*, 167.
33. Berg, 74.
34. Quoted in Oliver Daniel, "Rite of Spring: First Staging in America," *Ballet Review* 10:2 (Summer 1982): 69.
35. John Martin, *America Dancing* (New York: Dance Horizons, 1968), 195.
36. Eleanor King, *Transformations* (New York: Dance Horizons, 1978), 58.
37. Daniel, "Rite of Spring: First Staging in America," 70.
38. Massine, *My Life in Ballet*, 178.
39. Jean Bernier, "La Choreographie du Sacre du Printemps," *Commoedia dia Illustre* (Jan. 1921), 171.
40. André Levinson, "Stravinsky and the Dance," *Theatre Arts Monthly*, 8 (Nov. 1924): 754.
41. Grigoriev, 167.
42. [London] *Times*, 28 June 1921; cited in Macdonald, 264.
43. *Morning Post*, 28 June 1921; cited in *ibid.*, 266.
44. *Daily Mail*, 28 June 1921; cited in *ibid.*, 265.
45. [London] *Times*, 23 July 1929; cited in *ibid.*, 379.
46. Daniel, "Rite of Spring: First Staging in America," 68.
47. John Martin, *New York Times*, 27 April 1930.
48. Clement Crisp, "Massine's Ballets Revived in Nice," *London Financial Times*, 11 January 1995.
49. Berg, 87.
50. Bertil Hagman, "Massine Triumphs in Stockholm," *Dancing Times* (June 1956): 510.
51. Transcript of Dance Critics Association panel on Léonide Massine's *Le Sacre du printemps*, New York C987; cited in García-Márquez, *Massine*, 212.
52. "The Sitter Out," *Dancing Times* (March 1923): 601.
53. *Ibid.*, 600–01.
54. Sokolova, 198.
55. *Grove Dictionary of Art*, 1996, s.v. "Georges Braque," by Lewis Zurcher, 674.
56. Francis Ponge, "Braque or the Meditation of the Work," in Francis Ponge, Pierre Descargues, and Andre Malraux, eds., *G. Braque*, trans. Richard Howard (New York: Harry N. Abrams, 1971), 62.
57. Quoted by Anne Bertrand in "Les Soirées de Paris de Comte Etienne de Beaumont," unpublished dissertation, University de Paris X, Nanterre, 212; cited in García-Márquez, 181.
58. Massine, *My Life in Ballet*, 159.
59. *Grove Dictionary of Music and Musicians*, 1980, s.v. "Darius Milhaud," by Christopher Palmer, 305.
60. *Ibid.*, 307.
61. Quoted by Bertrand, "Les Soirées," 212; cited in García-Márquez, *Massine*, 181.
62. W. H. Haddon Squire, "A French Salad," *The Christian Science Monitor*, 11 February 1936.
63. Mme Milhaud in conversations with García-Márquez, *Massine*, 181.
64. Massine, *My Life in Ballet*, 158–59.
65. "The Soirées de Paris," *The Little Review*, 11:2, 76.
66. Massine, *My Life in Ballet*, 142.
67. Hugo, 175.
68. Gertrude Stein, *Picasso* (London: Scribner's Sons, 1939), 54.
69. Massine, *My Life in Ballet*, 160.
70. Hugo, 177.
71. Harding, *Erik Satie*, 211.
72. *Ibid.*
73. Virgil Thomson, "Music," *New York Herald Tribune*, 5 November 1940.
74. Harding, *Erik Satie*, 241–42.
75. "The Soirées de Paris," *The Little Review*, 56.
76. Ornella Volta, "Parade et Mercure," unpublished paper given at the conference

"Espanaylos Ballets Russos," Granada, 1989; cited in García-Márquez, *Massine*, 179.

77. Shaw, *The Criterion* (Oct. 1924); cited in Lincoln Kirstein, *Ballet, Bias and Belief* (New York: Dance Horizons, 1983), 16.
78. Buckle, *Diaghilev*, 434.
79. [London] *Times*, 12 July 1927; cited in Macdonald, 351.
80. Massine, *My Life in Ballet*, 159.
81. Polunin, 78.
82. *Observer*, 15 November 1925; cited in Macdonald, 317.
83. *Vogue*, December 1925; cited in *ibid*.
84. *Observer*, 15 November 1925; cited in *ibid*.
85. Alexandra Danilova, interviews by Peter Conway, 1978–79, typescript, Dance Collection, New York Public Library at Lincoln Center.
86. Grigoriev, 212.
87. Anton Dolin, *Divertissement* (London: Sampson Low, Marston and Co., n.d.), 106.
88. *Morning Post*, 13 November 1925; cited in Macdonald, 316.
89. Alicia Nikitina, *Nikitina*, trans. Moura Budberg (London: Allan Wingate, 1959), 46.
90. Danilova, typescript of interviews by Peter Conway, 1978–79.
91. Grigoriev, 212.
92. Dolin, 107.
93. Danilova, typescript of interviews by Conway, 1978–79.
94. *Observer*, 15 November 1925; cited in Macdonald, 318.
95. Massine, *My Life in Ballet*, 164–65.
96. Quoted in "The Sitter Out," *Dancing Times* (Aug. 1925): 1139.
97. "The Sitter Out," *Dancing Times* (June 1925): 954.
98. Massine, *My Life in Ballet*, 166.
99. "The Sitter Out," *Dancing Times* (June 1925): 953.
100. *Ibid*.
101. Kochno, 228.
102. André Levinson, *André Levinson on Dance*, ed. Joan Arocella and Lynn Garafola (Hanover, N.H.: Wesleyan University Press, 1991), 108.
103. *Les Matelots* (Motion Picture), 1956, 19 min. rehearsal film, si. b&w, 16 mm, Jerome Robbins Dance Division, New York Public Library at Lincoln Center.
104. Lifar, 295.
105. Rehearsal Film, Dance Collection.
106. [London] *Times*, 30 June 1925; cited in Macdonald, 310.
107. Svetloff, "The Diaghilev Ballet in Paris: Part II," 459.
108. *Observer*, 5 July 1925; cited in Macdonald, 310.
109. [London] *Times*, 30 June 1925; cited in *ibid.*, 312.
110. *Queen*, 8 July 1925; cited in *ibid.*, 310.
111. [London] *Times*, 30 June 1925; cited in *ibid.*, 310.
112. Arnold Haskell, *Diaghileff: His Artistic and Private Life* (London: Gollancz, 1935), 311.
113. Massine, *My Life in Ballet*, 168.

4. June 1927–January 1932

1. Kochno, 236.
2. Grigoriev, 237.
3. Lifar, 318, 320.
4. Grigoriev, 240.
5. Massine, *My Life in Ballet*, 174.
6. *Ibid*.
7. Danilova, typescript of interviews with Peter Conway, 1978–79.
8. Nicholas Nabokov, *Old Friends and New Music* (London: Hamish Hamilton, 1951), 81.
9. *Ibid.*, 95–96.
10. Kochno, 260.
11. Parker Tyler, *The Divine Comedy of Pavel Tchelitchew* (New York: Fleet, 1967), 333.
12. Nabokov, *Old Friends*, 106–07.
13. *Ibid.*, 112.
14. *Ibid*.
15. *Ibid.*, 124,126.
16. Grigoriev, 251.
17. John Martin, "A Ballet Master Is Imported," *New York Times*, 30 December 1930.
18. Massine, *My Life in Ballet*, 175.
19. Michael de Cossart, *Ida Rubenstein* (Liverpool: Liverpool University Press, 1987), 141.
20. Massine, *My Life in Ballet*, 176.
21. *Ibid.*, 177.
22. *Ibid.*, 185.
23. Christina Lodder, *Russian Constructivism* (New Haven: Yale University Press, 1983), 56.
24. *Ibid.*, 276; citing K. Umanskii, *Neue Kunst in Russland: 1914–1919* (Munich, 1920), 35–36.
25. *Grove Dictionary of Art and Artists*, 1996, s.v. "Georgy Yakulov," by V. Rakitin, 486.

26. Grigoriev, 242.
27. Harlow Robinson, *Sergei Prokofiev: A Biography* (New York: Viking, 1987), 96; citing S. Prokofiev, *Materialy dokumenty, vospominantie*, ed. S. I. Shlifshtein (Moscow, 1961).
28. Text for *Le Pas d'acier*, USSR Symphony Orchestra, Olympia Records, OCD103, 1987.
29. *Observer*, 10 July 1927; cited in Macdonald, 349.
30. [London] *Times*, 5 July 1927; cited in *ibid.*
31. Robinson, 211; citing Prokofiev, *Materialy, dokumenty, vospominantie*, 561.
32. Quoted in Robinson, 472.
33. Quoted in Alexander Worth, *Musical Uproar in Moscow* (London: Turnstile, 1949), 29.
34. Dmitri Shostakovich, *Testimony: The Memoirs of Dmitri Shostakovich*, as related to and edited by Solomon Volkov (New York: Dutton, 1979), 146.
35. Massine, *My Life in Ballet*, 171-72.
36. *Ibid.*, 172.
37. *Observer*, 10 July 1927; cited in Macdonald, 349.
38. Valerian Svetloff, "The Diaghilev Ballet in Paris: Part III," *Dancing Times* (Feb. 1930): 460.
39. André George, *Nouvelles Littéraires*, 21 June 1927.
40. Lifar, 321.
41. [London] *Times*, 5 July 1926; cited in Macdonald, 350.
42. *Observer*, 10 July 1927; cited in *ibid.*, 349.
43. Danilova, typescript of interviews with Peter Conway, 1978-79.
44. Alexandre Benois, *Reminiscences of the Russian Ballet*, trans. Mary Britnieva (London: Putnam, 1941), 381.
45. Tyler, 329-31.
46. A. V. Coton, *A Prejudice for Ballet* (London: Methuen and Co., 1938), 86.
47. "The Diaghilev Puzzle Ballet: Ode," *The Sketch*, 18 July 1928.
48. Svetloff, "The Diaghilev Ballet in Paris: Part III," 572.
49. *Morning Post*, 10 July 1928; cited in Macdonald, 362.
50. [London] *Times*, 10 July 1928; cited in *ibid.*, 361.
51. *Morning Post*, 10 July 1928; cited in *ibid.*, 362.
52. Danilova, typescript of interviews with Peter Conway, 1978-79.

53. Cyril Beaumont, *The Diaghilev Ballet in Paris* (London: Putnam, 1940), 288.
54. *Morning Post*, 10 July 1928; cited in Macdonald, 362.
55. Svetloff, "The Diaghilev Ballet in Paris: Part III," 572.
56. [London] *Times*, 10 July 1928; cited in Macdonald, 361.
57. Grigoriev, 250.
58. de Cossart, 141.
59. Massine, *My Life in Ballet*, 176-77.
60. [London] *Times*, 5 December 1928.
61. Arnold Haskell, *Balletomania Then and Now* (London: Weidenfeld and Nicholson, 1977), 153.
62. Sir Francis Rose, *Saying Life* (London: Cassell, 1961), 135-36.
63. A. Mangeot, "Opera: Les Ballets de Mme Ida Rubinstein," *Le Monde Musicale* (Dec. 1928), 413; cited in Charles S. Mayer, "Ida Rubinstein: Twentieth-Century Cleopatre," *Dance Research Journal* 20:2 (Winter 1989): 44.
64. "The Sitter Out," *Dancing Times* (Jan. 1929): 429.
65. de Cossart, 142.
66. Paul Bertrand, "Les Ballets de Mme Ida Rubinstein," *Le Menestrel*, 91:233 (May 1929); cited in de Cossart, 148.
67. James Harding, *The Ox on the Roof* (London: Macdonald, 1972), 206.
68. Bertrand, "Les Ballets de Ida Rubinstein"; cited in de Cossart, 148.
69. *Ibid.*
70. Henry A. Grubbs, *Paul Valéry* (New York: Twayne, 1968), 53-68.
71. Paul Valéry, *Lettres à quelques-uns* (Paris: Gallimard, 1952), 88.
72. *Revue de France*, August 1931; cited in García-Márquez, *Massine*, 214.
73. *Nouvelles Littéraires*, 18 July 1931; cited in *ibid.*, 214.
74. *Temps*, 1 July 1931; cited in *ibid.*, 214.
75. *Grove Dictionary of Music and Musicians*, 1980, s.v. "Arthur Honneger," by Fritz Muggler, 679.
76. *Ibid.*, 680.
77. Arthur Honneger, *I Am a Composer* (London: Faber and Faber, 1966), 109.
78. Marcel Delannoy, *Honneger* (Paris: Pierre Horay, 1953), 129.
79. Boris de Schloezer, "Amphion," *Nouvelle Revue Française*, 37 (1931): 348-49; cited in de Cossart, 155-56.
80. Prunières, "'Amphion' d'Arthur Honneger et de Paul Valéry," *Revue Musicale* 12:119 (Oct. 1931): 239-40; cited in de Cossart, 156.

81. André Levinson, *Les Visages de la Danse* (Paris: Editions Bernard Grasset, 1933), 111–12.
82. Gustave Bret, "Representation de Mme Ida Rubinstein: 'Amphion,'" *L'Intransigeant* (25 June 1931): 7; cited in de Cossart, 156.
83. Georges Guy, "Amphion," *Griffe Littéraire* (9 July 1931); cited in de Cossart, 156.
84. "A l'Opéra: Les Ballets de Ida Rubinstein: 'Amphion,'" Ida Rubinstein clipping file, Theatre Collection, New York Public Library at Lincoln Center, n.d.
85. F. Bonavia, "Notes and Comments," *New York Times*, 26 July 1931.
86. André Levinson, *Candide*, 2 July 1931; cited in García-Márquez, *Massine*, 214.
87. Lynn Garafola, "Ida Rubinstein (1885–1960): A Theatrical Life," *Dance Research Journal* 21:2 (Fall 1989): 26.
88. Name subsequently changed to David Lichine.
89. R. M. H., "Belkis Regina Di Saba," *Dancing Times* (March 1932): 669.
90. *Grove Dictionary of Music and Musicians*, 1980, s.v. "Ottorino Respighi," by John C. G. Waterhouse, 757.
91. *Ibid.*, 757–58.
92. Harvey Sachs, *Music in Fascist Italy* (New York: Norton, 1987), 132.
93. R. M. H., "Belkis Regina," 669–70.
94. Raymond Hall, text for *Belkis, Queen of Sheba*, Philharmonica Orchestra, Chandos Recordings, CHAN8405, 1985.
95. R. M. H., "Belkis Regina," 670.
96. *Ibid.*, 669.
97. Massine, *My Life in Ballet*, 182.

5. May 1932–July 1936

1. Danilova, typescript of interviews with Peter Conway, 1978–79.
2. Massine, *My Life in Ballet*, 190.
3. *Ibid.*
4. Agnes de Mille, *Dance to the Piper* (Boston: Little, Brown, 1952), 152.
5. Constant Lambert, "Dancing Seconds," *Sunday Referee*, 8 July 1934.
6. Edwin Evans, "The Symphonic Ballet," *Dancing Times* (Dec. 1936): 268.
7. Ernest Newman, "This Week's Music," *Sunday Times*, 4 August 1935.
8. Nicholas Nabokov, *Bagzah* (New York: Atheneum, 1975), 192.
9. Massine, *My Life in Ballet*, 197.
10. 1934 Ballet Russe de Monte Carlo program notes.
11. Nabokov, *Bagzah*, 193–94.
12. Vera Zorina, *Zorina* (New York: Farrar, Strauss & Giroux, 1986), 92–98.
13. Neither Massine's 1927 remake of *Les Facheux* nor his remake of *Le Bal* are included for analysis because they are derivative of the original versions choreographed by Nijinska and Balanchine, respectively.
14. Zorina, 98.
15. *Ibid.*, 117.
16. Anatol Dorati, *Notes of Seven Decades* (London: Hodder & Stoughton, 1979), 226.
17. Massine, *My Life in Ballet*, 203–04.
18. Quoted in *Grove Dictionary of Art and Artists*, 1996, s.v. "Joan Miró," by José Corregor-Matheos, 706.
19. Walter Erben, *Joan Miró* (New York: George Braziller, 1959), 124.
20. Gaston Diehl, *Miró* (New York: Crown Publishers, 1979), 52.
21. Manchester, "A Conversation," 76.
22. Coton, *A Prejudice for Ballet*, 73.
23. *Grove Dictionary of Music and Musicians*, 1980, s.v. "Georges Bizet," by Winton Dean, 751.
24. Frederick Robert, text *for Musique Français Pour Piano et Quatre Mains*, Philippe Corre and Edouard Exerjean, Le Chant du Monde Recordings, LDC 278–849/50, 1986.
25. *Grove Dictionary*, "Georges Bizet," 758.
26. Adrian Stokes, *To-night the Ballet* (London: Faber and Faber, 1935), 97.
27. Coton, 70–72.
28. *Ibid.*, 71.
29. Massine, *My Life in Ballet*, 184.
30. [London] *Times*, 9 July 1937.
31. Ernest Newman, "This Week's Music," *Sunday Times*, 16 July 1933.
32. [London] *Times*, 9 July 1937.
33. Fernau Hall, "De Basil and the Vic-Wells," *Dancing Times* (Nov. 1937): 144.
34. William Rubin and Carolyn Lanchner, *André Masson* (New York: Museum of Modern Art, 1976), 133.
35. Jean-Paul Clebart, *Mythologie d'André Masson* (Geneva: Pierre Cailler), 43; cited in Rubin and Lanchner, 133.
36. García-Márquez, 227.
37. John Percival, "Pushing Back the Frontiers," *Dance and Dancers* (May 1989): 20.
38. "Decor at the Alhambra and the Savoy," *Dancing Times* (Aug. 1933): 456.
39. *Ibid.*
40. *Grove Dictionary of Music and Musi-*

cians, 1980, s.v. "Peter Illych Tchaikovsky," by David Brown, 610–28.

41. Tchaikovsky, *To My Best Friend: Correspondence Between Tchaikovsky and Nadezhda von Meck*, ed. Edward Garden, trans. Galina von Meck (Oxford: Clarendon Press, 1913), 384–85.

42. *Muazkalnoe nasledie Chaikovskogo* (Moscow, 1958), 239; cited in Alexander Poznansky, *Tchaikovsky: The Quest for the Inner Man* (New York: Schirmer, 1991), 490.

43. P. I. Chaikovskii, *Perepiskar N. F. von Meck: 1876–1890* ("Correspondence with N. F. von Meck"), ed. Vladimir Zhdanov and Nikolai Zhegin, 3 vols. (Moscow, Leningrad, 1934–36), 559; cited in Poznansky, 495.

44. Massine, *My Life in Ballet*, 187.

45. Tamara Finch, "Les Présages Revisited," *Dance and Dancers* (April 1989): 638.

46. Percival, "Pushing Back the Frontiers," 20.

47. Massine, *My Life in Ballet*, 187.

48. Percival, "Pushing Back the Frontiers," 21.

49. Massine, *My Life in Ballet*, 187–88.

50. Anna Kisselgoff, "A Massine Revival by the Paris Opera Troupe," *New York Times*, 9 March 1989.

51. Manchester, "A Conversation," 62.

52. Kisselgoff, "A Massine Revival," 9 March 1989.

53. Ernest Newman, "The Case for Massine," *Sunday Times*, 26 July 1936.

54. In a 1977 interview for *Ballet Review*, P. W. Manchester said, "All the men in Les Présages looked as if they wore longjohns. And they were dreadful vile green. And puce—you know. And it was hideous in 1933."

55. John Martin, "The Dance: Ballet Russe," *New York Times*, 31 December 1933.

56. Kisselgoff, "A Massine Revival," 9 March 1989.

57. Percival, "Pushing Back the Frontiers," 21.

58. Kisselgoff, "A Massine Revival," 9 March 1989.

59. Alexandra Danilova replaced Tarakanova in this role shortly after the première.

60. Léonide Massine, "My First Sin," *Dance and Dancers* (April 1971): 19.

61. Alexandra Danilova, an open letter to *Dance* (March 1952): 20.

62. "Notes on Decor," *Dancing Times* (Aug. 1935): 529.

63. *Grove Dictionary of Music and Musicians*, 1980, s.v. "Johann Strauss," by Andrew Lamb, 210–11.

64. Massine, "My First Sin," 17.

65. *Ibid.*, 20.

66. P. W. Manchester, "Massine the Dancer," *Dancing Times* (Aug. 1972): 88–89.

67. *Ibid.*

68. Grace Robert, *The Borzoi Book of Ballets* (New York: Alfred A. Knopf, 1946), 52.

69. Richard Buckle, "Period Reproduction," *Observer*, 29 August 1960.

70. Massine, "My First Sin," 17–18.

71. *Grove Dictionary of Art and Artists*, 1996, s.v. "Raoul Dufy," by Dora Perez-Tiki, 373.

72. Ernest Newman, "This Week's Music," [London] *Times*, 6 August 1933.

73. Massine, *My Life in Ballet*, 190.

74. John Martin, "Ballet Russe Adds Lively Selections," *New York Times*, 3 January 1934.

75. G. E. Goodman, "Notes on Decor," *Dancing Times* (Sept. 1933): 619.

76. Ernest Newman, "This Week's Music," [London] *Times*, 15 July 1933.

77. "Chronicles: The Ballet Russe de Monte Carlo," *London Mercury* (Sept. 1933): 454.

78. Ernest Newman, "A Comedy of the Ballet," [London] *Times*, 15 July 1933.

79. Ernest Newman, "This Week's Music," [London] *Times*, 16 July 1933.

80. *Ibid.*

81. Martin, 3 January 1934.

82. G. E. Goodman, "Notes on Decor," *Dancing Times* (Sept. 1935): 619.

83. *Grolier's Encyclopedia*, 1993, s.v. "Johannes Brahms," by R. M. Longyear.

84. Igor Stravinsky, quoted in Allen Robertson, "Birmingham Royal Ballet," *Dancing Times* (Dec. 1991): 221.

85. Edwin Evans, "Choreartium—The Music and the Choreography," *Dancing Times* (Nov. 1933).

86. Notes on the source-theme of the Fourth Symphony from Edward T. Cone, "Harmonic Congruence in Brahms," in *Brahms Studies: Analytical and Historical Perspectives*, papers delivered at the International Brahms Conference, Washington, D.C., 8 May 1983 (Oxford: Clarendon, 1990), 185–86.

87. Evans, "Choreartium—The Music," 1104.

88. Lambert, "Dancing Seconds," 8 July 1934.

89. Ernest Newman, "The New Massine

Ballet," *Sunday Times*, 29 October 1933; and "This Week's Music," *Sunday Times*, 4 August 1933.

90. Robert, 73.
91. John Percival, "Choreartium," *Dance and Dancers* (Dec. 1991): 216.
92. Manchester, "A Conversation," 68.
93. Anna Kisselgoff, " A Long-Neglected Classic Still Amazes," *New York Times*, 1 December 1991.
94. Manchester, "A Conversation," 67.
95. Buckle, "Period Reproduction," 29 August 1960.
96. Robertson, "Birmingham Royal Ballet," 221.
97. Robert, 73.
98. Lambert, "Dancing Seconds," 8 July 1934.
99. Ernest Newman, "De Basil's Ballet Russe," [London] *Times*, 21 June 1936.
100. Alastair Macaulay, "The Best Bad Ballets," *Times Literary Supplement* [London], 26 April 1991.
101. Kisselgoff, "A Long-Neglected Classic," 1 December 1991.
102. Janet Sinclair, "Choreartium," *Dance and Dancers* (Jan. 1986): 28–29.
103. Constant Lambert, "Railroad Ballet," *Sunday Referee*, 15 July 1934; and Ernest Newman, "This Week's Music," *Sunday Times*, 25 July 1937.
104. Massine, *My Life in Ballet*, 198–99.
105. Manchester, "Massine the Dancer," 89.
106. Massine, *My Life in Ballet*, 199.
107. Nabokov, *Bagzah*, 194.
108. Kirstein, *Ballet, Bias and Belief*, 182.
109. Manchester, "A Conservation," 78.
110. Lambert, "Railroad Ballet," 15 July 1934.
111. Constant Lambert, "New Ballet at Covent Garden," *Sunday Referee*, 28 July 1935.
112. *Ibid.*; and Ernest Newman, "This Week's Music," *Sunday Times*, 28 July 1935.
113. "The Sitter Out," *Dancing Times* (Aug. 1936): 477.
114. Massine, *My Life in Ballet*, 201.
115. Newman, 28 July 1935; Lambert, "New Ballet at Covent Garden," 28 July 1935.
116. "The Sitter Out," *Dancing Times* (Aug. 1936): 477.
117. Lambert, "New Ballet at Covent Garden," 28 July 1935.
118. Much of this phraseology is Berlioz's own, which appeared in the 1910 edition of the *Symphonie fantastique* published by Breitkopf & Hartel, and was reprinted in the 1936 Ballet Russe de Monte Carlo program notes.
119. Robert, 326.
120. John Martin, "The Dance: 'Fantastique,'" *New York Times*, 8 November 1936; and Ernest Newman, "Berlioz and Massine," *Sunday Times*, 2 August 1936.
121. *Grove Dictionary of Music and Musicians*, 1980, s.v. "Hector Berlioz," by Hugh Macdonald, 582.
122. Hector Berlioz, *Memoirs of Hector Berlioz*, trans. Rachel Holmes and Eleanor Holmes, ed. Ernest Newman (New York: Tudor, 1932), 69.
123. As he stated, Berlioz later married Miss Smithson. Their union was not a success.
124. Cited in D. Kern Holoman, *Berlioz* (Cambridge: Harvard University Press, 1989), 101.
125. *Ibid.*
126. Newman, "Berlioz and Massine," 2 August 1936.
127. Massine, *My Life in Ballet*, 202.
128. Martin, "The Dance: 'Fantastique,'" 8 November 1936.
129. Diaries of Sir Lionel Bradley.
131. Arnold Haskell, "Massine's Finest Ballet," *Daily Telegraph*, 25 July 1936.
132. Newman, "Berlioz and Massine," 2 August 1936.
133. *Ibid.*
134. Constant Lambert, "Reviews," *Sunday Referee*, 2 August 1936.
135. Haskell, "Massine's Finest Ballet," 25 July 1936.
136. Russell Rhodes, "New York Letter," *Dancing Times* (Dec. 1936): 344.
137. Martin, "The Dance: 'Fantastique,'" 8 November 1936.
138. Manchester, "A Conversation," 71.

6. August 1936–May 1939

1. García-Márquez, *Massine*, 244; agreement between Col. de Basil and Massine, 10 August 1934, Mme de Basil Collection, Paris.
2. "Choreography to Court," *Time*, 30 August 1937, 27.
3. Heather Doughty, "The Choreographer in the Courtroom," proceedings, Dance History Scholars, Fifth Annual Conference, Harvard University, February 1982.
4. "Law Report, July 23," and "Law

Report, July 30," [London] *Times*, 24 July and 31 July 1937.
5. "Court of Appeal," [London] *Times*, 23 February 1938.
6. Manchester, "A Conversation," 80.
7. "Blum Ballet Sold to Company Here," *New York Times*, 20 November 1937.
8. Arnold Haskell, "Balletomanes Log Book," *Dancing Times* (July 1937): 413.
9. Kathrine Sorley Walker, *De Basil's Ballets Russes* (New York: Atheneum, 1983), 82.
10. John Martin, "Massine and de Basil Companies Merged," *New York Times*, 24 April 1938.
11. "The Sitter Out," *Dancing Times* (June 1938): 267.
12. "Head of Ballet Russe Must Pay $52,250 by Court Order for Breaking a Contract," *New York Times*, 18 September 1947.
13. Leo Kersley, "The Ballet Russe," *Ballet Today* (Dec. 1961): 26.
14. Massine, *My Life in Ballet*, 207.
15. Danilova, typescript of interviews with Peter Conway, 1978–79.
16. Paul Hindemith, *Selected Letters of Paul Hindemith*, ed. and trans. Geoffrey Skelton (London: Yale University Press, 1995), 16.
17. Massine, *My Life in Ballet*, 210.
18. Elizabeth McCausland, "The Ballet Russe Packs 'em In," *Dance Observer* (Nov. 1938): 128.
19. "Ballet Russe de Monte Carlo—A Variety of Sugary Anecdotes," *Daily Worker*, 26 October 1938.
20. "Fleischmann Donates $250,000 to World Art," *New York Times*, n.d., Massine Clipping File, Jerome Robbins Dance Division, New York Public Library at Lincoln Center.
21. Ruth Seinfel, "Big Man of Ballet," *Collier's*, 17 February 1940, 17.
22. Seinfel, 46; and Peter Avery, "Ballerinas; Handle With Care," *New York Herald Tribune*, n.d., Massine Clipping File, Jerome Robbins Dance Division, New York Public Library at Lincoln Center.
23. "Ballet Dancers' Duel Is Averted as Lifar Sails," *New York Herald Tribune*, 23 October 1938.
24. Kersley, 26.
25. "Ballet Dancers' Duel Is Averted," 23 October 1938.
26. Seinfel, 17.
27. Quoted in Avery, "Ballerinas; Handle With Care."

28. "Ballet Dancers' Duel is Averted," 23 October 1938.
29. This role was subsequently taken over by Alexandra Danilova.
30. Lawrence, *Victor Book of Ballets*, 199; and "Drury Lane Theatre," [London] *Times*, 15 July 1938.
31. Alexander Faris, *Jacques Offenbach* (New York: Charles Scribner's Sons, 1980), 69.
32. Sacheverell Sitwell, *La Vie Parisienne: A Tribute to Offenbach* (Boston: Houghton Mifflin Co., 1938), 23–24.
33. Manchester, "A Conversation," 82.
34. Robert, 143.
35. John Martin, "New Work Marks Opening of Ballet," *New York Times*, 13 October 1938.
36. Sophie Constanti, "American Ballet Theatre in London," *Dancing Times* (Sept. 1990): 1162.
37. Ann Barzel, "National Reviews," *Dance* (July 1989): 62.
38. John Percival, "In and Out of Favour," *Dance and Dancers* (Jan. 1989): 29.
39. Debra Cash, *Ballet News* (June 1979): 44.
40. Slavenska was replaced by Alicia Markova for the October New York premiere.
41. Italicized text is quoted from the 1938 Ballet Russe de Monte Carlo program notes. Other information derived from the Bradley diaries, 12 July 1938, and *Seventh Symphony* (Motion Picture), 1938, 34 min., sd. b&w, 16 mm, Dance Film Archives, University of Rochester, New York.
42. The fourth movement is missing from the only film version of *Seventh Symphony*, but fortunately, Lionel Bradley has left perhaps the only detailed description of this movement still extant.
43. Described in the Bradley diaries, 12 July 1938.
44. "Beethoven and Ballet," *Vogue* (Nov. 1938): 21.
45. Lincoln Kirstein, "Let's Go Native," *Town and Country* (Jan. 1939): 50.
46. *Grove Dictionary of Music and Musicians*, 1980, s.v. "Ludwig van Beethoven," by Joseph Kerman and Alan Tyson, 381.
47. *Ibid.*, 381–83.
48. Technical notes on the Seventh Symphony are taken from Hector Berlioz: *A Critical Study of Beethoven's Nine Symphonies*, trans. Edwin Evans (London: William Reeves, n.d.), 83–91.

49. *Grove Dictionary*, "Ludwig van Beethoven, 384.
50. Berlioz, 87.
51. *Ibid.*, 85.
52. Massine, *My Life in Ballet*, 206.
53. Lawrence, *Victor Book of Ballets*, 41.
54. *Ibid.*, and Ernest Newman, "This Week's Music," *Sunday Times*, 17 July 1938.
55. Robert, 279.
56. Leonid Sabaneev, "The Symphony in the Service of Ballet," *The Musical Times* (July 1940): 297.
57. Ernest Newman, "This Week's Music," 17 July 1938; and Anatole Vitak, "Dance Events Reviewed," *American Dancer* (Jan. 1940): 30.
58. Lawrence, *Victor Book of Ballets*, 414; and Arnold Haskell, "Ballet at Drury Lane," *The Bystander*, 27 July 1938.
59. "The Sitter Out," *Dancing Times* (Aug. 1938): 516; and *Modern Music* (Nov.-Dec. 1938), reprinted *Dance Index* (Jan. 1946): 42-43.
60. Interview with Pavel Tchelitchew in "New Mystical Ballet," *Observer*, 24 July 1938.
61. "Hands Seen on Scenery Spell Out Words—'Gloria!'" *Hartford Times*, 9 December 1938.
62. John Martin, "Massine's St. Francis," *New York Times*, 23 October 1938.
63. Tyler, 413.
64. *Grove Dictionary of Music and Musicians*, 1980, s.v. "Paul Hindemith," by Ian Kemp, 575.
65. *Ibid.*, 585.
66. Martin, "Massine's St. Francis," 23 October 1938.
67. Walter Terry, "Ballet Russe Makes First Appearance," *Boston Herald*, 13 November 1938.
68. Cyril Beaumont, *Supplement to the Complete Book of Ballets* (London: Putman, 1952), 54; and Robert, 266.
69. Letter from Paul Hindemith to Gertrude Hindemith, 26 February 1939; in Luther Noss, *Paul Hindemith in the United States* (Urbana: University of Illinois Press, 1989), 45-46.
70. Martin, "Massine's St. Francis," 23 October 1938.
71. Lawrence, *Victor Book of Ballets*, 388.
72. Martin, "Massine's St. Francis," 23 October 1938.
73. "The Sitter Out," *Dancing Times* (Sept. 1938): 623; and Arnold Haskell, "Ballet Extremes," *The Bystander*, 10 August 1938.
74. Terry, "Ballet Russe Makes First Appearance," 13 November 1938.
75. *Ibid.*
76. Quoted in Chamot, *Gontcharova*, 8.
77. *Grove Dictionary of Art and Artists*, 1996, s.v. "Natalie Gontcharova," by Anthony Parton, 894.
78. *Grove Dictionary of Music and Musicians*, 1980, s.v "Alexander Borodin," by Gerald Abraham, 58-59.
79. "The Sitter Out," *Dancing Times* (Dec. 1938): 320; and Kirstein, "Let's Go Native," 50.
80. John Martin, "Ballet Russe Returns," *New York Times*, 24 October 1941.
81. Kirstein, "Let's Go Native," 50.
82. George Dorris, "Massine in 1938: Style and Meaning," Society of Dance History Scholars, proceedings, 11th Annual Conference (1988), 211.
83. Argentinita was subsequently replaced by Mia Slavenska.
84. Rimsky-Korsakov, 246.
85. Lawrence, *Victor Book of Ballets*, 91.
86. John Martin, "Argentinita at the Met," *New York Times*, 5 April 1940; and Edwin Denby, "Ashton's 'Devil's Holiday' and More Monte Carlo," *Modern Music* (Oct.-Nov. 1939): 64.
87. Italicized text quoted from 1939 Ballet Russe de Monte Carlo program notes. Other information derived from *Rouge et noir* (Motion Picture), 1939, 42 min., si. b&w, 16 mm, Jerome Robbins Dance Division, New York Public Library at Lincoln Center.
88. Barr, *Matisse*, 254.
89. Set description taken from the Bradley diaries, 1 July 1939.
90. Walter Terry, "The Ballet," *New York Herald Tribune*, 29 September 1948.
91. Lincoln Kirstein, "Dance in Review," *Dance* (Nov. 1940): 5.
92. Roy Blokker and Robert Dearling, *Shostakovich: The Symphonies* (London: Tantivy Press, 1979), 43.
93. *Ibid.*, 43-45.
94. *Ibid.*, 35.
95. Sabaneev, "The Symphony in the Service of Ballet," 298.
96. Walter Terry, "The Dance," *New York Herald Tribune*, 30 October 1939.
97. Robert, 258.
98. A. E. Twysden, "Massine's New Ballets," *Dance* (Oct. 1939): 9; Lawrence, *Victor Book of Ballets*, 374; and Terry, "The Dance," 30 October 1939.
99. "Reviews," *Ballet*, 25 October 1940.

7. June 1939–February 1943

1. Seinfel, 46.
2. Lillian Moore, "War Time Adventures of a Company," *Dancing Times* (Dec. 1939): 133.
3. John Martin, "The Ballet Russe Hailed at Opening," *New York Times*, 27 October 1939.
4. "Tempo!" *Dance* (April 1940): 6.
5. "Ballet Theatre Can't Compete; Wants Ballet Russe Unionized," *New York Herald Tribune*, 22 March 1940.
6. "Tempo!" *Dance* (April 1940): 6.
7. Walter Terry, "Ballet Decor," *New York Herald Tribune*, 5 October 1940.
8. Massine, *My Life in Ballet*, 216.
9. A.E. Twysden, "Massine's New Ballets."
10. John Martin, "Monte Carlo Ballet Gives Way to De Basil," *New York Times*, 3 November 1940.
11. Walter Terry, "Season Closed by Ballet Russe de Monte Carlo," *New York Herald Tribune*, 4 November 1940.
12. Bradley diaries, 6 March 1941.
13. "Tempo!" *Dance* (Dec. 1940): 6.
14. García-Márquez; citing letter from Denham to Fleischmann, 5 July 1939, Denham Papers.
15. *Dance* (Nov. 1940): 9.
16. Jack Anderson, *The One and Only: The Ballet Russe de Monte Carlo* (New York: Dance Horizons, 1981), 50.
17. Walter Terry, "Magic Swan on Stadium's Ballet Program," *New York Herald Tribune*, 25 June 1942.
18. Anderson, *The One and Only*, 50.
19. Igor Youskevitch, interview by John Gruen, "Igor Youskevitch: Part II," *Dance* (May 1982): 52–53.
20. Massine, *My Life in Ballet*, 218.
21. *Ibid.*, 220.
22. García-Márquez, Massine, 289; citing letter from Denham to Fleischmann, 22 January 1942, Denham Papers.
23. Sol Hurok, *S. Hurok Presents ... the World of Ballet* (London: Robert Hale, 1955), 130.
24. Walter Terry, "Monte Carlo Case," *New York Herald Tribune*, 19 April 1942.
25. Massine, *My Life in Ballet*, 221.
26. *Ibid.*, 222.
27. "The Sitter Out," *Dancing Times* (Nov. 1946): 60.
28. "Choreography and the Law," *Dance* (June 1966): 8.
29. John Martin, "An American Sums Up," *Dancing Times* (Feb. 1943): 216.
30. So designated by Dalí in the 1939 Ballet Russe de Monte Carlo program notes.
31. Beaumont, *Supplement to the Complete Book of Ballets*, 60.
32. King Ludwig II, quoted in Martin Gregor-Dellin, *Wagner: His Life His Work, His Century*, trans. J. Maxwell Brownjohn (San Diego: Harcourt Brace Jovanovich, 1983), 337–38.
33. Hans Mayer, quoted in Oswald Georg Bauer, *Richard Wagner* (New York: Rizzoli, 1983), 79–80.
34. Gregor-Dellin, 302.
35. Ernst Bloch, *Gesamtausgabe*, Vol. 5, 972, Frankfurt, 1877; cited in *ibid.*, 301.
36. Massine, *My Life in Ballet*, 214.
37. Quoted in Ramón Gómez de la Serna, *Dalí*, ed. Franco Paone, trans. Nicholas Fry and Elisabeth Evans (New York: William Morrow and Company, 1979), 227–28.
38. Salvador Dalí, from André Breton, *Manifestoes of Surrealism*, trans. Richard Seaver and Helen R. Lane (University of Michigan Press, 1969); cited in Gómez de la Serna, 226–27.
39. Robert, 33–34.
40. Danilova says, "I can assure you that when these boys [the Fauns] came onstage everyone gasped. ... I think all vices of sex in that Bacchanale" (1978 interview by Conway).
41. When Ludwig drowned himself, his body was not discovered right away. At first his searchers found only an umbrella floating on the water.
42. John Martin, "Surrealism and America," *New York Times*, 19 November 1939.
43. Albertina Vitak, "Dance Events Reviewed," *American Dancer* (Jan. 1940): 15; and Martin, 19 November 1939.
44. Vitak, "Dance Events Reviewed," and Pitt Sanborn, *The Daily Worker*, 27 March 1940.
45. Martin, 19 November 1939; Robert, 35.
46. Martin, 19 November 1939.
47. Synopsis quoted from 1940 Ballet Russe de Monte Carlo program notes.
48. Irving Kolodin, "'New Yorker' Given

to Gershwin Music," *New York Sun*, 19 October 1940.
49. Quoted in Deena Rosenberg, *Fascinating Rhythm: The Collaboration of George and Ira Gershwin* (New York: Dutton, 1991), 38.
50. Steven E. Gilbert, *The Music of Gershwin* (New Haven and London: Yale University Press, 1995), 90.
51. Howard Taubman, *New York Times*, 17 August 1932.
52. Fred Astaire and Ginger Rogers walked their puppies on shipdeck to this tune in the 1937 movie musical, *Shall We Dance*.
53. Kolodin, 19 October 1940; and Robert Lawrence, "Massine's 'New Yorker' Danced to Music of George Gershwin," *New York Herald Tribune*, 19 October 1940.
54. Albertina Vitak, "'The New Yorker,'" *American Dancer* (Dec. 1940): 13; and Walter Terry, "Russian Ballet," *New York Herald Tribune*, 27 October 1940.
55. Kolodin, 19 October 1940; and Vitak, "'The New Yorker,'" 13.
56. Walter Terry, "'New Yorker' Premieres," *New York Herald Tribune*, 19 October 1940; and John Martin, "Massine Appears in Two Ballet Roles," *New York Times*, 30 October 1940.
57. Terry, 19 October 1940; Vitak, "'The New Yorker,'" 13; and Kolodin, 19 October 1940.
58. A. E. Twysden, "Massine's New Ballets," 9.
59. Synopsis quoted from 1940 Ballet Russe de Monte Carlo program notes.
60. A. E. Twysden, "Massine's New Ballets," 9.
61. John Warrack, *Carl Maria von Weber* (Cambridge: Cambridge University Press, 1976), 19.
62. *Grove Dictionary of Music and Musicians*, 1980, s.v. "Carl Maria von Weber," by Ronald Byrnside, 242.
63. *Ibid.*, 247.
64. Fokine used this music for *Le Spectre de la Rose* (1911), which gave Vaslav Nijinsky one of his most celebrated roles.
65. Lawrence, 27 October 1940.
66. Vitak, "Dance Events Reviewed," 13.
67. Robert Sabin, "Ballet Russe de Monte Carlo Opens Season," *Ballet*, 25 October 1940; and Russell Rhodes, "New York Letter," *Dancing Times* (Dec. 1940): 124.
68. Terry, 27 October 1940.
69. Quoted from 1941 Ballet Russe de Monte Carlo program notes.

70. Salvador Dalí, *The Secret Life of Salvador Dalí* (New York: Dial Press, 1942), 284–85.
71. Walter Terry, "Ballet and Books," *New York Herald Tribune*, 5 October 1941.
72. Terry, 5 October 1941; and John Martin, "Season of Ballet at the Metropolitan," *New York Times*, 14 April 1942.
73. *Grove Dictionary of Music and Musicians*, 1980, s.v. "Franz Schubert," by Maurice J. E. Brown, 776.
74. *Grove Dictionary of Music and Musicians*, 2001, s.v. "Franz Schubert," by Walter Winter, 688–89.
75. John Reed, *Schubert* (New York: Schirmer Books, 1997), 121–22.
76. Linton Martin, "Schubert Symphony Given Realistic Treatment," *U.S.* (New York), 9 November 1941.
77. Walter Terry, "The Ballet Russe," *New York Herald Tribune*, 19 October 1941.
78. Castor and Pollux were later lampooned as Ajax I and Ajax II in David Lichine's *Helen of Troy* (1942).
79. Beaumont, *Supplement to the Complete Book of Ballets*, 65.
80. Linton Martin, 9 November 1941; and Robert, 35.
81. Terry, 5 October 1941.
82. Robert Sabin, review of *Saratoga*, *Dance Observer* (Nov. 1941): 124.
83. Christopher Palmer, "Weinberger and Schwanda," text for *Schwanda*, Munich Radio Orchestra, cond. Heinz Walberg, CBS Records, 7934 CB: 273, 1981.
84. Sabin, review of *Saratoga*, 124.
85. "Ballet Russe Presents 'Saratoga,'" *Musical America*, 10 November 1941.
86. Massine and Toumanova performed their cakewalk in blackface, a practice which featured in several of Massine's ballets, including his 1947 *Mam'zelle Angot*.
87. Sabin, 124; Walter Terry, "The Week's Debuts," *New York Herald Tribune*, 26 October 1941; and Henry Simon, "Saratoga Misses the Spitoon," *P.M.* (New York, 20 October 1941).
88. Terry, 26 October 1941.
89. Sidney Alexander, *Marc Chagall* (New York: Putnam, 1978), 359.
90. Quoted in Selma Jeanne Cohen and A. J. Pischl, "The American Ballet Theatre, 1940–1960," *Dance Perspectives*, 6 (1960): 30.
91. Leland Windreich, "Massine's 'Aleko,'" *Dance Chronicle* 8:3 (1985): 160.
92. Robert, 25.
93. Robert Lawrence, "A Remarkable

Matinee," *New York Herald Tribune*, 25 October 1942.
94. Carl van Vechten, introduction to *Giselle and I* by Alicia Markova (New York: Vanguard Press, 1960), 12; and interview of George Skibine by Peter Anastos, "A Conversation with George Skibine," *Ballet Review* (Spring 1982): 80.
95. Robert, 26.
96. Martin, *World Book of Modern Ballet* (Cleveland: World Publishing Company, 1952): 80; Edwin Denby, *Looking at the Dance* (New York: Pelegrini and Cudahy, 1949), 237; and Winthrop Palmer, *Theatrical Dancing in America* (South Brunswick, N.J.: Barnes, 1978), 206–07.
97. Alexander, 359.
98. Sol Hurok, *S. Hurok Presents: A Memoir of the Dance World* (New York: Hermitage House, 1953), 146.
99. Croce, *Afterimages*, 331.
100. Jack Anderson, "Legends in the Flesh," *Ballet Review* 3:2 (1969): 34; and George Jackson, "American Ballet Theatre at the Met," *Ballet Today* (Sept.–Oct. 1968): 28.
101. Windreich, 175.
102. Synopsis quoted from 1942 American Ballet Theatre program notes.
103. *Grove Dictionary of Art and Artists*, 1996, s.v. "Julio Castellanos," by Ortiz Gaitan, 21.
104. Robert Lawrence, "Mexican Problem," *New York Herald Tribune*, 10 October 1942; and Anthony Fay, "Alicia Markova: Her Appearances in America," *Dance Magazine* (June 1977): 61.
105. Massine, *My Life in Ballet*, 225.
106. John Martin, "Mexican Ballet," *New York Times*, 10 October 1942.
107. Massine, *My Life in Ballet*, 225.
108. *Don Domingo*'s poor reception by the New York audience is substantiated in the Bradley diary entry of 16 December 1942, in which he records that some of the audience "actually hissed and booed" during curtain calls.
109. Lawrence, 10 October 1942.
110. Massine, *My Life in Ballet*, 226.
111. Mary Clarke, "Massine—in England and America," *Dancing Times* (April 1948): 294.
112. Wilson, "Reports from Abroad," *Dance News* (April 1980): 9.
113. Peter Williams, "The Case for Massine," *Dance and Dancers* (March 1968): 17.
114. Clarke, "Massine—in England and America," 294–95.
115. Massine, *My Life in Ballet*, 226.

8. March 1943–October 1954

1. *Musical Digest* 27:1 (Oct. 1945): 28.
2. Michael Powell, *A Life in Movies* (New York, Knopf, 1987), 242.
3. Massine, *My Life in Ballet*, 233.
4. Monk Gibbon, *The Red Shoes Ballet* (London: Saturn Press, 1948), 30, 17 and 14.
5. Michael Powell, "The Red Shoes," *American Film* (March 1987): 45.
6. "'Red Shoes' Sets 108-Week Film Record," *New York Herald Tribune*, 19 December 1950.
7. Memorandum, Eagle Lion Classics, Inc., 31 July 1950, Massine Clipping File, Jerome Robbins Dance Division, New York Public Library at Lincoln Center.
8. Massine, *My Life in Ballet*, 231.
9. Cited in *The Simon and Schuster Book of the Ballet* (New York: Simon and Schuster, 1979), 254.
10. García-Márquez, 186.
11. "First Lady Visits Massine's Island," *Philadelphia Enquirer*, 12 August 1962, Massine Clipping File, Jerome Robbins Dance Division, New York Public Library at Lincoln Center.
12. *Philadelphia Enquirer*, June 1964, n.d., Massine Clipping File, Jerome Robbins Dance Division, New York Public Library at Lincoln Center.
13. Notes on the choreography derived from *Le Peintre et son modèle* (Motion Picture), 1949, 16 min., si. b&w, 16mm, Jerome Robbins Dance Division, New York Public Library at Lincoln Center.
14. Notes on the choreography derived from *Concertino* (Motion Picture), 1950, 15 min., 16 mm, si b&w, and *Platée*, (Motion Picture), 1950, 21 min., si b&w, Jerome Robbins Dance Division, New York Public Library at Lincoln Center.
15. Pierre Tugal, "Paris," *Dancing Times* (July 1951): 596.
16. Monk Gibbon, *The Tales of Hoffmann: A Study of the Film* (London: Saturn Press, 1951), 58–59, 60, and 73–74.
17. Fernau Hall, *Anatomy of Ballet* (London: Andrew Melrose, 1953), 197.
18. Ian Christie, *Powell, Pressburger and Others* (London: British Film Institute, 1978), 62.

19. Massine, *My Life in Ballet*, 239.
20. "Ballet in San Domenico's," *Time*, 6 October 1952.
21. Laura Clandon, "Mediterranean Melange," *Dance* (Nov. 1961): 25.
22. Ernest Borneman, "The Most Remarkable Film—with Massine," *Ballet Today* (Nov. 1954): 9.
23. Massine, *My Life in Ballet*, 245; and interview with Tatiana Massine, conducted by John Gruen on 2 April 1973. Jerome Robbins Dance Division, New York Public Library at Lincoln Center.
24. "Venice Inaugurates Island Theatre," *Musical America* (Sept. 1954): 3; Anatole Chujoy, "A Great Choreographer Returns," *Dance News* (Oct. 1954): 8; and *Le Monde*, 16 July 1954.
25. Haskell, *Balletomania Then and Now*, 105.
26. Italicized text quoted from 1944 Ballet International program notes. Other information derived from *Mad Tristan* (Motion Picture), 1944, 24 min., si. b&w, 16 mm, Jerome Robbins Dance Division, New York Public Library at Lincoln Center.
27. Interview of Massine, "Dalí to Provide Scenario for a Massine Ballet," *New York Herald Tribune*, 22 January 1938.
28. Dalí, quoted in Nadeau, *Histoire du Surréalisme suivi des documents surréalistes* (Paris: Editions du Seuil, 1964); cited in de la Serna, 229.
29. Interview of Dalí, "Dalí—or a Dream Talking," *Cue*, 11 November 1944.
30. Robert, 37.
31. Robert Bagar, "First Paranoic Ballet," *World Telegram* (New York), 16 December 1944; and John Martin, "Ballet Premiere of 'Mad Tristan,'" *New York Times*, 16 December 1944.
32. Quoted in Bauer, 136.
33. *Ibid.*, 133.
34. *The New Grove Dictionary of Opera*, 1992, s.v. "*Tristan und Isolde*," by Barry Millington, 819.
35. *Ibid.*, 147.
36. Edwin Denby, "Dalí's 'Mad Tristan,'" *New York Herald Tribune*, 16 December 1944.
37. Review of *Mad Tristan*, *New Statesman*, 4 July 1949.
38. Denby, 16 December 1944; and Cyril Beaumont, cited in "What They Said," *Ballet and Opera* (Aug. 1949): 52.
39. A. V. Coton, *Sunday Times*, 4 July 1949; Arthur Berger, "Dalí's 'Tristan,'" *Dance News*, 16 December 1944; and Martin, 16 December 1944.
40. Carl Brahms, *Evening Standard*, 4 July 1949; and Denby, 16 December 1944.
41. Bagar, 16 December 1944.
42. John Martin, "Two Stadium Shows by Ballet Troupe," *New York Times*, 3 July 1945.
43. John Martin, "The Dance: Massine's Highlights," *New York Times*, 5 July 1945.
44. Martin, 3 July 1945.
45. Ann Barzel, "Ballets Down the Drain," *Ballet Annual* 17 (Fall 1963): 79.
46. Martin, 5 July 1945.
47. Robert Hague, "Ballet Borscht at the Stadium," *P.M.*, 2 July 1945.
48. Martin, 5 July 1945.
49. "The Sitter Out," *Dancing Times* (Aug. 1948): 578.
50. Arnold Haskell, "Outstanding Events of the Year," *Ballet Annual*, 3 (1949): 34.
51. *Grove Dictionary of Music and Musicians*, 1980, s.v. "Franz Joseph Haydn," by Jens Peter Larsen, 352.
52. H. C. Robbins Landon and David Wyn Jones, *Haydn: His Life and Music* (Bloomington: Indiana University Press, 1988), 265.
53. Cited in Landon and Jones, 248.
54. Massine, *My Life in Ballet*, 232.
55. Haskell, "Outstanding Events," 34.
56. Interview of Moira Shearer by Dale Harris, 29 August 1976, typescript, Jerome Robbins Dance Division, New York Public Library at Lincoln Center.
57. Alexander Grant in conversations with Vicente García-Márquez; cited in García-Márquez, *Massine*, 326.
58. "The Sitter Out," *Dancing Times* (Aug. 1948): 578.
59. Alastair Macaulay, "The Best Bad Ballets," *Times Literary Supplement* (London): 26 April 1996; and Massine, *My Life in Ballet*, 235.
60. Synopsis derived from *Donald of the Burthens* (Motion Picture), 1951, 41 min., si. b&w, 16 mm, Jerome Robbins Dance Division, New York Public Library at Lincoln Center.
61. Alexander Bland, "'Donald of the Burthens,'" *Dancing Times* (Feb. 1952) : 27.
62. *Grove Dictionary of Music and Musicians*, 1980, s.v. "Ian Whyte," by Conrad Wilson, 393.
63. Bland, 27.
64. "The Sitter Out," *Dancing Times* (Jan. 1952): 202; *Ballet Annual*, 7 (1953): 17; and

Clive Barnes, *Dance and Dancers* (Feb. 1953): 13–14.
65. Bland, 22 and 27.
66. Hall, *Anatomy of Ballet*, 134.
67. Bland, 25.
68. Hall, *Anatomy of Ballet*, 134–35.
69. Set description for *Laudes Evangelii* (Motion Picture), 1961, 84 min., sd. b&w, Associated Rediffusion (London) telecast. Directed by Joan Kemp-Welch. Jerome Robbins Dance Division, New York Public Library at Lincoln Center.
70. Valentino Bucchi, quoted in *The Simon and Schuster Book of the Ballet*, 260.
71. "Ballet in San Domenico's," *Time*, 6 October 1952.
72. Massine, *My Life in Ballet*, 241.
73. Signorini, quoted in *The Simon and Schuster Book of the Ballet*, 260.
74. "Ballet in San Domenico's," 6 October 1952.
75. Massine, *My Life in Ballet*, 241.
76. "Massine Ballet for Nantes," *Dance and Dancers* (July 1954): 23; and Haskell, *Balletomania Then and Now*, 105.
77. Cited in "Ballet in San Domenico's," 6 October 1952.
78. Quoted in "Massine Ballet for Nantes," 23.
79. Jack Iams, *New York Herald Tribune*, 9 April 1962; and Jack Gould, *New York Times*, 9 April 1962.
80. Massine, *My Life in Ballet*, 241–42.
81. P. W. Manchester, "The Season in Review," *Dance News* (Nov. 1954): 7; and Baird Hastings, "Massine's Symphonic Ballets," *Ballet Review* 23:1 (Spring 1995): 93.
82. *Grove Dictionary of Music and Musicians*, 1980, s.v. "Hector Berlioz," by Hugh Macdonald, 583.
83. Holoman, 247.
84. Manchester, "The Season in Review," 7.
85. Barzel, "Ballets Down the Drain," 78.
86. Doris Hering, "Reviews," *Dance* (Dec. 1954): 57.
87. Barzel, "Ballets Down the Drain," 78.

9. July 1955–July 1960

1. Charles Baudelaire, "Hymn to Beauty," in *The Flowers of Evil*, trans. Dorothy Martin, ed. Marthiel and Jackson Matthews (New York: New Directions, 1963), 30.
2. Notes on the choreography derived from *Hymne à la Beauté* (Motion Picture), 1955, 23 min., si. b&w, Jerome Robbins Dance Division, New York Public Library at Lincoln Center.
3. Gaia Servadio, *Luchino Visconti: A Biography* (New York: Franklin Watts, 1983), 127.
4. Quoted passages taken from Thomas Mann, *Mario and the Magician*, trans. H. T. Lowe-Porter (London: Martin Secker, 1930).
5. Gianni Caradente, "Ballet Re-awakens in Italy," *Dance and Dancers* (Aug. 1956): 29.
6. Jean Babilée in conversations with García-Márquez; cited in García-Márquez, *Massine*, 351.
7. Janet Sinclair, "Holland Festival," *Ballet Today* (Sept. 1958): 7.
8. García-Márquez, *Massine*, 355.
9. G. B. L. Wilson, "The Italian Renaissance," *Ballet Annual*, 15 (1961): 127–28.
10. Ibid., 261–62.
11. Clive Barnes, "Massine Goes North," *Dance and Dancers* (Nov. 1960): 7–8.
12. When Teatro Colón Ballet performed *Usher* in Paris in 1960, Neglia was awarded a special prize for his interpretation.
13. Quotations taken from Poe's "Fall of the House of Usher."
14. Victoria García, "Massine's New Ballet Is Praised," *Dance News* (Sept. 1955): 3.
15. Massine, *My Life in Ballet*, 247.
16. Descriptions of set and costumes taken from *Usher* (Motion Picture), 1955, 45 min., si. b&w, 16 mm, Jerome Robbins Dance Division, New York Public Library at Lincoln Center.
17. "Ballet by Massine Hailed in Argentina," *New York Times*, 3 July 1955; Hans Ehrmann-Ewart, "New Massine Ballet," *Dancing Times* (Sept. 1955); and García, "Massine's New Ballet," 3.
18. Quoted in *New York Times*, 3 July 1955.
19. Fernando Emery, *Lyra*, August 1955; cited in García-Márquez, *Massine*, 349.
20. "Ballet by Massine Hailed in Argentina," 3 July 1955; and García, "Massine's New Ballet," 3.
21. Ehrmann-Ewart, "New Massine Ballet."
22. J. M. Lybyer and James L. Roberts, *Poe's Short Stories* (New York: Wiley and Sons, 1980), 18.
23. Marc Vignal, text for *Don Juan*, English Baroque Chamber Orchestra, cond. John Eliot Gardner, Musical Heritage Society, MHS 4939M, 1982.
24. Hedwig M. von Aslow, introduction to *The Collected Correspondence and Papers of Christoph Willibald Gluck*, ed. Hedwig and E. H. Mueller von Aslow, trans. Stewart

Thompson (New York: St. Martin's Press, 1962), 10.
25. *Grove Dictionary of Music and Musicians*, 1980, s.v. "Christoph Willibald Gluck," by Winton Dean, 469.
26. Massine, *My Life in Ballet*, 256.
27. Robert Lawrence, "A New Massine Ballet," *Saturday Review*, 16 May 1959, 3.
28. *Ibid.*
29. The first episode in Act Three is actually a revival of *The Tub* from *Cochran's Revue 1926*.
30. Hamblen Sears, introduction to Giovanni Boccaccio, *Decameron*, trans. David McKay (Philadelphia: David McKay Co., n.d.), xv.
31. Lillian Moore, "The Nervi Festival," *Dancing Times* (Aug. 1960): 617; and Barnes, "Massine Goes North," 23.
32. *Grove Dictionary of Music and Musicians*, 1980, s.v. "Claude Arrieu," by Paul Griffiths, 635.
33. Buckle, "Period Reproduction," 8 July 1960; and Barnes, "Massine Goes North," 23.
34. García-Márquez, *Massine*, 358.
35. Barnes, "Massine Goes North," 23.
36. *Le Figaro*, 16 July 1960; cited in García-Márquez, *Massine*, 358.
37. *Ibid.*, and Buckle, "Period Reproduction," 8 July 1960.
38. Mary Clarke, "Tourists in Town," *Dancing Times* (July 1963): 585.
39. Peter Williams, "Le bal des voleurs," *Dance and Dancers* (July 1963): 29.
40. "Gala Performance," *Ballet Today* (July 1963): 10.
41. Massine, *My Life in Ballet*, 262.
42. Clarke, "Tourists in Town," 585.
43. Peter Williams, "The Case for Massine," *Dance and Dancers* (March 1968): 13.
44. Williams, "Le bal des voleurs," 29.
45. Clarke, "Tourists in Town," 585.
46. Beaurepaire in conversations with García-Márquez; cited in García-Márquez, *Massine*, 361.
47. Richard Osborne, *Rossini* (Boston: Northeastern University Press, 1986), 29–30.
48. Nicholas Till, *Rossini: His Life and Times* (New York: Hippocrene Books, 1983), 63.
49. Massine, *My Life in Ballet*, 260.

10. The Final Years

1. Massine, *My Life in Ballet*, 267.
2. García-Márquez, *Massine*, 370.
3. "Ballet Great Leonide Massine Still Going Strong," *Pittsburgh Post Gazette*, 15 December 1974, Massine Clipping File, Jerome Robbins Dance Division, New York Public Library at Lincoln Center.
4. Ann Hutchinson, "Massine Choreographic Course," Report to the Royal Academy of Dance, March 1969, Jerome Robbins Dance Division, New York Public Library at Lincoln Center.
5. Typescript of interview by John Gruen, September 1972, Jerome Robbins Dance Division, New York Public Library at Lincoln Center.
6. "A Conversation with Leonide Massine," *Dance* (Dec. 1977): 68.
7. Souren Melikian, "Art Market, a Personal Collection," *International Herald Tribune*, 3–4 July 1971.
8. García-Márquez, *Massine*, 377.
9. *Dance News* (Nov. 1977): 17.
10. De Vlieg in conversations with García-Márquez; cited in García-Márquez, *Massine*, 379.
11. *Ibid.*, 379–80.
12. *Ibid.*, 381.

Epilogue

1. Kirstein, "Let's Go Native," 79.
2. Amberg, *Ballet in America* (New York: Da Capo Press, 1983), 47.
3. *Ibid.*, 45.
4. Manchester, "A Conversation," 71.
5. Anna Kisselgoff, "Leonide Massine—Ripe for a Reappraisal," *New York Times*, 7 May 1989; Clement Crisp, *Financial Times*, 28 October 1991; cited in García-Márquez, *Massine*, 384; and Jack Anderson, "A Long Neglected Classic Still Amazes," *New York Times*, 1 December 1991.
6. García-Márquez, *Massine*, 385.
7. *Ibid.*, 46, 59 and 87.
8. Tamara Karsavina, "Dancers of the Twenties," *Dancing Times* (Feb. 1967): 252.
9. Interview of Tatiana Massine Weinbaum by John Gruen, 12 April 1973, typescript, Jerome Robbins Dance Division, New York Public Library at Lincoln Center.
10. Agnes de Mille, *Dance to the Piper*, cited in Pamela Gaye, "A Conversation with Léonide Massine," *Dance Scope* 13:4 (1979): 21.
11. "Massine's New Ballets," *Dance* (Nov. 1940).
12. Diane Menuhin, "Dancing for Balan-

chine: 1933," *Ballet Review* 16:3 (Fall 1988): 36.

13. Keith Lester, "Choreographers at Work," *Dancing Times* (Feb. 1941): 246, 276.

14. Interview of Charles Dickson by Katy Matheson, 12 February 1979, typescript, Jerome Robbins Dance Division, New York Public Library at Lincoln Center.

15. G. B. L. Wilson, "The Italian Renaissance," *Ballet Annual*, 15 (1961): 128.

16. *Ibid.*

17. "A Conversation with Leonide Massine," *Dance*, (Dec. 1977): 70.

18. Massine, *My Life in Ballet*, 277.

19. *Ibid.*, 278.

Bibliography

Alexander, Sidney. *Marc Chagall*. New York: Putnam, 1978.
Amberg, George. *Art in Modern Ballet*. New York: Pantheon, 1946.
_____. *Ballet in America*. New York: Da Capo, 1983.
Anderson, Jack. *The One and Only: The Ballet Russe de Monte Carlo*. New York: Dance Horizons, 1981.
Bakst, Leon. *Unedited Works of Bakst*. New York: Brentano's, 1927.
Barr, Alfred H., Jr. *Matisse: His Art and His Public*. New York: Museum of Modern Art, 1951.
_____. *Picasso: Fifty Years of His Art*. New York: The Museum of Modern Art & Arno Press, 1966.
Baudelaire, Charles. *The Flowers of Evil*. Translated by Dorothy Martin. Edited by Marthiel and Jackson Matthews. New York: New Directions, 1963.
Bauer, Oswald Georg. *Richard Wagner*. New York: Rizzoli, 1983.
Beaumont, Cyril. *Complete Book of Ballets*. London: Putnam, 1951.
_____. *The Diaghilev Ballet in London*. London: Putnam, 1949.
_____. *The Diaghilev Ballet in Paris*. London: Putnam, 1940.
_____. *Supplement to the Complete Book of Ballets*. London: Putnam, 1952.
Benois, Alexandre. *Reminiscences of the Russian Ballet*. Translated by Mary Britnieva. London: Putnam, 1941.
Berg, Shelley. *Le Sacre du Printemps: Seven Productions from Nijinsky to Martha Graham*. Ann Arbor: UMI Press, 1988.
Berlioz, Hector. *Memoirs of Hector Berlioz*. Translated by Rachel Holmes and Eleanor Holmes. Edited by Ernest Newman. New York: Tudor, 1932.
Blokker, Roy, and Robert Dearling. *Shostakovich: The Symphonies*. London: Tantivy Press, 1979.
Boccaccio, Giovanni. *Decameron*. Translated by David McKay. Philadelphia: David McKay Company, n.d.
Boyd, Malcolm. *Domenico Scarlatti—Master of Music*. New York: Schirmer, 1986.
Buckle, Richard. *Diaghilev*. New York: Atheneum, 1984.

Calvocoressi, M. D. *Musician's Gallery*. London: Faber, 1933.
Chamot, Mary. *Gontcharova: Stage Designs and Paintings*. London: Oresko Books Ltd., 1979.
Christie, Ian. *Powell, Pressburger and Others*. London: British Film Institute, 1978.
Compton, Susan. *Chagall*. London: Royal Academy of Arts in association with Weidenfeld and Nicholson, 1985.
de Cossart, Michael. *Ida Rubinstein*. Liverpool: Liverpool University Press, 1987.
Coton, A. V. *A Prejudice for Ballet*. London: Methuen & Co., 1938.
Croce, Arlene. *Afterimages*. New York: Alfred A. Knopf, 1977.
Dalí, Salvador. *The Secret Life of Salvador Dalí*. New York: Dial Press, 1942.
Delannoy, Marcel. *Honegger*. Paris: Pierre Horay, 1953.
Demidov, Alexander. *The Russian Ballet*. Translated by Guy Daniels. Garden City, N.Y.: Doubleday, 1977.
Denby, Edwin. *Looking at the Dance*. New York: Pelegrini & Cudahy, 1949.
Diehl, Gaston. *Miró*. New York: Crown Publishers, 1979.
Dolin, Anton. *Divertissement*. London: Sampson Low, Marston & Co., n.d.
Dorati, Anatol. *Notes of Seven Decades*. London: Hodder and Stoughton, 1979.
Duke, Vernon. *Passport to Paris*. Boston: Little, Brown, 1955.
Einstein, Alfred. *Schubert: A Musical Portrait*. New York: Oxford University Press, 1951.
Erben, Walter. *Joan Miró*. New York: George Braziller, 1959.
Faris, Alexander. *Jacques Offenbach*. New York: Charles Scribner's Sons, 1980.
Garafola, Lynn. *Diaghilev's Ballets Russes*. New York: Oxford University Press, 1989.
García-Márquez, Vicente. *The Ballets Russes*. New York: Knopf, 1990.
_____. *Massine: A Biography*. New York: Alfred A. Knopf, 1995.
Gibbon, Monk. *The Red Shoes Ballet*. London: Saturn Press, 1948.
_____. *The Tales of Hoffmann: A Study of the Film*. London: Saturn Press, 1951.
Gluck, Christoph Willibald. *The Collected Correspondence and Papers of Christoph Willibald Gluck*. Edited by Hedwig and E. H. Mueller von Aslow. Translated by Stewart Thompson. New York: St. Martin's Press, 1962.
Gold, Arthur, and Robert Fizdale. *Misia*. New York: Alfred A. Knopf, 1980.
Gilbert, Steven E. *The Music of Gershwin*. New Haven and London: Yale University Press, 1995.
Gregor-Dellin, Martin. *Wagner: His Life, His Work, His Century*. Translated by J. Maxwell Brownjohn. San Diego: Harcourt Brace Jovanovich, 1983.
Grigoriev, Serge. *The Diaghilev Ballet: 1909–1929*. Translated and edited by Vera Bowen. London: Constable, 1953.
Hall, Fernau. *Anatomy of Ballet*. London: Andrew Melrose, 1953.
Harding, James. *Erik Satie*. New York: Praeger Publishers, 1975.
_____. *The Ox on the Roof*. London: Macdonald, 1972.
Haskell, Arnold. *Balletomania Then and Now*. London: Weidenfeld and Nicholson, 1977.
_____. *Diaghileff: His Artistic and Private Life*. London: Gollancz, 1935.
Hill, Polly, and Richard Keynes. *Lydia and Maynard: The Letters of L.L. and J.M.K.* New York: Charles Scribner's Sons, 1989.
Hindemith, Paul. *Selected Letters of Paul Hindemith*. Edited and translated by Geoffrey Skelton. London: Yale University Press, 1995.
Holoman, D. Kern. *Berlioz*. Cambridge: Harvard University Press, 1989.
Honegger, Arthur. *I Am a Composer*. London: Faber and Faber, 1966.
Honour, Hugh, and John Fleming. *The Visual Arts: A History*. New Jersey: Prentice-Hall, 1982.

Hugo, Jean. *Avant d'Oublier*. Paris: Fayard, 1976.
Hurok, Sol. *S. Hurok Presents... The World of Ballet*. London: Robert Hale, 1955.
———. *S. Hurok Presents: A Memoir of the Dance World*. New York: Hermitage House, 1953.
Johnson, James H. *Listening in Paris: A Cultural History*. Berkeley: University of California Press, 1995.
Karsavina, Tamara. *Theatre Street*. London: Dance Books, 1981.
King, Eleanor. *Transformations*. New York: Dance Horizons, 1978.
Kirby, Michel. *Futurist Performance*. New York: Dutton, 1971.
Kirstein, Lincoln. *Ballet, Bias and Belief*. New York: Dance Horizons, 1983.
Kochno, Boris. *Diaghilev and the Ballets Russes*. Translated by Adrienne Foulke. New York: Harper & Row, 1960.
Landon, H. C. Robbins, and David Wyn Jones. *Haydn: His Life and Music*. Bloomington: Indiana University Press, 1988.
Lawrence, Robert. *The Victor Book of Ballets and Ballet Music*. New York: Simon and Schuster, 1950.
Leopold, Silke. *Monteverdi: Music in Transition*. Oxford: Clarendon Press, 1911.
Levinson, André. *André Levinson on Dance*. Edited by Joan Arocella and Lynn Garafola. Hanover, N.H.: Wesleyan University Press, 1991.
Lieven, Prince Peter. *The Birth of the Ballets Russes*. Translated by L. Zarine. New York: Dover, 1973.
Lifar, Serge. *Histoire du Ballet Russe depuis les origines jusqu'à nos jours*. Paris: Nage, 1950.
———. *A History of the Russian Ballet*. London: Hutchinsons, 1954.
Lodder, Christina. *Russian Constructivism*. New Haven: Yale University Press, 1983.
Lybyer, J. M., and James L. Roberts. *Poe's Short Stories*. New York: Wiley and Sons, 1980.
Macdonald, Nesta. *Diaghilev Observed*. New York: Dance Horizons, 1975.
Marco, Tomás. *Spanish Music in the Twentieth Century*. Translated by Cola Franzen. Cambridge: Harvard University Press, 1993.
Markova, Alicia. *Giselle and I*. New York: Vanguard Press, 1960.
Martin, John. *America Dancing*. New York: Dance Horizons, 1968.
Massine, Léonide. *My Life in Ballet*. London: Macmillan, 1968.
Milhaud, Darius. *Notes Without Music*. London: Dobson, 1952.
Nabokov, Nicholas. *Bagzah*. New York: Atheneum, 1975.
———. *Old Friends and New Music*. London: Hamish Hamilton, 1951.
Nectoux, Jean-Michel. *Gabriel Fauré: A Musical Life*. Translated by Roger Nichols. Cambridge: Cambridge University Press, 1991.
Nikitina, Alicia. *Nikitina*. Translated by Moura Budberg. London: Allan Wingate, 1959.
Noss, Luther. *Paul Hindemith in the United States*. Urbana: University of Illinois Press, 1989.
Orledge, Robert. *Gabriel Fauré*. London: Eulenburg Books, 1979.
Osborne, Richard. *Rossini*. Boston: Northeastern University Press, 1986.
Palmer, Winthrop. *Theatrical Dancing in America*. South Brunswick, N.J.: Barnes, 1978.
Penrose, Roland. *Picasso: His Life and Work*. New York: Harper & Row, 1971.
Polunin, Vladimir. *The Continental Method of Scene Painting*. London: Beaumont, 1927.
Powell, Michael. *A Life in Movies*. New York: Alfred A. Knopf, 1987.
Poznansky, Alexander. *Tchaikovsky: The Quest for the Inner Man*. New York: Schirmer, 1991.

Prokofiev, Sergei. *Prokofiev by Prokofiev*. Edited by David H. Appel. Translated by Guy Daniels. New York: Doubleday, 1979.
Propert, W. A. *The Russian Ballet in Western Europe: 1909–1929*. London: John Lane the Bodley Head, 1921.
Ricketts, Charles. *Self-Portrait*. Edited by Cecil Lewis. London: Peter Davies, 1939.
Ridenour, Robert C. *Nationalism, Modernism, and Personal Rivalry in Nineteenth-Century Russian Music*. Bloomington: UNI Research Press, 1981.
Rimsky-Korsakov, Nikolai. *My Musical Life*. Edited by Carl van Vechten. Translated by Judah A. Jofee. New York: Alfred A. Knopf, 1923.
Robert, Grace. *The Borzoi Book of Ballets*. New York: Alfred A. Knopf, 1946.
Robinson, Harlow. *Sergei Prokofiev: A Biography*. New York: Viking, 1987.
Rose, Sir Francis. *Saying Life*. London: Cassell, 1961.
Rosenberg, Deena. *Fascinating Rhythm: The Collaboration of George and Ira Gershwin*. New York: Dutton, 1991.
Rubin, William, and Carolyn Lanchner. *André Masson*. New York: Museum of Modern Art, 1976.
Sachs, Harvey. *Music in Fascist Italy*. New York: Norton, 1987.
Selz, Jean. *Matisse*. New York: Crown, 1990.
de la Serna, Ramón Gómez. *Dalí*. Edited by Franco Paone. Translated by Nicholas Fry and Elisabeth Evans. New York: William Morrow and Company, 1979.
Sert, Misia. *Two or Three Muses*. London: Museum Press, 1953.
Servadio, Gaia. *Luchino Visconti: A Biography*. New York: Franklin Watts, 1983.
Shostakovich, Dmitri. *Testimony: The Memoirs of Dmitri Shostakovich*. New York: Dutton, 1979.
The Simon and Schuster Book of the Ballet. New York: Simon and Schuster, 1979.
Sitwell, Sacheverell. *La Vie Parisienne: A Tribute to Offenbach*. Boston: Houghton Mifflin Company, 1938.
Sokolova, Lydia. *Dancing for Diaghilev*. London: John Murray, 1960.
Spate, Virginia. *Orphism: The Evolution of Non-Figurative Painting in Paris, 1910–1914*. Oxford: Clarendon Press, 1979.
Spencer, Charles. *Léon Bakst*. New York: Rizzoli, 1973.
Steegmuller, Francis. *Cocteau*. London: Macmillan, 1970.
Stein, Gertrude. *Picasso*. London: Scribner's Sons, 1939.
Stokes, Adrian. *To-night the Ballet*. London: Faber & Faber, 1935.
Stravinsky, Igor. *Chronicle of My Life*. London: Gollancz, 1936.
Stravinsky, Igor, and Robert Craft. *Conversations with Igor Stravinsky*. London: Faber, 1959.
_____. *Expositions and Developments*. Berkeley: University of California Press, 1981.
_____. *Memories and Commentaries*. Garden City, N.Y.: Doubleday, 1960.
Stravinsky, Vera, and Robert Craft. *Stravinsky in Pictures and Documents*. New York: Simon and Schuster, 1978.
Talbot, Michael. *Vivaldi*. London: J. M. Dent & Sons LTD, 1978.
Taper, Bernard. *Balanchine*. New York: Harper & Row, 1960.
Tchaikovsky, Peter Illych. *To My Best Friend: Correspondence Between Tchaikovsky and Nadezhda von Meck*. Edited by Edward Garden. Translated by Galina von Meck. Oxford: Clarendon Press, 1913.
Till, Nicholas. *Rossini: His Life and Times*. New York: Hippocrene Books, 1983.
Tyler, Parker. *The Divine Comedy of Pavel Tchelitchew*. New York: Fleet, 1967.
Valéry, Paul. *Lettres à quelques-uns* . Paris: Gallimard, 1952.
de Valois, Ninette. *Come Dance with Me*. London: Hamish Hamilton, 1957.

Volta, Ornella. *Satie Seen Through His Letters*. Translated by Michael Bullock. London: Marion Boyars, 1989.
Walker, Kathrine Sorley. *De Basil's Ballets Russes*. New York: Atheneum, 1983.
Warrack, John. *Carl Maria von Weber*. Cambridge: Cambridge University Press, 1976.
Werth, Alexander. *Musical Uproar in Moscow*. London: Turnstile, 1949.
White, E. Walter. *Stravinsky: The Composer and His Works*. Berkeley: University of California Press, 1966.
Zorina, Vera. *Zorina*. New York: Farrar, Straus & Giroux, 1986.

Index

Aleko (ballet) 237, 238, 261–66, 352
Alfonso XIII, King of Spain 16, 49
Alhambra Theatre 51–52, 55, 61, 81, 136, 138–9, 147, 166, 307, 346
Amberg, George 28, 334, 340, 356, 359
American Guild of Musical Artists 196, 232
El Amor brujo (opera-ballet) 47, 65, 307
Amphion (ballet) 112, 127–30, 345–6
Andersen, Hans Christian 68, 73–74, 274–75
Anderson, Jack 46, 67, 235, 265–66, 335, 341, 351, 353, 356, 359
Andreú, Mariano 222
Angiolini, Gasparo 307, 315
Annenkoff, Georges 166, 168
Anouilh, Jean 308, 320, 322
Apollinaire, Guillaume 37–38, 162
L'Après-midi d'un faune (ballet) 13, 15
Argentinita 198, 222–23, 350
Arrieu, Claude 316, 319, 356
Ashton, Frederick 279, 350
Le Astuzie femminili (opera) 53–55, 79
Auric, Georges 93, 102–4, 107, 123, 126, 320–21, 351

Babilée, Jean 306–7, 355
Bacchanale (ballet) 232, 239–46, 254, 256, 351
Bagar, Robert 286, 288, 354

Bakst, Leon 7, 26–29, 31, 51, 54, 64, 78, 123, 251, 277, 340, 359, 362
Le Bal (ballet) 141–42, 346
Le Bal des voleurs (ballet) 308, 320–22, 325, 356
Le Bal du Pont du Nord (ballet) 278–79
Balanchine, George 74, 83, 108, 112, 118, 124, 135–36, 141–42, 147, 170, 185, 204, 214, 235, 258, 272, 296, 334, 337, 342, 346, 356–57, 362
Ballet Caravan 196, 232
Ballet du XXI Siécle 327
Ballet Guild 233
Ballet Russe de Monte Carlo: and appearances in London 136, 138, 142; and appearances in the United States 139–42, 194, 196–98; formation of 111–12; photographs of 137, 149, 159, 172, 176, 184; and split with Massine 191–94; *see also* specific productions
Ballet Russe Highlights 273, 288–90
Ballet Theatre (American Ballet Theatre) 2, 203, 225, 232, 236–39, 260, 263, 265, 273, 329, 349, 351–53
Ballet Today 321, 349, 353–56
Ballets de Monte Carlo 191, 193, 222
Ballets des Champs-Elysées 79, 83, 85–86, 278
Ballets Européens 173
Ballets Ida Rubinstein 110, 123, 127, 130

Ballets Russes: and appearances in Great Britain 10–11, 48–52, 79, 81, 84; and appearances in Paris 10, 12, 31, 35, 53, 55, 68, 74, 79, 85, 102, 108, 113, 118; and appearances in Rome 18, 26, 80; and appearances in Spain 16–17, 24; and appearances in the United States 13–16; demise of 111; formation of 7; photographs of 9, 14, 22, 40, 44, 50, 54, 58, 60, 63, 120; *see also* specific productions
Ballets Suédois 82–83, 91, 195
Il Barbiere di Siviglia (ballet) 308, 322–25
Il Barbiere di Siviglia (opera) 58, 324–25, 354
Barnes, Clive 67, 295, 308, 319, 320, 341, 354–56
Baronova, Irina 135, 161, 164, 176, 288, 300
Barzel, Ann 203, 289, 303, 349, 354–55
Baudelaire, Charles 3, 305, 359
Beach (ballet) 136, 161–63
Le Beau Danube (ballet) 83, 136, 151–61, 204, 308, 330, 342
Beaumarchais, Pierre Augustin 322, 325
Beaumont, Cyril 28, 31, 35, 122, 214, 257, 287, 340–41, 345, 350–52, 354, 359
Beaumont, Etienne de 82–83, 95–98, 155, 157, 164, 194–95, 198, 200, 203–4, 342
Beaurepaire, André 322–23
Bederkhan, Lelia 131, 133
Beethoven, Ludwig van 186, 195, 204, 206–10, 256–57, 289, 349
Belkis (ballet) 112, 131–34, 346
Bellerive 12
Bennett, Robert Russell 250, 252
Benois, Alexandre 7, 27–28, 118, 122–24, 126–28, 345, 359
Benois, Nicola 131–32
Bérard, Christian 182, 185, 204, 206, 290–91
Berg, Shelley 87–88, 90, 343, 359
Berlioz, Hector 142, 186–88, 208–9, 282, 300–2, 348–49, 355, 359–60
Birmingham Royal Ballet 171, 173, 189, 335, 347–48
Bizet, Georges 142, 145–47, 346
Bland, Alexander 294–96, 354–55
Blasis, Carlo 17, 53, 98
Blum, René 112, 135–36, 191, 193, 222, 349
Boccaccio, Giovanni 3, 106, 308, 316, 318, 320, 356, 359
Boccherini, Luigi 163, 165
Bogatyri (ballet) 195, 218–21
Bolshoi Ballet 5–7, 116, 264

Borodin, Alexander 21, 218, 220, 350
La Boutique fantasque (ballet) 48, 51, 55–61, 177, 203, 238, 270, 274, 330–31
Boutnikov, Ivan 282, 287
Bradley, Sir Lionel 20, 187, 210, 234, 339, 348–51, 353
Brahms, Johannes 138, 166, 168–69, 173–74, 257, 347
Branca, Vittore 308, 316, 319
Braque, Georges 2, 38–39, 91–93, 95, 99, 101, 107, 277, 329, 343
Breton, André 144–45, 149, 243, 351
Bucchi, Valentino 297–98, 355
Buckle, Richard 97 160, 171, 319–20, 340, 342–44, 347–48, 356, 359
Bullet in the Ballet (play) 274
Byron, Lord George Gordon 253, 300–1, 330

Cannes Film Festival 279, 281, 307
Capell, Richard 89, 154
Capriccio (ballet) 277
Capriccio espagnol (ballet) 198, 221–25, 238
La Carmagnole (ballet) 106
Carnival in Costa Rica (motion picture) 274
Carosello Napolitano (motion picture) 280–81
Castellanos, Julio 266–67, 353
Cecchetti, Enrico 10–11, 17, 26, 31, 55, 74, 83, 330
Cecchetti, Giuseppini 17, 26, 31, 55
Chabelska, Marie 35, 143, 148
Chagall, Marc 2, 261, 263–66, 352, 359, 360
Chanel, Coco 79, 162
Chaney, Stewart 234, 250–51
Le Chant du rossignol (ballet) 53, 55, 68–74
Charbonnier, Pierre 118–19, 122
Chase, Lucia 261, 266, 273
Chauviré, Yvette 281, 305
Chinese Dance (ballet) 90
Chisea, Armando 309, 311
Choreartium (ballet) 138–39, 142, 166–74, 189, 209, 229–30, 257, 308, 335, 347–48
Cimarosa, Domenico 54
Cini, Count Vittorio 281–82
Clarke, Mary 61, 272, 321–22, 341, 353, 356
Clock Symphony (ballet) 277, 290–93
Cochran, Charles H. 84–85, 102, 106, 112, 356

Cochran's Revue 1926 (revue) 85, 106, 356
Cocteau, Jean 3, 18, 23, 35, 37, 41–43, 45, 83, 93–94, 103, 124, 136, 162, 340–41, 362
Collier's 197, 349
Colquhoun, Robert 293–94
Colt, Alvin 258–59
commedia dell' arte 17, 52–53, 74, 77, 91, 94, 165, 280–81
La commedia umana (ballet) 308, 316–20
Compañia de Bailes Rusos 81
Concertino (ballet) 278, 353
constructivism 2, 20, 113, 344, 361
Contes russes (ballet) 18, 20, 31–35, 49
Le Coq d'or (ballet) 20, 219
Le coq et l'arlequin 42, 93
El corregidor y la molinera (pantomime) 47, 65, 145–46
Coton, A. V. 119, 288, 345–46, 354, 360
Coward, Noël 101
Craft, Robert 72, 76, 342–43, 362
La Création du Monde (ballet) 94, 195
Crescendo (ballet) 101–2
Crisp, Clement 90, 335, 343, 356
Croce, Arlene 67–68, 265, 341–42, 353, 360
Csonka, Ariane 329–30
cubism 2, 28, 36–39, 41, 75, 92–93

Dalí, Salvador 2, 235, 354, 360, 362; and *Bacchanale* 232, 239–40, 242–43, 245–46; and *Labyrinth* 232, 235–36, 253–54, 256–58; and *Mad Tristan* 273, 282–86, 288
Dance (*Dance Magazine*) 329, 336–37, 342, 347, 349, 351, 353–57
Dance News 282, 311–12, 341, 353–56
Dance Observer 196, 340, 349, 352
Dancing Times 44, 90, 102, 132–33, 150, 157, 181, 339–48
Danilova, Alexandra 58, 60–61, 100–1, 135, 139, 157, 159–60, 166, 174, 179, 181–83, 203, 222, 246, 249, 251–52, 258, 328, 344–47, 349, 351
David (ballet) 111–12, 123–25
de Basil, Colonel Wassily 112, 154, 157, 160, 173, 189, 191–94, 346, 348
Debussy, Claude 25, 42, 93, 128–29
Delarova, Eugenia 108, 110–11, 142, 148, 164–65, 174, 179, 181, 195, 198, 231
Delysia, Alice 101–2, 105
de Mille, Agnes 1, 88, 138, 179, 336, 346, 356
Les Demoiselles d'Avignon (painting) 38, 92

Denby, Edwin 225, 265, 287–88, 350, 353–54, 360
Denham, Serge 157, 160, 193–94, 214, 232–36, 282, 303, 351
de Nobilii, Lila 306
Derain, André 31, 51, 55, 57, 82, 98, 104, 270, 277
Désormière, Roger 97, 155, 158
de Valois, Ninette 81, 90, 195, 272, 274, 362
de Vlieg, Mary Ann 330–31, 356
Diaghilev, Sergei and American censorship 13–15; artistic vision of 7–8, 307, 329, 338; and breakup with Massine 79–80; and career before 1909 7; death of 111; financial troubles of 48–49, 79, 81; and Kochno 84, 108–9; and Massine 7–12, 15–18, 47–55, 79–80, 83–85, 98, 107–11, 277, 327, 329–30, 335, 338; and Nijinsky 7–8, 13, 16, 23, 47, 79; research of 12, 17, 47–48, 52–54, 109; and Stravinsky 12, 53–54, 79; *see also* specific productions of Diaghilev's Ballets Russes
Dickson, Charles 204, 261, 337, 357
Dietrich, Marlene 177
Divertissement (ballet) 98
Dobujinsky, Mastislav 268, 270
Dolin, Anton 266, 360
Don Domingo de Don Blas (ballet) 238, 266–68, 353
Don Juan (ballet) 306–7, 313–16, 355
Donald of the Burthens (ballet) 278–79, 293–96, 354
"The Donkey's Tail" 19
Doubrovska, Felia 119
Drury Lane Theatre 10, 194, 197, 211, 349–50
Les Dryades (ballet) 281
Dufy, Raoul 161–62, 347
Dukelsky, Vladimir 84, 99–100, 141, 179–81

Eagle Lion Classics, Inc. 275–76, 353
Ecole de Paris 20, 168, 219, 263
Edinburgh Festival 320
Eglevsky, André 164, 166–67, 174, 205, 239, 246, 250, 252–53, 269–70, 288, 305
Egorova, Lubov 108, 135, 198
Elaborations and Variants (book) 328
Eliot, T. S. 52, 341
Les Enchantements d'Alcine (ballet) 111, 125–27
Evans, Edwin 24, 138, 340, 346–47, 349

Les Fâcheux (ballet) 107, 346
Falla, Manuel de 47–48, 61, 65, 223, 238, 307, 316, 341
Fancy Free (ballet) 105, 179
Fauré, Gabriel 16, 24–25, 340, 361
fauvism 19, 57, 70, 92, 144
Les Femmes de bonne humeur (ballet) 17–18, 26–31, 49, 53–54, 77–78, 136, 166, 293, 340
Feuillet, Raoul 17, 53, 98, 337
Fifty-first Street Theatre 234, 246, 250
The Firebird (ballet) 13, 34, 72, 107
The Five 21, 151, 220
Fleishmann, Julius 193, 196, 236, 349, 351
Fokine, Michel 6–8, 10, 23, 28, 80–81, 123, 153, 170–71, 178, 220, 222, 266, 274, 281, 288, 307–8, 315, 352
Fonteyn, Dame Margot 269–70
Fracci, Carla 313, 316, 320
Françaix, Jean 161–63, 165, 278
Franklin, Frederic 198, 202, 204–6, 211, 216, 218, 225, 229, 246, 250–53, 258, 305
Freud, Sigmund 144, 232, 240, 243, 245–46
Fry, Roger 49
Fuller, Loie 98
futurism 2, 28, 36–37, 44, 115, 340–41

Gaîté parisienne (ballet) 195, 199–204, 216, 260, 274, 328
Garafola, Lynn 130, 340, 344, 360–61
García, Felix Fernandez 47–48, 51–52, 66
García-Márquez, Vicente 319, 340, 342–46, 348, 351, 353–56, 360
The Gay Parisian (motion picture) 202–3
Gershwin, George 94, 234, 246–47, 249–50, 352, 360, 362
Giannini, Ettore 280
Gibbons, Monk 279, 353, 360
Gibson, Ian 246, 250, 252, 261
Gide, André 141, 179, 182
Gieliotti-Ford, Susan 329–30
Gigue (ballet) 98, 106
Giselle (ballet) 6, 197, 353, 361
Gluck, Christoph Willibald 2, 307, 313–15, 324, 355–56, 360
Goetz, Ray 111
Golden Fleece Salon 19, 219
Goldoni, Carlo 3, 17, 26, 30, 52, 136, 163, 166, 293
Gontcharova, Natalie 12, 17, 19–20, 54, 82, 218–19, 221, 277, 339, 350, 360
Goodman, G. E. 163, 168, 347

Gorsky, Alexander 6–7
Graham, Martha 288–90, 171, 181, 217, 343, 359
Grant, Alexander 269–71, 290, 292–93, 295–96, 354
Grant, Duncan 91
Grey, Beryl 293, 295–96
Grigoriev, Serge 12, 14–15, 23, 25, 28, 48, 54–55, 59, 68, 73, 80, 83–84, 89, 100, 108, 112, 114, 122, 127, 340–44, 360
Gruen, John 66, 329, 341, 351, 354, 356
Guérard, Roland 143, 148, 174, 179, 182, 197, 211, 246, 250, 252
Guys, Constantin 155, 157

Halicka, Alice 179, 181
Hall, Fernau 147, 279, 295, 353, 355
Harding, James 43, 97, 126, 341–43, 345, 360
Harmsworth, Harold Sidney (Lord Rothermere) 84, 100
Harold in Italy (ballet) 282, 300–3
Haskell, Arnold 125, 188–89, 193, 210, 282, 291–92, 299, 345, 348, 349–50, 354–55, 360
Hastings, Sir Patrick 192
Haydn, Franz Joseph 106, 256, 290–92, 354, 361
Heineman, Benjamin 275
Helen! (play) 112, 135
Helpmann, Robert 275, 279
Hindemith, Paul 2, 21, 195, 213–14, 349–50, 360–61
Holtwick, Hannelore 327–28, 330–31
Honegger, Arthur 94, 123, 127, 129–30, 360
Hungarian Wedding (ballet) 101, 105
Hurok, Sol 139–40, 193–94, 197–98, 232, 236–37, 265, 273, 351, 353, 361
Hymne à la Beauté (ballet) 305, 355

Idzikovsky, Stanislas 26, 31, 34–35, 56, 62, 74, 98
Irwin, Rea 234, 246–47
Isole dei Galli 52, 84, 107, 110, 112, 136, 142

Jack-in-the-Box (music score) 97
Jacob, Gordon 268, 270
Jardin public (ballet) 141–42, 179–82
Jasinski, Roman 166, 179, 182–83
Jeux d'enfants (ballet) 135, 142–47
Joffrey Ballet 44, 46, 67, 329
Johnson, Albert 141, 174, 176

Kahn, Otto 12, 16
Kamerny Theatre 107, 114
Karinska, Barbara 142, 147, 161, 164, 182, 239, 307
Karsavina, Tamara 10, 13, 34, 51–52, 62, 66, 68, 73–74, 335, 339–42, 356
Kaye, Nora 269–70
Kendall, Terry 101–2
Kennedy, Jacqueline Bouvier 278
Kerdyk, René 161, 163
Keynes, John Maynard 49, 82, 91, 342, 360
Kikimora (ballet) 17–18
Kirstein, Lincoln 1, 178, 196, 206, 221, 227, 232–33, 333, 344, 348–50, 356, 361
Kisselgoff, Anna 153–55, 171, 174, 334–35, 347–48, 356
Kochno, Boris 84, 98, 102, 107–10, 112, 118, 121, 136, 142, 278, 342, 344, 361
Kokhlova, Olga 14, 24, 26, 65
Kokitch, Casimir 199, 204, 239, 246, 255
Koribut-Kubitovitch, P. G. 108
Krassovska, Nathalie 196, 204, 206, 218, 225, 239, 246, 251
Kremnev, Nicholas 32, 56

Laban, Rudolf von 153, 329
Labyrinth (ballet) 237, 253–58
Lacroix, Christian 203
Laing, Hugh 261, 265
Laloy, Louis 71, 73, 125, 342
Lambert, Constant 59, 138, 154, 169, 173, 177–78, 180–82, 188–89, 341, 346–48
Lamotte, Bernard 300–1
Lanvin, Jeanne 161–62
Larionov, Mikhail 12–13, 17–20, 23, 31, 33–34, 54, 82, 219–20, 277
Laudes Evangelii (ballet) 280–82, 296–99, 307, 355
Laurencin, Marie 98
Lawrence, Robert 73, 200, 209–10, 216, 229, 249, 252, 264, 267–68, 315–16, 342, 349–50, 352–53, 356, 361
Lecocq, Alexandre 268, 270
Lee, Kathryn 288, 290
The Legend of Joseph (ballet) 7–8, 10–11, 23, 51
Leningrad Symphony (ballet) 289
Leskova, Tatiana 152–54, 173, 308
Lespagnol, Geneviéve 297–98
Levinson, André 30, 89, 103–4, 130, 344, 346, 361

Lewisholm Stadium 274
Lichine, David 131, 143, 148, 150, 161, 166–67, 170, 174, 346, 352
Lieven, Prince Peter 51, 341, 361
Lifar, Serge 28, 80, 95, 99–100, 103–4, 108, 113, 117–20, 127, 197–98, 340–42, 344–45, 349, 361
Liszt, Franz 208, 287
Liturgie (ballet) 12, 280
Lomonossov, Mikhail 109, 118
London Coliseum 28, 30, 49, 51, 81, 84
London Festival Ballet 46, 277, 329
London Pavilion 101, 105–6
Lopokova, Lydia 14, 19, 26, 31, 35, 42, 49, 56, 59, 81–82, 90–91, 95, 98
Loring, Eugene 1
Lourié, Eugéne 166, 168
Ludwig II, King of Bavaria 232, 239–40, 244–46, 351
Luna de miel (motion picture) 307
Lurcat, Jean 179–80
Lyadov, Anatole 17, 21, 31, 33–34, 340

Macaulay, Alastair 173–74, 293, 348, 354
MacBryde, Robert 293–94
Macdonald, Nesta 41, 339–45
MacLeish, Archibald 140, 174
Maclès, Jean-Denis 320–21
Mad Tristan (ballet) 273, 282–88, 306, 354
Mademoiselle Angot / Mam'zelle Angot (ballet) 238, 268–74, 352
Makarova, Natalia 330
Maly Theatre 6–8
Manchester, P. W. 31, 144–45, 153–54, 160, 170, 178, 189, 193, 201, 301, 303, 334, 340–41, 346–49, 355–56
Mann, Thomas 3, 306, 355
Mannino, Franco 306
Marchi, Virgilio 281
Maré, Rolf de 82–83
Marin Ballet 330
Marinetti, Filippo 36–37
Mario e il Mago (play) 306–7
Markova, Alicia 196–97, 205, 210, 225–26, 229, 251–52, 261, 264–66, 268, 349, 353, 361
Marquis de Cuevas Ballet International 31, 273, 277, 279, 284
Marra, Eleonora 83–84, 91, 98, 101–2, 105–6, 143, 164, 225
Martin, John 88–89, 110–11, 154, 163, 166, 186–87, 189, 193–94, 203, 213–14, 216–17, 221, 225, 232, 234, 245–46,

250, 255, 264–65, 267, 286, 288–90, 343–44, 347–48, 353–54, 361

Massine, Léonide: and American nationalism in dance 1, 2, 178–79, 196, 232–33, 235, 239, 250, 259–60, 273, 333–34; and Americana ballets 140, 174–79, 234, 236, 246–50, 258–60, 334; and appearances in the United States 13–16, 198, 231, 327–28, 330–31; art interest and collection of 277, 329; and Ballet Russe de Monte Carlo career 111–12, 135–94, *see also* specific productions; Ballet Theatre productions of 236–39, 261–73; and Ballets Russes career 7–80, 83–90, 98–105, 107–10, 113–22, *see also* specific productions *and* Diaghilev; birth and childhood of, 5–6; and breakup with Diaghilev 79–80, 83–84; children of 67, 203, 238, 273, 282, 329–30, 336; choreographic methods of 30, 34, 66, 73, 87, 152–54, 158, 169–71, 187–88, 201, 209, 216, 229, 264–65, 287, 292, 315, 319, 325, 328–29, 333, 337; and Cochran revues 84, 101–2, 105–6; Coliseum and Alhambra triumphs of 30, 35, 49, 51–52, 61, 66; contemporary relevance of 333–35; and copyright litigation 191–93, 238; and criticism of his choreography 46, 73, 89, 100–1, 121, 133, 154, 178–79, 181–82, 201, 203, 210–11, 217, 220–21, 229–30, 234, 237, 245, 249–50, 253, 257, 259–60, 265–66, 268, 287–88, 289–90, 292–93, 295–96, 303, 313, 319–20, 321–22, 325, 334; and Dalí 232, 235–36, 239–46, 253–58, 273, 282–88, *see also* Dalí; dance training of 6, 10–11, 330; death o, 331; and decline of his reputation 234–35, 237, 260, 296, 308–9, 333–34, 337–38; and Diaghilev 7–12, 15–18, 47–55, 79–80, 83–85, 98, 107–11, 277, 327, 329–30, 335, 338, *see also* specific productions *and* Diaghilev; and disputes with de Basil and Denham 191–94, 234–36, 238; and extra-marital relationships 83–84, 141–42, 327–28, 335; fame of 49, 52, 108, 136, 138–39, 234–37, 273, 316, 333; and film career 274–76, 279–81, 307; and final years 327–31; financial concerns of 273, 329; and foes and fans of his symphonic ballets 136, 138–39, 154, 171, 173–74, 188–89, 210, 229–30, 235, 303, 334–35, *see also* specific symphonic ballets; and Fokine

8, 10, 170, 281, 307, 315; and genius for characterization 30, 59–60, 67–68, 158, 160, 165, 201, 264–65, 270–71, 315, 333; greatest roles of 59, 68, 160, 177, 188, 201, 216, 223, 275, 279, 307, 333; independent troupes formed by 80–81, 273–74, 288–90; and Isole dei Galli 52, 84, 107, 110, 136, 277–78, 329–30, 338; and modern dance 88–90, 153–54, 170–71; musicality of 30, 73, 87, 139, 152–53, 170, 173–74, 187–88, 209–10, 214, 225, 229, 242, 250, 256–57, 264, 292–93, 303, 315, 325, 333; and Nervi Festival productions 173, 307–9, 316, 319–20, 322, 356; and One and Only Ballet Russe de Monte Carlo career 193–238, 282, 300–3, *see also* specific productions; photographs of 14, 22, 54, 60, 63, 159, 176, 184, 202, 215, 224, 248, 262, 271, 276, 302, 328, 336; and Picasso 18, 82, 103, 277, 329, *see also* specific Picasso productions; and play choreography 6, 112, 135, 274; and posthumous idolization of Diaghilev 111, 277, 329, 338; posthumous reputation of 334–35; religiosity of 5, 11, 335, 338, see also *Laudes Evangelii* and *Resurrezione et Vita*; and revivals of his ballets 23, 26, 30–31, 46, 61, 66–68, 78, 88–90, 97–98, 105, 118, 147, 154–55, 160, 173–74, 189, 203–4, 230, 245, 265–66, 272, 274, 276–77, 278, 288, 299, 305, 307, 320, 322, 329–31, 334–35; revues of, 81–82, 84–85, 90–91, 101–2, 105–6; and rivalry with Balanchine 136, 214, 235; and Roxy productions 88, 109–12, 163; and Rubinstein productions 110–12, 122–30; and Sadler's Wells productions 270, 272, 274–75, 277, 279, 292, 329, 331; and La Scala productions 78, 90, 112, 131, 133, 225, 276–78, 280, 298–99, 306–7, 313, 329; and *Soirées de Paris* 82–83, 91–98; and Stravinsky 12, 41–42, 73, 77, 87, 97, 277, *see also* specific Stravinsky productions; and symphonic ballets 1, 2, 136, 138–39, 147–55, 166–74, 182–89, 195, 204–11, 225–30, 235, 282, 300–3; wives of 108, 110–11, 142, 148, 164–65, 174, 179, 181, 195; work ethic of 51, 141–42, 231, 298, 330, 335–37

Massine, Lorca 203, 273, 330
Massine on Choreography (book) 328–29
Masson, André 147, 149–50, 278, 346, 362

Les Matelots (ballet) 83–84, 102–5, 344
Matisse, Henri 2, 57, 68, 70–71, 73, 198, 225, 227, 329, 342, 359, 362
Meck, Nadezhda von 151–52
Las Meninas (ballet) 16–17, 24–26, 340
Mercure (ballet) 83, 95–98, 107, 144, 343
Messiah (ballet) 330
Metropole Hotel 7–8, 327, 338
Metropolitan Opera 12–13, 16, 89, 196, 198, 210, 218, 230, 232–33, 236–37, 239, 245, 253, 258, 264–65, 268, 350, 352–53
Miassine, Konstantin 5–6, 327
Mignone, Francisco 305
Milhaud, Darius 82, 91, 93–94, 97, 123, 195, 343, 361
Millet, Jean-François 284
Mir Iskusstva (journal) 7, 27, 124
The Miracle (play) 112, 135
Miró, Joan 2, 142, 144–45, 149, 329, 360
Mladova, Milada 202–3, 239
Mohaupt, Richard 268, 270
Molière 107, 313
Monahan, James 46, 341
Moonlight Sonata (ballet) 273
Moore, Lillian 232, 319, 351, 356
Morillo, Roberto García 309, 311, 313
Morning Post (London) 89, 100, 102, 121–22, 343–45
Murphy, Gerald 140
Musical America 260, 282, 352, 354
My Life in Ballet (book) 68, 328, 339–51, 353–57, 361

Nabokov, Nicholas 109–10, 118, 121, 140–41, 174, 177–78, 344, 346, 348, 361
Neglia, José 309, 312, 355
Nemchinova, Vera 56, 74, 103
Neo-primitivism 2, 20, 219
Nervi Festival 173, 307–9, 316, 319–20, 322, 356
New York Herald Tribune 197, 233, 275, 284, 339, 349–54
New York Sun 13, 23, 339, 352
New York Times 110, 133, 311–12, 339, 341, 343–44, 346–56
The New Yorker (ballet) 234, 247–50, 253, 334, 351–52
Newman, Ernest 73, 78, 139, 147, 154, 162–63, 165–66, 170, 173, 177, 180–81, 186, 188, 210, 342, 346–48, 350, 359
Nijinska, Bronislava 55, 83, 107, 111, 123, 136, 217, 219, 221, 346

Nijinsky, Vaslav 7–8, 10, 13, 16, 23, 47, 52, 79, 85–89, 343, 352, 359
Nikitina, Alice 99–100, 113, 119, 344, 361
Les Noces (ballet) 217, 219, 221
Noverre, Jean-Georges 314–15
Nureyev, Rudolf 155
Nuvel, Walter 108

Oakland Ballet 23, 147, 330
Observer (London) 26, 30, 74, 78, 86–87, 99, 104, 115, 117–18, 340, 342–45, 347, 350
Ode (ballet) 109–10, 118–22, 345
Offenbach, Jacques 157, 195, 198, 200, 270, 279, 349, 360, 362
On with the Dance (revue) 84, 101–2
One and Only Ballet Russe de Monte Carlo: and appearances in London 194, 197, 211; and appearances in Monte Carlo 198, 204, 222, 225; and appearances in the United States 196–98, 218, 232–39, 246, 250, 253, 258; and Ballet Guild 234; and "Ballet War" 193–94; formation of 193–94; photographs of 202, 215, 224, 244, 248, 255; and severance of Massine 236–38; and unionization 196, 232–33; *see also* specific productions
opera buffa 2, 54, 76, 324
Opéra-Comique 65, 146–47, 276–78
opera seria 2, 75–76, 324
Original Ballet Russe 154, 194, 234
Orlova, Tatiana 198, 237

Paisiello, Giovanni 324–25
Palacio de Bellas Artes (Mexico) 261, 266
Parade (ballet) 18, 26, 35–46, 49, 52, 78, 96–97, 179, 341, 343
Paris Opéra (Académie Nationale de Musique et de Danse) 10, 13, 53, 55, 67, 74, 94–95, 122–23, 126–27, 130, 154–55, 173, 189, 197, 219, 241, 277
Parisina (ballet) 330
Le Pas d'acier (ballet) 107–8, 113–18, 178, 345
Le Peintre et son modéle (ballet) 278, 353
Penrose, Roland 39, 75, 341–42, 361
Percival, John 153, 155, 170, 203–4, 346–49
Pergolesi, Giovanni 53, 74–78, 342
Petipa, Marius 6–7, 45, 81, 104, 153, 158, 170, 178, 203, 252–53, 279, 288, 296
Petrouchka (ballet) 13, 15, 72, 86, 97, 124, 274
Petrov, Paul 143, 179, 181–83

Petrova, Vera 95, 98
Petrovna, Elizabeth, Empress of Russia 109, 121
Picasso, Pablo 2, 18, 82–83, 92–93, 144, 277, 316, 329, 341, 343, 359, 361–62; and *Mercure* 95–97; and *Parade* 35, 37–39, 41–42; and *Pulcinella* 74–75, 78; and *Le Tricorne* 61, 64–65; *see also* cubism
Pillar of Fire (ballet) 266
Platée (ballet) 278, 353
Platov, Marc 182, 218, 225, 229, 239, 250–51
Pleasant, Richard 232–33
Poe, Edgar Allan 3, 309, 311, 313, 355
Polunin, Vladimir 64–65, 68, 71, 95, 98, 155, 157, 341–42, 344, 361
Pompeii à la Massine (ballet) 105
Poueigh, Jean 45–46
Poulenc, Francis 93–94
Powell, Michael 274–75, 279, 307, 353, 360–61
Premier Amour (ballet) 98
Les Présages (ballet) 136, 138, 142, 147–55, 168, 170–71, 173–74, 335
Pressburger, Emeric 274, 279, 353, 360
Prix de Rome 145, 301
Prokofiev, Sergei 21, 108, 113–16, 228, 345, 362
Propert, W. A. 30, 340, 362
Pruna, Pedro 102–4
Pulcinella (ballet) 52–55, 74–79, 342
Die Puppenfee (ballet) 48, 51, 55
Pyjama Jazz (ballet) 105

Quattro stagione (ballet) 277

Radice, Attilia 131, 133
The Rake (ballet) 101–2, 105
Rameau, Jean-Philippe 17, 53, 278
Rapée, Erno 261, 264
Raskin, David 246, 249
rayonism 19–20, 219
The Red Shoes (motion picture) 274–76, 280, 353, 360
Reinhardt, Max 112
Reis, Claire 88
Respighi, Ottorino 48, 55, 59, 131–33, 346
Resurrezione e vita (ballet) 281–82
Revueltas, Silvestre 266–67
Rhodes, Russell 189, 253, 348, 352
Riabouchinska, Tatiana 135, 143, 146, 148, 156, 161, 163, 166–67, 182–83
Ricketts, Charles 10–11, 339, 362

Rimsky-Korsakov, Nikolai 12, 18, 21, 33–34, 71–72, 339–40, 350, 362
Robbins, Jerome 105, 179, 261
Robert, Grace 160, 170–71, 188, 201, 203, 210, 214, 229, 245, 257, 264, 284, 347–54, 362
Robey, George 81
Roerich, Nicholas 85–86
Romanov, Dimitri 266, 268
Rome Opera Ballet 277, 280–81
Rosenthal, Manuel 198, 200
Les Roses (ballet) 98, 124
Rossi, Ezio 297
Le Rossignol (opera) 53, 72
Rossini, Gioacchino 2, 48, 55, 58–59, 322, 324–25, 356, 361–62
Rostova, Lubov 143, 166, 198, 205, 225, 239
Rothafel, S. L. 109–11
Rouge et Noir (ballet) 198, 225–30, 350
Roxy Theatre 88, 109–12, 163
Royal Danish Ballet 189
Royal Opera House (Covent Garden) 55, 81, 90, 109, 139, 141–42, 173, 182, 194, 231, 268, 288, 290, 293, 320, 348
Royal Swedish Ballet 277
Ruanova, Maria 309, 312
Rubinstein, Ida 110–12, 122–28, 130, 345–46, 360

Sabaneev, Leonid 2, 10, 229, 350
Le Sacre du printemps (ballet) 72, 79–80, 85–90, 133, 277, 343, 359
Sadler's Wells Ballet 270, 272, 274–75, 277, 279, 292, 329, 331
St. Saavo 5, 11, 327, 335
St. Francis (ballet) 195, 211–17, 298, 350
Les Saisons (ballet) 279
Salade (ballet) 82, 91–95
Saratoga (ballet) 236–37, 258–260, 352
Satie, Erik 18, 35, 37, 42, 45–46, 82–83, 93–98, 124, 126, 129, 341, 363
Sauguet, Henri 79, 81, 83–84, 98, 122–24, 279
Savina, Vera 49, 80
La Scala (Milan) 78, 90, 112, 131, 133, 225, 276–78, 280, 298–99, 306–7, 313, 329
Scarlatti, Domenico 2, 17, 26, 29, 98, 340, 359
Scheherazade (ballet) 13, 21, 28, 70, 123, 222, 235, 308
Schervachidze, Prince A. 142, 147, 161, 164, 182, 239

Schopenhauer, Arthur 286–87
Schubert, Franz 235, 253–58, 352, 360
Scuola di ballo (ballet) 136, 163–66
Sert, José Maria 10, 23–24
Sert, Misia Edwards 10, 18, 23, 37, 79–80, 95, 339, 362
Seventh Symphony (ballet) 195, 204–11, 349
Shearer, Moira 269, 275, 279, 290–93, 354
Shostakovich, Dmitri 116, 198, 225, 227–28, 289, 345, 350, 359, 362
Siciliani, Francesco 280–81, 308
Sierra, Martínez 47, 61, 65
Signorini, Giorgio 296, 298, 355
"The Sitter Out" 102, 194, 292–93, 295, 343–45, 348–51, 354
Les Six 93–94, 103–4, 115, 129
Skibine, George (Yura) 204, 261, 265–66, 268, 353
Slavinska, Mia 143, 156, 204, 218, 224, 250–51, 349–50
Slavinsky, Taddeus 81, 90, 103
The Sleeping Beauty (ballet) 84, 152
The Sleeping Princess (ballet) 81, 84, 251
Smith, Oliver 258–59
Smithson, Harriet 186, 348
The Snow Maiden (opera) 18, 21
Les Soirées de Paris 82–83, 91–98
Sokolova, Lydia 15–16, 20, 24, 31, 34–35, 47–48, 51–52, 56, 68, 79–81, 84–85, 87–88, 90–91, 103, 339–40, 341–43, 362
Le Soleil de nuit (ballet) 12–13, 18–24, 34, 49, 331, 340
Somes, Michael 269–70, 290
Spanish Fiesta (motion picture) 225
Stanislavsky, Konstantin 6, 85
Stein, Gertrude 96, 343, 362
Stepanov, Vladimir 328–29
Still Dancing (revue) 85, 105
Stokowski, Leopold 88, 139, 173
Stoll, Sir Oswald 48, 51, 81
Strange Sarabande (ballet) 289
Strauss, Johann 155, 157–58, 347
Strauss, Richard 10
Stravinsky, Igor 12, 21, 34, 41–42, 54, 93, 97, 168, 219, 277, 342–43, 347, 362–63; and *Le Chant du rossignol* 53, 68, 71–74; and *Pulcinella* 53, 76–79; and *Le Sacre du printemps* 85–87
Sunday Times (London) 46, 341–42, 346–48, 350, 354
surrealism 2, 38, 109, 119, 144, 147, 149–50, 180, 232, 242–43, 245, 254–55, 257, 263, 265, 287–88, 354
Svetloff, Valerian 61, 71, 73, 104, 117, 121–22, 340, 342, 344–45
Swan Lake (ballet) 7, 104, 151–52, 196–97
Les Sylphides (ballet) 72, 79, 102, 170, 281
Symphonie fantastique (ballet) 142, 182–89, 206, 282, 348

Tairov, Alexander 107, 114
The Tales of Hoffman (motion picture) 279, 281
Tannhäuser (opera) 239–42
Tarakanova, Nina 148, 156, 166–67, 198, 328, 347
Taylor, Elizabeth 278
Tchaikovsky, Peter Illych 72, 86, 136, 138, 147–48, 150–52, 173, 257, 261, 264, 347, 361–62
Tchelitchew, Pavel 109–10, 118–20, 122, 211–13, 344, 350, 362
Tchernicheva, Lubov 14–15, 26, 31, 56, 74, 113
Teatro Colón (Buenos Aires) 147, 173, 189, 276, 305, 309, 355
Teatro Costanzi (Rome) 18, 26
Teatro Municipal (Rio de Janeiro) 305
Teatro Real (Madrid) 16, 47–48
Terechkovitch, Constantin 166, 168
Terry, Walter 214, 217, 229–30, 234–35, 237, 249–50, 253–55, 257–58, 260, 350–52
Théâtre de la Cigale (Paris) 82–83, 91, 93, 95
Théâtre de la Gaité-Lyrique (Paris) 102
Théâtre de Monte Carlo 55, 99, 142, 147, 155, 161, 164, 198, 204, 222, 225
Théâtre des Champs-Elysées (Paris) 79, 83, 85–86, 278
Théâtre du Châtelet (Paris) 7, 18, 26, 35, 45
Théâtre Sarah Bernhardt (Paris) 95, 113, 118
Theilade, Nini 204–6, 211, 215–16, 239
Times (London) 35, 73–74, 89, 98, 104–5, 115, 118, 121–22, 125, 139, 146–47, 166–67, 174, 179, 181–83, 196, 200, 342–49
Togo; Or, The Noble Savage (ballet) 90–91
Tommasini, Vincenzo 26, 29, 78
Toumanova, Tamara 63, 135, 143, 176, 179, 184, 253, 255, 257–58, 260, 273
Le Train bleu (ballet) 136, 162

Le Tricorne (ballet) 37, 47, 51–52, 61–68, 134, 177, 198, 225, 238, 274, 296, 307, 316, 329, 334
Tristan und Isolde (opera) 241, 282–83, 286–87, 354
The Tub (ballet) 106, 356
Tudor, Anthony 261, 265–66
Twysden, A. E. 229, 350–52

Union Pacific (ballet) 140–41, 175–79, 334
Universal Art 193–94, 232–33, 236
Usher (ballet) 305, 309–13, 316, 355

Valéry, Paul 3, 127–30, 345, 362
Vauxcelle, Louis 38, 92
Vegh, Maria 330
Verchinina, Nina 148, 153, 166, 171–72, 183
Vesak, Norbert 330
Vienna—1814 (ballet) 234, 250–53, 351
Visconti, Luchino 306, 355, 362
Vitak, Albertina 210, 245, 249–50, 252, 350–52
von Weber, Carl Maria 234, 250–52, 351–52, 363

Wagner, Richard 2, 11, 93, 208–9, 232, 239–42, 245–46, 256, 282–84, 286–87, 351

Wakhevitch, Georges 313–14
Wanger, Walter 81
Weinbaum, Tatiana Massine 67, 203, 237–38, 282, 307, 317, 336, 354, 356
Weinberger, Jaromir 258–59, 352
Whyte, Ian 293, 295, 354
Wigman, Mary 153, 171
Williams, Peter 31, 61, 270, 321–22, 340–41, 356
Wilson, G. B. L. 270, 308, 337, 355, 357
Woizikowsky, Leon 24, 26, 31, 35, 56, 62, 66, 81, 88, 90, 103, 119, 143, 148, 161, 163–64, 166–67

Yakulov, Georgi 107–8, 113–14, 117–18, 344
You'd Be Surprised (revue) 90–91
Youskevitch, Igor 204–5, 210, 218, 225–26, 235, 246, 250–52, 288, 330, 351

Zéphyr et Flore (ballet) 83–84, 98–101, 105, 122, 180
Zhadanov, Andrei 116, 228
Zorina, Vera 141–42, 179, 183, 346, 363
Zoritch, George 182, 204, 218, 246, 250, 252–53
Zvenigorod-Moskovsky 5–6, 327
Zverev, Nicholas 19, 22, 35, 74, 101–2, 106

www.ingramcontent.com/pod-product-compliance
Lightning Source LLC
Chambersburg PA
CBHW051205300426
44116CB00006B/446